# INFLUENCE IN EARLY STUART ELECTIONS, 1604–1640

# INFLUENCE
# IN EARLY STUART
# ELECTIONS

## 1604–1640

John K. Gruenfelder

OHIO STATE UNIVERSITY PRESS : COLUMBUS

**Library of Congress Cataloguing in Publication Data**

Gruenfelder, John K.    1932–
   Influence in early Stuart elections, 1604–1640.

   Bibliography: p.

   Includes index.

   1. Elections—England—History. 2. Great Britain—Politics and
government—1603–1649. I. Title

JN948.G78                    324.94106                    80-28226

ISBN 0-8142-0316-7

# CONTENTS

|  | ACKNOWLEDGMENTS | vii |
|---|---|---|
|  | LIST OF ABBREVIATIONS | ix |
|  | INTRODUCTION | xi |
| ONE: | THE PATH TO WESTMINSTER | 3 |
| TWO: | THE ELECTIONS OF 1604–1610 | 33 |
| THREE: | THE COURT AND ELECTIONS | 59 |
|  | 1. THE LORD WARDENS AND ELECTIONS, 1614–1628 | 65 |
|  | 2. THE DUCHY OF LANCASTER AND ELECTIONS, 1614–1628 | 73 |
|  | 3. THE DUCHY OF CORNWALL, THE PRINCE'S COUNCIL AND ELECTIONS, 1614–1628 | 85 |
|  | 4. THE COUNCIL OF THE NORTH AND ELECTIONS, 1614–1628 | 97 |
|  | 5. THE COUNCIL OF THE MARCHES OF WALES AND ELECTIONS, 1614–1628 | 103 |
|  | 6. THE PRIVY COUNCIL AND ELECTIONS, 1614–1628 | 107 |
| FOUR: | ARISTOCRATIC PATRONAGE, 1614–1628 | 123 |
|  | 1. THE GREAT PATRONS | 123 |
|  | 2. THE MIDDLE RANK OF PATRONAGE | 152 |
| FIVE: | THE ELECTIONS OF 1640 | 183 |
| SIX: | CONCLUSION | 213 |
|  | APPENDIXES | 221 |
|  | BIBLIOGRAPHY | 253 |
|  | INDEX | 271 |

# Acknowledgments

Unfortunately, it is impossible to list all those who have been of help in the preparation of this book. However, I remember, with gratitude and respect, the late Professor David H. Willson, of the University of Minnesota, who first introduced me to the study of early Stuart England. I also wish to thank the staffs of the Public Record Office, the Duchy of Cornwall Record Office, the Bodleian Library, the students' room and reading room of the British Library, the National Register of Archives, and, in particular, the numerous county and borough archivists and town clerks and their staffs, who made my research so pleasant and rewarding.

I would also like to express my gratitude to the inter-library loan staff of the University of Wyoming and to the librarians of the Sterling Memorial Library at Yale University and the University of Minnesota, who gave me every possible assistance. Several of my colleagues, past and present, contributed generously of their time and patience in reading the manuscript in its various stages. In particular, I wish to thank Professor J. Quentin Cook and Professor Roger Daniels and his wife, Judith, for their comments and criticism. I also owe a debt of gratitude to Professor Wallace MacCaffrey and Professor Roger L. Williams for their encouragement. Robert C. Johnson and Maija Cole, of the Yale Parliamentary Diaries Project, were of especial help.

I also wish to acknowledge the generous research support I received from the National Endowment for the Humanities (grant no. H68-I-178) and the University of Wyoming, which awarded me two summer research grants, a leave of absence, and a sabbatical leave so that my work could be completed.

My thanks, too, to Mrs. Irene Walker and Mrs. Diane Alexander for their valuable assistance. I also want to acknowledge the help I received from the late Mr. Thomas Woodforde Scott and his wife, Angela, of Impala House, the Zebra Trust, and Hans Fellner. My wife and family provided constant encouragement and endless patience.

Finally, my thanks to my parents. This book is dedicated to them.

# List of Abbreviations

Bean, *Northern Counties* — W. W. Bean, *The Parliamentary Representation of the Six Northern Counties of England*

Blomefield, *Hist. Norfolk* — F. Blomefield, *An Essay towards a Topographical History of the County of Norfolk*

Brayley, *Hist. Surrey* — E. W. Brayley, *A Topographical History of Surrey*

CDNB — *Concise Dictionary of National Biography*

CSPD — *Calendar of State Papers, Domestic, Reigns of James I and Charles I*

CSPV — *Calendar of State Papers, Venetian*

Clutterbuck, *Hist. Hertfordshire* — R. Clutterbuck, *The History and Antiquities of the County of Hertfordshire*

Cussans, *Hist. Hertfordshire* — J. E. Cussans, *History of Hertfordshire*

DNB — *Dictionary of National Biography*

Fletcher, *County Community* — A. Fletcher, *A County Community in Peace and War: Sussex 1600–1660*

Gleason, *JP's* — J. H. Gleason, *The Justices of the Peace in England*

Hasted, *Kent* — E. Hasted, *The History and Topographical Survey of the County of Kent*

Hoare, *Wiltshire* — R. C. Hoare et al., *The History of South Wiltshire*

Horsfield, *Hist. Sussex* — T. W. Horsfield, *The History, Antiquities, and Topography of the County of Sussex*

Hutchins, *Hist. Dorset* — J. Hutchins, *The History and Antiquities of the County of Dorset*

| | |
|---|---|
| *HMC* | Publications and reports of the Historical Manuscripts Commission |
| Lipscombe, *Buckinghamshire* | G. Lipscombe, *The History and Antiquities of the County of Buckingham* |
| Manning and Bray, *Hist. Surrey* | Q. Manning and W. Bray, *The History and Antiquities of the County of Surrey* |
| Morant, *Hist. Essex* | P. Morant, *The History and Antiquities of the County of Essex* |
| Nichols, *Progresses* | J. Nichols, ed., *The Progresses, Processions . . . of King James the First* |
| Nichols, *Hist. Leicestershire* | J. Nichols, *The History and Antiquities of the County of Leicester* |
| NLW | National Library of Wales |
| *OR* | *Return of the Names of Every Member of the Lower House of Parliament of England* (commonly known as the Official Return) |
| Ormerod, *Hist. Cheshire* | G. Ormerod, *The History of the County Palatine and City of Chester* |
| P.R.O., St. P. Dom. | Public Record Office, State Papers, Domestic |
| Rymer, *Foedera* | Rymer and Sanderson, eds., *Foedera, conventiones, literae . . .* |
| Spedding, *Bacon* | J. Spedding et al., eds., *The Works of Sir Francis Bacon* |
| Suckling, *Hist. Suffolk* | A. Suckling, *The History and Antiquities of the County of Suffolk* |
| Thompson, *Hist. Leicester* | J. Thompson, *The History of Leicester from the Time of the Romans to the End of the Seventeenth Century* |
| *VCH* | *Victoria History of the Counties of England* |
| Willcox, *Gloucestershire* | W. B. Willcox, *Gloucestershire: A Study in Local Government, 1590–1640* |
| Wright, *Hist. Essex* | T. Wright, *The History and Topography of the County of Essex* |

# Introduction

Sir John Neale's masterly portrait of the Elizabethan electoral scene needs no detailed review, nor, for that matter, does the pioneering work of Sir Lewis Namier, who has illuminated the structure of electoral politics in the eighteenth century. Both noted the influence of the county squirearchy and peerage, and, in Namier's exhaustive analysis, the electioneering of the court received its first detailed exposition. The local rivalries and quarrels, the strategems and campaigns, the very motives that drove men in the Elizabethan and Georgian ages to seek that coveted prize, a place in the House of Commons, have been explored. The political and electoral landscape, too, of Queen Anne's England has been examined in the excellent studies of Geoffrey Holmes and William A. Speck.[1]

Derek Hirst's excellent study *The Representative of the People?* examines early Stuart elections from a new and provocative perspective. His focus is upon England's surprisingly large electorate and not upon its customary "leaders," the peerage and gentry. He carefully traces the emergence of that electorate as an increasingly aware and responsive body that not only begins to make its wishes known to those returned to Westminster but that was, in turn, "courted" by the local elite. The gentry, anxious about the growth of influence in elections, saw the electorate as a potential ally in their struggle to maintain parliament as a "free" institution — free, that is, from the influences of the peerage and an increasingly interventionist court. Unfortunately, Hirst's study does not discuss electoral patronage or influence, the very factor that caused the gentry's growing concern over "free" parliaments. Two books that treat James I's parliaments, *The Addled Parliament* and *The Parliament of 1624*, discuss elections in a serious and useful way. A number of articles dealing with county and borough elections or the influence wielded by a member of the elite have also appeared. Two excellent studies of the membership of the Long Parliament have been published and in one, *The Long Parliament*, by Mary Frear Keeler, the elections for the autumn parliament have been comprehensively reviewed. M. B. Rex has provided a definitive study of the university constituencies, and, with that, the bibliography of works dealing with early Stuart elections is exhausted.[2]

Elizabeth's last elections were marked by the bitter rivalry between her favorite, the egocentric earl of Essex, and Lord Burghley's son, Robert Cecil, rewarded by James with the earldom of Salisbury in 1605. Both employed electoral patronage to reward their clients, increase their following, and illustrate their importance in the Elizabethan political marketplace. And though the influence of the peerage had been a constant factor in Elizabethan elections, the contest between Essex and Cecil marked, as Neale realized, a new development: it was a glimpse of the early Stuart election scene. Doubts have been raised, however, that the nobility was able to maintain its grip on electoral patronage. It has been suggested that, as the territorial holdings of the nobility declined, so did its capacity to influence elections.[3]

England was still, however, a structured society; rank retained meaning and privilege. Landholdings, court, and local office still gave the peerage a powerful electoral voice. A borough might need powerful friends at court or an ally against another pushing patron. A burgess-ship could be bargained in return for favor. That probably explained Rochester's offer to James's favorite, the earl of Somerset, of the disposal of a place in 1614, or the decision reached by the corporation of Wells in 1625 that the local bishop "shall commend some discreet and sufficiently worthy Burgess to serve in the next parliament." Canterbury's corporation quarreled with the archbishop and sought the earl of Montgomery's help. In return, Montgomery's clients won Canterbury burgess-ships. Contemporaries recognized the importance of aristocratic influence as surviving requests for burgess-ships to Pembroke, Buckingham, and Zouch suggest. The early Stuart peerage was a force to be reckoned with in any analysis of elections between 1604 and 1640.[4]

In contrast to Elizabeth's reign, the court became a significant electoral patron. In 1614 the lord warden and court agencies like the Duchy of Cornwall and the Prince's Council probably intervened in thirty-nine elections; in 1624 they were active in fifty-one. The Duchy of Lancaster was also involved; it usually nominated its own officials and, like the Duchy of Cornwall and the Prince's Council, relied upon its territorial holdings for its influence. The Prince's Council and the Duchy of Cornwall nominated courtiers and officials linked with the central administration. The Duchy of Cornwall's nominees for 1621 included four privy councillors; its other candidates were courtiers, one a kinsman to a great farmer of the customs, another a future chancellor of the Duchy of Lancaster. The Councils of the North and Marches of Wales, however, usually relied upon the influence and zeal of their lord presidents for their electoral patronage. The court's electioneering intensified competition for places in parliament; it also exemplified its centralizing energies. It was another challenge to the autonomy of the local community.

Parliament, as G. R. Elton perceptively observed, was a "point of contact between rulers and ruled" wherein private causes were advanced, careers launched, and necessary change effected. Parliament, for Elizabethan Norfolk's county community, was increasingly regarded as an institution that could be used for its own purposes. Elton's "point of contact" was, for Norfolk, a reality. It was the forum wherein the local gentry, spokesmen for their "partially independent shire-states, each with its own distinct ethos and loyalty," voiced the concerns and wishes of their "country," their local community. That is reflected in the instructions, listing local needs, issues, and problems, sent by boroughs and even counties to their members serving at Westminster.[5]

Representation in parliament became even more important for the county community as the crown's intervention in its affairs increased. Elizabethan Norfolk was a battleground between the community's own interests and independence and the centralizing energies of the monarchy. Norfolk's leadership divided between the defenders of local autonomy and those that, often for selfish motives, backed the crown's activities. In Durham a body of influential gentry, recruited from the Newcastle coal trade, found their hopes for influence dashed by its bishops, acting as agents for the crown. To challenge that authority and to advance their own political hopes, the Newcastle group allied themselves with some of Durham's older families suffering from similar frustrations and demanded parliamentary representation, a goal blocked by the crown. Durham's dissatisfied gentry, like those of Elizabethan Norfolk, saw parliament as a barrier against the crown's intervention; they also, like Norfolk's gentry, needed it to defend and advance their own interests.[6]

The gentry's ambitions for a place in parliament was not met by a corresponding increase in the number of available places. The expansion of parliamentary representation that had marked the previous century was over by 1603. There were 473 places in the Parliament of 1604; only twenty more were added by the autumn of 1640. And while the number of places remained nearly static, the competition the gentry faced in their bid for representation did not; in fact, thanks to the continuing influence of the peerage and the intervention of the court, it probably increased.

The elections of 1604 and 1640 are treated separately. James's first election had a closer link with the elections of Elizabeth than to succeeding elections. Nothing suggests the court took an innovative elec-

toral stance. James apparently left everything to Cecil, whose intervention followed customary Elizabethan practices. And since the elections of 1640 were unique, they deserve and receive separate treatment.

The influence of the peerage and court are discussed in a more
topical fashion for the elections of 1614–28. The court's electioneering
developed a more organized character after 1614, and its record as a
patron, through a discussion of the intervention of the lord wardens
and its agencies, is a necessary part of the early Stuart election story.
The influence of three peers, Arundel, Pembroke, and Buckingham,
indicates the influence that territorial holdings, office, or a combination of both brought to the peerage. The patronage of a group of
minor — in terms of influence — peers is also reviewed in the discussion of aristocratic electioneering between 1614 and 1628.

Borough corporations, as at York, Salisbury, or Bristol, exercised
their own influence to control elections. Such boroughs, however,
were in the minority; the gentry's invasion of borough seats, noted in
Elizabeth's reign, continued apace. But the competition was fierce;
different patrons challenged each other for electoral victory. Indeed,
the electoral history of early Stuart England could be summarized as a
story of patronage. Little wonder, then, that a foreign observer could
comment on the "tricks" and "devices" employed, in almost bewil-
dering variety, by a candidate seeking that great prize, a place at
Westminster.[7] And it is to those tactics, the strategems of influence in
a story of patronage, that we must turn.

1. Sir J. Neale, *The Elizabethan House of Commons*; Sir L. Namier, *The Structure of Politics
at the Accession of George III*, 2d ed. (London, 1957), and *England in the Age of the American
Revolution*, 2d ed. (London, 1963); Sir L. Namier and J. Brook, *The History of Parliament:
The House of Commons, 1754–1790*, 3 vols. (London, 1964); G. Holmes, *British Politics in
the Age of Anne* (New York, 1967); W. A. Speck, *Tory and Whig* (London, 1970).

2. The four books on James's parliaments are W. Notestein, *The House of Commons,
1604–1610*; T. Moir, *The Addled Parliament of 1614*; R. Zaller, *The Parliament of 1621* (Los
Angeles, 1971); and R. Ruigh, *The Parliament of 1624*. Notestein and Zaller pay practically no attention to elections, but Moir offers a more complete treatment. Ruigh's
analysis of the elections of 1624 is the best. Many articles on particular elections have
appeared in English local history journals and are cited throughout the text and listed
in the bibliography. However, the most important articles on elections and influence
must include M. E. Bohannon, "The Essex Election of 1604"; E. Farnham, "The Somerset Election of 1614"; M. R. Frear, "The Election at Great Marlow in 1640"; R. W.
Kenny, "Parliamentary Influence of Charles Howard, Earl of Nottingham, 1536–1624";
V. A. Rowe, "The Influence of the Earls of Pembroke on Parliamentary Elections,
1625–41"; L. Stone, "The Electoral Influence of the second Earl of Salisbury, 1614–68";
J. K. Gruenfelder, "The Elections to the Short Parliament, 1640"; R. N. Kershaw, "The
Elections for the Long Parliament 1640"; J. K. Gruenfelder, "The Lord Wardens and

Elections, 1604–1628," "The Electoral influence of the Earls of Huntingdon, 1603–1640"; "The Electoral Patronage of Sir Thomas Wentworth, Earl of Strafford, 1614–1640"; Two other articles of importance for elections are Lady E. De Villiers, "Parliamentary Boroughs Restored by the House of Commons, 1621–41," and J. H. Plumb, "The Growth of the Electorate in England from 1600 to 1715." On the Long Parliament, see D. Brunton and D. H. Pennington, *Members of the Long Parliament*, and M. F. Keeler, *The Long Parliament, 1640–1641*. The university electoral story is told by M. B. Rex, *University Representation in England, 1604–1690*.

3. L. Stone, *The Crisis of the Aristocracy, 1558–1614*, pp. 258–63.

4. Mayor and Citizens of Rochester to the Earl of Somerset, 13 Feb. 1614, P.R.O., St. P. Dom. 14/76:21. All transcripts of Crown-copyright records in the Public Record Office appear by the kind permission of the Controller of H. M. Stationery Office. Sandys to the Mayor of Rochester, the same to Burke and Others at Rochester, 3 Mar., 4 Apr. 1614; Burke and Others to Sandys, 3 Apr., 1614, Staffordshire RO, D593S/4/60/11, 12; Sir R. Mansell to the Earl of Somerset, 23 Feb. 1614, *Gentleman's Magazine*, vol. 96, pt. 1, (1826), pp. 483–84; Wells City MSS, Acts of the Corporation, 1615–25, f. 186v, 187, 187v; P. M. Hembry, *The Bishops of Bath and Wells*, p. 217; Scott Manuscript," Canterbury Citizens for Parliament," by Thomas Scott, 1626, in the possession of William Urry of St. Edmund's Hall, Oxford, 1–10, 15–38, 40–43. I am indebted to Mr. Urry for bringing this manuscript to my attention and allowing me to use it in the preparation of this book. *CSPV 1623–1625*, p. 201; *CSPV 1625–1626*, pp. 20, 63, 598; Bosvile to Lord Zouch, 9 Nov. 1620, Wotton to the same, 11 Nov. 1620, Goodere to Buckingham, 20 Nov. 1620, P.R.O., St. P. Dom. 15/117:67, 72, 83; Drury to Zouch, 10 Dec. 1623, P.R.O. St. P. Dom. 14/155:32; Nethersole to Carleton, 24 Apr. 1625, P.R.O., St. P. Dom. 16:1:83; Apsley to Nicholas, 2 Feb. 1628, P.R.O., St. P. Dom. 16/92:28. The terms *aristocracy, peerage,* and *nobility* are used synonymously throughout and refer to members of the English nobility who were entitled to a place in the House of Lords.

5. G. R. Elton, "Tudor Government: The Points of Contact: I. Parliament," pp. 191, 195, 198–200; A. Hassell Smith, *County and Court: Government and Politics in Norfolk, 1558–1603*, pp. 108, 276, 331–32; A. Everitt, "Social Mobility in Early Modern England," p. 59; Hirst, *Representative of the People?* pp. 160, 161–63, 174–75.

6. I. Roots, "The Central Government and the Local Community," in E. W. Ives, ed., *The English Revolution, 1600–1660*, soft cover ed. (New York, 1971), p. 37; Hassell Smith, *County and Court*, pp. 16, 112, 126–33, 138, 181, 242, 246, 247–76, 314–32, 335–39; Hirst, *Representative of the People?*, pp. 8, 10, 11; M. James, *Family, Lineage, and Civil Society*, pp. 156–59, 160–61, 164–67; L. Stone, *The Causes of the English Revolution, 1529–1642*, pp. 106–8.

7. *CSPV 1623 1625*, p. 201; *CSPV 1625 1626*, pp. 20, 63, 598.

**INFLUENCE IN EARLY STUART ELECTIONS, 1604–1640**

# ONE

## The Path to Westminster

The path to Westminster for a prospective member of parliament was most easily pursued when he could rely upon influence or patronage to get him his parliamentary place, and that influence or patronage came in many forms in early Stuart elections. Patronage meant more than just the influence of a great peer or court agency; it included the power exercised by a borough's corporation to control elections or the supremacy enjoyed by a family or group of families over their county's returns. Salisbury's corporation directed its elections, whereas the Montagu and Spencer families usually determined the outcome of Northamptonshire's returns. A manor lord could control a borough's elections; another borough's choices might be dictated by its high steward or recorder. Borough oligarchies and the leaders of a county community held fast to one principle: neither wanted contested elections and did all that they could, through preelection agreements, negotiations, and consultation, to prevent them. Contested elections were anathema to the elite; they were unsettling, factious affairs that could ruin the control the elite enjoyed. Electoral tactics — canvassing, entertainment, intimidation — were the elite's methods of preserving its authority over an occasionally capricious electorate. The elite's patronage was just as important as the influence a Pembroke could wield, for, like a peer's influence, it determined the course of parliamentary elections.

Given the substantial increase in the number of gentry in the century ending in 1640, and the ensuing "intense competition for posts in county government," it is surprising that there were not more contested county elections between 1604 and 1640. The prestige that went with a county return was still the ultimate recognition of a squire's position within his county community. However, unless the evidence is deceptive, most county elections were tranquil affairs.[1] And the county's leadership clearly wanted it that way.

Preelection consultation, negotiation, and agreement enabled many a county's gentry to avoid the nightmare of a quarrelsome contest. The Spencer-Montagu alliance customarily decided upon Northamptonshire's candidates before an election. Sir Robert Harley probably owed his return for Herefordshire in 1624 to just such an arrangement. He urged "Sir T. C. " (presumably Sir Thomas Coningsby) to take no action "till we all meet to deliberate of the fittest persons for that attendance." Suffolk's 1626 election followed a similar course. John Winthrop asked for Sir Robert Crane's opinion of the possible election of Sir Robert Naunton as knight of the shire. Winthrop and Crane consulted other leaders of Suffolk's community, agreement was reached, and Naunton was returned. Shropshire's gentlemen discussed beforehand who their candidates should be, and in 1628 they "resolved to support Sir Richard Newport and Sir Andrew Corbett for Parliament," who were dutifully elected knights of the shire. Had the evidence survived, it is likely that similar agreements were reached in counties like Devonshire, Staffordshire, Sussex, and Westmorland, which apparently never suffered through a contested election from 1604 to 1640.[2]

Influence dominated borough elections. Indeed, of England's 207 parliamentary boroughs that returned one, two, or, as in London's case, four members to parliament, 124, or nearly 60 percent, can be described as patronage boroughs. And of those 124 patronage boroughs, the returns indicate that neighboring gentry dominated 65, the peerage 26, and urban corporations 27. A lonely six were under the crown's influence.[3] A borough might be controlled by its oligarchy, determined to return local men for local purposes; it could also mean that a corporation willingly surrendered a burgess-ship in return for a promise of support and favor from an influential peer or neighboring squire. The great or near-great could be potentially useful to a borough. And just as boroughs increasingly expected their members to defend local interests and secure aid for local projects, so too did they hope for the assistance of their patron or high steward. Canterbury turned to the earl of Montgomery as a counterweight to the archbishop's influence; in return, Montgomery expected burgess-ships for his friends. The corporation, an alderman admitted, "durst not deny" Montgomery since "they had great enemies, and need of great friends."[4]

The ultimate expression of influence was in the use of "blanks." The patron secured the blank indenture and inserted the name of his nominee; its employment made an election unnecessary. Blanks were employed in Elizabethan elections; indeed, James's proclamation summoning his first parliament outlawed "blanks," a possible indication of widespread usage.[5] Despite the proclamation's strictures, the use of blanks continued. Cecil, the first earl of Salisbury, employed them at Hedon and Bossiney in 1609. He was sent the Bossiney "indenture subscribed and sealed together with our seal itself to alter and dispose the same with our allowance and consent." Blanks were used in Penryn in 1625, 1626, and 1628, at West Looe in 1628, and probably at Helston in 1614. Lord Sheffield, president of the Council of the North, employed a blank at Scarborough in 1614; the earl of Bridgewater used one in Flint's 1621 election, and, if objections were made, its corporation was welcome to insert his nominee's name in the indenture. Pembroke employed a blank at Wilton in 1626. Sheffield claimed he was following the "usual course" in elections; and though his remark was an exaggeration — to persuade Scarborough's corporation — it suggested that blanks were used more often than remaining evidence indicates. Their use guaranteed an uncontested election; it was striking evidence of the power of the elite in borough elections.[6]

Manor lords could dominate a borough's elections. Thomas Arundell, later Baron Arundell of Wardour, bought the manor and borough of Christchurch in 1601 and gained the right to nominate a burgess to parliament. However, his nominees took both places in 1604 and nine (possibly ten) further places through 1628. Nine men served for Christchurch; seven (perhaps eight) owed their choice to Arundell. And, as he promised the little borough in 1614, they served without charge. That must have been an added incentive; the burden of paying its burgesses could have been disastrous for the borough.[7]

Cambridge's elections from 1614 through 1628 illustrated the price a borough could pay for having illustrious high stewards. Despite ordinances against the choice of strangers, its stewards, Lord Chancellors Ellesmere, Bacon, and Coventry, nominated four outsiders who took seven of Cambridge's twelve burgess-ships. The corporation, in continual conflict with its freemen over its control of municipal elections, kept its grip on parliamentary elections without trouble through 1628. The oligarchy's acceptance of the freemen's gradual involvement in such elections may explain the absence of contests and emphasizes the lack of interest parliamentary elections aroused, since, even with a wider electorate, Cambridge's returns continued to reflect the corporation's control and steward's influence.[8]

Bedford, an oligarchic borough with a narrow franchise, had as its neighbor and recorder Oliver, Baron St. John of Bletsho and earl of Bolingbroke (1624); and, given those connections, it is hardly surprising that its elections showed his imprint. His brothers, Sir Alexander St. John (1614–25), Sir Beauchamp St. John (1626–28), and his deputy recorder, Richard Taylor (1621–28), were Bedford's burgesses. Taylor, whose election was challenged by the earl of Cleveland's nominee in 1628, reminded the corporation of his faithful service, noted he would serve without pay, and emphasized that if he were not returned, the "honour of the honourable lord, whose servent I am in this place" would be besmirched. He was elected. Bedford's corporation, at least in parliamentary elections, was under Bolingbroke's control.[9]

The office of recorder could be a stepping stone to parliament. Sir Henry Yelverton, Northampton's recorder, was M. P. for the borough in 1604 and 1614 and probably supported the election of three other burgesses, who filled six of its places, through 1628.[10] Chester's 1621 election testified to the influence of its recorder; Sir James Whitelocke, Woodstock's recorder, was returned in 1610, 1614, and 1621, and his office was responsible, since in 1614, when Woodstock "was hardly pressed for another by the Earl of Montgomery," Whitelocke was still elected. Lord Conway nominated Sir Robert Harley for Evesham in 1628, but its corporation refused to take any action "before they had spoken with Mr. Cresheld, their recorder," who approved Harley's choice. The office was no guarantee, however, of influence, as Sir Richard Buller, Saltash's recorder, discovered in 1628. He fought the borough's choice of Sir Francis Cottington, but, thanks to the mayor, "who deserves exceeding well," Cottington was returned.[11]

Urban oligarchies controlled election returns in a few cities or boroughs. These urban elites were patrons for their own members. Such corporations, unlike those at Cambridge or Bedford, resisted any form of influence. Gloucester and York went through contested elections; in neither was the electoral predominance of the oligarchy impaired. Plymouth and Salisbury had narrow, restrictive franchises; Gloucester, York, and Newcastle-on-Tyne had large electorates. In all of them, however, Plymouth, Salisbury, Newcastle-on-Tyne, Gloucester, York, and Bristol, their urban oligarchies directed their parliamentary returns.[12]

Salisbury and Plymouth returned their recorders and members of their ruling oligarchies. Both rejected outside intervention. Salisbury, which accepted nominees of the earls of Pembroke in 1572 and 1640, turned down Pembroke and the king's attorney general, Sir Robert Heath, in 1626; Plymouth, which had accepted outsiders in Elizabeth's reign, refused the Duchy of Cornwall in 1621 and 1624. Salisbury exemplified Hirst's argument that boroughs wanted members "who could bring home local goods," for, as its corporation pointed out to its prospective patrons in 1626, poverty was so serious in the town that it needed an Act of Parliament to preserve its "common brewhouse." Other issues, too, required that "two of our own company" serve in parliament. Local men for local goods was Salisbury's position through the election of 1628. Plymouth may have felt the same way; it generously rewarded its recorders for their services following the Parliaments of 1614 and 1621.[13]

Newcastle-on-Tyne, Bristol, and Gloucester's elections through 1628 were controlled by their oligarchies, men of similar economic backgrounds and often connected by marriage. Their urban elites dominated their town's economic and political life. Gloucester and Newcastle had large electorates that could be factious (Gloucester, 1604) but never overturned their corporation's domination. Newcastle's members had all served as mayors, sheriffs, and aldermen; all were coal merchants and leaders of the Hostmen. Bristol's freemen demanded the "vote . . . in the midst of depression" in 1625, but it still consistently returned its recorders or, more often, merchants who had served Bristol as mayors, sheriffs, and aldermen.[14]

York's corporation also managed its elections. Only one contest occurred (1628), and the House of Commons confirmed the corporation's choices. Its members were instructed to give constant attention to the city's parliamentary needs, and York paid a high price for such service. Christopher Brooke (1604–10) received £132, and that was after he reduced his claim. Sir Robert Askwith (1604–10, 1614, 1621) received travel expenses, ten shillings a day, and was given an additional £20 in 1621. Sir Arthur Ingram (1624–28) served, no doubt to York's relief, without pay; but another member, alderman Thomas Hoyle (1628), was still after his pay in 1630 and finally received it after a special tax was levied to satisfy his claim.[15] Given York's bills, it is not surprising that many a borough corporation accepted candidates who served without charge.

Cost probably forced Worcester's corporation to turn to outsiders; at Nottingham it certainly did. Through 1624 Worcester elected its own to parliament. The usual charges were paid, half by a tax of "one double fifteen" by the commons, the other half by the corporation. The bill was steep, totaling nearly £91 for the Parliaments of 1614–24, and that was probably too much for Worcester, already "much impoverished" by the clothing depression. Three of its next four members (1625–26) were outsiders, the likely result of its financial woes, since there is no mention of wages or taxation in the Chamber Orders book. In 1628 it chose two residents, but, despite the best efforts of the corporation, John Cowcher, owed £37, was still unpaid at Christmas 1629, and his colleague, John Haselock, was probably never paid for his service in 1626 and 1628.[16] Cost forced Nottingham's corporation to decide, before the election of 1621, that "2 foreigners be chosen

. . . to serve in this Parliament for the easing of the town's charge," and they were in both 1621 and 1624. It reversed itself in 1625 and chose townsmen, but that was the end, since, in 1626 and 1628, Nottingham accepted nominees. Cost was a factor; however, the corporation also wanted "the friendship and favour of those two noble families [Viscount Mansfield and Viscount Newark], and have their assistance to the town." Nottingham's reasons showed why the influence of the gentry and peerage was so successful in early Stuart elections.[17]

County elections were the province of the gentry, the county community. Between 1604 and 1640, fifty-one counties elected 810 knights of the shire, and, of those that can be identified, the gentry, through their own influence, accounted for 544 (67.1 percent) knightships. Other patronage, chiefly aristocratic, secured 254 places.[18] Gentry influence predominated in twenty-five English and ten Welsh counties, and eight counties returned candidates of the gentry and peerage on a fairly even basis. Aristocratic influence dominated the returns of six English and two Welsh counties.[19]

Gentry influence was increasingly felt in borough elections. In 1604, 111 boroughs chose at least one county resident, a figure that increased to 130 boroughs in 1626 and 1628. In 1628, 62 boroughs filled both burgess-ships with county residents; 192 local gentry captured borough places in 1628. And since the number of local residents returned to parliament had leveled off at about 81 in 1625–28, the outsider was the loser in the gentry's invasion. In 1614, 121 outsiders were elected; a slow decline followed until, in 1628, only 103 strangers were returned.[20] Borough self-interest was, perhaps, behind the gentry's success. The neighboring squire, experienced in local government, aware of local needs, and known to a borough corporation and its electorate, enjoyed substantial advantages over an outsider, a stranger to the community and its requirements. The increasing fiscal demands of the early Stuarts, as Hirst has shown, strengthened the tie between a constituency and its members; local men could be kept responsible to the community's wishes more readily than a stranger.[21]

The influence of a Sir Thomas Grantham in Lincolnshire, a Sir John Strangways in Dorsetshire, or a Sir Thomas Bludder in Surrey accounted for their elections. Gentry influence was responsible for more than 36 percent of available burgess-ships through 1628; indeed, it peaked at 46 percent in 1628. Gentry, thanks to their own and other electoral influence, won more than four out of every ten burgess-ships through 1626 and over half (51.0 percent) in 1628. And when the electoral intervention of the gentry is added to that wielded by the peerage, royal agencies, and great clerics, it is clear that patronage dominated early Stuart elections and that the gentry, leaders of their county communities, enjoyed a preponderant electoral voice in county and borough.[22]

Many counties avoided conflict through preelection agreements reached by the community's elite; however, if such agreements collapsed or negotiations failed, troublesome elections followed. Contested elections were nightmares for the elite. Challenges to a family's electoral eminence could turn a county's elections upside down; so, too, could a battle between two equal contenders for election victory. Faction within a borough corporation could lead to election contests; disputes between a corporation and a great neighbor or resident also led to trouble. Dissatisfaction among the governed produced serious municipal problems that could spill over into parliamentary elections. Economic issues, poverty, concern over the use of the town's revenues, local quarrels over the selection of ministers, the election of a mayor, all could set the town's oligarchy at odds with its citizenry. Such quarrels could be exploited by a neighboring squire, anxious to extend his influence at the corporation's expense. Contested elections often grew out of local disputes, and that combination, of local faction and a bitter election, could wreck a community's harmony for years.[23]

Contested elections could result from a challenge to one family's predominance (the Wynns in Caernarvonshire) or because two ambitious contenders wanted sole eminence (Yorkshire). They could also develop from the failure of the candidates to reach a preelection accord. In 1614 Sir Robert Phelips, Sir Maurice Berkeley, and Sir John Poulett, despite their professed desire to maintain the "long continued peace and quiet of our country," fell out over who would stand with Berkeley. Berkeley and Poulett were elected for Somersetshire, but the fight was so bitter that it scarred the county for years.[24] When preelection agreements were reached in Northamptonshire, elections passed quietly; but when such planning failed and the county's leadership divided, contested elections, as in 1624 and 1626, were the result. In Dorsetshire a preelection agreement broke down in 1624, and a contest followed; in 1626 the county's elite, led by Sir John Strangways, held their usual meeting to "agree among themselves who should stand" but reached no decision since Strangways had to leave the meeting early. Nothing was resolved and Dorsetshire went through not one, but two, faction-plagued elections.[25]

Three candidates, leaders of Hampshire's county community, sought election in 1614. The gentry, anxious to obtain agreement and preserve tranquility, tried as late as 2 March 1614 to settle the election. During a sessions meeting, the three were pressed to resolve their differences "by lot or hazard" to decide which two would stand; agreement failed, and a contested election and a Star Chamber suit were the results. Cheshire's gentry tried the same approach in 1626 and 1628 in the hopes of avoiding contested elections. On both occasions they pressured candidates either to withdraw or to settle their differences by drawing lots. In 1626, they gained a partial success; one candidate withdrew.[26]

Contested elections at Chester and Gloucester were the outgrowth of disputes within the governing body. Gloucester's factious 1604 election was caused by an alderman, John Jones, who may have been backed by the local bishop. Jones refused to accept his colleague's choices as the city's members for parliament. His campaign, among the "meaner sort," stressed local issues of benefit to the citizens' pocketbooks, liberal drinking, deceit, and the votes of the "vulgar." There was further trouble in 1614 when the corporation, after selecting two candidates, reversed itself, and two others, members of the oligarchy, were returned. Jones's campaign did not change Gloucester's habit of choosing members of its governing body or their relatives. He did, however, manage to upset the oligarchy's plans in 1604.[27] Municipal bitterness was pronounced at Chester and surfaced in its 1621 election. The corporation was at odds with the freemen and divided against itself. The bitter dispute intensified in 1619 when the mayor tried to sack recorder Edward Whitby and forced his allies off the governing body. The quarrel grew so hot that an assize judge and the Privy Council intervened. A reconciliation was effected but came unstuck during the election, which was further enlivened by the intervention of the Prince's Council. Whitby, the outraged recorder, and his allies revenged themselves on the corporation by overturning its plan to elect Sir Thomas Edmondes, the prince's nominee. The corporation, of course, complained of Whitby's campaign among the "vulgar," but, again, his victory marked no reversal of Chester's habit of returning members of its oligarchy or its officials to parliament. The disputes at Gloucester and Chester confirm Hirst's view that election contests were "almost incidental" to the main quarrels, which were rooted in municipal issues.[28]

Canterbury's elections from 1621 through 1628 were bitter affairs. Local grievances, intensified by increasing poverty, the plague, and a developing quarrel between the corporation and the archbishop, were further enlivened by the intervention of two peers, the duke of Lennox, in the elections of 1621–24, and the earl of Montgomery, in the contests of 1625–28. Their intervention only made the situation worse. The corporation's divisions grew, the commons became even more alienated, and several local ministers became zealous electoral opponents of the municipal regime. The election of 1626 brought such discontents to a head. Montgomery's nominee, backed by most of the oligarchy including the mayor, the sheriff, and a majority of the aldermen, was challenged by two local residents, Thomas Scott and Sir John Wylde, a friend of the archbishop. The common councillors and "other honest commoners" favored Scott and Wylde, who lost. It was Canterbury's fourth contested election in a row; all were reflections of the grievances that plagued the city.[29]

At Colchester and Exeter, rebellious freemen overthrew corporate electoral control. Exeter's oligarchy ruled its elections, but, thanks to growing urban discontent, the situation was ripe for the change that came in 1626, following a serious outbreak of the plague. The oligarchy's response to the crisis was flight; one magistrate, Ignatius Jourdain (M.P. 1621, 1625), remained, took charge of the city, and became the hero of the commons, who, over the resistance of the oligarchy, twice elected him to parliament (1626, 1628). They also won (1628) an extension of the franchise. Jourdain, although a popular hero, was no outsider; he had been mayor and deputy mayor of Exeter and was just as much a part of the urban oligarchy as the corporation's candidates that the freemen refused.[30] Colchester's freemen, thanks to the clothing depression, had been at odds with its corporation since at least 1612. Their discontent was a constant factor in the town's politics, which were further complicated by the earl of Warwick's interest in the town. A minor election dispute in 1625 may have involved the freemen. Sir Henry Hobart and Robert Radcliffe, earl of Sussex, intervened in the election; but when the town clerk, William Towse, with corporation approval, gave up his place in favor of Hobart's son, the "whole company . . . consisting of a multitude" refused to allow it. The freemen's discontent overturned the corporation's electoral control in 1628 when they refused the oligarchy's choice, the outsider Edward Alford (M.P. for Colchester 1604–25), and instead chose Warwick's friend Sir William Masham. They petitioned the House of Commons, which overturned Alford's election, Colchester's narrow franchise, and, as another result, turned Colchester into a safe borough for Warwick's friends.[31]

Disputes over corporate control of town lands and growing poverty were behind election quarrels that vexed Chippenham and Warwick and led to the overthrow of narrow franchises and customary electoral influences. At Warwick, Sir Fulke Greville, Lord Brooke (1621), was allied with its corporation, which was repeatedly challenged by the commons. Economic grievances were compounded by the commons' belief that the oligarchy was appropriating town revenues for its own use. Neighboring gentry became involved in the quarrel, and in the 1621 election, the commons, led by several gentry, questioned the oligarchy's choices. Serious trouble began in 1625 when a more determined neighbor, Sir Thomas Puckering, contested the influence of Brooke and the corporation by petitioning the House of Commons over the election. Parliament's dissolution probably frustrated Puckering's plans, but Puckering, the ally of the factious commoners, tried again in 1626 and finally succeeded in 1628. The House of Commons overthrew Warwick's narrow franchise, and, by so doing, temporarily ended Brooke's electoral influence. Puckering's selfish alliance with Warwick's commoners had triumphed.[32]

Chippenham's patron, Sir Anthony Mildmay of Apethorpe, Northamptonshire, had, thanks to his marriage connections, a financial tie to the town. However, his nominee, Edward Wymarke, had been refused in 1604; perhaps his candidacy was caught up in the simmering dispute between the freemen and the corporation over the use of the profits from the town's lands. Economic troubles plagued Chippenham; it had great difficulty in paying John Roberts, elected in 1604, the only townsman returned in the early seventeenth century. Another disputed election followed in 1614 when Mildmay and his son-in-law, Sir Francis Fane of Mereworth Castle, Kent, forced through the choice of a Kent squire, Thomas Culpeper. Other patrons, including William, second earl of Salisbury, John Hungerford, a neighboring squire, and Cicely, countess of Rutland, were also involved.[33] The commoners, already hard hit by the clothing depression, were angered even more by the crown's enclosure of Chippenham forest. In the 1624 election, the outraged commons rebelled against the corporation's nominee, John Pym, who was the royal receiver closely connected with the enclosure. Sir Francis Popham of Littlecote, Wiltshire, and Wellington, Somersetshire, was the commoners' ally. On petition the House of Commons denied Pym's election and threw out the borough's narrow franchise. Popham served from 1624 through 1628 and became Chippenham's benefactor, granting £6 "forever to three poor freemen, yearly." If it was the commons' reward for their support in 1624, it was only a beginning; he repaid their loyalty with service and generosity. The enlarged franchise made no difference in Chippenham's elections. It was, actually from 1621 onward, another Wiltshire gentry borough.[34]

Discontented freemen were ready allies for ambitious gentry at Shrewsbury (1604) and Sandwich (1621), but in neither case was the electoral pattern of the borough substantially altered. The story was different at Dartmouth. Its merchant oligarchy, which had denied two patrons on the grounds of local necessity in 1614, could not prevent the intervention of a neighbor, Sir John Upton of Brixham and Lupton, elected in 1625 and 1626. Upton probably used discontented freemen for his own purposes since, in 1626, the angry corporation prepared a "constitution" for the election of future burgesses which noted that some freemen (supporters of Upton?) "out of contentious, malicious and turbulent humor" had ignored "their oaths and duties" to only elect freemen by recently (1625 and 1626?) supporting "foreigners, men neither free of the borough nor inhabitants of the same," presumably Upton. But, in spite of strong penalties and the denial of the earl of Manchester's nominee, Upton was still returned in 1628. Upton, unlike three other powerful patrons, had upset the electoral control of the town's oligarchy.[35]

Disputed elections meant an appeal to the electorate, and, as Hirst has shown, it was a much larger electorate than hitherto realized. Inflation had made the forty-shilling freehold qualification largely meaningless, and, to swell the crowds even more, tenurial distinctions were very blurred. Confusion existed over just who could vote, a confusion that was further compounded by the obvious difficulties in attempting to ascertain voter eligibility. Listing freeholders was a difficult and time-consuming task at best, and, in populous counties, it was practically impossible. The House of Commons, too, opposed such practices since it smacked of intimidation. The county electorate was large, "socially heterogeneous," and volatile to a frightening degree for the place-seeking squire. It could not be easily controlled. In 1659 Richard Baxter claimed, "Our common people ordinarily choose such as their landlords do desire them to choose," but reality was probably quite different from Baxter's patronizing view. Tenants were "expected to comply with their landlord's wishes," but, given the variety of tactics employed to control voters, tenants could not be trusted to do so. Norfolk's candidates in Elizabeth's reign, at least, were seldom sure of the electorate's favor since "many Norfolk freeholders refused to be martialled as pawns on the electoral board." Wentworth's concern over freeholder reliability in Yorkshire, based on his experience in its hotly contested elections of 1621, 1625, and 1628, suggests a similar problem. Indeed, Baxter's views would have been vigorously denied by the gentry of Worcestershire (1604), Hampshire and Somersetshire (1614), Caernarvonshire (1621, 1624, 1625), Cambridgeshire (1624), Northamptonshire (1625), Cornwall and Essex (1628), or Gloucestershire (spring 1640), who, in those contested elections, found their tenants challenging their leadership.

It may be, as Hassell Smith suggests, that Norfolk's freeholders were developing a political consciousness; it is also possible that they simply refused to be easily swayed and were determined to show their independence.[36] Borough electorates could also be difficult, especially in the larger towns that had the freemen's franchise. Such franchises were the most numerous and often included "some hundreds of voters," a potentially troublesome prospect for a patron or town corporation.[37]

Contested elections brought this volatile and sometimes large electorate into action and put the plans and hopes of the elite, in borough or county, at risk. Electoral tactics were attempts at voter control. An oligarchy's or patron's influence could vanish in a flood of freemen's votes; a county's leaders might see their plans and hopes dashed by an unruly flock of freeholders. Uncontested elections were the goal of the elite, and some schemes—the capture of the writ, the suborning of the sheriff, or the use of "blanks"—were used to prevent electoral challenges, to ensure "quiet" elections. Other tactics—canvassing, the employment of clergy as campaign orators, entertainment, even force and violence—were variations on the same theme: voter control.

Office, a symbol of status in a socially conscious society, could be profitably employed in elections. Justices of the peace, deputy lieutenants, sheriffs, and mayors could play strong electoral roles. Worcestershire's justices were active participants in its 1604 election, and Wentworth's candidacies in Yorkshire relied heavily upon such support. Anglesey's election of Sir Sackville Trevor in 1625 was the work of its justices, who "subscribed under their hands to be for him" before the election. The Essex election of 1628 was a blatant example of what justices could do in an attempt to control an election. Deputy lieutenants could also try to influence elections. Voters in Caernarvonshire's 1621 contest were threatened with military penalties by two of Wynn's supporters, both deputy lieutenants. Sir John Stawell, a deputy lieutenant in Somersetshire, billeted more than one hundred rude soldiers in Taunton, even putting some in the homes of the mayor and recorder, in an effort to pressure the town's voters to oppose his foe, Sir Robert Phelips, in the county's 1628 election.[38]

"Mr. Coryton moved against the sheriff of Flint. Divers misdemeanours about the last election of the Knight of the Shire there." It was a common complaint for, as Neale observed, the sheriff was "the key man" in a contested election; indeed, it was always important to have the sheriff as an ally. He was the presiding electoral officer, decided on the necessity of a poll, and made the return. His actions could, if unchallenged, nullify the electorate's wishes. And since he was deeply involved with his county, Neale's remark that "he was rarely impartial" was an understatement. His support was much in demand, especially if a contest threatened to develop. Henry Wynn was finally advised to stand for Merionethshire in 1624 because "the shreive shall do what you please." Sir Thomas Wentworth made sure of the sheriff before Yorkshire's elections in 1621 and 1625. Norfolk's 1614 election was decided by the sheriff's decision to move the election site. The sheriff was so important to the Wynns in Caernarvonshire's 1621 election that they bribed him. Radnorshire's sheriff determined the outcome of its 1621 election by spinning out the poll, by counting only those backing his friend James Price, including clergymen rounded up for the occasion, and by ignoring the voices of Price's foe William Vaughan. Finally, he went to a leisurely dinner with Price, and Vaughan's backers, patience exhausted, "departed thence away much discontented." Cambridgeshire's 1624 election was decided by the tactics of a scheming undersheriff since the sheriff, astonishingly enough a young and inexperienced man of around twenty-two, simply abandoned his responsibilities. In every case of shreival chicanery, some part of the electorate was affected; the sheriff's power, if forcefully used, could disfranchise voters and ensure a favored member of the elite election victory.[39]

Mayors could play decisive roles in elections. Pembroke's mayor, thanks to his canvassing, intimidation, and a promise to "admit no election" unless his brother-in-law was elected in 1621, had his way until the House of Commons threw out the election. In 1624 Pontefract's mayor endeavored to control its election by shutting voters out, and Arundel's mayor kept an election going until he secured a majority for his candidate. The House threw out both elections. Winchelsea's mayor blocked Sir Alexander Temple's return in 1624 despite two petitions and two elections. He failed to give adequate notice of the first election, accused Temple of being a papist, hid or destroyed his letters of recommendation, and disqualified two of Temple's supporters from voting so that he could cast the decisive vote. The House ordered another election, but its results duplicated the first; Temple petitioned again but to no avail. Winchelsea's mayor, unlike his colleagues at Pontefract, Arundel, and Pembroke, had triumphed.[40]

Everyone, from the Privy Council on down, condemned canvassing, the solicitation of votes. It was often a sign of friction among the elite, it invited the electorate's active participation (under appropriate leadership, of course), and signaled that electoral trouble was ahead. Canvassing, despite such objections, remained a commonly employed tactic. Letters flew from competitor's pens, alliances were formed, friendships were tested, all in order to win the backing of as many influential men as possible. It was their task to rally the freeholders to a candidate's side, to organize and lead their tenants to an election. Canvassing marked both borough and county elections; it was part of the 1604 elections at Gloucester and Shrewsbury, the bitter Sandwich election in 1621, and the contested elections of 1604, 1624, and 1626 in Northamptonshire. Both sides, Protestant and papist, vigorously canvassed Worcestershire's electorate in 1604, but opposition to such tactics surfaced there in 1614. Sir Samuel Sandys's labors—"he writes to divers about the country for their voices,"— made his neighbor, William Russell, angry enough to condemn Sandys's canvass as "impudent folly." The furious Russell promptly launched a similar campaign against Sandys. Yorkshire's elections of 1621, 1625, 1626, and 1628 were all marked by zealous canvassing. The battles between Wentworth and Savile in 1621 and 1625 were intensified by Savile's canvassing among the "vulgar," which probably rebounded against him among the county's leadership. In 1625 one of Wentworth's supporters, Sir Richard Beaumont, was outraged by what he saw: it was "more like a rebellion than an election: the gentry are wronged, the freeholders are wronged." For Beaumont the social implications were intolerable, and Wentworth heartily agreed. He saw the campaigns of 1625 as challenges to the gentry's customary authority. He pictured Savile's campaign as one conducted against his candidacy and "against all the gentlemen too besides." Savile's electioneering aroused the "vulgar," Yorkshire's large and volatile electorate; it was too much for Yorkshire's gentry to accept. Canvassing, of course, was not always fruitful, as Sir Thomas Thynne discovered in Wiltshire's elections of 1625 and 1628. In spite of appeals to his friends for their "kind assistance . . . by the voice of all your friends and tenants of this county at the election" and of promises of help from the sheriff in 1628, he was twice rebuffed. Electoral predominance in Wiltshire, at least in 1625 and 1628, was in the hands of the earls of Pembroke and Hertford, and nothing that Thynne attempted could alter that.[41]

County canvassing often included appeals to urban voters, who could, as Hirst observed, play decisive roles in shire contests. In 1621 Wentworth recruited York's citizens to help "mend our cry" and, as an inducement, promised Sir George Calvert's aid to the city. James

Price's friends in Radnorshire's 1621 contest busily canvassed voters from New Radnor and Prestigne, and Dorchester's citizens almost gave Dorsetshire's 1626 election to their favorite, "John Brown of Dorchester." In hotly fought contests, competitors occasionally went further and created bogus freeholders. Both sides did it in Caernarvonshire's 1621 election. The Wynn's foes were hard at work "creating of [sic] new freeholders," and the Wynns did the same to such an extent that news of their apparently bountiful creations even reached London.[42]

Clergymen, from humble parish vicars to mitred bishops, were often vociferous electoral campaigners. They could lend their authority to rally and control potential voters. Such activity could be expected; their ties were usually with the elite, frequently patrons of their livings.[43] The bishop of Worcester's interest in Worcestershire's 1604 election must have led to electoral homilies before the election, and campaigns in Essex were undoubtedly enlivened by the earl of Warwick's clergymen, holders of those reformist views so dear to the earl and his friends. Bishop Bayly, following a Sunday sermon, exhorted "all his parishoners & tenants to pass their voices" for Sir Richard Wynn in Caernarvonshire's 1621 election, and James Price might well have credited his return for Radnorshire in 1621 to his clerical son-in-law, Dr. Vaughan, who was his most effective campaigner. Vaughan used Sunday services for canvassing, suborned the sheriff, enlisted his fellow clergy around New Radnor in Price's behalf, and threatened reluctant voters with appearances "before the ordinary of the diocese of St. Davids," an expensive and time-consuming prospect. Sandwich's 1621 election was further stirred by a "precise preacher"; at Blechingley in 1624, Dr. Nathaniel Harris became so involved that he was punished by the House of Commons for his electioneering. Wentworth and Savile employed ministers in Yorkshire's 1625 election, and a Canterbury clergyman, the Reverend Aldey of St. Andrews', got so mixed up in its 1626 election that he attracted the "very earnest and fierce" attentions of the mayor and town clerk, who demanded to know why Aldey "meddle[d] in civil businesses? He did contrary to religion in it." Cornwall's clergy were probably active participants in its 1628 election.[44]

Canvassing, even when enhanced by the fulminations of the clergy, was still not enough to ensure voter loyalty; indeed, a landlord could hardly be sure of his tenant's constancy. It was, for the worried candidate, a short step from persuasion to threats and intimidation; and, in some contested elections, it was an easy step to take. A form of more subtle intimidation that aroused the wrath of the House of

Commons occurred in Yorkshire's 1621 election when Sir Thomas Wentworth directed that the constables prepare lists of freeholders' names committed to his, and Calvert's, cause. But it was not a new practice; it had been used in Northamptonshire (1604) and Hampshire (1614) and was probably more common than the surviving evidence indicates.[45]

More direct action, however, was often taken, testimony to the lack of control the elite enjoyed and their determination to maintain voter discipline by any means at hand. Clergymen were not immune to such action; Bishop Bayly's friends feared that parliament would call him to account "for threatening his tenants to give their voices with him" in Caernarvonshire's quarrelsome 1621 election. Indeed, the situation was so threatening in Caernarvonshire and Worcestershire, too, that the Council of the Marches of Wales intervened, ordering that only "the Sheriff and his servants in livery and officers do bear any weapons" to the elections.[46]

Threats, intimidation, and violence, then, were desperate tactics used to control the voter. In 1621 Huntingdonshire's sheriff, Thomas Maples, allegedly pressured freeholders for their voices by warning them that if they refused, he "would punish them by making them continually to attend your Majesty's service at the Assizes and Sessions." Maples, it seems, kept his word. James Price's followers mounted a parade in Prestigne to mark Radnorshire's election day in 1621. Accompanied by ringing bells and with drums beating, they trooped through the town "in warlike manner, armed with swords, daggers and other unlawful weapons" threatening any freeholders who might "pass their voices" against Price. John Wogan and his men had, it was claimed in a disputed Pembrokeshire election in 1625, threatened and beaten up many, impressed some as soldiers, and prevented others (the lucky ones?) "from coming to the election." Some of Stockbridge's voters in its 1614 election found themselves jailed for their refusal to back the Duchy of Lancaster's nominee, and Bishop Castle's corporation was so fearful of tumult at its 1621 election that it ordered every householder "be that day ready with his halberd" to prevent disturbances. Some elections could be exciting and, for the prospective voters, potentially damaging affairs.[47]

"Double dealing" could win an election, as Sir Nathaniel Napier learned to his cost in Dorsetshire's 1624 election. Napier believed Sir George Horsey's denials of any intention to stand, but, on election day, the trusting Napier came up short and Horsey took the seat. A similar deceit was tried at Lewes in 1628. Another trick was to secretly secure the election writ so supporters could be mustered and a snap election held during the subsequent county court day. The Wynns were constantly on the lookout for the writ for Caernarvonshire's elections. Sir James Perrot was positive he owed his loss to Sir Thomas Canon at Haverfordwest in 1626 to Canon's interception of the writ. The 1628 Essex election was a textbook example of the scheme and, for that matter, of many of the other tactics and tricks that could be used to attempt election victory.[48]

Surviving evidence suggests that elections could be expensive affairs. Sir John Wynn spent over £100 in Caernarvonshire's 1621 election, and that did not include his friends' expenses. Little wonder, then, that before the next election, Owen Wynn cautioned his father against involvement since it would cost him "£50 at least," a conservative estimate given the expenses run up in 1621. Henry Wynn was urged to stand for Merionethshire, but only "if it may be done, without charge." Such concern was understandable; the cost of Wentworth's preelection dinners for many of his friends before Yorkshire's 1621 election must have been substantial. Sir Albertus Morton allegedly spent "two or three hundred pounds at the least" in winning the Kent election of 1625. Borough elections could also be expensive. Sir Henry Wotton spent £50 in losing Canterbury's 1625 election; the city's next contest cost Thomas Scott £100. Such sums might explain why Warwick's town clerk was so concerned when, in 1628, the borough's franchise was enlarged by the House of Commons. He was haunted by visions of widespread corruption as candidates courted almsmen and "all sorts of ill conditioned people."[49]

The money usually went for food, drink, and lodgings for the voters; occasionally it was used to pay "alleged" freeholders for their time and trouble in coming to the election. Worcestershire's 1604 election illustrated such expenditures. Similar allegations, of the creation of freeholders by "divers bribes, rewards and sums of money" were made in Radnorshire's 1621 election and in the Essex contest of 1628.[50] Food, drink, and lodgings were arranged for voters at Gloucester and Essex (1604) and Northamptonshire (1626). Such preparations could prove essential for voter loyalty, as Sir Henry Wallop discovered in Hampshire's 1614 contest. A late start, delays caused by demonstrations, two views, and a wearying poll made it a long day. Sir Richard Tichborne, Wallop's opponent, was ready: ample supplies of food and drink sustained his supporters while Wallop's went without. His hungry and thirsty followers melted away as the day wore on. Sir Thomas Wentworth made sure that supplies of beer and wine had been laid in to "refresh" his voters in

Yorkshire's 1625 election. East Retford's voters, too, were a thirsty lot: they ran up a tavern bill of £40 in its 1624 election, and Wotton's £50 at Canterbury in 1625 was mostly spent, it was claimed, on drink. Occasionally custom dictated expenditure, as Lord Conway discovered at Andover in 1628 when, following his son's election, he was expected to host a celebratory dinner.[51]

Other rewards or "gifts" might also be made by candidates. Sir Dudley Digges of Kent was so grateful to faithful Tewkesbury (it elected him six times) that he sent the corporation £160 for land purchases, the beginning of a number of benefactions Digges showered on the loyal borough. And, though nothing directly connects Scarborough's 1614 election of William Conyers to his uncle's generous loan to the corporation, it is hard to believe it was simply coincidence. Gifts, however, could be withdrawn; in 1625 Lady Howard threatened to take away her benevolence of fourteen nobles at Blechingly if her nominee was not returned.[52] But where was the line drawn between these "gifts" and bribery?

Only one case of bribery is known for Elizabeth's reign; no one admitted a similar action to the House of Commons from 1604 to 1628. However, bribery was employed by the Wynns in Caernarvonshire's 1621 election; it allegedly occurred at East Retford and Blechingley in 1624 and at Bridport in 1626. The Wynns bribed the sheriff. Sir William Thomas suggested it, fearful that their opponents might "outbid" them for the sheriff's favor. The Wynns lost the election, and an outraged Sir John Wynn contemplated Star Chamber action against the sheriff but was dissuaded by his son Owen, who had given the bribe to the sheriff's wife. The sheriff, Owen argued, could deny knowledge of it; furthermore, Sir William Thomas could be challenged for his "petty briberies in the country, which he has committed under colour of his office of lieutenant." It was a mare's nest and best left undisturbed.[53]

Henry Lovell, a candidate at Blechingley in 1624, denied before the House of Commons that he knew that a supporter "offered any money for him" to be elected. Voters at East Retford were allegedly offered from £2 to £10 for their votes. In 1626 Sir Richard Strode denounced the "foul corruption in buying of burgess-ships" in Bridport's election. Strode, who had unsuccessfully backed Buckingham's client, Edward Clarke, asserted that Sir Lewis Dyve's friends had used corrupt practices, presumably a "gift" of £5 to the town's poor, to win Dyve's election. The House of Commons ignored the complaint, but Bridport's corporation was very pleased with "one silver salt cellar" that Dyve gave them following his choice.[54]

The variety and ingenuity of the strategems employed by the early Stuart candidate was a singular comment on his tenacious pursuit of a parliamentary seat. The following table, based on direct evidence from 440 elections from 1604 to 1628, suggests the methods employed on the path to Westminster.

| Method | Employment in Number of Elections |
|---|---|
| Aristocratic, court, clerical letters of recommendation | 307 |
| Gentry letters of recommendation | 106 |
| Canvassing and campaigning | 150 |
| Intimidation and the creation of voices | 82 |
| Interception of the writ | 14 |
| Violence | 12 |
| Use of blanks | 10 |
| Employment of office: | |
| Sheriff | 40 |
| JP, Dep. Lt. | 29 |
| Borough office or corporation decision | 92 |
| Employment of ministers as campaign agents | 9 |
| Financial intervention | |
| Serve without pay | 49 |
| Entertainments | 25 |
| Bribery | 2 |

The candidate's motivation — political, social, or, more likely, a mixture of both — brought out his most inventive qualities. Faced with a potentially volatile electorate, he stopped at nothing to win his place; friends and relatives were canvassed, the sheriff consulted and, if possible, won over; local officers, the justices of the peace or the borough mayor, were rallied to his cause. Clergymen spread the election gospel. Freeholders could be created, writs intercepted, expenses paid, food and drink provided, even wages were available when necessary. Bribery was not beyond him, nor was he reluctant to threaten, intimidate, and, if necessary, use force to win his electoral goal. The prize was great; the prestige of election victory a compelling force. Election methods mirrored the turbulent, striving, and egotistical society that was early Stuart England.[55]

1. According to Hirst, 28 counties went through only three (or less) contested elections between 1604 and 1640. For the 11 Welsh counties not included in his totals, only one, Caernarvonshire, was consistently contested. There were contested elections for Radnorshire (1621) and Merionethshire (1626). Otherwise, Welsh counties seem to have been relatively quiet. Hirst, *Representative of the People?*, app. 4, pp. 216–22; Stone, *The Causes of the English Revolution, 1529–1642*, pp. 73–75; C. Russell, Ed., *The Origins of the English Civil War*, p. 9.

2. T. T. Lewis, ed., *Letters of the Lady Brilliana Harley*, pp. xliii–xliv; Winthrop to Crane, 14 Nov. 1625, Crane to Winthrop, n.d. 1627, Bodleian Library, Tanner MSS 72, fols. 69, 69v; Pierson to Harley, 16 Feb. 1628, *HMC Portland*, 3:23; Hirst, *Representative of the People?*, app. 4, pp. 216–22.

3. A two-member borough is defined as a patronage borough if eleven of its eighteen members or if 60% of its burgesses owed their return to a particular form of patronage. Single-member constituencies are given that title if six of nine members owe their choice to a special form of patronage, i.e., gentry, urban corporation, crown, or aristocratic influence. This determination and the figures used are taken from the returns set out in Appendix Six.

4. Examples of this relationship between patron and borough can be found at the Northamptonshire RO, Ellesmere (Brackley) MSS, E(B) 510/1 & 2, 512/1, 513/1, 514/2, 515, 516, covering 1616–21. Brackley was involved in a dispute over its privileges and sought Bridgewater's aid; for his part Bridgewater found at least two places for his nominees at Brackley between 1614 and 1628. Thomas Wentworth, who enjoyed considerable influence over Pontefract at election time, was also sought out by the borough in 1628 for help (Mayor and Corporation of Pontefract to Wentworth, 6 May 1628, Sheffield City Library, Wentworth Woodhouse MSS 12 [31]. I should like to thank the Trustees of the Fitzwilliam (Wentworth) Estates and the Director of Sheffield City Libraries for their courtesy in allowing me to use the Wentworth Woodhouse MSS.) The lord wardens, who normally secured one place at each of the Cinque ports, were also expected to assist the ports as much as they could. See, for example, Gruenfelder, "Rye and the Parliament of 1621," pp. 25–35; and note too that some of Rye's candidates in that election, and in the elections of 1624 and 1625, made much of local issues facing the port in their bid for its seats. See also the Hythe Borough Assembly Book, 209, f. 191v, of 22 Apr. 1624, wherein the assembly prepared a petition to its patron, the lord warden, asking for his assistance in "the obtaining of a subsidy of tonnage towards the amending & new making of the haven & harbour of this town." Scott MSS, 13, 13v; P. Clarke, "Thomas Scott and the Growth of Urban Opposition to the Early Stuart Regime," *Historical Journal* 21 (1978): 13; Hirst, *Representative of the People?*, pp. 160–62, 170.

5. Rymer, *Foedera*, 16:562–63; Neale, *Elizabethan House of Commons*, pp. 144, 197, 198, 211, 225.

6. Hender to the Earl of Salisbury, 21 Oct. 1609, P.R.O. St. P. Dom. 14/48:116; the Mayor of Hedon to the same, 13 Nov. 1609, P.R.O., St. P. Dom. 14/49:25; the same to the same, 2 Mar. 1610, P.R.O., St. P. Dom. 14/53:2; J. Bruce, ed., *Liber Famelicus of Sir James Whitelocke*, pp. 40–41; Scott MSS, 19; Bagg to Buckingham, 17 Mar. 1628, P.R.O., St. P. Dom. 16/96:36; Sheffield to the Bailiffs and Burgesses of Scarborough, 14 Feb., 7 Mar. 1614, Hickson to Thompson and Lacey, 28 Mar. 1614, Scarborough Borough MSS, General Letters B. 1., 1597–1642; Earl of Bridgewater to Ravenscroft et al., 7 Nov. 1620, *HMC 3rd Report*, p. 258; Pembroke's letter to the mayor and corporation of Wilton is

cited in Stone, "The Electoral Influence of the Second Earl of Salisbury, 1614–68," p. 395.

7. Arundell's nominees were Richard Martyn and Nicholas Hyde (1604), Sir Thomas Norton and Henry Breton (1614), Nathaniel Tomkins (1621–28), Sir Thomas Wilsford (1625), and Sir Henry Croke (1628). He may have backed Sir George Hastings (1621), kinsman to the previous owner of Christchurch, but Hastings won, in a contest with Arundell's candidate, John Eltonhead, in 1624. Robert Mason, a local gentleman, was returned without Arundell's known backing, in 1626. *VCH Hampshire*, 5:87, 92; Arundell to the Mayor and Burgesses of Christchurch, 14 Feb. 1614, p. 12; Phelips to the Mayor, 6 Jan., Phelips to Goldwyne, 7 Jan., Talbot to the same, 7 Jan., all 1621, unpaginated letters; Arundell to the Mayor and Burgesses of Christchurch, 21 Jan. 1624, p. 15, G. Hastings to the same, 31 Jan. 1624, p. 17, Arundell to the same, 24 Jan. 1624, p. 18; Woodeson to the same, 6 Feb. 1628, p. 20, Arundell, to the same, 3 Feb. 1628, p. 32 (all Christchurch Borough MSS, bound volume of election letters for the sixteenth and seventeenth centuries, in the custody of the town clerk of Christchurch); H. A. C. Sturgess, ed., *Register of Admissions to . . . the Middle Temple*, 1:90. Arundell also intervened in the 1625 bye-election when Edward Boys, junior, replaced Sir Thomas Wilsford.

8. Oligarchic control can be seen in the election of Cambridge's recorders, Francis Brackin (1614, 1624) and Talbot Pepys (1628). Robert Lukyn, a county gentleman (1624) and alderman Thomas Purchas (1628) also were returned. Ellesmere nominated Sir Robert Hitcham (1614), Bacon saw to the choice of Thomas Meautys, later a clerk of the privy council, and Sir John Hobart (both 1621). Coventry recommended Meautys (1625, 1626, 1628) and his secretary and kinsman through marriage, John Thompson (1626). The borough, given the University, no doubt felt it needed the most influential high stewards it could find. *VCH Cambridge and the Isle of Ely*, 3:60, 70; Neale, *Elizabethan House of Commons*, pp. 165–66; Keeler, *Long Parliament*, p. 36; C. H. Cooper, ed., *Annals of Cambridge*, 3:60–61, 136–37, 140, 176, 183–84, 200; Moir, *Addled Parliament*, p. 43; *Commons Journal*, 1:569; Notestein et al.; eds., *Commons Debates, 1621*, 1:211–13, 4:181–82; Mead to Stuteville, 31 Mar. 1621, Birch, *Court and Times of James I*, 2:245; Mead to Stuteville, 28 Jan. 1626, BM Harleian MSS 390, f. 18; J. W. Clay, ed., *Visitation of Cambridgeshire*, Harleian Soc. (London, 1897), p. 110; Hirst, *Representative of the People?*, pp. 53, 134.

9. Cokayne, *Peerage*, 1:367, 8:97–98; "Oliver St. John, fourth Baron St. John of Bletsho and first Earl Bolingbroke," *DNB*, 17:639–40; Keeler, *Long Parliament*, pp. 33, 330, 385; F. A. Blades, ed., *Visitations of Bedfordshire*, Harleian Soc. (London, 1884), pp. 144–45; Nichols, *Progresses*, 2:203 & n; 3:557; G. D. Gilmore, ed., *The Papers of Richard Taylor of Clapham*, 25:105; Taylor's speech can be found in the Bedford Corporation MSS, and I would like to thank Mr. G. F. Simmonds, Esq., town clerk of Bedford, for supplying me with a copy of that address. The earl of Cleveland, who nominated Sir Henry Astry at Bedford in 1628, was a friend of Buckingham's and may have intervened to help the duke. Cleveland waited until the 1640 elections for Bedfordshire before his influence was rewarded. Bedford's franchise was enlarged in the 1640 elections, but Bolingbroke's influence was unaffected; Sir Beauchamp St. John was chosen for both 1640 parliaments (Hirst, *Representative of the People?*, pp. 63, 99; Keeler, *Long Parliament*, pp. 33, 330).

10. Yelverton probably supported Northampton's election of his brother-in-law, Francis Beale (1614), a fellow county lawyer Sir Thomas Crew (1621), and his nephew Christopher Sherland (1624–28), whom he successfully recommended as his successor as recorder in 1623. "Sir Henry Yelverton," *DNB*, 21:1231–33; "Sir Thomas Crew or Crewe," *DNB*, 5:82–83; *VCH Northamptonshire*, 3:14, 17; Markham and Cox, eds., *Records of the Borough of Northampton*, 2:105, 108—9, 493, 495–96; Notestein et al., eds., *Commons Debates, 1621*, 6:475; M. E. Finch, *Five Northamptonshire Families*, pp. 58, 59 & n. Northampton, with its narrow franchise and tight corporation control, was a patronage borough; Lord Spencer's son, Richard, served for it in five parliaments (1621–28).

Local troubles between the oligarchy and the freemen did not develop until the later 1630s; they had no apparent impact on the borough's elections through 1628. Hirst, *Representative of the People?*, pp. 59, 75, 88, 89, 92, 135.

11. Gruenfelder, "The Parliamentary Election at Chester, 1621," pp. 35–44; "Sir James Whitelocke," *DNB*, 21:117–19; Bruce, ed., *Liber familicus*, pp. 40–41; Reed to Conway, 14 Feb. 1628, P.R.O., St. P. Dom. 16/93:32; Bagg to Buckingham, 6 Apr. 1628, P.R.O., St. P. Dom. 16/100:47; Evesham Public Library, the Barnard Collection, vi, 125–26; Keeler, *Long Parliament*, pp. 121–22, 146–47, 203; "Sir Robert Harley," *DNB*, 8:1282–83; W. R. Williams, *Parl. Hist. Worcestershire*, p. 142. In any early Stuart election, about 28 boroughs in England and Wales could be expected to elect their legal adviser, i.e., their recorder, deputy recorder, town clerk, or "counselor." That figure also includes those boroughs that returned nominees or kinsmen of their legal officials.

12. Hirst, *Representative of the People?*, p. 92, app. 1, p. 195; app. 3, pp. 213–15.

13. Sir William Strode, Plymouth's recorder, was given £20 for his services in the Parliament of 1614 and for "assisting the two withstanding the Patent for packing and salting of fish and for other things," and his successor as recorder, John Glanville, received a basin and ewer worth £33 17 s. 2 d. from a grateful corporation after the Parliament of 1621. R. N. Worth, ed. *Calendar of the Plymouth Municipal Records*, pp. 62, 148, 151, 155, 205, 206; R. N. Worth, *History of Plymouth*, pp. 148, 153, 155, 162–63; "Sir John Glanville the younger," *DNB* 7:1291–92; Hirst, *Representative of the People?*, pp. 56–58, 92, 135, 136, 137, 160; Neale, *Elizabethan House of Commons*, pp. 164–65, 179; Keeler, *Long Parliament*, pp. 72, 256–57; Salisbury Corporation MSS, General Entry Book, D/34, Ledger C, fols. 238v, 279v, 295, 299v, 323v, 337, held by the Chief Executive of the Salisbury District Council in the Muniment Room, Salisbury District Council office; Corporation of Salisbury to Heath, 16 Jan. 1626, Hoare, *Wiltshire*, 6:348–49; *VCH Wiltshire*, 5:113, 6:104, 121; "Henry Sherfield," *DNB*, 18:74; Hoare, *Wiltshire*, 2:37, 39, 67; 6:290, 301, 312, 313, 333, 356, 372, 375. For an excellent discussion of Salisbury's attempts to deal with its serious poverty problem, see P. Slack, "Poverty and Politics in Salisbury, 1597–1666," in P. Clark and P. Slack, eds., *Crisis and Order in English Towns, 1500–1700*, pp. 164–94. Eventually, the town's economic problems led to trouble with the corporation based on a belief, in the 1630s, that the oligarchy was using its powers for its own benefit; this attitude merged with other issues in 1640 and caused considerable election trouble for the corporation.

14. Newcastle's corporation had trouble with its freemen over municipal issues in the 1630s, trouble that erupted in its election for the short parliament in 1640. For Gloucester see Gruenfelder, "Gloucester's Parliamentary Elections, 1604–1640," pp. 53–59; Keeler, *Long Parliament*, pp. 59, 86–87; Bean, *Northern Counties*, p. 564; J. Brand, *The History and Antiquities of Newcastle*, 2:209, 216, 240; R. Howell, Jr., *Newcastle-Upon-Tyne and the Puritan Revolution*, pp. 3, 14, 28, 46, 47, 113 & n; J. Latimer, *Annals of Bristol in the 17th Century*, pp. 23, 35, 51–53, 76, 85, 89, 93, 114; City of Bristol Record Office, Common Council Proceedings, vol. 2, 1608–27, fols. 133v–134; G. Pryce, *A Popular History of Bristol*, pp. 142, 156–57; W. R. Williams, *Parl. Hist. Gloucestershire*, pp. 112–14; Hirst, *Representative of the People?*, pp. 17, 55, 56, 57, 58, 95, 136, 195, 196.

15. Gruenfelder, "Yorkshire Borough Elections, 1603–1640," pp. 103, 105, n; *Commons Journal*, 1:879, 887, 888, 890, 891; Keeler, *Long Parliament*, pp. 224–25, 229; *VCH Yorkshire, City of York*, pp. 128–29, 168–69, 186, 196, Hirst, *Representative of the People?*, pp. 15, 58, 94–95, 161–62, 164, 175–76, 179, app. 3, p. 215; R. Carroll, "Yorkshire Parliamentary Elections, 1625–1660," pp. 56, 57–58, 80–81; A. F. Upton, *Sir Arthur Ingram*, pp. 148–49, 155, 247–48, 250–51.

16. Three outsiders chosen by Worcester were Sir Henry Spelman (1625) and his son John (1626), who were probably the nominees of its recorder, Sir Thomas Coventry. The earl of Essex may have been behind the return of his kinsman Sir Walter Devereux (1625) of Castle Bromwich, Staffordshire. Williams *Parl. Hist. Worcestershire*, pp. 38–39, 92–96; City of Worcester MSS, Chamber Orders Book, fols. 7, 7v, 8, 10v, 15, 27v, 39, 40, 70v, 77, 86v, 89, 91, 111v, 114v, 118v, 122v; S. Bond, ed., *The Chamber Order Book of*

*Worcester, 1602–1650,* Worcestershire Hist. Soc., New Series, vol. 8 (1974), pp. 82–83, 84, 87, 93, 96, 109, 112, 125, 126, 167, 175–76, 190–91, 196, 202, 203, 222, 225, 230, 234; Keeler, *Long Parliament,* p. 144; *CSPD 1619–1623,* p. 391; "Sir Henry Spelman," *DNB,* 18:736–41; "Sir John Spelman," *DNB,* 18:741–12; *VCH Worcestershire,* 2:231.

17. Nottingham returned the nominee of Viscount Mansfield, Sir Charles Cavendish, in both 1624 and 1628 and elected Viscount Newark's eldest son, Henry Pierrepont, in 1628. Mansfield's nominee, Cavendish, was refused by the corporation in 1625. W. H. Stevenson et al., eds., *Records of the Borough of Nottingham,* 4:317, 326, 272, 275, 385, 387; 5:102, 129; Nottinghamshire Record Office, City of Nottingham Hall Books, 1623–24, CA 2398, 42, 45; 1624–25, CA 3399, 37, 60; 1627–28, CA 3402, 57; J. Blackner, *The Hist. of Nottingham,* pp. 287, 291; T. Bailey, *Annals of Nottinghamshire,* 2:599–600, 611, 612, 617–18; G. Marshall, ed., *Visitation of Nottingham,* Harleian Soc. (London, 1871), pp. 2, 42, 52–53, 59; "Sir Charles Cavendish," *DNB,* supplement, 1:399. The control Nottingham's corporation enjoyed over its elections was, no doubt, much helped by its restricted franchise, Hirst, *Representative of the People?,* p. 92.

18. See Appendix Five for an assignment of gentry residency and patronage in county elections, 1604–40.

19. Gentry influence accounted for at least 11 of 18 county places for Berkshire, Buckinghamshire, Cambridgeshire, Cheshire, Cornwall, Cumberland, Devonshire, Dorsetshire, Gloucestershire, Hampshire, Kent, Lancashire, Middlesex, Nottinghamshire, Norfolk, Northumberland, Oxfordshire, Shropshire, Somersetshire, Suffolk, Surry, Sussex, Westmorland, Worcestershire, and Yorkshire in England; and in Anglesey, Breconshire, Caernarvonshire, Cardiganshire, Carmarthenshire, Denbighshire, Flintshire, Merionethshire, Pembrokeshire and Radnorshire in Wales. Derbyshire, Herefordshire, Huntingdonshire, Leicestershire, Lincolnshire, Monmouthshire, Warwickshire, and Wiltshire's returns reflected a mixture of gentry and aristocratic influence, and the returns for Bedfordshire, Essex, Hertfordshire, Northamptonshire, Rutlandshire, Staffordshire, Glamorganshire, and Montgomeryshire indicated the power of aristocratic influence.

20. These figures are taken from the tables for two-member borough constituencies in Appendix Four.

21. Hirst, *Representative of the People?,* pp. 160, 161–62, 164, 168–69, 170, 176, 179–80. See also C. Russell's excellent article, "Parliamentary History in Perspective, 1604–1629," esp. pp. 13–14, 25–26.

22. For an example of gentry influence in a county's borough elections, see Gruenfelder, "Yorkshire Borough Elections, 1603–1640." The figures employed above are taken from Appendix Four.

23. Hirst, *Representative of the People?,* pp. 54, 56–57, 60, 109, 110.

24. E. Farnham, "The Somersetshire Election of 1614," pp. 579–99; T. G. Barnes, *Somerset, 1625–1640,* pp. 133, 281–98; Moir, *Addled Parliament,* p. 33. Sir Thomas Wentworth and Sir John Savile fought it out in Yorkshire in the elections of 1621, 1625, and 1628. The 1624 election may have passed quietly, but another contest, involving Savile, broke out in 1626. The electoral dominion of the Wynns in Caernarvonshire was challenged successfully by the Griffiths of Cefnamwlch and their allies; contested elections resulted in 1621, 1624, 1625, and 1626; they may have also fought it out in 1628 and again, though perhaps with less intensity, in 1640. Star Chamber suits were another constant feature of the quarrel. Gruenfelder, "The Electoral Patronage of Sir Thomas Wentworth, Earl of Strafford, 1614–1640"; Gruenfelder, "The Wynns of Gwydir and Parliamentary Elections in Wales, 1604–1640"; Keeler, *Long Parliament,* pp. 79, 197, 402–3.

25. Gruenfelder, "Two Midland Parliamentary Elections of 1604, Northamptonshire and Worcestershire"; Gruenfelder, "The Parliamentary Election in Northamptonshire, 1626"; Gruenfelder, "Dorsetshire Elections, 1604–1640." In 1626 Strangways lent his support to the choice of Sir George Morton for Dorset, who, although still connected to

the county, was regarded by many as an outsider since he maintained his principal residence in Oxfordshire. For information about Dorset's gentry who served the county as knights of the shire, see Gruenfelder, "Dorsetshire Elections, 1604–1640," and sources cited therein.

26. J. S. Morrill, *Cheshire, 1630–1660*, p. 31; Gifford to Whitehead, 16 Feb., West, Paulet, Kingswell, Sandys, and Others to the Earl of Southampton, 2 Mar., Wallop to Whitehead, 11 Mar., Gifford to Whitehead, 14 Mar., Wallop to Whitehead, 16, 17 Mar., all 1614, Hampshire RO, Whitehead's letter book, H.R.O. 4M53/140. I should like to thank Mrs. Borthwick-Norton for her kind permission to use the Whithed MS and the Hampshire Record Office for making it available for my use. Keeler, *Long Parliament*, pp. 369–70, 376–78, 391–92; "Sir Henry Wallop," *DNB*, 20:613; Nichols, *Progresses*, 1:27 & n; *VCH Hampshire*, 2:85; 4:12. Sir Henry Wallop, probably the leading candidate, lost, possibly because the earl of Southampton finally intervened in behalf of Wallop's foes, Sir William Uvedale of Wickham and Sir Richard Tichborne, son of one of Hampshire's leading recusants, Sir Benjamin Tichborne. Hirst, *Representative of the People?*, pp. 16, 116.

27. Gruenfelder, "Gloucester's Parliamentary Elections, 1604–1640."

28. Gruenfelder, "The Parliamentary Election at Chester, 1621"; Hirst, *Representative of the People?*, pp. 49, 60, app. 2, pp. 197–98.

29. Scott MSS, 3–7v, 13–31, 33–34; Hasted, *Kent*, 7:21, 24; 8:79; 11:421; 12:103; Everitt, *Kent*, p. 48; *CSPD 1628–1629*, pp. 86, 185, 206, 227; *CSPD 1634–1635*, p. 511; Hirst, *Representative of the People?*, p. 56. One aspect of the feud between the archbishop and the corporation involved the city's disputes with its recorder, John Finch, which was only settled with Finch's restoration, through Privy Council intervention (*CSPD 1619–1623*, pp. 108, 144, 146, 148). For an excellent discussion of Canterbury's problems and the growing spirit of urban radicalism that marked its bitter quarrels, see P. Clarke, "Thomas Scott and the Growth of Urban Opposition to the Early Stuart Regime," *Historical Journal* 21 (1978): 1–28, and especially 11–23. Clarke clearly shows, too, the importance of more "national" issues in the development of Canterbury's urban opposition.

30. Exeter's M.P.'s, including Jourdain, were prominent merchants and civic leaders; the sole exception was the return of its recorder, Nicholas Duck, in 1624 and 1625. Exeter, unlike several other boroughs controlled by their corporations (Salisbury, Plymouth), did not make a practice of electing its recorder. *Commons Journal*, 1:875, 920, 924, 926; Hirst, *Representative of the People?*, pp. 57, 77, 176, app. 2, pp. 203–4; Devon RO, Exeter City Archives, Act Book VII, 647, 693, 710, 717, 729, 740, 741, 749; Wright to the Mayor and Corporation of Exeter, 5 Feb. 1629, letter 319, Devon RO, Exeter City Archives; W. MacCaffrey, *Exeter, 1540–1640*, pp. 64, 215, 216, 223–25, 253, 267, 270; G. Oliver, *The History of the City of Exeter*, pp. 232–33, 236, 238, 245; *HMC Lonsdale*, p. 59; "Ignatuis Jourdaine," *DNB*, 10:1103; J. J. Alexander, "Members of Parliament for Exeter," pp. 202–3.

31. Sir H. Hobart to the Bailiffs of Colchester, 31 Mar. 1625, Earl of Sussex to the Mayor and Corporation of Colchester, 7 Apr. 1625, Bailiffs of Colchester to the Earl of Sussex, 14 Apr. 1625, Bailiffs of Colchester to Sir H. Hobart, n.d. Apr. (?) 1625, the same to the Earl of Sussex, 19 Apr. 1625, Essex RO, Morant MSS, vol. 43, fols. 23, 25, 27, 29, 77; Hirst *Representative of the People?*, p. 134, app. 2, pp. 199–201; *Essex Review* 5:193–95; Walter C. Metcalfe, ed., *Visitations of Essex*, 2 pts., Harleian Soc. (London, 1878), pt. 1, p. 505; Morant, *Hist. Essex*, 2:507, 574, 575.

32. Brooke's influence probably helped elect every member for Warwick from 1614 to 1628. It temporarily ended, however, with the overthrow of the election of his cousin Robert Brooke in 1628. The Prince's Council had tried to place Sir Francis Cottington at Warwick in 1624 without success. Puckering, whom the corporation wanted to choose in 1628, refused and served for Tamworth. His successful nominee in the bye-election of 1628, held under the enlarged franchise, was one Anthony Stoughton. T. Kemp, ed., *The*

*Black Book of Warwick*, pp. 409–11; Warwickshire RO, Warwick Borough Muniments, Minute Book 1610–62, W. 21/6, fols. 83, 268–71; Prince's Council to Mallett, Deputy Steward of Warwick Manor, 1 Jan. 1624, Duchy of Cornwall RO, "Burgesses for Parliament, 1623–1624," f. 34v; *Commons Journal*, 1:800, 807, 816, 867, 907, 920; *VCH Warwickshire*, 8:496–97; Hirst, *Representative of the People?*, pp. 52, 62, 77, 93, 101–2, 152, app. 2., pp. 210–12; D. H. Willson, *Privy Councillors*, p. 70; John Fetherston, ed., *Visitation of Warwickshire*, Harleian Soc. (London, 1877), p. 183; Nichols, *Progresses*, 3:439 & n; "Sir John Coke," *DNB*, 4:700–702; "Francis Lucy," 16:444; "Robert Greville, second Baron Brooke," *DNB* 8:606–7.

33. Roberts's wages through 1607 exceeded £34, a huge sum for Chippenham. John Hungerford, his colleague in 1604–10, served without pay, which probably saved Chippenham from bankruptcy and made subsequent elections of neighboring gentry all the more attractive. The election of Sir Roger Owen of Condover, Shropshire, in 1614 remains a mystery. He chose to serve for Shropshire and was replaced by an Essex courtier, Sir William Maynard, the likely nominee of Sir Edward Bayntun, who was Maynard's son-in-law and owner of Stanley Abbey near Chippenham. Salisbury's nominee was elected elsewhere before Chippenham's election. The countess of Rutland's candidate, Humphrey Tufton, stood against Culpeper. Her ties to the borough were close; her first husband, Sir Edward Hungerford, held property near the town and her second marriage, to the earl of Rutland, was celebrated in Chippenham. Goldney mistakenly dates the marriage in September 1625, but it must have taken place earlier since she is referred to, in the town correspondence, as the countess of Rutland; see also Cokayne, *Peerage*, 6:465, and Nichols, *Progresses*, 4:682 & n, the marriage taking place after October 1608 or later in that year. BM ADD MSS 18, 597, f. 110; F. H. Goldney, ed., *Records of Chippenham*, pp. xviii, 30, 189, 191, 192, 195, 197, 301–2, 327 & n, 338–39; Mildmay to the Burgesses of Chippenham, 15 Feb., the same to the same, 6 Mar., Cicely Tufton to R. Wastfield, 20 Feb., Fane to the Bailiff and Burgesses, 3 Mar., Wastfield to the same, 18 Mar., "Precept for the Election," 8 Mar., "Indenture for the Election," 16 Mar., all 1614, Chippenham Borough MSS, Yelde Hall, nos. 252, 253, 254, 255, 256, 258, 267; Keeler, *Long Parliament*, pp. 101, 366–67; Cokayne, *Peerage*, 8:115–16; "Sir Anthony Mildmay," *DNB*, 8:376; "Sir Thomas Culpeper," *DNB*, 5:287–88; "Francis Fane, first Baron Burghersh, first Earl Westmorland," *DNB*, 6:1042–43, 1044–45; "Sir Roger Owen." *DNB*, 14:1349; *VCH* Shropshire, 8:40, 134–35, 165, 180–181, 265–66, 313–14, 319; *Trans. Shrop. Arch. and Nat. Hist. Soc.*, 4th series, 11 (1927–28): 161–62; Precept and return of "Sir William Maynard loco Roger Owen," 15 Apr. 1614, Chippenham borough MSS, Yelde Hall, nos. 261, 262; W. P. Courtney, *Parl. Repr. Cornwall*, pp. 17–18; E. A. Fitch, "The Lord Lieutenants of Essex," p. 239; Morant, *Hist. Essex*, 2:432; *VCH Wiltshire*, 5:123; Hirst, *Representative of the People?*, pp. 52, 71–72, app. 2, p. 198.

34. Edward Hungerford, owner of three nearby manors, was elected in 1621 along with John Bayliffe, another country squire. Bayntun was chosen in 1626 and probably aided the return of Sir William Maynard's brother, Sir John Maynard, in 1624 and 1625. Another Wiltshire neighbor, Sir John Eyre, was elected in 1628. List of freemen's names, 23 Jan. 1624, Chippenham Borough MSS, Yelde Hall, no. 264; BM Harleian MSS 6806, fols. 262, 262v; *Commons Journal*, 1:673; 678, 684, 686, 717, 729, 732, 735, 737, 745, 749, 759; Hirst, *Representative of the People?*, pp. 52, 63, 134, 176, app. 2, pp. 198–99; Goldney, ed., *Chippenham*, pp. xi, xii, xiv, xv, 19, 27, 33, 206–7, 332; *VCH Wiltshire*, 5:122; Hoare, *Wiltshire*, 6:53, 107, Keeler, *Long Parliament*, pp. 101, 225–26, 310–11; Morant, *Hist. Essex*, 2:432, "Sir John Maynard," *DNB*, 13:155–56.

35. Dartmouth, which probably accepted a nominee of Northampton in 1604, refused Sir George Carey and the earl in 1614, informing Northampton "that in hope their grievances might be the better made known, and themselves thereof relieved, they would be at the charge to send burgesses" of their own to parliament. In 1628 the earl of Manchester's nominee, his servant Robert Dixon, was refused. Dartmouth returned resident merchants Thomas Howard and Thomas Gourney (1614), William Nyell (1621,

1624), and, when Nyell died, replaced him with another merchant, Roger Mathew, who had served before (1621). William Plumleigh, three times mayor, also served in parliament (1624). Carey to the Mayor of Dartmouth, 14 Feb., Northampton to the same, 20 Feb., the Mayor of Dartmouth to Northampton, n.d. 1614, Devon RO, Dartmouth Borough Records, D.D. 61850, S.M. 1420; Dartmouth Court Book, S.M. 1989, f. 20; Devon RO, Exeter City Archives, "A Constitution for the more orderly and legal choosing . . . of burgesses," 18 Jan. 1626, Dartmouth Borough Records, S.M. 2004, f. 7; Earl of Manchester to the Mayor of Dartmouth, 29 Jan., Mayor and Corporation of Dartmouth to the Earl of Manchester, 25 Feb., both 1628, Devon RO, Dartmouth Borough Records, Dartmouth Court Book, S.M. 1989, f. 34; H. A. Merewether and A. J. Stephens, *The History of the Boroughs and Municipal Corporations of the United Kingdom,* 2:982; *Reports and Trans. Devonshire Assoc.* 43. (1911): 361, 367, 368, 369, 370.

36. Hirst, *Representative of the People?,* pp. 29–40, 43, 104, 113, 115–16; C. Hill, *Puritanism and Revolution,* p. 308 & n; Hassell Smith, *County and Court,* pp. 314–30.

37. Hirst, *Representative of the People?,* pp. 104–5, app. 5, pp. 223–26.

38. Gruenfelder, "Two Midland Parliamentary Elections of 1604, Northamptonshire and Worcestershire," pp. 244, 247, 248; Gruenfelder, "The Electoral Patronage of Sir Thomas Wentworth, Earl of Strafford, 1614–1640"; Sir Wm. Thomas to Sir Jo. Wynn, 10 Dec. [1620], NLW, Wynn MSS (9057E), 925; Sir Jo. Wynn to his Son, Richard?, 24 Dec. 1620, NLW, Wynn MSS (9057E), 932; Mostyn to Sir Jo. Wynn, 15 Apr. 1625, NLW, Wynn MSS (9060E), 1324; J. Rushworth, *Collections,* 3:26–27; *Commons Journal,* 1, 759, 886, 898. William Walrond, another Somersetshire deputy lieutenant, was deeply involved with Stawell at Taunton and, like Stawell, was a close friend of Baron Poulett, an avowed enemy of Phelips (Barnes, *Somerset,* pp. 43, 297). Any office could have its electoral uses: two subsidy commissioners in Gloucestershire ordered their assessors, all freeholders, to attend them on election day for a county bye-election in 1624, in order to prevent them from voting (Willcox, *Gloucestershire,* pp. 29–30; Williams, *Parl. Hist. Gloucestershire,* pp. 51–52; BM ADD MSS 18, 597, f. 125).

39. Appeals for the support of the sheriff were made before elections for Norfolk (1603), Northamptonshire (1604), and Cambridgeshire (1614); and his role in a contested election is also shown at Cambridgeshire (1614), Northumberland (1614), Caernarvonshire (1625), Flintshire (1626), and Essex (1628). There were, no doubt, many other unrecorded examples. Neale, *Elizabethan House of Commons,* pp. 74, 76, 77; *Commons Journal,* 1:457–58, 463, 468, 485, 494, 495–96, 677–78, 686, 687, 714, 729, 737–38, 739, 798, 855; Hassell Smith, *County and Court,* pp. 153, 329–30; Montagu to Spencer, 18 Apr. 1603, *HMC Buccleuch and Queensberry,* 3: 73–74; Moir, *Addled Parliament,* pp. 37–38; *HMC De L'Isle and Dudley,* 5:174; C. H. Hunter Blair, "Knights of the Shire for Northumberland," pp. 110–13; Sir Wm. Thomas to Sir Jo. Wynn, 10 Dec. [1620], Sir Jo. Wynn to His Son [Richard?], 24 Dec. 1620, Owen Wynn to Sir Jo. Wynn, 20 Apr. 1621, NLW, Wynn MSS (9057E), 925, 932, 948; Sir Jo. Wynn to Mutton, 14 Apr. 1625, NLW, Wynn MSS (9060E), 1320; Cooper, ed., *Annals of Cambridge,* 3:62, 161, 166; *HMC Rutland,* 1:470; BM ADD MSS 18, 587, fols. 49v–50v, 53v–54, 63v, 67, 87v, 90v, 197; L. Stone, *An Elizabethan, Sir Horatio Palavicino,* pp. 312–13; P.R.O., St. Ch. 8/288/9; Gruenfelder, "The Electoral Patronage of Sir Thomas Wentworth, Earl of Strafford, 1614–1640," pp. 560, 562, 564, 565–66.

40. Cooper, ed., *Annals of Cambridge,* 3:136–37, 140; Notestein et al., eds., *Commons Debates, 1621,* 1:211–13; 2:380; 3:285–86; 4:181–82, 360; 6:164; *Commons Journal,* 1:569, 624, 677, 714, 726, 739–40, 745, 748, 751, 797–98; Tyrwhitt, ed., *Proceedings and Debates,* 2:89–90; Mead to Stuteville, 31 Mar. 1621, Birch, *Court and Times of James I,* 2:245; BM ADD MSS 18, 597, fols. 46v–47, 88, 103, 179v, 196, 196v; Nethersole to Carleton, 25 Mar. 1624, P.R.O., St. P. Dom. 14/161:36; *VCH Sussex,* 1:521; Horsfield, *Hist. Sussex,* vol. 2, app. 3, pp. 29, 72; Somersetshire RO, Phelips MSS, vol. 4, fols. 11–11v; Lloyd, *Gentry of south-west Wales,* p. 104; W. R. Williams, *Parl. Hist. Wales,* p. 161; Buckingham to the Mayor of Winchelsea, 30 Jan., Buckingham to Sir Allen [Alexander] Temple, 5 Feb., Buckingham to Eversfield, 6 Feb., all 1624, BM ADD MSS 37, 818, fols. 145v, 146,

147v–148; Young to Zouch, 7 Apr. 1624, P.R.O., St. P. Dom. 14/162:26; East Sussex RO, Winchelsea Borough MSS 55, Court Book 1597–1627, f. 283v.

41. Other elections marked by canvassing included Huntingdonshire, Hampshire, and Somersetshire (all 1614); Chester (1621); Suffolk (1621); Shropshire (1621); Caernarvonshire (1621–25); Poole (1624); Dorsetshire (1624–26); Merionethshire (1624–26); Norfolk, Pembrokeshire, and Denbighshire (all 1625); and York, Essex, and Cornwall (all 1628). There were many more. Gruenfelder, "Two Midland Parliamentary Elections of 1604, Northamptonshire and Worcestershire," pp. 241–42, 243, 246–47; Gruenfelder, "The Parliamentary Election for Shrewsbury, 1604," pp. 273–75; Gruenfelder, "Gloucester's Parliamentary Elections, 1604–40", pp. 54–55; Gruenfelder, "The Electoral Patronage of Sir Thomas Wentworth, Earl of Strafford, 1614–1640"; Gruenfelder, "The Parliamentary Election in Northamptonshire, 1626"; "The Parliamentary Election at Chester, 1621"; Gruenfelder, "The Lord Wardens and Elections, 1604–1628," pp. 10–12; Hirst, *Representative of the People?*, pp. 14, 115–16, 143–45; Russell to Forifould, n.d. 1614? Worcestershire RO, Berington family papers, 705:24/647/(3); Geo. Lehunt? to Crane, 14 Nov. 1620, Hitcham to the same, 20 Dec. 1620, Bodleian Library, Tanner MSS 69, fols. 150, 151; Tollemache to Jo. Hobart, 6 Dec. 1620, Bodleian Library, Tanner MSS 283, f. 174; Crane? to?, 29 Nov. 1620, Ward to Crane, 29 Nov. 1620, Sir Henry Hobart to Crane, 23 Nov. 1620, Bodleian Library, Tanner MSS 290, fols. 28, 37, 54; Vernon to Mitton, 9 Dec. 1620, Local Studies Library, County Library, Shrewsbury, deed No. 16140; Walden to Cotton, 18 Mar. 1614, BM Harleian MSS 7002, f. 308; Wallop to Whitehead, 11 Mar. 1614, Gifford to the same, 14 Mar. 1614, Wallop to the same, 16, 17 Mar. 1614, Hampshire RO, Whitehead's letter book, H.R.O. 4M53/140 fols. 68v–70; P.R.O., St. Ch. 8/293/11; Moir, *Addled Parliament*, pp. 35–37; G. Gawdy to Framlingham Gawdy, 10? Apr. 1625, BM Egerton MSS 2715, f. 283, in *HMC Gawdy*, p. 122; *Commons Journal*, 1:800, 806; S. R. Gardiner, ed., *Commons Debates 1625*, pp. 53–54; and *Dorset Notes & Queries* 4 (1894–95): 23–24; Thynne to Ludlow, 13 Apr. 1625, P.R.O., St. P. Dom. 16/1:55; Long to Thynne, 21 Feb. 1628, in *VCH Wiltshire*, 5:131 & n. 89; Ruigh, *The Parliament of 1624*, p. 127 & n. 56; Powell to Mostyn, 3 Nov. 1620, Owen Wynn to Sir Jc. Wynn, 11 Nov. 1620, Sir Wm. Thomas to the same, 24 Nov. 1620, the same to the same, 10 Dec. 1620, NLW, Wynn MSS (9057E), 916, 918, 921, 925; Owen Wynn to Sir Jo Wynn, 2 Dec. 1623, the same to the same, n.d. 1623, Sir Wm. Thomas to the same, 21 Jan. 1624, NLW, Wynn MSS (9059E), 1172, 1178, 1189; Wm. Salusbury to Sir Jo. Wynn, 4 Apr. 1625, Sir Thos. Myddleton to the same, 7 Apr. 1625, Sir Jo. Wynn to Sir Thos. Myddleton, 8 Apr. 1625, Edward Wynn to Sir Jo. Wynn, 15 Apr. 1625, Sir Jo. Wynn to Mutton, 17 Apr. 1625, Wm. Wynn to Sir Jo. Wynn, 7 Dec. 1625, NLW, Wynn MSS (9060E), 1312, 1315, 1317, 1323, 1329, 1380.

42. Other elections that included appeals to urban voters occurred in Caernarvonshire (1621) and Northamptonshire (1626), and allegations of freeholder creation were made in Worcestershire (1604), Hampshire (1614), Somersetshire (1614), East Retford (1624), Maldon (1624), and Essex (1628). Hirst, *Representative of the People?*, pp. 23, 24, 40–41; Gruenfelder, "The Electoral Patronage of Sir Thomas Wentworth, Earl of Strafford, 1614–1640," pp. 559–60, 562; Gruenfelder, "The Parliamentary Election in Northamptonshire, 1626," pp. 159–65; Gruenfelder, "Two Midland Parliamentary Elections of 1604, Northamptonshire and Worcestershire," pp. 246–47, *Somerset and Dorset Notes & Queries*, 4 (1894–95): 23–24; P.R.O., St. Ch. 8/288/9, 8/293/11; Sir Wm. Thomas to Sir Jo. Wynn, 24 Nov. 1620, the same to the same, 10 Dec. [1620], Sir Rich. Wynn to the same, 20 Dec. 1620, NLW, Wynn MSS (9057E), 921, 925, 995.

43. Secular control over advowsons had expanded greatly thanks to the reformation, which provided a veritable flood of advowsons and lay rectories for the gentry and peerage. The earl of Pembroke, for example, held about 38 livings by 1575, and the earl of Dorset, in the mid 1620s, controlled 39. The earl of Warwick was not far behind; by 1632 at least 24 livings were within his sphere of influence; 44 livings in Northamptonshire alone were under aristocratic control. However, nothing indicates, at least through 1628, that reformist clergy participated in an organized electoral campaign as

they apparently had in the 1580s. Neale, *Queen Elizabeth and Her Parliaments*, 2:60–64, 146–65, 216–32, and his *Elizabethan House of Commons*, pp. 241, 251–54; P. Collinson, *The Elizabethan Puritan Movement*, pp. 278, 306, 397–98; C. Hill, *The Economic Problems of the Church*, p. 261, and his *Society and Puritanism in Pre-Revolutionary England*, pp. 98, 100–101, 106–7; Stone, *Crisis of the Aristocracy*, p. 260; M. Walzer, *The Revolution of the Saints*, pp. 128–29, 259–60.

44. Gruenfelder, "Two Midland Elections of 1604, Northamptonshire and Worcestershire," pp. 245–48; Gruenfelder, "The Electoral Patronage of Sir Thomas Wentworth, Earl of Strafford, 1614–1640," pp. 564–65; *Commons Journal*, 1:624, 677, 694, 695, 726, 745–46, 753–54, 779, 781; Owen Wynn to Sir Jo. Wynn, 11 Nov. 1620, NLW, Wynn MSS (9057E), 918; Notestein et al., eds., *Commons Debates 1621*, 5:172–73; Dodd, *Studies in Stuart Wales*, p. 187; J. Williams, *Hist. of Radnorshire*, p. 83; Williams, *Parl. Hist. Wales*, p. 173; P.R.O., St. Ch. 8/288/9; Neale, *Elizabethan House of Commons*, pp. 80–81; Kenny, "Parliamentary Influence of Charles Howard, Earl of Nottingham," pp. 218–19; Brayley, *Hist. Surrey*, 2:326; Manning and Bray, *Hist. Surrey*, 2:295–96; *VCH Surrey*, 4:255–56; U. Lambert, *Blechingley: A Parish History*, 2:424–25; Keeler, *Long Parliament*, pp. 178–79, 261–62; Scott MSS 13–13v, 17, 18–18v, 20, 22–22v, 24–28; Hasted, *Hist. Kent*, 7:21, 24; 7:79; 11:421; 12:103; Everitt, *Kent* p. 48; *CSPD 1628–1629*, pp. 86, 185, 206, 227; *CSPD 1634–1635*, p. 511.

45. Wallop to Whitehead, 17 Mar. 1614, Hampshire RO, Whitehead's letter book, H.R.O. 4M53/140 fol. 70; P.R.O., St. Ch. 8/293/11; Gruenfelder, "The Electoral Patronage Sir Thomas Wentworth, Earl of Strafford, 1614–1640," pp. 561, 562; Gruenfelder, "Two Midland Parliamentary Elections of 1604, Northamptonshire and Worcestershire," p. 242; Hirst, *Representative of the People?*, pp. 39, 117–78.

46. Sir Jo. Wynn to Rich. Wynn, 24 Dec. 1620, NLW, Wynn MSS (9057E), 932; *HMC Rye and Hereford*, p. 260.

47. Other contests that involved threats and violence occurred at Shrewsbury, Gloucester, and Worcestershire (1604); Cambridgeshire and Pembroke (1614); Northampton (1621); Cornwall and Lewes (1628), to note but a few. *Commons Journal*, 1:457, 468, 477, 485, 624, 800, 806; Gardiner, ed., *Commons Debates 1625*, pp. 53–54; P.R.O., St. Ch. 8/288/9; P.R.O., St. Ch. 8/47/7; Somersetshire RO, Phelips MSS, vol. v, fols. 11–11v; Tyrwhitt, ed., *Proceedings and Debates*, 1621, 2:89–90; Notestein et al., eds., *Commons Debates*, *1621*, 2:380; 3:285–86; 4:360; 6:164, 475; Lloyd, *Gentry of south-west Wales*, p. 104; *HMC Portland*, 9:132; *HMC De L'Isle and Dudley*, 5:175; Borough of Bishop's Castle MSS, 1st minute book, fols. 1020–1021v; Bagg to Buckingham, 17 Mar. 1628, P.R.O., St. P. Dom. 16/96:36; BM Harleian MSS 2313, fols. 8v–9; Gruenfelder, "Two Midland Elections of 1604, Northamptonshire and Worcestershire," pp. 246, 247, 249; Gruenfelder, "The Parliamentary Election for Shrewsbury, 1604," pp. 273–74; Gruenfelder, "Gloucester's Parliamentary Elections, 1604–1640," pp. 54–55; Gruenfelder, "Radnorshire's Parliamentary Elections, 1604–1640," pp. 27–28.

48. BM Egerton MSS 784, f. 38; BM Harleian MSS 2313, fols. 8v–9; Jo. Williams to Sir Jo. Wynn, 14 Dec. 1620, Sir Rich. Wynn to the same, 20, 25 Dec. 1620, NLW, Wynn MSS (9057E), 926, 933, 995; Sir Rich. Wynn to Sir Jo. Wynn, 24 Dec. 1623, Owen Wynn to the same, n.d. 1623, Sir Rich. Wynn to the same, 3 Jan. 1624, NLW, Wynn MSS (9058E), 1177, (9059E), 1178, 1185; Sir Edw. Littleton to Sir Wm. Thomas, 12 Apr. 1625, Sir Wm. Thomas to Sir Jo. Wynn, 14, 16 Apr. 1625, Mostyn to the same, 15 Apr. 1625, NLW, Wynn MSS (9060E), 1318, 1322, 1324, 1326; Perrot to Conway, 14 Jan. 1626, P.R.O., St. P. Dom. 16/18:63.

49. Owen Wynn to Sir Jo. Wynn, 6 Dec. 1620, NLW, Wynn MSS (9057E), 924; the same to the same, 2 Dec. 1623, NLW, Wynn MSS (9059E), 1172; Sir Rich. Wynn to Sir Jo. Wynn, 24 Dec. 1623, NLW, Wynn MSS (9059E), 1177; Chamberlain to Carleton, 6 May 1625, P.R.O., St. P. Dom. 16/2:27, in McClure, ed., *Chamberlain's Letters*, 2:614–15, and Birch, *Court and Times of Charles I*, 2:18–19; Scott MSS, 22; Warwickshire RO, Warwick Borough Minute Book, 1610–62, W. 21/6, f. 270.

50. Gruenfelder, "Two Midland Elections of 1604, Northamptonshire and Worcestershire," p. 246; Gruenfelder, "Radnorshire's Parliamentary Elections, 1604–1640," pp. 26–29; P.R.O., St. Ch. 8/288/9; Nuttall to Nicholas, 4 Mar. 1628, P.R.O., St. P. Dom. 16/95:35.

51. Gruenfelder, "Gloucester's Parliamentary Elections, 1604–1640," p. 55; Willcox, *Gloucestershire*, pp. 31–33; Lord Rich to Barrington, 15 Feb. 1604, Mildmay to the same, 20 Feb. 1604, Lord Rich to the same, 1 Mar. 1604, in *Trans. Essex Arch. Soc.*, New Series, 2 (1884): 14–17, 21–22; Barrington to Mildmay, 20 Feb. 1604, BM Egerton MSS 2644, f. 130; P.R.O., St. Ch. 8/293/11; Jenyson to Lord Montagu, 9 Jan. 1626, Northamptonshire RO, Montagu MSS, V, 48, in *HMC Buccleuch and Queensberry*, 3:262; P. R. Seddon, "A Parliamentary Election at East Retford 1624," p. 30; Hirst, *Representative of the People?*, pp. 118–19; Lord Conway to Jervoise, 2 Feb. 1628, P.R.O., St. P. Dom. 16/92:14; the same to the Bailiff and Burgesses of Andover, the same to Jervoise, both 15 Feb. 1628, P.R.O., St. P. Dom. 16/93:47, 48.

52. Willcox, *Gloucestershire*, p. 30; J. B. Baker, *The History of Scarborough*, p. 250; Conyers to the Bailiffs and Burgesses of Scarborough, 15 Feb. 1614, 20 Apr. 1614, 13 Feb. 1615, Scarborough Borough MSS, General Letters B.1., 1597–1642; *Commons Journal*, 1:695; Manning and Bray, *Hist. Surrey*, 2:295–96.

53. Neale, *Elizabethan House of Commons*, pp. 157–58; Sir Wm. Thomas to Sir Jo. Wynn, 24 Nov., 10, 15, Dec. 1620, Sir Jo. Wynn to Sir Rich. Wynn, 24 Dec. 1620, extracts from Sir Jo. Wynn's letter by Owen Wynn, 20 Mar. 1621, Owen Wynn to Sir Jo. Wynn, 20 Apr. 1621, Sir Jo. Wynn to Bodvel, 28 Apr. 1621, NLW, Wynn MSS (9057E), 921, 925, 928, 932, 942, 948, 952.

54. *Commons Journal*, 1:753–54, 820; Lambert, *Blechingley*, 2:424–25; Manning and Bray, *Hist. Surrey*, 2:295–96; Seddon, "A Parliamentary Election at East Retford 1624," p. 30; Hutchins, *Hist. Dorset*, 2:12; Strode to Sir Jo. Coke, 5 May 1627, *HMC Cowper*, 1:305; Bailiffs of Bridport to Buckingham, 28 Jan. 1626, P.R.O., St. P. Dom 16/19:69; H. G. Tibbut, ed., *The Life and Letters of Sir Lewis Dyve, 1599–1669*, pp. 8–9; Hirst, *Representative of the People?*, p. 119.

55. Electioneering and the independence of the electorate is discussed in Hirst, *Representative of the People?*, pp. 108–31. The methods employed in the 1640 elections are given, with those for 1604–28, in Appendix Eight.

# TWO

## The Elections of 1604–1610

The hunt for places began within a month of James I's accession, for, by April 1603, election planning was already afoot in Norfolk and Northamptonshire. Baron Zouch, whose patronage depended on his office as lord president of the Council of the Marches of Wales, was anxiously awaiting news of a parliament and urged Robert Cecil, earl of Salisbury,[1] the king's principal adviser, to keep him fully informed of developments, and Lord Cobham, still the lord warden of the Cinque Ports, wrote Rye in May 1603 to remind it "that I expect you should yield me the nomination of one of your burgesses." The lord admiral, the earl of Nottingham, nominated a candidate for Scarborough in August. Cobham, thanks to the "Main" plot, was replaced as lord warden by Henry Howard, earl of Northampton, who was just as eager for places; he wrote Hastings in October to make sure it and its sister ports recognized his right "to have the denomination of one of the burgesses for any port and town" within his jurisdiction. Salisbury, too, was concerned; he wrote the earl of Shrewsbury in December 1603 to "remember that you forget me not for a burgess-ship." Little Dunwich, though, must take highest honors for speed; it made its choice of burgesses in April 1603 although parliament's summons was still months away![2] The customary patronage system was functioning well before the proclamation for James's first parliament even appeared.[3]

Save for an essay on the Essex election, nothing has been done to explore the elections of 1604. The roles of Robert Cecil, earl of Salisbury, of court agencies like the Duchy of Lancaster, and of the aristocracy have remained a mystery. Despite the fact that "the number of officials and courtiers" elected "was greater than is commonly supposed," no one has disagreed with David H. Willson's remark that "it seems clear that elections, broadly speaking, were neglected." But why were Salisbury and the court so negligent? It has been suggested that Salisbury was too busy to pay attention to the elections; however, given his prudent management of the Crown's affairs and his enthusiastic place-hunting from 1593 to 1601, that suggestion seems altogether inadequate. Another, and possibly more attractive thesis rests on the "consensus" argument. The enthusiasm that greeted the new king made electioneering unnecessary. Salisbury's keen interest in the bye-elections of 1605–10 seems to verify this explanation. The "consensus" was fading away. Salisbury's intervention was a part of his attempt to smooth the crown's path in an increasingly difficult House of Commons. His bye-election activities may also indicate previous neglect. This suggestion gains additional weight from the Venetian ambassador's claim in 1605 that James wanted new elections since he realized "how much his neglect of the elections cost him last year." Furthermore, when Sir Francis Bacon was urging another parliament in 1613, he suggested that some consideration be given to ensure the return "of courtiers and the K's servants to be as they have ever in former times (except the last Parliament)." Were such allegations valid? After all, numerous royal officials and courtiers were returned in the very election that Salisbury and the court presumably ignored.[4]

Bacon's criticism is the most important and, at the same time, the most questionable. His experience at court and service in parliament might, at first glance, make his views practically unimpeachable. However, he had constantly competed with his cousin, Salisbury, for court favor and influence, and he had lost. Furthermore, Bacon's task in 1613 was a formidable one: he was trying to convince James that another parliament was necessary. He knew that James had blamed Salisbury for the collapse of the Great Contract, for the failure of the last session of parliament in 1610. Criticisms of the late earl could hardly harm Bacon's cause. He had to prove to James that his advice was superior to Salisbury's and that he would not repeat the earl's mistakes. Bacon's remarks about the election of 1604 should be taken with strong reservations. His frustrations and probable jealousy of Salisbury's successful career hardly make him a credible witness in any evaluation of Salisbury's role in James's first election. In addition, any allegation of electoral negligence on Salisbury's part ignores the last ten years of his Elizabethan service.

The full-scale battle that raged between Essex and Salisbury carried over into the elections of 1593 and 1597. The patronage of Elizabethan England was changing from what Sir John Neale has called "clientage, a vestige of feudalism adapted to new social purposes" into a struggle for domination of the Elizabethan court. "Patronage," Sir John Neale aptly noted, "was being turned into a political weapon." This was the hard school of politics in which Salisbury grew to political maturity. He and Essex were forerunners of Pembroke and Buckingham. Salisbury interfered in the elections of 1593 and 1597, and in 1601, although Essex was out of the way, his place-hunting continued; his patronage accounted for twenty or more seats. Is it possible that he was, in 1604, so out of character as to ignore what had become, for him, standard electoral planning? That is a question that must be answered, if only tentatively, for the first election of James's reign.[5]

The proclamation summoning parliament called for free elections. Faction must be avoided; knights and burgesses must be elected "without desire in any particular men to please parents or friends"; men of factious religious humors should be ignored; blanks must not be employed. Boroughs were ordered to choose their representatives "according to the law." The proclamation's tone must have suited the "Schoolmaster of the Realm" very well. It was not, however, as forthright a document as Lord Keeper Ellesmere or Judge Popham, who drafted it, would have liked. Perhaps Salisbury's hand can be seen in its modification. The original draft specified the choice of "free men of the cities, boroughs, or places for which they shall be chosen." If that was impossible, then county residents must be elected. Presumably, these clauses went too far for Salisbury. The final draft was far more ambiguous about residency and recommendations. The call for free elections had been abandoned in favor of carefully contrived generalities. Even this version, however, as events proved in the Cinque Ports, offered scope for opposition to patronage.[6] Indeed, while Popham and Ellesmere worked on its clauses, customary electoral practices were already making it meaningless.

Aristocratic patronage was probably involved in four of every ten 1604 elections (102 of 250, or 40.8 percent), and from 1604 to 1610, such patronage can be traced in over 40 percent (41 of 95) of the bye-elections. Aristocratic place-hunting was not a new development. The duke of Norfolk and the earls of Leicester and Essex were great Elizabethan place-hunters. So was, of course, Salisbury, whose intervention in 1601 had accounted for twenty or more places; he did a little better as a patron in 1604. Save for an interesting analysis in his papers of Old Sarum's electoral history, no direct evidence has survived to detail his electioneering in 1604; but thanks to the connections of various members chosen by patronage boroughs, it is possible to form a fairly accurate picture of his activities. At Queenborough, where he placed his friend Sir George Carew in 1597, he probably nominated Sir Edward Strafford, the Elizabethan diplomat. Cornish boroughs were his main targets. His friends or clients, Sir Thomas Lake (Launceston), Sir Thomas Chaloner (Lostwithiel), Thomas Provis (Penryn), Dudley Carleton (St. Mawes), and the lieutenant of the Tower, Sir George Harvey (West Looe) probably owed their elections to his influence. Indeed, his patronage possibly accounted for both places at West Looe and Penryn, and it is likely that his candidates could have also taken burgess-ships at Bossiney, Callington, Grampound, Helston, East Looe, St. Ives, and Saltash. He was active elsewhere as well. Sir Arthur Atye, a veteran courtier whose electoral history reads like a list of patronage boroughs, was chosen at Beeralston; and Salisbury's servant, Sir Hugh Beeston, was returned for Stafford and Shoreham, although his choice for Shoreham was probably not the earl's work. Westminister's election of Sir Walter Cope was a sure sign of Salisbury's intervention, which might have accounted for both of Westminster's places. Stamford was a family borough, and its election of Salisbury's friend and distant kinsman Sir Robert Wingfield testified to his patronage. Bewdley may have granted him a place while Peterborough surrendered one. Altogether, Salisbury's patronage may have accounted for a maximum of twenty-two places in eighteen elections. It is an impressive total, but, recalling his zealous electioneering in 1597 or 1601, it is not unrealistic. It is impossible to imagine that one of the most skillful of Elizabethan patrons would or could, suddenly and inexplicably in 1604, abandon customary electoral practices. Election management was part of the late Elizabethan political system. Salisbury was, if not its leading exponent, one of its most able and active. He could not have done otherwise in 1604. And his efforts were not simply confined to the employment of his own credit. In 1604, as in the past, he was quite willing to use the power of other patrons to place his nominees.[7]

As parliament became increasingly difficult for Salisbury and the crown, bye-elections gained in importance. They offered Salisbury an opportunity to place more sympathetic members in a reluctant House of Commons. There is, happily, considerable evidence to show his zealous efforts. Between 1605 and 1610, he intervened in twenty bye-elections, or in about one-fifth of the total of ninety-five. His electioneering won a harvest of sixteen places; he lost five. Salisbury's place-hunting was a model of efficiency. His friends and clients kept him in mind whenever the possibility of a place arose, as did those ready to bargain a possible burgess-ship for his favor. In addition, the methodical Salisbury kept his own list of deceased M.P.'s whose places his nominees might capture. His planning is typified in Penryn's election story. In 1605 Thomas Provis, one of its members, expressed his desire to be rid of his parliamentary obligations since his "trade and adventure" required his full attention. He wanted Salisbury to "appoint some other more sufficient in my room." His request was impossible to fulfill in 1605; he could not simply give over his burgess-ship. Natural causes, however, took Provis and his fellow M.P. from Penryn, Sir Richard Warburton, from the scene in 1609, and its return of Sir William Maynard and Sir Edward Conway in the succeeding bye-election looks very much like Salisbury's work.

Salisbury's power is also illustrated by the bye-elections at Beeralston and West Looe in 1605. He successfully nominated Sir William Waad, the lieutenant of the Tower, for Beeralston but then shifted him to West Looe and put Humphrey May, the future chancellor of the Duchy of Lancaster, in at Beeralston. In 1610 Eye, Suffolk, reversed its election at Salisbury's request but also made sure that his nominee, Sir John Kaye, would "not be further chargeable unto us," the same promise that Hedon received for electing Sir John Digby. Boroughbridge could not refuse his nominee because "(even in our simplest judgment)," it would be "worse to us than death itself." All towns, however, were not that servile. In 1605 Hereford's corporation, despite the added pressures put upon them by the local bishop, refused Salisbury's nominee as did proud and independent Ludlow, which denied both the earl and Lord Eure. It would not elect anyone "that was not a resident Burgess among us." Ludlow's own regulations, "the stature laws and his majesty's proclamation" made it impossible. Ludlow and Hereford, though, were in the minority; Penryn, Beeralston, Eye, West Looe, Hedon, and Boroughbridge represented the majority. Salisbury's bye-election success reflected his customary skill and foresight. It was eloquent testimony to his career as a patron, begun in Elizabeth's election of 1593.[8]

Salisbury, of course, was not the only patron hard at work in the elections. In 1601 a Catholic gentleman, Sir Thomas Arundell, elevated to the peerage as Lord Arundell of Wardour in 1605, bought the manor of Christchurch, Hampshire, and with his purchase gained a controlling voice in the little borough's elections. He used his power to such advantage that Christchurch became his pocket borough. In 1604 he nominated two outsiders, Richard Martyn and John Foyle; and, when Foyle could not serve, Arundell replaced him with another stranger, Nicholas Hyde of Wiltshire and London.[9] Henry Wriothesley, earl of Southampton, was another and more industrious patron. He had been restored to favor at James's accession and had been appointed captain of Carisbrooke Castle and governor of the Isle of Wight, an office that provided election patronage over the island's three parliamentary boroughs. Sir George Carey, the late queen's kinsman, had held that post in 1584 when, thanks to his intervention, parliament restored Yarmouth and Newport to the franchise and granted Newtown the right to choose burgesses. Newport had been so grateful that it rashly promised Carey that he could have, as long as he lived, the right to nominate one of its burgesses. Southampton held Newport and its sister boroughs to that promise. The earl did have, however, some trouble with Yarmouth, where his candidate, Sir Thomas Cheeke, ran into unexpected opposition. Southampton was shocked and angry. He found it "strange," he wrote Yarmouth, "that by way of prevention and cunning, you have provided rather to make excuses, than to yield satisfaction to my reasonable request." Yarmouth tried to explain, in vain, that it had promised its places to others, an explanation that outraged Southampton even more. The earl tersely noted that he would "have occasion to note your little love and respect to me" and warned the borough his servant was on his way to conduct a personal investigation and to make sure that the corporation clearly understood Southampton's "mind." Yarmouth understood: it returned Cheeke and Arthur Bromfield, which possibly gave the determined earl both places. Perhaps that was the price Yarmouth had to pay for its ill-advised effort at independence. Newtown and Newport, however, apparently surrendered one place each to the earl's nominees and, by so doing, were able to preserve the other place for their own candidates.[10] Arundell of Wardour was a manor lord; Southampton's influence was the result of the offices he held. Their stories offer a brief but important example of how and why aristocratic patronage could be brought to bear.

Local office also contributed to the electoral influence of the peerage. Baron Ellesmere employed his offices as high steward of both Oxford and St. Albans to place a nominee at each borough. Baron Knollys probably saw to the choice of Sir Jerome Bowes at Reading, where Knollys was high steward, and his position as Berkshire's lord lieutenant, combined with his prestige and territorial influence, must have aided the election of his brother, Sir Francis Knollys, for Berkshire. Lord Buckhurst (earl of Dorset in 1604), was lord lieutenant of Sussex; his son and heir was returned for that county in 1604, a choice that provides another example of the electoral prestige land and office could provide. He may have helped another kinsman, Sir Henry Compton, find a place at East Grinstead, and recommended Joseph Tey, of an Essex family, at Arundel although the town must have regretted its choice. Tey, who had promised — as an election inducement — to forgo any parliamentary wages, was, by 1610, pushing the borough so hard for money that it petitioned the House of Commons for relief.[11]

Territorial influence and prestige provided its customary foundation for electioneering. Lord Sheffield's son won a seat for Lincolnshire, a county whose representation was altogether aristocratic, for Sir Edmund Sheffield's colleague was Thomas, Lord Clinton. The earl of Shrewsbury was involved in Nottinghamshire's choices, and Richard Spencer had the backing of the countess of Derby for his place at Brackley. The earl of Pembroke's nominees took both places at Old Sarum and Wilton, where he was lord of the manor, and captured one place each at Shaftesbury, Cardiff, and Downton. His family's influence accounted for his brother's choice for Glamorganshire, and another Herbert, Sir William, won Montgomeryshire's election. Lord Paget's insistence that Sir Robert Stanford stand for Staffordshire possibly accounted for his return in what may have been a contested election.[11]

No discussion of aristocratic patronage, however, would be complete without a review of the influence wielded by the Howard family. Henry Howard, earl of Northampton and lord warden of the Cinque Ports, Thomas, earl of Suffolk and lord chamberlain, and Charles, earl of Nottingham and lord admiral, were the most important patrons, but the electioneering of Thomas, earl of Arundel, and Thomas, viscount Bindon, can be quickly considered. Arundel's influence probably accounted for one place at Steyning and possibly two more at Horsham, and Bindon's patronage left even less of a mark. He had some influence in Dorsetshire and, in 1601, even offered Cecil some burgess-ships there, but little can be said about his role in 1604. He was involved at Weymouth, where Edward Reynolds, returned for Weymouth, 1601, hoped to repeat his success. But the outcome of his brother Owen's campaign for him at Weymouth was in doubt since, as Edward complained, "I do forbear the urging thereof" because "I would not cross my L[ord] V[iscount] Bindon the second time, having had so honorable a testimony of his own opinion, and with such difficulty passed the suit the last election." Reynolds failed, but Weymouth's return gives no hint that Bindon enjoyed any success either. He may have found Francis James, the chancellor of Bath and Wells, a place at Wareham, but, save for those two boroughs, Bindon's patronage leaves no trace.[13]

Nottingham's influence in Shropshire, Carmarthenshire, Sussex, Reigate, Blechingley, and Harwich has already been examined, but some additions can be made. His influence as lord admiral apparently gave him a place at Portsmouth, which he kept in its bye-election in 1607 when John Corbett, a clerk of the Privy Council, was chosen. Harwich probably gave up both its places to Nottingham since Sir

Richard Brown, Trevor's colleague in 1604, had previously served for the Howard's patronage boroughs of Steyning, Arundel, and Midhurst. Nottingham's influence possibly accounted for the choices made in the bye-elections at Harwich (1605) and Blechingly (1610). Windsor may have granted him one place in 1604 and probably did in its bye-election in 1610, and the election of Salisbury's servant Beeston at Shoreham looks very much like Nottingham's work. Scarborough, too, respected his power enough to reserve a place for his nominee. He first suggested his officer "and your recorder Mr. Desworth" but shifted his support to Sir Thomas Posthumous Hoby's candidacy. Counting the bye-elections, Nottingham was probably involved in fourteen elections and may have won as many as sixteen places.[14]

Northampton, thanks to his office as lord warden, was another influential patron. But he was also lord of the manor of Bishop's Castle, and its election of an outsider, the patentee William Twinehoe, was the result. In 1610 it returned another Northampton nominee, Sir William Cavendish, son of the earl of Devonshire. Sir Robert Drury may have had his aid in Suffolk's election, and the choice of his Norfolk agent, Sir Thomas Holland, at Dartmouth was another sign of his influence. Another of the earl's agents, Sir Thomas Cornwallis, served for Norfolk. James's physician, Sir William Paddy, probably owed his Thetford burgess-ship to Northampton, although the earl of Suffolk could have been responsible; they were the principal property owners in and around the borough. Castle Rising chose Northampton's friend and associate Thomas Monson. Counting the ports and the bye-elections, he intervened in eighteen elections and won a possible eighteen places for his friends and dependents. Save for Salisbury, he was the most influential patron in 1604–10.[15]

The bitterly fought Essex election was only a part of the earl of Suffolk's electoral enterprise. He intervened at Maldon, either requesting a blank indenture or, and it is not certain, assurances that the borough would reserve a place for his candidate. Maldon did neither since its "election stands upon the consent of a great multitude wherein we may doubt of the certain election of any man." Besides, Suffolk "should nominate a man by name other wise we are not able to satisfy your Lord's request." Suffolk apparently complied, and the borough's return of Sir Edward Lewkenor, possibly a past Howard client at Shoreham, may have been the result. Maldon's bye-election in 1605 definitely involved the earl, who must have been embarrassed since, as in the Essex election of 1604, he was compelled to ask for the Privy Council's assistance in his effort to have the borough choose his son, Theophilus. The borough had already promised the vacancy to a neighbor, Sir John Sams; but possibly because of the council's intervention, it consulted with Sams and reported, perhaps with a sigh of relief, that he had agreed to withdraw, "not willing to oppose himself against so worthy a man as my Lord of Walden." At least, in his other elections, Suffolk did not have to rely on the Privy Council. He was Ipswich's high steward, which probably explained its return of Sir Francis Bacon and Sir Henry Glemham. Bacon had won at Ipswich before, thanks to the nomination of its former high steward, the earl of Essex; and Glemham, married to the earl of Dorset's daughter, owed his later elections to the patronage of the earl of Arundel. Morpeth, too, probably gave Suffolk at least one place, thanks, no doubt, to the help of his brother, Lord William Howard. Suffolk's marriage to Catherine Knyvett, daughter of an influential Wiltshire squire, Sir Henry Knyvett, provided him with an estate at Charlton Park, near Malmesbury, and enough Wiltshire influence to account for one burgess-ship each at Calne and Wootton Bassett and both at Malmesbury, where his client Sir Roger Dallison and his kinsman Sir Thomas Dallison were elected.[16] Suffolk, including the bye-election at Maldon, contributed a possible ten places in eight elections to the Howards' total. Together, the Howards probably intervened in forty-four elections for forty-eight places, a significant comment on the electoral power of England's aristocracy.

There were 250 elections in 1604 and the peerage, including the great churchmen, intervened in 102, or slightly better than forty percent. In the ninety-five bye-elections held from 1604 to 1610, forty-one showed evidence of such intervention or about four in ten.[17] Given its electioneering for James's first parliament, it is clear that the aristocracy was still a significant force in parliamentary elections.

Royal officials and agencies were also part of the electoral story. Officers like the lord warden of the Cinque Ports or the lord president of the Council of the North exercised an authority that could provide scope for patronage. Much depended, of course, on the electoral zeal of the official who directed the agency and the influence of any local competitors for places. The place-hunting of such officials and agencies must be evaluated in any election.

The Cinque Ports, traditionally England's gateway to Europe, enjoyed their own unique franchise, courts, and organization. They were under the authority of the lord warden, who was also constable of Dover Castle, and, happily for his patronage, the ports returned representatives—called barons—to parliament. Two of Elizabeth's lord wardens, the Lords Cobham, father and son, William and Henry

Brooke, held the office from 1558 to 1603. In 1563 William, Lord Cobham, may have placed as many as five nominees; but eight years later he failed at Sandwich, Hastings, and possibly Winchelsea, and Hythe gave him but one of the two places he sought. But the threat was clear to the ports, and in the summer of 1572, following another election wherein Cobham's patronage reached its lowest ebb, the ports tried to define their electoral position. The General Brotherhood decreed that "none but resident freemen, or those of counsel with the Ports and receiving a fee from them" should be elected. The decree was easy to publish but hard to enforce since, in 1584, aided by the Privy Council's request that the warden "deal with all the Cinque Ports" to see to the choice of "loyal and responsible representatives," only Rye and Sandwich avoided Cobham's interference. In the next elections (1586–1601), Hythe, Dover, Winchelsea, and Hastings always surrendered at least one place. Rye may have refused the warden in 1586 and 1593 but gave way in 1597 and surrendered both its places in 1601. New Romney maintained its independence in 1586 and 1588 but gave up one seat in 1597 and 1601. Only Sandwich successfully withstood the warden's admonitions, refusing his nominees in the last four Elizabethan parliaments, a proud and lonely record of independence. The stage was set by 1603: the ports would either have to make a stand or be swallowed up by the warden.[18]

Before he lost his post as lord warden in 1603, Henry, Lord Cobham, had requested that each port reserve a place for his nominees. This might have contributed to the ports' decision, reached at a General Brotherhood meeting in July 1603, to fine any port £20 for not electing "a mayor or freeman inhibitant as burgess for Parliament." These were brave words, indeed, but it remained to be seen just how staunch the ports would be. Testing time was near at hand; in October, the new lord warden, Northampton, launched his electoral campaign. His agent, Sir Thomas Fane, visited the ports to inform them of his nominees and stressed that Northampton expected "satisfaction in this my first request." Only Dover, which had probably already agreed to the election of Northampton's lieutenant, Sir Thomas Waller, was not on his list.[19]

The ports' unanimity was short-lived. Hythe, Dover, and Rye surrendered a place without apparent trouble; and although Sandwich was, as it had been before, plagued by a bitter quarrel between the corporation and "'the mutinous opposition . . . sailors and others of the meaner sort'," Northampton's nominee was elected. More serious difficulties arose, however, over his candidates at Winchelsea, New Romney, and Hastings, but Northampton's response was swift and effective. Winchelsea's surrender can be best described as humiliating. It had already elected two jurats, but, under the earl's unrelenting pressure, one of them, Thomas Eglestone, resigned so that Northampton's nominee, Thomas Unton, could take his place. New Romney and Hastings also put up a brave show of resistance but soon gave way. The ports, for better or worse, had apparently decided that they could not do without the assistance and influence of the lord warden. Northampton's electoral successes continued in the ports' bye-elections through 1610. In fact, after 1607, both of Sandwich's members were his nominees, a clear indication that the corporation, with his assistance, had asserted their control over their opponents. His success boded well for the future prospects of any lord warden's election hopes.[20]

The Duchy of Lancaster was composed of the estates of Henry IV, duke of Lancaster, which he had kept separate from the crown's holdings on his accession in 1399. Although its headquarters were in London, its bureacracy, headed by the chancellor of the duchy, administered large holdings throughout England, the core of which was the County Palatine of Lancaster. Seventeen boroughs showed, in Elizabeth's years, the results of its electoral influence. Not all were consistently in the duchy's grasp; its success varied and often reflected nothing more than the place-hunting enthusiasm of its current chancellor. Six of the boroughs—Lancaster, Preston, Wigan, Newton-in-Makersfield, Liverpool and Clitheroe—were within Lancashire. The remaining eleven were scattered about the realm. Monmouth was the duchy's Welsh borough; three others, Aldborough, Knaresborough, and Boroughbridge, were in Yorkshire, and Sudbury and Thetford were in East Anglia. Leicester, Newcastle-under-Lyme, Stockbridge, Huntingdon, and Higham Ferrers completed the roster. East Grinstead, another duchy town, was apparently outside its election patronage. In Lancashire, Preston, Wigan, Clitheroe, and Lancaster were the most receptive to its influence. Liverpool's electoral pattern was complicated by the presence of the earl of Derby, but the duchy usually managed to secure a place, as it did at Newton-in-Makersfield, in spite of its local patrons, the Langtons and Fleetwoods. Outside Lancashire, Huntingdon, Sudbury, and Boroughbridge were the most cooperative, and Knaresborough and Newcastle-under-Lyme were nearly as quiescent. Results in the other boroughs were mixed: Thetford, Leicester, and Monmouth were the most independent.[21]

The chancellors, Sir Thomas Heneage and his successor, Cecil, were zealous patrons. In 1593 Heneage intervened in ten elections and won thirteen places, and Cecil, four years later, saw his candidates take twelve burgess-ships. But the duchy's election story changed with the appointment of the aging Sir John Fortescue as chancellor in 1601, an appointment that has all the appearance of a court compromise. Fortescue's selection came late in the election season of 1601, which might explain the duchy's relatively poor showing (eight elections for ten places); but in 1604 Fortescue's electioneering continued on its uninspired course. At least evidence has survived to tell the tale of the duchy's intervention at Leicester.

The duchy had enjoyed little previous success at Leicester. It may have won a place in 1572 and certainly had in 1584. Leicester's independence, though, was increasingly endangered since its close neighbor, George Hastings, the fourth earl of Huntingdon, had been actively engaged in four of its last six elections. In 1604 Huntingdon and the duchy became electoral allies. Local conditions complicated the election, since the duchy and Huntingdon were backing one of the town's neighbors, a Mr. Tamworth, who was being sued by the corporation. Leicester's recorder, Augustine Nicholls, was defending the town's interests, and, perhaps as a reward, the corporation wanted Nicholls as a burgess. Nicholls, however, refused; instead, he nominated Sir William Skipwith, a county gentleman and close friend. Sir John Fortescue, with Huntingdon's support, nominated his son-in-law, Sir John Poulteney; but Huntingdon went even further, urging Leicester to "offer him [Fortescue] the placing of the other." That was too much; it meant the complete surrender of Leicester's independence to the duchy and the earl. The town's leaders fought back with considerable skill. They fenced with Huntingdon, pointing out that they could not accept his proposal because the "greatest number" of the corporation's membership were absent and, since their consent was required, no answer could be given to the earl's request. It was a fair excuse, a good delaying tactic. Presumably, the town was seeking another suitable applicant, and, as luck (or planning?) would have it, another county gentleman, Sir Henry Beaumont, announced his candidacy. Beaumont was a perfect candidate: he was a free burgess of Leicester, and his past services to the town entitled him to its grateful reward. Skipwith and Beaumont were elected even though Poulteney, so Fortescue promised, would serve without charge. The town's independence, however, was worth any cost in wages. There was, for the corporation, the added satisfaction of knowing that Tamworth's influential supporters had, electorally at least, been dealt a hard blow. Leicester had escaped its prospective patrons. It was, alas, a short-lived victory. Skipwith died, and, in the bye-election to replace him in 1610, Henry Hastings, the fifth earl of Huntingdon, nominated his "cousin, Mr. Henry Rich [son of the first earl of Warwick]" whom

Leicester dutifully returned. The story of its losing battle against Huntingdon and the duchy that occupied Leicester throughout the early Stuart period was well begun.[22]

The duchy found seats at Wigan for Poulteney and another nominee, Sir William Cooke, Salisbury's kinsman. Loyal Lancaster returned two of its candidates, Sir Thomas Fanshawe, a duchy auditor, and an attorney for the Court of Wards, Sir Thomas Hesketh, who, following his death in 1605, was replaced by another duchy nominee, Sir Thomas Howard, a son of the earl of Suffolk. Clitheroe probably surrendered one place, and Preston's choice of Sir Vincent Skinner was probably the duchy's work. The choice of an officer of the ordnance, Sir Robert Johnson at Monmouth, can also be credited to it. Newcastle-under-Lyme's return of Salisbury's former nominee, Bowyer, and Stockbridge's election of Chancellor Fortescue's son, Sir William, completes the duchy's 1604 election story. Compared with the success the earls of Nottingham and Northampton enjoyed in 1604–10, the duchy's showing can hardly be described as very effective. It intervened in eight elections and took no more than nine places.[23]

The Councils of the North and of the Marches of Wales differed considerably from the Duchy of Lancaster. Their function was to bring the king's authority, justice, and administration to England's distant borders. Furthermore, the Welsh and Yorkshire gentry were an influential and electioneering lot. Their appointments to the councils recognized local status, and, since this was so, it seems far more realistic to disregard council patronage as a key to any understanding of the elections that occurred under their jurisdiction. The absence, too, of hard evidence makes the distinction between the two types of patronage practically impossible. Boroughbridge, Aldborough (when they were not listening to the Duchy of Lancaster), Beverley, Ripon, and, on one occasion at least, Hull enjoyed the election attentions of the Council of the North before 1603. But, despite the electoral zeal displayed by its great Elizabethan president, the earl of Huntingdon, the council's electioneering was spasmodic at best; it was clearly not as influential as the Duchy of Lancaster.[24]

In 1604 the council, led by Lord Sheffield, probably accounted for almost half (nine of twenty-two) of Yorkshire's parliamentary places. Sheffield canvassed for Francis Clifford and Sir John Savile as knights of the shire, urging William Wentworth "to give your voices of yourselves, your tenants and such other friends as you can procure with these two gentlemen only, and to take pains to be with them at the day of the election." The earl of Shrewsbury's agents were also gathering freeholders for Clifford when Shrewsbury ordered them to attend the council meetings at York, which led to a joint and, as Yorkshire's election proved, successful campaign for Savile and Clifford. It was one of the few peaceful Yorkshire elections between 1604 and 1640. At Scarborough, Sir Thomas Posthumous Hoby sought a place and, although a neighbor to the port, thought it worthwhile to clear his candidacy with Sheffield. Hoby profited, too, from the earl of Nottingham's backing, but the very fact that he sought Sheffield's approval was testimony of the influence of the lord president. Another council member, Lord Eure, placed his second son, Francis, at Scarborough as well. Aldborough's return of Sheffield's son, Sir Edmund, was probably another sign of council intervention. William Gee, a secretary of the council and Beverley's recorder, took a place there, a neat union of compelling electoral advantages, and John Ferne's election—he was another council secretary—at Boroughbridge was possibly due to the council's intervention. Richmond chose one of Burghley's former clients, Richard Percival, and Ripon divided its places between the patronage of the archbishop of York and Lord Eure. Altogether, Sheffield and the council were probably involved in seven elections, its best early Stuart record. Why did it do so well? Sheffield, its lord president, was powerful enough in his own right and an energetic place-hunter. The council enjoyed another compelling advantage: only one of its nominees was a stranger; the rest, through their family connections, marriages, property holdings, and local offices, were known to the county and borough electorates. As a result, its prospects of success were greatly enhanced; it was a lesson other prospective patrons might well have learned.[25]

The Council of the Marches of Wales made practically no impression at all on Elizabethan elections. County families and the patronage of the earls of Pembroke barred its path. When it did have a voice in an election, as at Ludlow in 1597, it was the result of either the sheriff's chicanery or because of the power of the earl of Pembroke, then lord president.[26] The first parliament of James's reign was no exception.

Ludlow was council headquarters, but its Elizabethan story only served to reveal the council's impotence. Nothing changed in 1604. Ludlow returned Robert Berry, burgess of the town since 1597 and its M.P. in five previous parliaments, and bailiff Richard Benson. There is nothing even to hint that the council or its president, Baron Zouch, played any role in the election. Indeed, both of Ludlow's members served at the town's expense, a sure sign of independence.[27]

Shrewsbury's election was far different from Ludlow's. Lord Zouch nominated his son-in-law's brother, Francis Tate, and endorsed the candidacy of Shrewsbury's recorder and former (1601) M.P., Richard Barker. But Barker's candidacy caused a furious controversy that

Zouch was unable to stop; indeed, it seemed as if no one could control the town's "malignant spirit," Sheriff Sir Roger Owen, a rather unstable firebrand who was determined to prevent Barker's election. Owen hid the election writ and even altered its date, supplied drink in liberal amounts to his followers, and even compiled a "roll" of those intimidated citizens who had promised to support his cause. Tumult and riot marked the first election, which ended in the return of different indentures to the House of Commons, which promptly ordered another election. Owen and his followers, however, were equal to the challenge; their actions so frightened the town's bailiffs that they fled the Common Hall rather than attempt a second election. Finally, on its third try, Shrewsbury managed to finish its election, although it was only accomplished under armed guard and in such a tense atmosphere that bloodshed nearly resulted. However, much to everyone's surprise and relief, Owen gave way and agreed to Barker's return. Zouch's nominee, Tate, was never an issue in the election, but it was the last time that the council enjoyed any electoral success at Shrewsbury. From 1614 through 1640, the borough contented itself with quiet elections of neighboring gentlemen or borough officials. It was, for Shrewsbury's baliffs, just as well; they had suffered enough in 1604.[28]

The election of 1604 was typical for the Council of the Marches of Wales. Save for Tate's choice at Shrewsbury, its patronage left no trace. Even at Ludlow, its headquarters, it made no impression. Of the crown's agencies, it was the least important electoral patron. And so it would remain throughout the early Stuart years.

At the heart of early seventeenth-century administration was, of course, the Privy Council, and though its involvement in the elections for Essex (1604) and Maldon (1605) has been mentioned, its other electioneering requires a brief review. London's recorder was traditionally an appointee of the crown, and his election to parliament probably was the council's work. Sir Henry Montagu, later earl of Manchester, was appointed recorder of London in 1603 and served for the city in James's first parliament. It is possible, too, that Sir William Fleetwood may have had council support for his election for Middlesex, and the council's intervention in two 1606 bye-elections completes the patronage picture of the court's agencies. The two men involved in the disputed Buckinghamshire election of 1604, Sir Francis Goodwin and Sir John Fortescue, were the council's 1606 candidates. It placed Goodwin at Buckingham and was, in all likelihood, responsible for Fortescue's return for Middlesex.[29]

The lord warden and the court's agencies were involved in twenty-six elections in 1604 and can be credited with a voice in the probable return of twenty-eight members of parliament.[30] One of every ten elections, in other words, involved the court. Save for the lord warden's success, however, the court's role in the election of 1604 was in keeping with its Elizabethan past. The electioneering of the Duchy of Cornwall, the Prince's Council, and the Queen's Council was yet to come.

Most county elections passed off quietly in 1604, although in Worcestershire, Northamptonshire, and Essex contested elections set the stage for future troubles; and Buckinghamshire's election, the famous clash between Goodwin and Fortescue, had important implications for electoral history.[31] Worcestershire's election grew out of the county's deep religious divisions; it provided a glimpse of the future when such issues often mirrored England's worsening situation. The contests in Northamptonshire and Essex were quite similar: both involved county factions struggling for political dominance. The Spencers and Montagus of Boughton were bent on establishing their hegemony in Northamptonshire, and in Essex the Rich family was adamantly trying to defend its stake in Essex politics in a contest that became so heated that it involved the Privy Council.

Northamptonshire's previous electoral calm had been largely based on the influence of the Mildmays, led by Sir Walter Mildmay, chancellor of the Exchequer and privy councillor to Elizabeth I, who first appeared for the county in 1557 and continued to serve it until his death in 1589. In 1604 the first of several contested elections occurred, caused by the struggle for power that had been slowly developing in Northamptonshire. The ambitious Spencer-Montagu alliance was challenged by Lord Mordaunt and Bishop Dove of Peterborough, who were backing Sir Anthony Mildmay in an apparent attempt to restore the Mildmays' former influence.

Mildmay's challenge was hardly a serious one, but Sir Edward Montagu and his ally, Sir Robert Spencer, treated it as such. Canvassing began as early as mid-April 1603; the sheriff was won over to their side, and, in at least fifteen of Northamptonshire's hundreds, Montagu's agents prepared lists of their committed supporters. Montagu and Spencer would know on election day where county loyalties lay. It was a subtle threat, for should a voter switch sides retribution could be swift. Even Spencer's elevation to the peerage in the summer of 1603 did nothing to harm the alliance. Spencer and Montagu chose Sir Valentine Knightley to take Spencer's place, and, thanks to their skillful campaign, Mildmay's candidacy simply withered away. By election time there was no opposition. Spencer and Montagu had every reason to feel satisfied. Montagu and Knightley were elected and the county's tranquility maintained. In Essex and Worcestershire, though, the story was different.

In Essex, as in Northamptonshire, county prestige was at stake. The Rich family, with its properties and links to other county families like the influential Barringtons, found their county preeminence challenged in the election by the earl of Suffolk, Thomas Howard, privy councillor and lord chamberlain, who was backing Sir Edward Denny. When it appeared that Denny's bid might fail, the Privy Council stepped in, as it had in a somewhat similar situation in 1588 to save Denny's return and Suffolk's credit. Mary Bohannon, the historian of the Essex election, suggested that the religious issue, specifically Rich's puritanism, provoked the council's intervention. But if that were so, why did the council ignore the far more explosive Worcestershire election, where the religious issue was openly flaunted? Papist and Protestant battled in Worcestershire; that was hardly true in Essex. In 1601 Worcestershire's election had been plagued by a bitter religious quarrel that put the return of a prominent courtier at risk. The council intervened to save his election; it stepped into the Essex election for the same reason in 1604. It did nothing in Worcestershire's factious election; no courtier peer or prominent official was involved.[32]

Recusancy was a problem of long-standing in Worcestershire, as its bitter elections of 1601 and 1604 revealed. James I had courted Protestant and Catholic alike before reaching the throne, and his accession raised the hopes of both sides. Prospects of a parliament led to rumors that recusants were "labouring tooth and nail for places," a rumor that was certainly well founded in Worcestershire. They had organized themselves "for the election of knights" who would "stand fast . . . for the advancing of their religion." Their planning, however, was revealed to all on the day before Christmas, 1603, when they mistakenly mustered to carry the election only to discover that the writ had not yet arrived and that no election would be held. Their mistake alerted the Protestants, who quickly organized their campaign and guaranteed for Worcestershire another quarrelsome contest.

Both sides reviewed their positions and carefully selected candidates with the widest possible appeal. Sir Henry Bromley of Holt Castle and Sir William Ligon stood for the reformed religion, and the recusants, after considerable thought, backed a suspected Papist, Sir Edmond Harwell of Besford. Their efforts, however, to join Harwell with the popular and widely respected Sir John Packington, the famous "lusty Packington" of Elizabeth's court, failed. Packington would have been, had he consented to stand, an excellent ally for Harwell; his apparent

Protestantism and county reputation might well have carried Harwell with him to Westminister.

The county's leadership was deeply divided by the contest. Canvassing was intense, and threats, violence, and fraud marked the campaign. Bromley and Ligon, promising "rewards for such their labour and travel," herded together anyone they could lay their hands on and marched them off to occupy Worcester's Castle Green—the election site—on election eve. They were to deny it, by force if necessary, to Harwell's supporters on election day. Little wonder, then, that passions boiled over; in a scene marred by fisticuffs and the threat of sword play, Bromley and Ligon were duly returned. Everything the proclamation denounced—factions, combinations, the candidacy of men "noted for their superstitious blindness" —occurred in Worcestershire's election. Yet the Privy Council did nothing. Its inaction emphasizes even more that it was the earl of Suffolk's prestige and not the religious issue that led to its interference in Essex. For Worcestershire the end of such divisions was not yet in sight. There may have been trouble in 1614; there was in the 1640s, but by then the impact of religious issues upon elections was a more common symptom of impending calamity.[33]

Boroughs found it difficult to maintain electoral independence. Poverty might force the election of outsiders who would serve without pay; the borough's lord might be too powerful to deny, or, for the borough anxious about its own interests, the choice of a nominee might serve as a *quid pro quo* for the help of a patron. Sir Edward Coke, the attorney general, owed his electoral success at Corfe Castle and Dunwich to those very reasons. Dunwich was too poor to maintain its independence, and Corfe Castle, where Coke was lord, wanted its charter confirmed. Both boroughs followed their Elizabethan path.[34]

Gloucester's 1604 election was a continuation of its Elizabethan history, which Sir John Neale summarized as a constant "division of opinion—a cleavage between the few and the many, with some of the few in the role of demagogues." It was exciting: contested elections were fought in 1571, 1572, and 1597, and the earl of Leicester's intervention in 1580 and 1584 kept the pot boiling; and if contested elections were not enough, the appointment of a recorder led to a confrontation with the Privy Council in 1586–87! James's first election was no exception.[35]

The city corporation, despite the objections of Alderman John Jones, agreed that Recorder Nicholas Overbury and Alderman Thomas Machen should be elected. Jones, presumably encouraged by Godfrey

Goldsborough, bishop of Gloucester, wanted a burgess-ship for himself. He feared that his position as registrar of the diocese and a lease he held from the bishop might be challenged in parliament. Jones gulled the corporation by apparently promising he would back Overbury and Machen while, at the same time, he allied himself with a dissident faction among the city's freemen by promising to cure the city's economic ills. If elected, Jones claimed he would "procure an Act" of parliament that would confine malt-making and the growth of "pease" to city residents and promised that he "would procure a grant of more fairs to be kept" in Gloucester than ever before. His campaign shrewdly focused on local issues that affected citizen's pocketbooks, and it worked. Even his enemies admitted that Jones "did allure many of the meaner sort of Burgesses to promise to give their voices with him." On election day a mob of his supporters, allegedly well served with drink, invaded the hall and, in a rousing scene, overwhelmed the mayor, corporation, and sheriff. Jones and Overbury were elected.[36]

What was the fate, in 1604, of the Elizabethan independents, Bath, Bristol, Ludlow, Newcastle-on-Tyne, Worcester, and the nearly independent city of York? York returned to the ranks of the electorally "pure" when it chose an alderman, Sir Robert Askwith, and Christopher Brooke, son of a former mayor and civic official. The archbishop of York, who had broken the city's defenses in 1601 when Dr. John Bennett was chosen, could not repeat his success. York, perhaps buoyed by this victory, would follow an independent path through the next six elections.[37] Ludlow steadily pursued its former course while Bath, for the last time, kept its place among the proud few by electing resident aldermen. Bristol, Newcastle-on-Tyne, and Worcester continued in their independent ways. Sir George Snigge, Bristol's recorder, son of a former mayor and twice previously (1597, 1601) an M.P. for the city, was returned along with an alderman, Thomas James, who had been Snigge's parliamentary partner (1597) and who, in 1605, would be chosen mayor. And this in spite of the fact that Bristol's high steward was no less a personage than Thomas Sackville, earl of Dorset and England's lord treasurer! Newcastle-on-Tyne chose two influential aldermen, Sir George Selby and Henry Chapman. Worcester returned two residents, John Cowcher and Christopher Dighton, but the end was drawing near; in 1625 its record of electoral virtue would be broken. It would, like other cities and towns, fall victim to the increasing patronage pressures of the early Stuart years.[38]

James's first election clearly emphasized the gentry's invasion of borough elections. In comparison with Sir John Neale's figures for two member borough constituencies for the parliaments of 1584 and 1593, there is a marked increase in the return of county residents.[39] Eighty-four boroughs elected at least one county resident in 1584, and eighty-three did so in 1593. However, in 1604, 111 boroughs chose a county resident. They did so, it seems, at the expense of the foreigner. The number of boroughs that elected a foreigner declined sharply in 1604. In 1584, 94 boroughs chose at least one stranger, a total that increased to 101 boroughs in 1593. But only 78 boroughs chose a stranger in 1604. It is still a high figure (78 of 177, or about 44% of identified borough elections); but the number of boroughs that elected two foreigners absolutely declined from 36 in 1593 to only 15 in 1604. Thirty-three boroughs returned residents in 1604, a show of independence from influence that was never matched again, although in 1624, 28 boroughs chose their own. Of the 33 "independents" in 1604, only 9 continued to escape any form of outside intervention; the others gave way to the influence of either neighboring squires, aristocrats, or the Duchy of Lancaster (Liverpool) or the Council of the Marches of Wales (Ludlow).[40]

The election of 1604 was unique in that so few strangers were returned. Only fifteen boroughs chose two foreigners in 1604, a figure that would not be surpassed until the elections of 1640.[41] What can explain the absence of strangers and, too, the surprising show of independence by thirty-three boroughs? There is no firm answer. Perhaps James's proclamation did have some effect, especially in boroughs where no overwhelming patron was at hand. The Cinque Ports tried to use the proclamation to justify their resistance to the lord warden, but his power was too much for them to overcome. Perhaps other boroughs had better luck in defying possible patrons. Furthermore, the combined figures for the electoral involvement of the peerage and the court's agencies is the lowest for the first seven elections (1604–28) of the early Stuarts.[42] The intervention of the Duchy of Cornwall and the Prince's Council, agencies of the crown that customarily nominated strangers, was for the future; neither was active in 1604. In other respects, too, the election of 1604 belonged more to Elizabeth's reign than to those of her early Stuart successors. Contested elections were fought over local quarrels and rivalries. Worcestershire's election was, as in 1601, marked by strong anti-Catholic sentiment, and, in that sense, reflected a consistent theme of early Stuart elections.[43] The changes of the early Stuart elections, the growth of patronage, the increasing outcry against the choice of outsiders, the development of a court electoral effort, all were still in the future. The election of 1604 may well have been one of the last memories of Elizabeth's reign.

1. Cecil, although not elevated to the earldom of Salisbury until May 1605, will be referred to throughout this chapter by his final title.

2. Zouch to Lord Cecil, 6 Sept. 1603, 22 Jan. 1604, *HMC Salisbury*, 15:245; 16:11–12; Heveningham to Sir Bassingbourne Gawdy, 2 Apr. 1603, *HMC Gawdy*, 87; Montagu to Spencer, 18 Apr., Andrewe to Montagu, 19 Apr., "An Election Paper" of 19 Apr., Montagu to Yelverton, Rooe to Montagu, Apr. 1603, *HMC Buccleuch and Queensberry*, 73–75; Lord Cobham to the Mayor and Jurats of Rye, 26 May 1603, Rye Corp. MSS, East Sussex RO, 47/64, 22:10; Beverly Borough Minute Book 1597–1642, East Riding RO, DDBC/1/2, 34, which I was allowed to use thanks to the permission of the Beverley Borough Council; Nottingham to the Bailiffs and Burgesses of Scarborough, 17 Aug. 1603, Scarborough Borough MSS, General Letters B.1., 1597–1642; *HMC Various Collections*, 7:28; Dunwich Borough MSS, Suffolk RO, Ipswich Branch, Dunwich Borough Minute Book, 1595–1619, EE 6:1144/10, fols. 117, 117v; I should like to thank the Suffolk Record Office for its kind permission to use these documents. Corporation of Hastings MSS, Common Book of Assembly C/A (a) 1, fols, 88v, 89; Cecil to the Earl of Shrewsbury, 23 Dec. 1604, in E. Lodge, ed., *Illustrations of British History*, 3:83.

3. For aristocratic patronage and electioneering methods in Elizabeth's reign, see Neale, *The Elizabethan House of Commons* passim; and for discussion of earlier patronage, see J. S. Roskell, *The Commons in the Parliament of 1422*, pp. 130–34, 144, and M. McKisack, *The Parliamentary Representation of the English Boroughs*, pp. 60–61.

4. Spedding, *Bacon*, 4:368; Willson, *Privy Councillors*, pp. 104–5; *CSPV 1603–1607*, p. 268.

5. Neale, *Elizabethan House of Commons*, pp. 24–26, 233–45; and his *Elizabeth I and Her Parliaments*, 2:370–71; Willson, *Privy Councillors*, pp. 17–20, 114, 132, 133.

6. J. P. Collier, ed., *The Egerton Papers*, pp. 384–86; Rymer, *Foedera*, 16:562–63; Proclamation Summoning Parliament, 11 Jan. 1604, P.R.O., St. P. Dom. 14/73:57.

7. Salisbury probably used the Duchy of Lancaster as his agent in placing John Bowyer (his nominee in 1597) again at Newcastle-under-Lyme, and the duchy also backed another of his kinsmen, Sir William Cooke, for Wigan. Preston returned one of his father's former secretaries, Sir Vincent Skinner, and he probably was behind the Council of the North's likely support for the choice of another of his father's former agents, Richard Percival at Richmond. The earl of Pembroke backed another of his friends and clients, Sir Thomas Edmondes, at Wilton, and Salisbury used Howard patronage to his client's advantage at both Horsham and Morpeth. Willson, *Privy Councillors*, pp. 104–9, 112, 128; Neale, *Elizabethan House of Commons*, pp. 189, 193, 195, 224–25, 227–30, 242–43, 312, 314, and his *Elizabeth I and Her Parliaments*, 2:370–71; *HMC Salisbury*, 15:386; Pape, *Newcastle-under-Lyme*, pp. 133–35; Courtney, *Parl. Repr. Cornwall*, pp. 17–18, 41–42, 84–85, 114–16, 130–32, 148–50, 186–88, 209–12, 268–69, 283–86, 325–27, 363–64; Pink and Beaven, *Parl. Repr. Lancashire*, pp. 147–48, 223; D. Sinclair, *Hist. of Wigan*, 1:191; J. Drakard, *Hist. Samford*, pp. 138, 148, 153; Nevinson, *Hist. Stamford*, pp. 100–101; A. Rogers, Ed., *The Making of Stamford*, pp. 92, 96; *Devonshire Reports and Transactions* 41 (1909): 163; Walter Rye, ed., *Visitation of Norfolk*, Harleian Soc. (London, 1891), pp. 158, 201; W. Harry Rylands, ed., *Visitation of Berkshire*, 2 pts. (London, 1908), pt. 2, p. 191; Bean, *Northern Counties*, p. 1019; Gleason, *JP's*, pp. 170, 172; W. Notestein, *The House of Commons, 1604–1610*, pp. 44, 81, 97, 117; Keeler, *Long Parliament*, p. 97; W. J. Jones, "Ellesmere and Politics, 1603–1617," and T. M. Coakley, "Robert Cecil in Power: Elizabethan Politics in Two Reigns," both in H. Reinmuth, ed., *Early Stuart Studies*, pp. 18, 80 & n; M. Prestwich, *Cranfield*, pp. 23, 27, 30, 32; "Sir John Doderidge," *DNB*, 5:1062–63; "Sir Peter Manwood," *DNB*, 12:990–91; "Sir George Carew," *DNB*, 3:959–60; "Sir Thomas Chaloner," *DNB*, 3:1367–68; "Sir Francis Barnham," *DNB* 1:1184; "Sir Michael Hicks," *DNB*, 9:810–11; L. Stone, *Family and Fortune*, p. 36.

8. *CSPV 1603–1607*, pp. 268, 270, 501, 509; *CSPV 1607–1610*, p. 516; *CSPV 1610–1613*, pp. 100, 110; Willson, *Privy Councillors*, pp. 105, 109–26; Neale, *Elizabethan House of Commons*, pp. 163–64; Upton, *Sir Arthur Ingram*, pp. 30–31; Notestein, *House of Com-*

*mons 1604–1610*, p. 171; H. T. Weyman, "Members of Parliament for Ludlow," p. 18; *HMC, 3rd Report*, p. 180; *VCH Staffordshire*, 7:42–43; G. May, *Hist. of Evesham*, pp. 280, 281; Salisbury to Kirkham, n.d. 1605, E. Lodge, ed., *Illustrations of British History*, 3:171–72; Carew to Salisbury, 27 July 1605, Sneyde to the same, 9 Aug. 1605, Bishop of Hereford to the same, 9 Aug. 1605, Salisbury to the Mayor of Beeralston, 3 Oct. 1605, Provis to Salisbury, 21 Oct. 1605, Cross to Salisbury, 24 Oct. 1605, *HMC Salisbury*, 17:339, 358, 360, 445, 461, 465; Salisbury to Edmondes, 17 Oct. 1605, BM Stowe MSS 168, fols. 181–181v; Mayor and Burgesses of Hull to Salisbury, 12 Mar. 1607, Hatfield House MSS; Shropshire RO, Ludlow Corporation Minute Book 1590–1648, 356/2/1, fols. 80v, 81v, Carew to Phelips, Carew to Ellesmere, 12 Sept. 1605, P.R.O., St. P. Dom. 14/15:59, 60; Hender to Salisbury, 21 Oct., 1605, P.R.O., St. P. Dom. 14/48:116; Lok to Salisbury, 8 Nov. 1605, P.R.O., St. P. Dom., 14/16:27; Carew to Phelips, 12 Sept. 1608, P.R.O., St. P. Dom. 14/48:109; Bailiffs of Boroughbridge to Salisbury, 5 Nov. 1609, P.R.O., St. P. Dom. 14/49:10; Corp. of Ludlow to Salisbury, 1 Dec. 1609, P.R.O., St. P. Dom. 14/50:5; Mayor of Hedon to Salisbury, 13 Nov. 1609, 2 Mar. 1610, P.R.O., St. P. Dom. 14/49:25, 53:2; Mayor and Bailiffs of Weymouth and Melcombe Regis to Caesar, 13, 16 June 1610, P.R.O., St. P. Dom. 14/55:20, 23; Willcox, *Gloucestershire*, p. 31; Tewkesbury Corporation MSS, Rec. 1, f. 43; J. Bennett, *Hist. of Tewkesbury*, pp. 244–45; Williams, *Parl. Hist. Gloucestershire*, pp. 232–33.

9. *VCH Hampshire*, 5:86–87; Arundell to the Mayor of Christchurch, 10 Feb. 1604, 2 Mar. 1604, Martyn to the same, 14 Feb. 1604, Arundell to the same, 14 Feb. 1614, Christchurch Borough MSS, in the custody of the town clerk, whom I would like to thank, along with the courteous and helpful staff of the Hampshire Record Office, for their assistance in making it possible for me to use these documents; "Sir Nicholas Hyde or Hide," *DNB*, 10:399–400.

10. Neale, *Elizabethan House of Commons*, p. 143; "Henry Wriothesley, second Earl Southampton," *CDNB*, p. 1442; Hunsdon to the Burgesses of Yarmouth, 10 Sept. 1601, Southampton to the same, 19 Feb. 1604, Isle of Wight RO, Yarmouth Borough MSS, unnumbered borough letters; Sir F. Black, *The Parl. Hist. of the Isle of Wight*, pp. 9, 11–13, app. 2, pp. 32–33; *VCH Hampshire*, 5:224; "John Stanhope, first Baron Stanhope," *DNB*, 28:906–7; Keeler, *Long Parliament* pp. 132–33. In 1614 Southampton nominated Bromfield for one place at Yarmouth, and when Sir Thomas Cheeke preferred to serve for Newport in Cornwall, Southampton's son, Thomas Wriothesley, took his place. Wriothesley to the Burgesses of Yarmouth, n.d., 1614?, Isle of Wight RO, Yarmouth Borough MSS, unnumbered borough letters. Southampton was probably also behind Newtown's bye-election choice of the earl of Salisbury's servant Thomas Wilson in 1605 (Stone, *Family and Fortune*, pp. 66, 227).

11. A. Aspinal, ed., *Parliament through Seven Centuries: Reading and Its MP's*, pp. 48–49; Neale, *Elizabethan House of Commons*, pp. 166–68, 236; H. E. Salter, ed., *Oxford Council Acts, 1583–1626*, pp. 142, 158; W. R. Williams, *Parl. Hist. Oxfordshire*, p. 113; Clutterbuck, *Hist. Hertfordshire*, 1:2, 50, 53; A. E. Gibbs, *Corp. Records of St. Albans*, p. 296; Stone, "The Electoral Influence of the Second Earl of Salisbury, 1614–68," p. 388; Keeler, *Long Parliament*, pp. 66–67, 243–44; *VCH Sussex*, 7:7, 33–36; Horsfield, *Hist. Sussex*, vol. 2, app., pp. 23–28; "Robert Sackville, second Earl of Dorset," *DNB*, 17:585–89; E. R. Foster, ed., *Proceedings in Parliament, 1610*, 2:373; W. H. Hills, *Hist. East Grinstead*, pp. 2, 5, 32, 96–97, 108–9, 113; Sainty, *Lieutenants of Counties, 1585–1642*, pp. 12, 34.

12. Somerscales, Bouth, and Morehouse to the Earl of Shrewsbury, 12 Mar. 1604, Lambeth Palace Library, MS 708, f. 151; Hacker to the Earl of Shrewsbury, 4 Apr. 1604, Lodge, ed., *Illustrations of British History*, 3:114; R. Spencer to Clark, 8 Mar. 1604, Northamptonshire RO, Ellesmere (Brackley) MSS, E(B) 566; Gleason, *JP's*, pp. 230, 232, 233; Keeler, *Long Parliament*, pp. 45, 70–72; C. H. Mayo, "Shaftesbury," p. 41; Hoare, *Hist. Wiltshire*, 2:73, 3:18–21; Rowe, "The Influence of the Earls of Pembroke on Parliamentary Elections, 1625–41," p. 245; Harcourt to Bagot, 11 Feb. 1604, *HMC, 4th*

*Report*, p. 333; Williams, *Parl. Hist. Wales*, pp. 142–43; A. H. Dodd, *Studies in Stuart Wales*, pp. 180–81; "Philip Herbert, Earl of Montgomery and fourth Earl of Pembroke," *DNB*, 9:659–63.

I should like to thank Mrs. Judith Daniels for drawing my attention to a letter in the Bagot MSS, dated 14 Feb. 1604 from Stanford to Bagot, which sheds some light on the Staffordshire election of 1604.

13. Neale, *Elizabethan House of Commons*, pp. 44–46, 59, 188–89, 194–95, 238–40, 243, 249, 262–63, 265, 272, 317; Edw. Reynolds to Owen Reynolds, 26 Apr. 1603, 22, 28 Feb., 2, 12 Mar. 1604, P.R.O., St. P. Dom. 14/1:48, 6:74, 82, 85, 96; Gleason, *JP's*, p. 194.

14. R. East, ed., *Extracts from the Records of Portsmouth*, p. 627; Kenny, "Parliamentary Influence of Charles Howard, Earl of Nottingham, 1536–1624," pp. 215–32; Brayley, *Hist. Surrey*, 3:326; Lambert, *Blechingley*, 1:327–28; Nottingham to the Bailiffs and Burgesses of Scarborough, 17 Aug. 1603, Hoby to the same, 26 Feb. 1604, Scarborough Borough MSS, General Letters, 1597–1642, B. 1; Tighe and Davis, eds., *Annals of Windsor*, 2:60–61; J. C. Wedgwood, *Parl. Hist. of Staffordshire*, 1:380–81. Harwich, a borough restored by the crown in 1604, had a small electorate of around thirty-two, which probably contributed to its role as a patronage borough. Of its fourteen burgess-ships from 1604 to 1628, Nottingham's nominees took three and the earl of Warwick's friends probably captured another six (Plumb, "The Growth of the Electorate in England from 1600 to 1715," p. 99 & n).

15. Borough of Bishop's Castle MSS, Minute Book 1, fols. 53, 66, and, in its reverse pagination from the back of the book, Northampton to the Bailiff and Burgesses of Bishop's Castle, 21 Oct. 1610, f. 4v; Cavendish's election, first pagination in the same book, 24 Oct. 1610, f. 54; "William Cavendish, second Earl of Devonshire," *DNB*, 3:1273; *Trans. of the Shropshire Arch. and Nat. Hist. Soc.*, 2d series, (1898): 40–41; Willson, *Privy Councillors*, p. 141; W. Notestein, *House of Commons 1604–1610*, p. 168; Blomefield, *Hist. Norfolk*, 1:410–11; 4:668; H. L. Bradfer-Lawrence, *Castle Rising*, p. 60, 118; "Sir Thomas Monson," *DNB*, 13:645–46; "Sir William Paddy," *DNB*, 15:35–36; Neale, *Elizabethan House of Commons*, pp. 200–201.

16. According to Hirst, Maldon's electorate may have had as many as 131 voters in 1624 (*Representative of the People?*, app. 5, p. 224); *VCH, Essex*, 2:242–44; Bohannon, "The Essex Election of 1604," pp. 395–413; Wiseman to the Bailiffs, Aldermen, and Burgesses of Maldon, 20 Feb. 1604, Corporation of Maldon to the Earl of Suffolk?, n.d. Essex RO, D/B 3/33205/1, 6; Baliffs of Maldon to the Privy Council, 16 Oct. 1605, *HMC Salisbury*, 17:455; Neale, *Elizabethan House of Commons*, pp. 180–82; Wedgwood, *Staffordshire MP's*, 1:368; G. R. Clarke, *The Hist. of Ipswich*, pp. 434, 437; Prestwich, *Cranfield*, pp. 392–93; N. Bacon, *Annals of Ipswich*, ed. W. H. Richardson, pp. 417, 435–36; Cokayne, *Peerage*, 7:311; J. Hodgson, *A Hist. of Northumberland*, vol. 2, pt. 2, pp. 379, 381, 517; Stone, *Family and Fortune*, p. 280; R. Ashton, *The City and the Court, 1603–1643*, p. 22.

17. These totals do not include those of the lord warden or the lord presidents of the Councils of the North and the Marches of Wales. Their intervention is included with that of the court in Appendix Two. The patronage of the peerage from 1604 to 1640 is set out in Appendix Two, and Appendix Seven lists the boroughs and counties affected by possible, probable, and certain electoral intervention by the peerage.

18. Neale, *Elizabethan House of Commons*, pp. 215–21; F. Hull, ed., *The White and Black Books of the Cinque Ports*, p. xxxi.

19. Hull, ed., *The White and Black Books*, p. 375; the nominees were Sir George Carew (Hastings), Thomas Unton (Winchelsea), John Young (Rye), Sir Robert Remington (New Romney), Sir George Fane (Sandwich), and Mr. Christopher Tolderrey (Hythe) (Hastings Borough MSS, Common Book of Assembly, C/A (a)1, fols. 88, 88v).

20. For a detailed discussion of Northampton's electioneering in the ports and that of his successors, Lord Zouch and George Villiers, duke of Buckingham, see Gruenfelder, "The Lord Wardens and Elections, 1604–1628," and the sources cited therein; for a

discussion of the local problems that caused the nearly continuous quarrel between the corporation and the commons at Sandwich, see Hirst, *Representative of the People?*, app. 2, pp. 207–9.

21. Neale, *Elizabethan House of Commons*, pp. 189, 190, 224–30; *VCH Lancashire*, 4:88, 135, 168 & n.

22. C. Cross, *The Puritan Earl*, pp. 128–29; Neale, *Elizabethan House of Commons*, pp. 171–75; J. Thompson, *Hist. Leicester*, pp. 326–27, 342; J. Nichols, *Hist. Leicestershire*, vol. 2, pt. 1, p. 418; E. Baines, *The History of the County Palatine and Duchy of Lancaster*, ed. James Croston, 1:134; *VCH Leicestershire*, 4:60, 65–66; "Sir Henry Rich, first Baron Kensington and first Earl of Holland," *CDNB*, p. 1100; Nicholls to the Mayor of Leicester, 15 Jan. 1604, the Earl of Huntingdon to the same, Jan. 1604, Mayor and Corporation of Leicester to Huntingdon, 31 Jan. 1604, Beaumont to the Mayor and Corporation of Leicester, 14 Feb. 1604, Leicester Museum, City of Leicester MSS, Hall Papers Bound 1600–1606, BR II/18/8: 421, 428, 431, 440; meetings of the corporation of Leicester, Hall Papers Bound 1600–1606, BR II/18/8: 432, 434; Earl of Huntingdon to the Mayor of Leicester, 3, 9 May 1610, Common Hall Meeting of 19 May 1610, Hall Papers Bound 1608–10, BR II/18/9:433, 437, 442; Hall Book 1587–1708, BR/II/1/3: 367. I should like to thank the Leicestershire Museums, Art Galleries and Records Services, and, in particular, Mr. G. A. Chinnery, the assistant director, for making Leicester's material available for my use.

23. Neale, *Elizabethan House of Commons*, pp. 223–24; Pink and Beaven, *Parl. Repr. Lancashire*, pp. 115–16, 147–48, 185, 223, 250–51, 277–78; Keeler, *Long Parliament*, pp. 172–73; Willson, *Privy Councillors*, pp. 77, 83, 107; *OR* 1:444, 445, 447; F. C. D. Sperling, *Hodson's Hist. of the Borough of Sudbury*, pp. 45, 92, 209–10; W. C. Metcalfe, ed., *Visitation of Essex*, pt. 1, p. 149; Williams, *Parl. Hist. Wales*, p. 134; Pape, *Newcastle-under-Lyme*, pp. 133–35; W. S. Weeks. *Clitheroe in the 17th Century*, p. 224; Nichols, *Progresses of James I*, 1:165; W. H. Rylands, ed., *Visitation of Buckinghamshire*, p. 58. R. Somerville, *Office-Holders in the Duchy and County Palatine of Lancaster*, pp. 67, 94, 100, 164, 187–88.

24. Neale, *Elizabethan House of Commons*, pp. 164, 228–29; Cross, *The Puritan Earl*, pp. 174–75; F. W. Brooks, *The Council of the North*, p. 26.

25. Earl of Nottingham to the Bailiffs and Burgesses of Scarborough, 17 Aug. 1603, Posthumous Hoby to the same, 26 Feb. 1604, Scarborough Borough MSS, General Letters, 1597–1642, B. 1; Sir Edmund, Baron Sheffield, to Wm. Wentworth 19 Feb. 1604, Sheffield City Library, Wentworth Woodhouse MSS, 20(189); Somerscales, Bouth, and Morehouse to the Earl of Shrewsbury, 12 Mar. 1604, Shrewsbury and Talbot Papers, Lambeth Palace Library, MS 708, f. 151; York City Library, City of York Housebooks, vol. 32, 1598–1605, fols. 313v–315; Neale, *Elizabethan House of Commons*, p. 164; A. Gooder, *Parliamentary Representation of Yorkshire*, 2:41–45; Bean, *Northern Counties*, pp. 644, 685, 706, 716, 736, 740, 759, 769, 783, 1019, 1032, 1058, 1122–23; Lawson-Tancred, *Records of a Yorkshire Manor*, pp. 374–76; G. Oliver, *The Hist. and Antiquities of the Town and Minister of Beverley*, p. 382; W. Harrison, ed., *Ripon Millenary Record*, pp. ii, xiii; Baker, *Hist. of Scarborough*, pp. 245, 433; VCH *City of York*, 186; R. R. Reid, *The Council of the North*, app. 2, pp. 489, 496–97. For a discussion of Yorkshire borough elections, see J. K. Gruenfelder, "Yorkshire Borough Elections, 1603–1640."

26. Neale, *Elizabethan House of Commons*, pp. 163, 288, 317. Not one of the eleven men listed by Penry Williams as members of Parliament who served on the Council of Wales would have relied upon it to secure their election to parliament. All of them had sufficient influence or connections of their own to win their places (Penry Williams, *The Council in the Marches of Wales*, app. 4, pp. 342–61).

27. H. T. Weyman, "Members of Parliament for Ludlow," pp. 3–4, 16–18; Shropshire RO, Ludlow Corporation Minute Book, 1590–1648, 356/2/1, fols. 50, 51.

28. For a thorough discussion of Shrewsbury's 1604 election and its subsequent electoral history, see Gruenfelder, "The Parliamentary Election for Shrewsbury, 1604," pp. 272–77, and sources cited therein.

29. V. Pearl, *London and the Outbreak of the Puritan Revolution*, p. 66; "Sir Henry Montagu, Earl of Manchester," *DNB*, 13:696–98; R. R. Sharpe, *London and the Kingdom*, 2:8; Privy Council to the Bailiffs and Burgesses of Buckingham, 21 Feb. 1606, BM ADD MSS 11,042, f. 110; Willson, *Privy Councillors*, pp. 57–58.

30. The figures for the court and its agencies include the patronage of the lord warden (Northampton), the Council of the North (Lords Sheffield and Eure), and the Council of the Marches of Wales (Lord Zouch). For a breakdown, in tabular form, of the court's influence, see Appendix One.

31. For a recent and judicious appraisal of the importance of the Buckinghamshire contest and its implications for constitutional history and the powers of the House of Commons and elections, see Hirst, "Elections and the Privileges of the House of Commons in the Early Seventeenth Century: Confrontation or Compromise?"

32. Gruenfelder, "Two Midland Parliamentary Elections of 1604, Northamptonshire and Worcestershire"; Bohannon, "The Essex Election of 1604"; Neale, *Elizabethan House of Commons*, pp, 293–96.

33. For a more detailed account of Worcestershire's 1604 election, see Gruenfelder, "Two Midland Parliamentary Elections of 1604, Northamptonshire and Worcestershire," and sources cited therein; for the impact of recusancy in other elections, see Hirst, *Representative of the People?*, pp. 145–48.

34. Coke's marriage to Lady Elizabeth Hatton gave him influence at Corfe Castle, and at Dunwich his nominee Valentine Knightley was elected but preferred to serve for Northamptonshire. "Sir Edward Coke," *DNB* 4:685–700; G. Bankes, *The Story of Corfe Castle*, p. 38; Mayor of Corfe Castle to Sir Jo. Hobart?, 10 Mar. 1604; Merewether and Stephens, *Hist. of Boroughs*, 2:1350–51; Hutchins, *Hist. Dorset*, 1:471, 472; A Suckling, *Hist. Suffolk*, 2:256; Neale, *Elizabethan House of Commons*, p. 155; Dunwich Borough MSS, Suffolk RO, Ipswich Branch, Dunwich Borough Minute Book, 1595–1619, EE 6:1144/10, fols. 117, 117v, 131v; *HMC Various Collections*, 7:88, 89.

35. Neale, *Elizabethan House of Commons*, pp. 272–81; Willcox, *Gloucestershire*, p. 32.

36. For a full discussion of Gloucester's 1604 election and its subsequent electoral history, see Gruenfelder, "Gloucester's Parliamentary Elections, 1604–40." Gloucester's contest, involving a self-seeking member of its corporation whose campaign among the freemen stressed local economic issues parallels, in some respects at least, similar developments noted by Hirst at Coventry, Warwick, Chippenham, Exeter, and Oxford (*Representative of the People?*, pp. 46–47, 51–52, app. 2, pp. 198–99, 203–4, 205, 210–12).

37. *VCH City of York*, p. 186; Neale, *Elizabethan House of Commons*, p. 164; York City Library, City of York Housebooks, 32, 1598–1605, pp. 314v–315; "Christopher Brooke," *DNB*, 2:1327. Bennett was nothing if not zealous: he tried for each of York's places, losing to Askwith by a vote of 61 to 14 and then to Brooke, for the second place, by a vote of 60 to 29.

38. There is no evidence to suggest that Dorset tried to intervene at Bristol, but if he did, he was rebuffed. Neale, *Elizabethan House of Commons*, p. 163; A. B. Beaven, *The Aldermen of the City of London*, 1:276; Latimer, *Annals of Bristol in the 17th Century*, p. 8; J. Evans, *A Hist. of Bristol*, p. 163; Pryce, *A Popular Hist. of Bristol*, p. 468; Williams, *Parl. Hist. Glouscestershire*, pp. 112–13; Bean, *Northern Counties*, pp. 564, 581, 589; Brand, *Hist. Newcastle*, 2:240; Keeler, *Long Parliament*, p. 144; Williams, *Parl. Hist. Worcestershire*, pp. 92–94

39. This discussion is based on the tables for borough elections in Appendix Four.

40. The nine boroughs that avoided outside intervention through the election of 1628 were Chester, Exeter, Plymouth, Bristol, Gloucester, Newcastle-on-Tyne, Salisbury, Norwich, and York. Influential high stewards or neighboring peers became the electoral patrons of Cambridge, Carlisle, Hull, and Chichester, and county gentry eventually had their way at Tregony, Truro, Totness, Dorchester, Lyme Regis, Poole, Weymouth, Melcombe Regis, Winchester, Worcester, Great Yarmouth, Nottingham, Coventry, and Warwick. Indeed, nonresidents were returned in the 1614 elections at Cambridge, Tre-

gony, Carlisle, Totness, Dorchester, Lyme Regis, Poole, Weymouth, Melcombe Regis, Winchester, Liverpool, Great Yarmouth, Ludlow, Chichester, Warwick, and Hull. Nottingham and Truro became patronage boroughs in 1621, Worcester in 1625, and Coventry in 1628. In at least two cases, Nottingham and Worcester, the cost of parliamentary wages was probably responsible for the change in their electoral pattern.

41. In the spring 1640 election, twelve boroughs elected two outsiders as burgesses, and in the autumn only ten boroughs chose two strangers.

42. The total for 1604 is 128. The highest figure for such electoral involvement came in 1624 when 167 elections probably showed such electioneering. For the other elections, the number of elections that reflected such intervention is 142 (1614), 140 (1621), 145 (1625), 135 (1626), and 131 (1628).

43. Hirst, *Representative of the People?*, pp. 145–47.

# THREE

## The Court and Elections

Court intervention in elections may have dated from the fifteenth century, although such intervention was hardly consistent policy. Edward IV's Parliament of 1478 was particularly affected by such manipulation; it is also possible that crown electioneering marked several other Edwardian parliaments. However, it is not until the reign of Henry VIII and specifically during Cromwell's tenure of office that such intervention can again be identified in 1532–33, 1534, 1536, and 1539. Electioneering continued, albeit sporadically, throughout the Tudor years. There was, though, a reduction in direct intervention during Elizabeth's reign. On four occasions her government issued circular letters that usually urged the election of "wise and well-affected gentlemen," but in 1586 the crisis she faced and her satisfaction with the Parliament of 1584 led her to issue a letter that specifically urged the reelection of its former members to her new parliament. Indeed, in contrast to the fierce electoral battle waged between Essex and Cecil in the elections of 1593 and 1597 and Cecil's place-hunting in 1601, the court's lack of involvement justifies Sir John Neale's assessment that "the election of royal officials and courtiers was a haphazard business, achieved without government planning, and with no official policy behind it." The same cannot be said for the elections of 1614–40. At least four, and perhaps as many as five, of those eight elections demonstrated a notable contrast between Elizabethan and early Stuart politics, for under James I and Charles I, electoral planning and government interference became an election tactic.[1]

James's first parliament showed little sign of the court involvement that was to come. Salisbury's intervention was personal, as it had been from 1593 to 1601. He did not, as Buckingham and the king did in 1620, suggest nominees to Zouch as lord warden; nothing suggests, either, that he ever perceived the potential electoral influence of a lord warden, Duchy of Lancaster, or Duchy of Cornwall, as Bacon would in 1613.[2]

Even before the overworked Salisbury died in May 1612, rumors of another parliament were in the air, rumors that reflected the discontent felt by James and others with the outcome of the first parliament. Sir

Henry Neville, a "popular" spokesman in James's first parliament, was an early candidate for a secretaryship who had confidently promised he could "undertake to deal with the Lower House" and pressed on the reluctant James a program of concessions designed to establish a bond of confidence between king and commons should another parliament be summoned. But Neville's plan—which said nothing about electioneering—and his hopes for advancement vanished in 1613: he was "too popular a candidate for the king's taste." Sir Francis Bacon was another contender for the post who also tried to win the king over to the calling of a new parliament, basing his appeal on James's worsening financial situation, but the year (1612) ended without any shift in the royal opinion.[3]

Bacon raised the whole question again in 1613 as the king's financial situation grew increasingly difficult. Bacon's plan was detailed, carefully prepared, and reflected the pragmatic mind of a realistic politician. He believed it necessary to discover "what persons in particular, in respect of their gravity, discretion, temper, and ability to persuade, are fit to be brought in to be of the house, *bonis artibus*, without labouring or packing" and suggested that "violent and turbulent" men should be kept out of the House of Commons, a course the court later twice attempted, in 1624 and 1626. Practically, what tools did the crown have to implement Bacon's suggestions? Bacon knew. "What use," he asked, "may be made of the Boroughs of the Cinq Ports, and of the Duchy, and other boroughs at the devotion of diverse the K's councillors, for the placing persons well affected and discreet?" They were, of course, to be employed to place royal nominees in forthcoming parliaments. Everything, however, must be done with great care and subtlety: "What course may be taken that though the K. do use such providence as is before remembered and leave not things to chance, yet it may be so handled as it may have no show nor scandal nor nature of the packing or briguing [intrigue] of a Parliament, but contrariwise that it tends to have a Parliament truly free and not packed against him?" Careful preparations and discretion were Bacon's linchpins. His shrewd appraisal of the court's electoral requirements would have won the warm approval of that great electoral manager of the eighteenth century, the duke of Newcastle![4]

The plan was Bacon's response to the growing crisis in the king's affairs; it was also, no doubt, a way of displaying his potential value as a principal adviser to the king. And it appears that James accepted his advice. For the first time, the Duchy of Cornwall joined other royal agencies as an election patron; furthermore, James realized the importance of the elections. Fearful that they were going badly, the king urged Sir Thomas Lake to recommend "your Lordship's special care to do your endeavor with other of the Lords of the Council, to whom (in his Majesty's name) your Lordships are to recommend the same providence in places where you have credit or power that the house is furnished of men of good disposition, and apt to have due consideration of him and his estate, or else his Majesty shall have little comfort in the Assembly!" Bacon's advice had been accepted. The court had probably intervened in twenty-six elections in 1604; in 1614 it was probably involved in thirty-nine elections. In 1604 it is possible that the crown may have secured as many as twenty-eight places; in 1614 it probably captured forty-eight. And the election of 1614 was only the first that witnessed a court campaign. An even greater effort was made in 1621 and 1624, and in the crisis elections of 1640 the court probably made its most comprehensive effort of all.[5]

The fulfillment of Bacon's scheme had one serious, and potentially disastrous, weakness: it must be discreet; however, it soon attracted attention. "Here is much bustling for places in parliament, and letters fly from great personages extraordinarily, wherein, methinks, they do the king no great service, seeing the world is apt to conceive it is a kind of packing." Chamberlain was right. The electioneering that preceded the parliament so aroused attention that James felt compelled, in his opening speech to parliament, to deny any intention that he "should have a packed parliament. . . . I assure you there is no such thing, for whosoever should do this I should hold him a knave and you might account me a fool." His denials were fruitless; the commons scented interference, feared packing, and brooded loud and long over the repeatedly rumored undertaking. There was nothing anyone could do about their attitudes, which contributed, in a substantial way, to that sad result of Bacon's hopes and plans, the Addled Parliament.[6]

Bacon's proposals invite ready comparison to eighteenth-century electioneering, a parallel made more noteworthy by the reaction of his contemporaries on the Privy Council to electoral management. It was debating the prospect of another parliament in September 1615, and its conclusion on elections was hardly in keeping with Bacon's views. Eighteen councillors spoke to the problem, and, among the variety of topics covered, the question of elections was discussed by three of them, Sir Edward Coke, Lord Zouch, and Lancelot Andrews. Their views won general agreement and reflected the belief that the electioneering before the previous parliament had badly backfired against the crown. Coke was outspokenly critical, hoping "that none of their Lordships or other of the Council or any other great men of the land should meddle with the election of knights or burgesses; but leave the people to their own choice; for he had observed in the last Parliament that such interposing of great men and recommendations in those elections had been very offensive; and withal that many had crept in by those means, who had showed themselves most adverse from the King [Northampton's friends, no doubt!]." His remarks were seconded by Zouch, lord warden of the Cinque Ports, and Andrews, the bishop of Winchester, and endorsed by the remainder of the councillors. And while it is clear that it was most critical of recent factional interference, the council's summary of its views included an agreement "not to meddle with the election of knights and burgesses" should a parliament be summoned. Perhaps Bacon's planning was too advanced for his peers. [7]

The prospect of a new parliament faded into the background following the council's autumn debate. The Spanish faction worked its will, and it was not until the European explosion—the Spanish invasion of the Palatinate in the late summer of 1620—that James's attitude reversed itself and parliament was again under consideration. Bacon, now a privy councillor, was again directly concerned, when James ordered him in early October to "advise with the two Chief Justices (Old Parliament men) and Sir Edward Cook [Coke] (who is also their senior in that school) and Sir Randall Crewe the last Speaker, and such other Judges as we should think fit, touching that which mought [may] in true policy, without packing or degenerate arts, prepare to a Parliament." James's favorite, Buckingham, was deeply involved, and it was to him that Bacon made his first report of the group's deliberations. Its suggestions were in four parts, two of which focused on the election question. The planners had agreed that the proclamation for the parliament should contain some "clauses . . . especially touching Elections; which clauses nevertheless we think should be rather monitory than binding and exclusive." Their views were clearly a far cry from those expressed by Ellesmere and Popham in 1603. [8] They were concerned too with "what persons were fit to be of the House . . . and of the means to place such persons without novelty or much observation." They had even prepared "some lists of names of the privy councillors and principal statesmen or courtiers; of the gravest and wisest lawyers; of the most respected and best tempered knights and gentlemen of the country." If only those lists had survived! What an insight into election planning, what a tool to evaluate the court's success or failure as an election agent!

Although the planners had not forgotten the effect of "packing" in 1614, it was clear that electioneering was still central to the preparations for a parliament. The proclamation was a smoke screen; it might allay fears of "packing" while the court undertook, quietly of course, to place its candidates "without novelty or much observation." Stealthy electioneering was the watchword. Indeed, James, perhaps concerned that rumors of election planning might leak out, ordered that the lists of possible nominees "is fit to be kept from the knowledge of the council-table, and to be carried with all secrecy." Did James remember or suspect the work of court factions in 1614? Or was he just concerned at the prospect of another outraged House of Commons roaring on and on about "undertaking" or "packing"?[9]

Much was expected of the proclamation and its expected condemnation of electioneering. Chamberlain forecast it would "give encouragement for a free election of knights and burgesses, and to forbid all recommendations by letters and, in case any be sent, to return them to him [the King] or his council." Those were foolish hopes. The proclamation was intended to be "rather monitory than binding and exclusive," and so it was. If boroughs could not find the best candidates among their residents, then "other grave and discreet men, fit to serve" were to be elected. Nothing further was said of any residency qualifications; in fact, nothing was said, as had been in 1604, about free elections or against the use of blanks or letters of recommendation. And that was just as Bacon, the judges, Buckingham, and the king intended it to be.[10]

Despite some concern at the court about the outcome of the elections—Bacon for one admitting his worries—there can be no doubt that the court made an intensive election effort. Buckingham and the king personally intervened, much to Zouch's surprise, in the Cinque Ports elections; the Duchy of Cornwall mounted its greatest campaign, and, for the first time, the Prince's Council made an electoral appearance. The Duchy of Lancaster was, as usual, active, as were the court's other agencies. The Venetian ambassador, although sometimes wrong in his assessments, was correct when he reported that "both the realm and the King have devoted extraordinary attention to choosing the members." The court's electioneering was repeated in 1624 when the Prince's Council and the Duchy of Lancaster made their strongest attempts to sway elections. Indeed, the court, aided by the alliance Charles and Buckingham effected with the "popular" group against Spain, reached its pre-1640 peak as an electoral patron.[11]

There was, of course, another way to influence elections: by trying to prevent particular members from being eligible for a seat. In return for his agreement to call parliament in 1624, James wanted his outspoken parliamentary foes, men like Sir Edward Coke and Sir Edwyn Sandys, exiled to Ireland through the means of a royal commission. James had apparently not forgotten Bacon's advice of 1613. The king saw the plan as the only way to prevent their election, but cooler heads prevailed. Even Charles and Buckingham opposed James's scheme; it was part of the price they had to pay for their alliance with the "popular" group. [12] A more effective device to secure similar ends was employed before Charles's Parliament of 1626 when a group of royal critics were selected as sheriffs by the king to prevent their probable attendance in parliament. [13]

Electoral interference was routine by 1625, as the discussion between Charles I and his lord keeper, Williams, showed just after Charles's accession. Charles wanted the writs for a new parliament to go out immediately, but Williams tried to delay the king's order since "it was usual in times before, that the King's servants, and trustiest friends, did deal with the countries, cities and boroughs, where they were known, to procure a promise for their elections, before the precise time of an insequent parliament was published."[14] Williams was restating what was customary practice for the court before a parliament, a practice that was pursued, though in a somewhat different way, through the elections of 1625–28. While the Duchy of Lancaster continued its electioneering, although with gradually declining results, the Duchy of Cornwall and Prince's Council disappear from electoral history, not to reappear until the elections of 1640. [15] Buckingham, the leading patron of 1625–28, stepped into the gap and extended his influence into some of the boroughs formerly under the sway of those agencies. The court's agencies, however, played an even more aggressive and sweeping role in 1640. Charles, well aware of the importance of the elections, made sure that the Prince's Council, the Duchy of Lancaster, the Councils of the North and of Wales, the Duchy of Cornwall, and the Queen's Council did all that they could to intervene in the elections for the Short and Long Parliaments. [16]

Bacon was the first to appreciate the importance of skillful electoral management and to evaluate the resources for such a program at the crown's disposal. And his suggestions were followed, especially in the Parliaments of 1614, 1621, 1624, and 1640. Electoral patronage was changing. Buckingham followed in the path of Cecil, the first earl of Salisbury, and Elizabeth's Essex; his electioneering was the best example of how, as Neale so aptly observed, "patronage . . . was being turned into a political weapon." However, by becoming an electioneer, the court itself was guilty of further emphasizing the political nature of patronage. It was also infringing on local electoral patrimonies and challenging local interests. It might not have mattered had a political consensus obtained, particularly in Charles's reign, but it did not.

Indeed, electoral management had become so political by 1640 that the court was paid what might be called the highest possible compliment: its opponents, the "popular" or country group, devoted far more attention to the elections than ever before. Indeed, it is even possible to delineate the electioneering of an aristocratic opposition group. [17]

Distinctions need to be made, however, about the electioneering of the various court agencies, especially the Duchies of Cornwall and Lancaster. Thanks perhaps to its long patronage history and the energetic leadership of Sir Humphrey May (chancellor during the elections of 1621–28), the Duchy of Lancaster pursued its own electoral path. It nominated "outsiders," as did the lord wardens and other royal agencies, but in most instances the Duchy of Lancaster's nominees were its officials. On the other hand, the Duchy of Cornwall attempted to reserve the majority of its places for privy councillors, courtiers, and royal servants who had no tie to the duchy whatsoever. It seems safe to say that while the Duchy of Lancaster pursued an independent course, the electioneering of the Duchy of Cornwall (and the Prince's Council, too) were closely directed by the court. Zouch found himself in a somewhat similar situation in 1620 when James and Buckingham attempted to intervene in the choice of the candidates Zouch would nominate as lord warden. Perhaps the short-lived alliance between Buckingham and the popular, or anti-Spanish, party explained why there is nothing to suggest similar interference in Zouch's 1624 electioneering, and Buckingham's acquisition of the lord warden's office clearly ended any possible need for such interference from 1625 to 1628. However, the number of "outsiders" nominated by the court's agencies and lord wardens was very high. Of the 276 nominees that can be identified, 177, or slightly more than 64 percent, were strangers. Such nominees emphasized the threat to local electoral interests and made the political nature of such intervention all the more apparent. By 1640, when the issues were thrown into bold relief, it cannot be surprising that the "outsiders" nominated by the crown's agencies fared so badly. [18] The patronage of the lord warden, the Duchy of Lancaster, the Prince's Council and the Duchy of Cornwall, the Councils of the North and of Wales, and that of the Privy Council must now be examined.

## 1. The Lord Wardens and Elections, 1614–1628

Once the court had committed itself to an active election role, its resources to effect such an undertaking were substantial. Bacon's plans, before the Parliament of 1614, had focused on, among other things, the use of the ports "for the placing [of] persons well affected and discreet."[19] What use was made of the Cinque Ports? Given the evidence, Bacon's suggestion clearly bore fruit. The wardens tried, with varying degrees of success, to make the ports their patronage boroughs. At first glance, their election record through the six parliaments of this fifteen-year span is pretty good. Eighty-four burgesses, or barons, as the ports described them, were chosen; and forty-nine owed, in some measure at least, their election to the lord wardens, Henry Howard, earl of Northampton (1614), Edward, Lord Zouch (1621, 1624), and George Villiers, duke of Buckingham (1625, 1626, 1628). On closer examination, however, the record shows surprising evidence of determined and increasing opposition to the persuasive powers of the lord warden. The returns also reveal the incompetence of the third lord warden, Buckingham, who suffered, by far, the worst record. Northampton placed ten of fourteen burgesses in 1614, and Zouch, in two elections, accounted for twenty of a possible twenty-eight seats. Buckingham, on the other hand, had all kinds of trouble: he managed to secure only nineteen places, out of a possible forty-two, in three elections.

### The Earl of Northampton as Lord Warden, 1614

Northampton's recommendations in 1614 met with greater success than they had in 1604.[20] His achievement testified to the accuracy of contemporary reports about the "great preparations" undertaken for the parliament. Dover, Rye, and Winchelsea returned two of his candidates; and Hastings, New Romney, Hythe, and Sandwich accepted one. There was some difficulty over the election at Sandwich, continuing evidence of the feud between Northampton, the corporation, and the commons. The port surprised Northampton by forcefully refusing his first nominee, Sir George Fane. Northampton gave way since Fane was "so much against your appetite," and nominated, in Fane's stead, Sir Thomas Smyth, brother of one of Hythe's members, Sir Richard Smyth.

Why was Northampton so successful? Two reasons may be suggested for his triumph. First, his powerful assertion of his rights in 1604 stood him in good stead in 1614. Winchelsea, Hastings, and New Romney, which had offered resistance in 1604, could not have been more compliant on this occasion. Another reason for Northampton's mastery was his choice of nominees. Of the ten men he recommended, only Sir Arthur Ingram and Sir Lionel Cranfield can be described as outsiders, men without connections in either Sussex or Kent. They were both his clients, close friends, and associates. The other men he supported had strong Kentish connections.[21]

Out of fourteen possible places, Northampton played a significant role in the filling of ten of them. Of the other barons elected, only two were residents of the ports themselves, Lasher, at Hastings, and Willock, elected for New Romney. Sir Samuel Peyton, returned by Sandwich, held property in the port but, like Sir Richard Smyth at Hythe, was more representative of the Kentish gentry, spilling over into obtainable seats within the ports. The independence of the ports had certainly vanished; brave words and resolutions were clearly not enough. It certainly seemed, in 1614 at least, that the lord warden had found secure seats for the court's electioneering.[22]

### Lord Zouch as Lord Warden, 1621, 1624

Northampton died shortly after the dissolution of the Addled Parliament and Edward, Baron Zouch, succeeded him as lord warden in 1615, holding the post through the elections of 1624. He had been lord president of the Council of the Marches of Wales, and we have already seen his patronage efforts in the Shrewsbury election of 1604. Zouch was not part of Buckingham's faction, a factor that may have been behind the crown's review of his electoral plans in 1621 and contributed to his problems in the Dover election of 1624. The ports, too, presumably concerned over Northampton's success as a patron, tried to limit the warden's patronage. At a General Brotherhood meeting at New Romney in July 1615, they reaffirmed their declaration of 1572, increased the fine for a violation of their rules to £50, but also admitted the warden's right to nominate one baron at each port as long as that nominee became a freeman of the port that returned him. It was hardly a bold declaration of electoral independence and caused Zouch little difficulty in the elections.[23]

Zouch was surprised by the crown's "commandment" in December 1620 that he "should nominate 3 particular gentlemen to 3 places within my government for burgesses places to serve in this parliament"; but after his list of nominees was inspected by James and Buckingham, they dropped the matter, James assuring Zouch of his confidence that he would "nominate such as will be serviceable to his Majesty and his kingdom."[24] The incident illustrated the court's interest in elections; it also cost Zouch precious time in making his nominations. It was not, however, repeated in the elections of 1624, probably because Zouch's anti-Spanish sentiments matched Buckingham's temporary views.

In the elections of 1621 and 1624, Zouch enjoyed substantial success. New Romney and Hastings each accepted his nominee in both elections without apparent resistance, as did Hythe and Rye. Indeed, at Hythe and Rye, where that port's elections were complicated by other powerful place-seekers, other candidates sought and won Zouch's approval. And although Dover's 1624 election was a nightmare for Zouch, in 1621 it returned his nominee Sir Richard Young and one of his officials, Sir Henry Mainwaring, who, three years later, would be responsible for Dover's bitter election dispute. However, local quarrels at Sandwich, where Zouch's candidate was finally refused, and Winchelsea gave him some anxious moments in the election of 1621.[25]

Winchelsea's elections in 1621 and 1624 were troublesome affairs, primarily because of an acrimonious dispute that divided the corporation. In 1621 the mayor sought Zouch's approval for two local candidates, including Sir Thomas Finch, against one "Mr. Amscombe, a lawyer," backed by the dissidents. Zouch indicated a modest support for Finch and reserved a place for his nominee, Edward Nicholas. Zouch had his way: Finch and Nicholas were chosen without apparent trouble, and although the quarrel dragged on, Zouch's electoral "rights" had not been endangered. Perhaps that was why in 1624, when Winchelsea's corporation was again embroiled in a bitter dispute, Zouch's nominee Nicholas was once more returned without challenge.[26]

Zouch was not as fortunate at Sandwich, at least in 1621. The port had been vexed by a running quarrel between the corporation and the commons over the latter's right to vote in municipal elections, a quarrel that had involved both Cobham and Northampton, former wardens, on the corporation's side. Economic difficulties compounded the situation, and popular feeling against Zouch was running high. The election provided the spark that set the port aflame. There were eight candidates in all, including Zouch's nominee, Sir Robert Hatton of Bishopsbourne, Kent, and Sir Edwyn Sandys, the popular candidate. Sandys backed the commons in their battle for voting rights, proclaimed his antagonism toward the East India Company's trading monopoly, and noted the sad condition of Sandwich's harbor. His campaign was ably assisted by a Londoner who held property near Sandwich, one Thomas Gookyn, who campaigned with enough skill to win members of the corporation over to Sandys's side. And, to make the situation all the more volatile, Sandys also had the backing of a "precise preacher" named Marston who had been deprived by Archbishop Abbot and, perhaps understandably enough, raged against all bishops. Since Hatton was claimed to be Abbot's man, Marston happily lent his oratorical powers to Sandy's campaign with good effect among the freemen.

On election day the mayor compounded Hatton's difficulties even more. Flustered, perhaps, by opposition to Hatton from within and without the corporation, he tried the manipulate the port's customary electoral procedures and, when that failed, made the outrageous claim that only the port's corporation could vote, thereby forcing Hatton's return. The results of such a turmoil can be readily imagined. On petition the House of Commons denied Hatton's election, threw out the mayor's claims for a narrow franchise, and ordered a new election, which Hatton lost. Zouch had suffered his first — and only — defeat as lord warden. For Zouch the election was an unfortunate mixture of local issues, including antagonism toward the warden, and a popular candidate who, ably backed by a clever election agent and a vociferous preacher, ruined Hatton's chances. The defeat, however, had no long-term effect; in 1624 Sandwich elected Zouch's nominee, the same Hatton, without apparent trouble.[27]

Dover's contested election in 1624 was a bitter quarrel between Zouch and one of Buckingham's clients, Sir Henry Mainwaring, who, until Zouch dismissed him for misconduct, had been lieutenant of Dover Castle. Mainwaring fought his dismissal and even enlisted the support of Prince Charles. The election, however, gave him the perfect opportunity to embarrass his former superior. And at Dover as at Sandwich in 1621, the local situation was ripe for selfish exploitation. Zouch was in disfavor with the commons; he had, with the corporation's help, forced them to accept an unpopular lecturer in 1621–22. There was, as well, a general undercurrent of discontent with the corporation among the freemen, a discontent that may well have included a growing opposition to Dover's narrow electoral franchise. At least, it was the franchise issue that Mainwaring and his local ally, Jasper Fowler, used against the corporation and Zouch.

Although the mayor had misgivings about the narrow franchise, Dover's corporation returned Zouch's nominees, Sir Richard Young and Sir Edward Cecil, on election day. And, by so doing, the corporation played right into Mainwaring's hands. Petitions were quickly lodged questioning the franchise and the election, and the House of Commons, "violent for free elections," threw out both the narrow franchise and the return. In his campaign for the second election, Mainwaring was joined with an outspoken critic of the corporation, Sir Thomas Wilsford, the son-in-law of Sir Edwyn Sandys, staunch friend of popular franchises, and a recent friend of Buckingham. Mainwaring and Wilsford, however, never stood against Young and Cecil in a second election. Without the freedom of the port, they could not stand; and the corporation, at Zouch's prodding, made sure their bid for freemen's status was denied. Another spectacular row ensued between Wilsford and the corporation, and star chamber suits were threatened; but the storm finally blew over. Cecil and Young were finally returned.[28]

The Sandwich and Dover elections illustrate the powerful impact local grievances and personal quarrels could have on elections. They also reflect the growing enthusiasm for wide or popular franchises in the House of Commons, a reaction against patronage, which the House believed was facilitated by narrow franchises.[29] The returns for Dover and Sandwich, however, indicate that the wider franchise had little impact on the warden's influence.

Zouch was the most successful lord warden of the early Stuart period. In two elections men he either nominated or supported claimed twenty of the ports' twenty-eight places. And, unlike Northampton, his nominees were usually outsiders; only three men that enjoyed his support had local connections. Of the other ten, two were his kinsman, and eight were courtiers or servants of the crown. The ports' shaky claim to independence was gone; they had, it seemed, become patronage boroughs for the lord warden.[30]

### The Duke of Buckingham as Lord Warden, 1625–1628

Buckingham's electoral record as lord warden was the worst for any warden between 1604 and 1628. His nominees and those that he supported managed to capture less than half of the ports' places; his two predecessors, Northampton and Zouch, supported candidates that took two-thirds of the ports' burgess-ships.

Winchelsea alone gave Buckingham no trouble. Candidates that he backed gained four places there between 1625 and 1628. Rye, however, because of its very servility to other patrons like the earl of Dorset in 1625–26, could only grant Buckingham one place in spite of his double nominations. Hythe and New Romney, which had each granted the warden a burgess-ship since 1593, elected Buckingham's nominees in 1625 but refused his candidates in both 1626 and 1628.[31]

Dover chose two of the duke's nominees in 1625 and then, much to Buckingham's surprise, was the scene of a contested election in 1626. One of his nominees was refused; the other, Sir John Hippisley, barely scraped through by a margin of "but three voices." No evidence has survived to explain what happened, although it seems likely that local issues, marked by "some stirrings among the freemen" against the corporation, contributed to the quarrel. Dover's franchise had been widened in 1624; however, the municipal struggle apparently continued, and the duke's nominees may have been caught in the middle of it. However, all was well by 1628: Dover elected both his candidates.[32]

Buckingham had little success at Hastings and Sandwich. Hastings chose one of his candidates in 1625, but when he tried for both places in 1626, he was refused. Hastings accepted one nominee, Sir Dudley Carleton, but in a subsequent bye-election to replace Carleton, elevated to the peerage, Buckingham's candidate was rejected. He settled for one place at Hastings in 1628. Sandwich would only take one of two Buckingham nominees in 1625, and in 1626 when his successful candidate, Sir John Suckling, decided to serve for Norwich, the port refused the duke's nominee for Suckling's vacant place. The port turned him down completely in 1628 when his nominee was Sir Edwyn Sandys. It is impossible not to wonder about the reaction of Sandys's former friends when they realized that their late "popular" candidate was now a nominee of the lord warden. Local problems, too, further complicated Sandwich's election.[33]

It is difficult, indeed, to suggest why Buckingham's intervention was so unsuccessful. But some explanations, at least, can be offered. It was clearly not because of any lack of advice; in 1626 and 1628, his friends urged him, in clear and unmistakable terms, to "make as many burgesses as you can," advice he followed in the ports. He did, however, commit a cardinal error in 1626 when, in spite of his agent's warnings, his letters were grievously late and helped turn the ports' elections into a disaster for his candidates. Yet, it must be remembered that even when his letters arrived at some of the ports before their elections, his nominees were in trouble and that in two bye-elections they were refused. Furthermore, his tardiness involved but one election, 1626, and cannot explain the problems his nominees faced in 1628. In both 1626 and 1628, Buckingham failed to place a candidate at each port, a customary practice for the lord wardens since 1604.

Buckingham may have made a major mistake when he tried for two places at Rye, New Romney, Hythe, and Sandwich in 1625. At first glance, there were apparent precedents for such action. Northampton had, in 1614, placed two candidates in three of the ports, an action that was probably behind the brotherhood's resolution against such practices in 1615. Save for Dover, Zouch observed the letter of the resolution. Although his approval was sought by candidates at Hythe and Rye and Winchelsea's mayor asked for his advice in 1621, Zouch always reserved the right to nominate his candidate while backing the choice of others. And of the three men that he supported, two were local men of considerable stature. Buckingham, however, made his nominations directly, and in three elections only six of the men he backed had any local connections. His double nominations, usually of strangers, possibly put the ports on notice that whatever rights they wanted to maintain to choose one of their own could easily vanish if they were not careful.

Resistance probably grew because of Buckingham's persistent nomination of outsiders. It is clear that by the early seventeenth century, there was a growing opposition to the return of strangers. The gentry's parliamentary ambitions were a major factor in the increasing resistance. Ambitious gentry from Kent and Sussex looked longingly at the Cinque Ports as suitable stepping stones to parliament while, at the same time, the wardens were even more vigorous in pressing their electoral claims. The nomination of outsiders could only heighten such tensions. Northampton had often supported men with local connections, but Zouch had not. His nominees were usually strangers. Buckingham, in three elections, backed the choice of twenty-three identified nominees; seventeen were outsiders. At the same time, local gentry were moving into the ports. In 1621 and 1624 seven of the nineteen men elected in the ports, or slightly more than one-third, were local gentry. During Buckingham's tenure the ports elected thirty-one, and, of those, nineteen, or nearly two-thirds, were from Kent and Sussex. The number of local men, members of the county community, that won election in the ports was clearly increasing. But even that does not fully explain why Buckingham's patronage record was the worst of the early seventeenth century. After all, Zouch had nominated outsiders; ten of the thirteen men he successfully backed were strangers to the ports.

Another explanation, and a tentative one, may rest in the increasingly "political" atmosphere of the 1620s. Zouch had never been one of the duke's followers at court; if labeled at all, he was identified with the more "popular" faction.[34] Buckingham, however, personified unpopular and unsuccessful policies. His ties to the court, his domination of it, were conceivably becoming electoral liabilities. It might suggest why Hastings, Sandwich, and Hythe chose men who were locally known and who were, in addition, reputed to be opponents of the court. Nicholas Eversfield led the opposition to Buckingham's nominee at Hastings in 1626. A man of substance in Hastings and Sussex, he had opposed the court as early as 1621. He might have had strong reformist religious views, and was clearly, in the Parliament of 1626, a member of the "popular" group. Sandwich, in its bye-election of 1626, returned the son of a man with similar credentials, Sir Edward Boys, whose family had noteworthy Puritan connections. Sir

Peter Heyman, educated at Emmanuel College, Cambridge, was chosen at Hythe in 1626 and 1628. He was another leading critic of royal policy; indeed, he was so outspoken that he would eventually be clapped in the Tower for his views. And, like Boys and Eversfield, he had impeccable local connections. These men were elected; Buckingham's were not. Indeed, when it is recalled that Zouch, in two elections, lost only one candidate and Buckingham, in three, had thirteen nominees refused, Buckingham's failure is all the more remarkable. And not all those who had his backing and lost were strangers. Sir William Twysden, Sir Edward Dering, and Sir Edwyn Sandys, father and son, were among those who, even with their local connections and his backing, still failed in their election bids.[35]

Buckingham's electioneering undoubtedly suffered from a combination of these factors. He nominated too many too often, and his nominees were usually outsiders, candidates who were, as a result, all the more vulnerable to the opposition of the county gentry, clearly bent on intruding themselves into the ports' returns. Local quarrels over the power of a corporation or the choice of a minister further complicated an already difficult situation, which was probably made even worse by the emergence of men who were determined critics of royal policy. Together, such developments may suggest why Buckingham, as lord warden, had such a sorry electoral record.[36]

## 2. The Duchy of Lancaster and Elections, 1614–1628

Two chancellors directed the Duchy of Lancaster's patronage between 1614 and 1628. Sir Thomas Parry was responsible for the election of 1614, and his eventual successor, Sir Humphrey May, directed the duchy's efforts for all the parliaments of the 1620s. Parry was an Elizabethan who had served as ambassador to France until 1605. On his return to England, he acted as Lady Arabella Stuart's custodian and finally, in 1607, secured a post on the Privy Council and the office of chancellor of the duchy. But his best days were behind him. By 1612 Chamberlain described him as "the old chancellor of the duchy," and there may well have been some truth in his defender's assertions, in the Parliament of 1614 when the Stockbridge election was thrashed out, that Parry was guiltless since he did not know what his servants were doing. Then, Chamberlain reported, Parry "is grown so dull and stupid . . . he is thought scant sensible of anything that befalls or concerns him." His advice was seldom sought and, it would seem, little regarded. It is hard to credit Parry with more than ten places for his electioneering in 1614; it is significant to note that his greatest claim to fame was the disaster at Stockbridge.[37]

The duchy had enjoyed mixed success at Stockbridge. It placed a nominee there in 1588 and again in 1593, missed in 1597, and probably took both places in 1601. It won one seat in 1604. Stockbridge was beginning to show signs of becoming a duchy borough. But Stockbridge's tiny electorate—it had only twenty-eight voters—had enough; and when the parliament of 1614 was summoned, it rebelled.

Four candidates sought its favors: two influential neighboring squires, Sir Richard Gifford of King's Somborne and Sir Henry St. John of Farley, and the duchy's nominees, Sir Henry Wallop and courtier Sir Walter Cope, master of the Court of Wards. By substantial margins Stockbridge's voters chose Gifford and St. John, leaving Wallop and Cope out in the cold. Parry was quick to respond to this surprising independence. He sent threatening letters to the borough and warned St. John "that if he did resist [Parry's electioneering] he should feel a greater power than he could resist." The borough's bailiff gave way under such pressure and returned Cope and Wallop, but Stockbridge's hardy voters petitioned the House of Commons, protesting the illegal return. Parry countered by sending a pursuivant down to silence the courageous electorate. He carried out his instructions with vigor, arresting some "with great extremity." Gifford, among others, was arrested and "refused all bail." One Cook, with more courage than discretion, announced his willingness to testify against the bailiff, "if it cost him [Cook] £100." He was arrested, not allowed to go home to his children whom he had to care for (his wife was dead), and was beaten, as was, for some reason, his horse! To top off Cook's problems, the pursuivant demanded over £6 in fees from him! Cook's account no doubt gained in the telling, but it won the sympathy of the House. Parry was defended in the Commons on the grounds that he was old, tired, and unaware; it was really his servants who carried vengeance to Stockbridge. Bacon made the most revealing comment about it all (given his election plans for the court), when he noted in the House that they were not living "in Plato his Commonwealth." The House, though, acted as if it were: the election was declared void, Parry was expelled from the House, and, thanks to James's displeasure, he was suspended from both the chancellorship and the Privy Council. For Parry, Stockbridge was a sad end to an official career; for the borough's twenty-eight voters, it was vindication for their temerity in denying the power of the duchy.[38]

In only one borough was the duchy able to extend its influence, and that was Leicester, caught between the power of the duchy and its great neighbors, the earls of Huntingdon. In 1604 Leicester denied them both; in 1614 Leicester's story was altogether different. With the arrival of Parry's letter nominating one Henry Felton, Leicester found itself with five candidates: Huntingdon had recommended his brother Sir George Hastings and Sir Henry Rich, and a former M.P., Sir William Heyrick, wanted a place and sought, too, the election of Leicester's recorder, Francis Harvey. To complicate matters further, the town was anxiously trying to secure a new charter for its almshouse. If it denied Huntingdon, the corporation was afraid he would "speak concerning the Hospital to the Chancellor [Parry], to the King, nay, if there be cause, my Lord will move the Parliament House" to block Leicester's bid for the charter. The same fate might obtain if it denied Parry's candidate. It was a dangerous situation for the hard-pressed corporation. Harvey came to Leicester's rescue. He withdrew his candidacy and urged that the town accept one nominee from each patron, thereby satisfying everyone and saving the hospital. Harvey's proposal was all the more feasible since Huntingdon's brother, Sir George Hastings, had won a shire seat. Huntingdon and Parry agreed although Parry made it abundantly clear that if Leicester expected "any favor at his hand any way [the hospital?], not to say him nay in this his request." Leicester meekly submitted; it had no other course. It returned Sir Henry Rich and Parry's second nominee, Sir Francis Leigh, a master of requests. Leicester won the support of its patrons for the hospital but paid the price, in 1614 at least, of electoral independence.[39]

Although evidence fails us in the effort to assess the duchy's other successes, it seems likely that Sir William Beecher, chosen at Knaresborough, had the duchy's support. Sir Henry Slingsby, whose family practically controlled Knaresborough, was a minor duchy official, a connection that must have aided Beecher and the duchy in the election. Newcastle-under-Lyme's choice of Edward Wymarke, a minor courtier who lived in London, was the duchy's work; he was also returned at Liverpool. Henry Binge, the duchy's steward for Sudbury, was one of that borough's M.P.'s, and Sir Robert Johnson of London, an officer of the ordnance, presumably owed his election at Monmouth to the duchy's intervention. Within Lancashire's boroughs, the duchy's record was surprisingly poor. Liverpool's election of Wymarke and Thomas Ireland, a Lancashire-born duchy official, was probably the duchy's work, as was the choice of Sir Edward Moseley, attorney general of the duchy, at Preston. Sir Thomas Fanshawe, clerk of the crown and surveyor general of crown lands, and his son, William, an auditor for the duchy, were returned at Lancaster in the duchy's interest.[40] Clitheroe, Newton-in-Makersfield, and Wigan showed no sign of duchy intervention. If Parry tried, the evidence is lost, but the returns reflect the power of Lancashire's gentry, not the duchy. Perhaps, and it seems likely, Parry was simply too old and tired to do more. The same, however, could not be said about his eventual successor as chancellor, Sir Humphrey May.

Parry died in 1616; Sir John Dacombe, who followed him as chancellor, died in 1618. And as Dacombe lay dying, an alleged forty-three suitors, including some of the "greats" and "near-greats" of James's court, engaged in a heated contest for his office. Sir Humphrey May finally won; he had better "goods" to trade for it than Sir Lionel Cranfield, including his post as surveyor of the wards and a position in the Star Chamber, which went to the ever-grasping Buckingham clan. It did not harm May, either, that he was "much liked by the King and Buckingham." May had entered the court about 1604 and won both a pension and a knighthood by 1613. Despite the bargaining tone of the transaction, his advancement to the chancellorship of the duchy was one of the few first-class appointments made by James and his favorite. He has received high praise for his effectiveness as a privy councillor and government member in the Commons from the expert on that subject, David H. Willson. In Willson's careful evaluation of the privy councillors that served the first Stuarts, Sir Humphrey May was described as having the "makings of a great parliamentarian." May's growing coolness toward the great favorite's policies condemned him to minor offices and prevented him from realizing what must have been his considerable potential as a servant of the crown. His career was another example of that personal power the duke of Buckingham enjoyed which so demoralized the court. He labored long and hard, sometimes even with success, as a defender of royal policy, protector of Buckingham, and as a moderating influence on an increasingly factious and antagonistic House of Commons.[41]

May performed creditably as an election agent, especially in the elections of 1624–26, but nothing that he could do would restore the duchy's patronage to its Elizabethan level; the growing pressures exerted by the local squirearchy were simply too great. May's nominees probably took eleven seats in 1621; he then succeeded in raising duchy influence to a fairly high level. He was probably involved in placing sixteen in 1624, twelve in 1625 and 1626, but in 1628 the number of places fell back to nine.

May went right to work in his first election (1621), claiming "a right in the election of every corporation within this country [Lancashire]." And since there is no reason to doubt that he continued such efforts through 1628, let us review his Lancashire record.[42] Of the six Lancashire towns, two—Lancaster and Preston—were duchy pocket boroughs. Lancaster elected Sir Thomas Fanshawe, a clerk of the crown, and Sir Humphrey May to each parliament of the 1620s, although May chose to serve for the borough only twice, in 1621 and 1625. May's place was taken by outsiders, duchy nominees John Selden (1624) and Sir Thomas Jermyn (1626). Preston's record is equally vivid testimony of the duchy's patronage. Sir Edward Moseley, first chosen in 1614, was reelected in 1621 and 1624 when he served with another duchy nominee, Sir William Poley of Suffolk, who was Sir Humphrey May's father-in-law. Poley, however, chose to serve for Sudbury in 1624, and the duchy filled his place with Francis Nicholls, a clerk in the prince's service. Nicholls died, and the duchy replaced him with Sir William Harvey of Suffolk, who was elected again at Preston in 1625. George Gerrard, chosen in 1626 and 1628, was the grandson of a former duchy official and Elizabethan M.P. for Wigan and, like his grandfather, probably owed his elections to the duchy's influence. Another outsider, Sir Robert Carr, elected in 1628, probably had the duchy's blessing although Carr's marriage in 1621 to Anne, daughter of William, earl of Derby, must have also contributed to his return. Together between 1614 and 1628, Lancaster (11 of 12 places) and Preston (10 of 12 places) filled 21 of their 24 seats with the duchy's nominees.[43]

Clitheroe, which had avoided the duchy's attentions in 1614, became a safe seat for at least one nominee from 1621 to 1628. In 1621, despite local gentry support, Sir Richard Beaumont's bid for a place was foiled. The corporation had already committee itself to a neighboring squire, Sir Thomas Walmesley of Dunkenhalgh and Hacking Hall, Lancashire, and was also being hard pressed by May, who was asserting his claim to one place. May nominated "one Mr. Shelton," but, instead, Clitheroe matched William Fanshawe, a duchy auditor, with Walmesley. Shelton may have withdrawn, or May may have changed his nominee. Fanshawe's election was evidence of duchy influence, an influence that captured both places in 1624 when two duchy candidates, Fanshawe and Kentish attorney Ralph Whitfield of Gray's Inn, a stranger to both Clitheroe and Lancashire, were returned. The duchy tried to capitalize on this double triumph, for in the next election (1625), May nominated Sir Thomas Trevor, another duchy auditor, but without success. Fanshawe was again elected, presumably at the duchy's behest, and served with Ralph Assheton, probably of the Assheton family of Middleton, Lancashire. The 1625 election set the pattern for Clitheroe's returns in 1626 and 1628. The borough divided its electoral favors between a duchy nominee and a representative of Lancashire's squirearchy. In 1626 Assheton was reelected, and duchy influence must account for the surprising choice of George Kirke, a Scotsman who had never been naturalized. Kirke was rejected by the House, and, in his stead, Clitheroe elected Sir Christopher Hatton, who looks very much like another duchy nominee. The duchy pressed for both of the borough's places in 1628, nominating Thomas Jermyn and auditor William Fanshawe. Fanshawe's claim that he wished "to serve for the town of Clitheroe [more] than another borough whatsoever" was not enough to sway the borough's corportion. It remained loyal to its custom of choosing one duchy candidate (Jermyn) and a member of the country's gentry (William Nowell of Little Mearley, Lancashire). Despite the duchy's failure to place anyone at the borough in 1614, its influence was still significant. Duchy patronage controlled six of Clitheroe's twelve places, and though it obviously hoped for more, as its double nominations in 1624, 1625, and 1628 showed, it could still count on Clitheroe for at least one place. May's electioneering, unlike that of Buckingham as lord warden, apparently never antagonized the corporations to such an extent that he lost all electoral influence.[44]

The other Lancashire's boroughs, Wigan, Liverpool, and Newton-in-Makersfield, showed varying degrees of duchy influence. Wigan's story was similar to Clitheroe's. It avoided Duchy patronage in 1614, but it still probably gave up six of its twelve places to candidates who possibly had the duchy's support. Roger Downes, elected in 1621, may have been a duchy candidate. He had served before (1601) for Wigan and was vice-chamberlain of Chester by 1627. His son Francis, of Pythchley, Northamptonshire, was returned in 1624 and 1625, thanks to his father's influence and possible duchy backing. Sir William Poley's election in 1626 was a sure sign of duchy patronage, and another burgess, Edward Bridgeman, chosen in 1625 and 1628, would have had the duchy's approval. Bridgeman, of Warrington, Lancashire, was the younger brother of John, bishop of Chester and lord of the manor at Wigan, who, no doubt, also supported his brother's candidacy. Bridgeman's nephew was Sir Orlando Bridgeman, later a solicitor general to the Prince of Wales and king's counsel for the duchy. Duchy influence also accounted for the bye-election choice in 1621 of George Gerrard, who later, in 1626 and 1628, served for the duchy pocket borough of Preston.[45] Liverpool showed flashes of independence, but in spite of momentary lapses of loyalty to the duchy its record reflected successful duchy intervention. It granted both places to the duchy in 1614 and again in 1621 when it returned Thomas May, brother of the chancellor of the duchy, and William Johnson, "servant unto the . . . Lord Chancellor," Sir Francis Bacon.

Sir Thomas Gerrard, a courtier with connections to the duke of Buckingham, probably had the duchy's approval for his election in 1624 but, in the following election of 1625, the duchy missed out altogether. Liverpool chose Edward Moore of Bank Hall, whose port connections were both ancient and influential, and James, Lord Strange, eldest son of the earl of Derby. In 1626 Edward Bridgeman's election probably had duchy approval. Another successful duchy nominee was Henry Jermyn, returned in 1628, a courtier and vice-chamberlain to the queen. Liverpool, like Wigan and Clitheroe, granted half its places between 1614 and 1628 to men who either were duchy nominees or would have had its support.[46]

Of all the Lancashire boroughs, tiny Newton-in-Makersfield was the most independent of duchy interference. It owed its liberty to the power of the Fleetwood family, which had bought the barony of Newton in 1594 and had, with that purchase, gained the predominant voice in the borough's elections. Only four of Newton's burgesses, Richard Kippax (1621), Edmond Breres (1624), Sir Henry Edmondes (1625–26), and Sir Henry Holcroft (1628), have possible links with the duchy. Kippax, of a minor county family, was a vice-chancellor of the duchy and probably also served as an "examiner in the Star Chamber," and Breres, also a Lancashire native, was a duchy attorney. Edmondes was the evidently worthless son of Sir Thomas Edmondes, ambassador and privy councillor; and Holcroft, who also served for the duchy borough of Stockbridge, was an officer of the Signet and active in Irish affairs. Both were strangers to Newton and Lancashire. The other members for Newton were either Lancashire gentry or kinsmen of the Fleetwoods. They won their places "with the consent" of Sir Richard Fleetwood and not the duchy of Lancaster.[47]

The six Lancashire boroughs, from 1604 through 1628, had 84 parliamentary places at their disposal. Duchy patronage took approximately 51, with Lancaster (13) and Preston (11) accounting for almost half of the duchy's total. Wigan (eight), Clitheroe (seven), and Liverpool (seven) followed, while Newton (five) practically left the duchy's orbit. The duchy's chief competitors were the local gentry. Except at Lancaster and Preston, the county squirearchy was moving in and threatening to become, as it already had at Newton-in-Makersfield, the principal patron of Lancashire's boroughs. It was the same challenge patrons elsewhere in early Stuart England had to face. Other changes from the immediate Elizabethan past could also be seen. Lancaster, Preston, and Liverpool remained fixed in their Elizabethan electoral customs; but Newton, which had apparently granted a place to the duchy in each Elizabethan election, had now almost escaped its electoral grasp. Wigan and Clitheroe, too, were showing signs of slipping away. They had often been ready to grant two places to duchy nominees in Elizabeth's reign, but their story changed after James's accession. From 1604 through 1628, the duchy had to usually settle for one place; the county gentry were taking the other. Elizabethan chancellors could count on between eight and ten places in Lancashire alone in any election.[48] Their early Stuart successors were forced to settle for seven. Under Fortescue in 1604, the duchy took six of Lancashire's twelve borough seats but under Parry the result was worse: his nominees won only five places. May's efforts were more fruitful: he was responsible for five elections (1621–28) in which men who were either the nominees of the duchy or would have had its support captured 40 of the available 60 places. It was the best early Stuart record, but despite May's exertions, the trend toward gentry influence remained clear.

Eleven other boroughs, outside Lancashire, had been targets for duchy intervention in the past. Of those eleven, between 1621 and 1628, only one (Leicester) came increasingly under the duchy's sway, and at one other (Stockbridge) the duchy was able to hold its own. Five (Huntingdon, Boroughbridge, Sudbury, Newcastle-under-Lyme, and Monmouth) were clearly less willing to listen to the duchy's recommendations, and four (Higham Ferrers, Thetford, Aldborough, and Knaresborough after 1614) escaped its influence altogether.

Leicester did not surrender to the duchy without a struggle. Five candidates sought Leicester's burgess-ships in 1621. The earl of Huntingdon nominated two, Sir Richard Morison and Sir William Harrington. Morison was a veteran soldier who had served in Ireland for some fifteen years but, frustrated in his hopes for the presidency of Munster, was back in England about 1615. He won appointment as lieutenant general of the ordnance for life; his brother-in-law, Harrington, may have secured a reversion to the post; he succeeded to it in November 1625. Morison, who held property in Leicester, settled at Tooley Park, Leicestershire. Harrington, whose main interests were in Hertfordshire, also had local connections. There is no evidence that the duchy made any nomination, but Harrington could have been its candidate. He was nominated by the Prince's Council at Hertford in 1624 and finally won election there in 1626.[49] Sir William Heyrick, who had failed in his bid in 1614, wanted a place as did Stephen Harvey, nominated to Leicester by his father, the town's recorder. The countess of Devonshire was also involved: she recommended her son. Leicester took a bold stand. It would take one of Huntingdon's nominees, Morison, but only if he came to take his freeman's oath. And if he did not, Leicester courteously but firmly informed Huntingdon that it hoped he would "not take any displeasure against us if we choose another"! The earl wanted the oath taken by commission; whether Morison finally appeared is not clear although an undated copy of his oath survives in Leicester's archives.[50] Morison and Sir William Heyrick were elected. Whether Heyrick took his brother's advice (given after Sir William's failure in 1614) and secured the duchy's backing is unknown. It would seem he hardly needed it. His father had lived in Leicester, and although Sir William had made his career in London and at the court, serving as the principal jeweler to James I, he never severed his ties to his birthplace. He had bought, as his career flourished and he waxed prosperous, Beaumanor Park, Leicestershire; he would be buried in St. Martin's Church, Leicester. At any rate, it seems possible that Leicester had denied one of its eager patrons, the duchy of Lancaster.[51]

The duchy's probable failure in 1621 may have contributed to May's actions before the 1624 election. He nominated himself at Leicester but was careful to seek the earl of Huntingdon's support, a realistic appreciation of where the predominant election patronage for Leicester lay. Huntingdon graciously consented—to his own cost as events proved—and, in his own right, nominated his brother Sir George Hastings. Hastings was refused; May was chosen along with William Ive, a Leicester property-owner. As might be expected, the earl received a full explanation. In spite of the mayor's "best endeavours," the "greater part" of Leicester's corporation voted for May and Ive. The mayor hoped Huntingdon would not be offended; after all, the choice of May was made "at your honor's request." Clever Leicester! It had again avoided entrapment at the hands of its two influential patrons and maintained a tenuous grip on independence by returning Ive. The earl's reaction is unknown, but he must have read May's letter of thanks with some chagrin.[52] It was, for Leicester, its last success. Henceforward, patronage dominated Leicester's electoral story.

Leicester gave way without resistance in 1625. May successfully nominated himself, and Huntingdon won a place for Sir George Hastings. Ive, who sought reelection, was easily outdistanced in the poll, and Arthur Hesilrige, recommended by his father, Thomas, was not even listed as a candidate. Leicester had bidden good-bye to its precarious independence. Both great patrons had been satisfied; it was the first such election since 1614.[53] Leicester's surrender was more

blatantly exposed that summer. May, who had also been chosen for
Lancaster, gave up his Leicester place and nominated, in his stead,
the Suffolk courtier Sir Thomas Jermyn. The election was dutifully
held; Ive tried again but Jermyn easily won. Leicester's subservience
was clearly revealed in the mayor's report to May. They had, he
wrote, elected Jermyn "although he be altogether unknown to any of
us." It was a sad comment on Leicester's defeat and a forecast of
things to come.[54]

May was again returned at Leicester in 1626 and 1628; his fellow
burgesses were Huntingdon's nominees, Sir George Hastings (1626)
and Sir John Stanhope (1628) of Elvaston, Derbyshire, whose brother
had married into the Hastings family.[55] In the elections from 1614
through 1628, Leicester's independence had withered away under the
unrelenting pressure of its eager patrons. The return of Sir Francis
Leigh in 1614 and Sir Humphrey May, chosen in every parliament
from 1624 through 1628, was eloquent testimony of the duchy's
newly found success, something that the town had avoided during
Elizabeth's long reign.

Stockbridge's courageous fight in 1614 did not bring duchy intervention to an end. It may, however, have forced the duchy to rest
content with one place from 1621 to 1626. Sir William Ayloffe, an
outsider from Essex who was deeply involved in various fen-draining
projects, could have been its successful candidate in 1621, and there is
no doubt that Sir Henry Holcroft, elected in 1624, was a duchy
nominee. Holcroft was also recommended by the Prince's Council at
Pontefract in 1624 and, in 1628, was returned for Newton-in-
Makersfield. Another outsider, the courtier Sir Thomas Badger was
one of Stockbridge's burgesses in 1625–26. He was James's master of
the harriers and a client of Buckingham's, having accompanied the
great favorite to France in 1625. Badger, too, was probably a duchy
nominee. At Stockbridge, as elsewhere, the duchy shared its influence with locally influential squires. Sir Richard Gifford was chosen
from 1621 through 1628, and when he was joined, in 1628, by another
powerful county gentleman, Sir Henry Whitehead, the duchy's influence apparently received a temporary setback. It was another example of the successful invasion of borough seats by prestigious county
families, but it was, too, the only election between 1621 and 1628
when the duchy missed a Stockbridge place. It had placed its first
candidate at the borough in 1588, and, save for the elections of 1597
and 1614, Stockbridge remained safely in the duchy's credit col-
umns.[56]

Monmouth, too, was a latecomer to the duchy's list, not giving up a place to its patronage until 1593. Its record, between 1621 and 1628, hardly reflected great duchy success, but the election of a Scottish alien, Walter Steward of Westminster, one of the gentlemen of James's Privy Chamber, was probably the duchy's work. Refused his seat in 1624 as an alien, he was allowed to serve in the succeeding parliament. He seems to have had no connection to Monmouth save as a possible duchy nominee.[57] Boroughbridge, Yorkshire, which had been consistently loyal to the duchy from 1588 to 1601, changed patrons in the first parliament of James, listening instead to the Council of the North. However, its election of Sir Philip Mainwaring in 1624–26 might have indicated a renewal of duchy influence. Mainwaring, of the Cheshire family at Over Peover, was a courtier who had briefly been the rumored future husband of the countess of Berkshire, Bridget, the second daughter of the earl of Oxford. He was a nephew of an Elizabethan M.P. and courtier, Sir Edward Fitten, who had served for both Wigan and Boroughbridge under the duchy's banner. He would later receive a job in the Irish administration from Sir Thomas Wentworth. Boroughbridge was far more under the electoral control of an influential Yorkshire family, the Fairfaxes of Denton. Sir Ferdinando Fairfax was chosen there for every parliament from 1614 through the spring of 1640, continuing evidence of the encroachment of local gentry on what had been, for the duchy, a safe and receptive borough.[58] Another borough where duchy influence was declining rapidly was Newcastle-under-Lyme, which had been, in Elizabeth's years and in 1604 and 1614, a fairly compliant duchy town. Only three men, Sir John Davies, returned in 1621, and Charles Glemham, who replaced the outsider Sir Edward Vere elected in a bye-election in 1624, might have been duchy nominees. Davies was a royal official who served as attorney general for Ireland from 1616 to 1619; he had no connections to Newcastle-under-Lyme save his elections. Vere was a soldier; Glemham, another outsider, was a gentleman of the Privy Chamber and master of the household to James I. His mother was a daughter of Thomas Sackville, earl of Dorset. By 1614 Glemham had become a client of the earl of Arundel, who nominated him at Aldeburgh, Suffolk, in the elections of 1621, 1624, and 1625. The remainder, except one, of Newcastle-under-Lyme's places went to men either directly connected to the town or representative of local Staffordshire families. The only exception was the return of Edward Kirton of Somersetshire in 1621. Kirton was closely tied to the Seymour family, and his election is best explained by the influence of

Robert Devereux, earl of Essex. Essex was a close friend of Kirton's patron, William Seymour, later Earl of Hertford, whose second wife was a sister of Essex. The duchy's grip at Newcastle-under-Lyme had been broken by Staffordshire's gentry.[59]

Two of the duchy's traditionally reliable boroughs, Huntingdon and Sudbury, showed remarkable independence after 1614. From 1563 through 1604 Huntingdon returned at least one duchy nominee, and in 1563 and 1571, it elected two. Sudbury's record was similar, save that it surrendered to the duchy in every Elizabethan election and, after slipping the duchy's grasp in 1604, returned to the fold in 1614. After that, however, the duchy's influence nearly disappeared. Only the election of Sir William Poley, in 1624 and 1628, can be credited to the duchy. Poley's cause was, no doubt, aided by his Suffolk connections, but, as at Preston and Wigan, his elections must have been strongly assisted by his son-in-law, the duchy chancellor, Sir Humphrey May. Poley's parliamentary career only began after his daughter's marriage, and it was confined to service from duchy boroughs. Sudbury's growing independence was shown by its refusal of a duchy nominee in 1621 when Sir Henry Hobart, member of the Prince's Council, suggested that May nominate Phillip Bell to the borough. Bell was nominated but to no avail. Sudbury, like Newcastle-under-Lyme, Boroughbridge, and many other formerly safe duchy boroughs, was becoming the property of neighboring county families like the Cranes of Chilton, near Sudbury, and the Barnardistons, another powerful Suffolk family. Huntingdon's story was just as bad from the duchy's point of view. Only the election of Sir Arthur Mainwaring, chosen from 1624 to 1626, might be credited to the duchy's declining influence. Mainwaring, also nominated by the Prince's Council for Knaresborough in 1624, had a long court career, serving as clerk of the Pipe, prince's carver, and gentleman of the Privy Chamber for Charles I, and lieutenant of the Castle and Forest of Windsor. He had no discernible connections with Huntingdon except his parliamentary service in its name. Huntingdon's other places were usually filled by the nominees of the powerful Montagu family of Northamptonshire or through the recommendations of the Lords St. John of Bletsoe, lord lieutenants of Huntingdonshire throughout the early seventeenth century.[60] Sudbury and Huntingdon were no longer part of the duchy's patronage story.

Higham Ferrers, Northamptonshire, and Aldborough, Yorkshire, were the electoral property of neighboring families even before Elizabeth I died. Knaresborough, after the election of 1614, also escaped the duchy's influence. It became, like so many others, the patronage borough of local families. Thetford's story differed in only one respect: its elections reflected the joint influence of Thomas Howard, earl of Arundel, and of the Gawdy family of West Harling, Norfolk.[61]

Even before the queen's death, the number of boroughs outside Lancashire that might be expected to return duchy nominees had fallen from eleven to eight. Thetford, Aldborough, and Higham Ferrers were already gone. What of the other eight? The duchy's record can only be described as dismal. Knaresborough provided a place in 1614 and was heard of no more, and Huntingdon and Sudbury, strongly loyal before 1603, were of little value after that date. The same can be said for Boroughbridge and Newcastle-under-Lyme. Stockbridge and Monmouth remained fairly constant; only at Leicester did the duchy make any solid gain. Before James's accession, non-Lancashire boroughs presented the duchy with approximately 60 places or, roughly 10 in each Elizabethan election.[62] After 1603 the duchy could only find 29 places.

The Duchy of Lancaster from 1604 to 1628 may have secured as many as 80 places, 51 in Lancashire boroughs and a lowly 29 outside that county. Without its Lancashire base, its record would have been very bad indeed. In Elizabethan elections the duchy usually secured between 18 and 20 places. The major reason for the substantial decline in duchy patronage after 1603 seems abundantly clear; the gentry were taking over. Families like the Gawdys, Slingsbys, Cranes, Fairfaxes, and Barnardistons, to name but a few, had replaced the duchy as borough patrons. The election records of Boroughbridge, Knaresborough, Sudbury, Newcastle-under-Lyme, and Newton-in-Makersfield tell the tale, and Wigan and Clitheroe show the signs of increasing gentry influence. Huntingdon, too, was no longer safe for duchy nominees, although there aristocratic influence was chiefly responsible. What remains a mystery, however, is what role antagonism to outside patrons or disaffection with the Stuart court played in this story of duchy electoral decline. The evidence has not survived that might have permitted an answer. What is clear, however, is that the Duchy of Lancaster, even with the redoubtable Sir Humphrey May as its chancellor, failed to repeat its Elizabethan successes at a time when the court was systematically attempting to influence elections.[63]

### 3. The Duchy of Cornwall, the Prince's Council, and Elections, 1614–1624

Twenty-one boroughs dotted the Cornish landscape, and most of them, fifteen to be exact, were Tudor creations. Local families—the Rashleighs, the Robartes, the Bullers, the Killigrews—often played dominant roles in determining the course of Cornish election history. The only challenger they faced for election dominance was the king's heir, the duke of Cornwall, who was, following the death of his brother Henry in 1612, Prince Charles. The Duchy of Cornwall had an impressive array of officials and was involved in many aspects of Cornish activity; it was, potentially, an influential election agent. Most Cornish boroughs were poor or small, even tiny, or both; they provided, or so it appeared, an easy avenue to Westminster for crown nominees. Bacon's program for a parliament in 1614 made much of electioneering as a necessary prelude to any meeting at Westminster, and the Cornish boroughs, possible electoral prey for the duchy, could hardly have been ignored.[64]

Ten of Cornwall's boroughs show evidence of possible duchy intervention in 1614, but without nominee lists or letters of recommendation, which have happily survived for the elections of 1621, 1624, and the spring and fall of 1640, any assessment of the duchy's influence is, at best, problematical. The choice, however, of Sir Robert Naunton at Camelford, Sir Henry Vane at Lostwithiel, and a Kentishman, Sir Francis Barnham at Grampound shows the duchy's hand; their only connection to Cornwall was their election. Another courtier, Sir Francis Crane, returned for Penryn, was a duchy nominee in 1624, but his election in 1614 was probably the work of Penryn's patron, the Cornish courtier Sir Robert Killigrew. Crane's intimate connections with Cornish families must have also contributed to his choice. Vane, Naunton, and Thomas Trevor, presumably the earl of Nottingham's nominee at Newport in 1614, were all listed as duchy candidates in 1621, and William Crofts, chosen at Launceston in 1614, made the duchy nominee list in 1624.[65]

Launceston probably surrendered both places to the duchy, for Crofts was joined, in the Parliament of 1614, by Sir Charles Wilmot, who had made his career in Ireland and was a stranger to the town and Cornwall. Sir Jerome Horsey, elected at Bossiney, had served there before, but his post with the Duchy of Lancaster and Bossiney's subservience make it possible that he was duchy nominee.[66] St. Ives, which returned Sir Anthony Maney, a Kentish gentleman, and St. Mawes, which sent a customs official, Sir Nicholas Smith, to Westminster, were other likely duchy boroughs. Michael and Saltash, too, might have been successfully influenced by the duchy. Christopher Hodson, chosen at Michael, was a stranger in Cornwall, and Sir Ranulph Crew's return for Saltash was probably at the insistence of the duchy. A legal careerist in London, he was the Speaker for the 1614 parliament. Sir Robert Phelips, his colleague at Saltash, was of an influential Somersetshire family; his father was master of the rolls, and it is likely that the duchy found him the Saltash place after he had been beaten in the hotly fought Somersetshire contest. His father had sought the prince's help in the Somersetshire struggle, and perhaps the prince's response also included the Saltash seat. Sir Edward Lewkenor, of Sussex, was returned at West Looe, apparently at the request of the duchy.[67]

Two other officials of the duchy, the auditor Richard Connock, chosen at both Bodmin and Liskeard, and Francis Vivian, captain of St. Mawes Castle, elected for St. Mawes, might have had duchy approval but undoubtedly owed their elections to their local Cornish prestige.[68] To summarize what must be an educated guess: the duchy could have been responsible for the return of twelve men in ten borough elections in 1614. The duchy's success was all the greater when it is realized that, of the twelve men it conceivably placed in Cornish constituencies, ten of them were outsiders.

Surviving lists of nominees bear witness to the duchy's continuing electoral involvement in the elections of 1621 and 1624. In 1621 the duchy nominated fourteen men at fourteen boroughs, including in its list the names of four privy councillors. On 1 December 1620, duchy officers were ordered "to make known withall speed to the Mayors, Bailiffs or other chief officers of the borough" listed that the prince was recommending "one person for every of the said boroughs" and did not expect "to be disappointed."[69]

Four of the nominees—Sir John Walter, Sir Henry Vane, Sir Thomas Trevor, and Sir Robert Carey—were in the prince's service, and four privy councillors, Sir Edward Coke, Sir Robert Naunton (principal secretary of state), Sir Fulke Greville (chancellor of the Exchequer), and Sir Lionel Cranfield (master of the Court of Wards) held significant Stuart appointments. Only four—Thomas Bond, William Noy, Trevor, and Carey—had Cornish connections. Trevor's mother was a Trevanion, and Noy, another Cornishman, was a bencher of Lincoln's Inn with a promising court career ahead of him. Carey, an impoverished courtier, had married into the Trevanion family of Caerhayes, Cornwall, a marriage that must have contributed, too, to his electoral success. The remaining duchy nominees (ten men) were all outsiders. Greville was from a great Warwickshire family, and Vane, from Kent, was a London-based courtier. Sir Oliver Cromwell's ties were with Huntingdonshire and the court; his lavish living and court ambitions would soon bring him to financial disaster. (He was an uncle of the more famous Oliver Cromwell.) Henry Finch was another Kentishman who had been knighted in 1616 and had been consulted by the king on the question of monopoly patents; following his loyal service to the crown in the 1614 parliament, he had been made a serjeant-at-law. Sir Edward Barrett was from Essex; his career, like that of Vane, Noy, and Trevor, was in the future. He would serve as ambassador to France in 1625 and become, in turn, chancellor of the Duchy of Lancaster and chancellor of the Exchequer. Edward Salter, soon to be knighted, was another courtier; he won a place as king's carver and was rewarded, in November 1625, with an annual pension of £150. His brother, Sir Nicholas Salter, was one of the Great Farmers of the Customs.[70]

Eight of the fourteen boroughs listened to the duchy's recommendations. Grampound (Carey), Launceston (Bond), East Looe (Walter), and Newport (Barrett) elected their original nominees, and, after some shifting around, four other boroughs also returned duchy candidates. Coke, recommended at Bossiney, found a place at Liskeard, and Vane, although originally listed for Liskeard, was actually chosen for Lostwithiel. Vane, however, had also been elected for Carlisle, and his preference for that seat allowed Salter, refused at Plymouth, to replace him. Sir Thomas Trevor, although nominated for West Looe, found an apparently safer place at Saltash, where, it would seem, Cromwell was unacceptable. Perhaps Trevor's Cornish connections pulled him through. Noy, too, turned up at Helston instead of Fowey, and Cranfield, under other patronage auspices, found a place at Arundel, Sussex. Greville's candidacy at Camelford may have been simply insurance; he was returned as a knight of the shire for his home county of Warwick. Naunton, too, was chosen elsewhere. Only Cromwell and Henry Finch failed to find a place in the parliament.[71]

The shifting of nominees from borough to borough may indicate that the surviving list was not the duchy's sole electoral word. Sir Heneage Finch, the Kentish barrister who made his career in the court's service, was probably substituted for Sir Thomas Trevor at West Looe, and Sir Henry Carey, a duchy nominee in 1624, could have been its candidate in Greville's place at Camelford. St. Mawes elected a duchy auditor, William Hockmore, and an outsider, Edward Wrightington of Lancashire, later a member of the Council of the North and a reader at Gray's Inn who was a friend of the earl of Derby. Wrightington's election may have represented a double triumph for duchy patronage at St. Mawes. Saltash and East Looe may have returned additional duchy candidates. East Looe's choice of Sir Jerome Horsey, Bossiney's member in 1614, and the election of Sir Thomas Smyth, the lord warden's candidate at Sandwich in 1614, for

Saltash might have been further testimony to the duchy's endeavours.[72]

If the probables are included, the duchy succeeded in placing fourteen burgesses in Cornish constituencies, failing only at Bossiney, St. Ives, and Fowey, where the interests of the Cornish gentry were too strong to overcome. It had intervened, all told, in fifteen elections, including Plymouth, where the corporation, despite the duchy's pressure, remained loyal to its own.

In 1624 the duchy repeated its previous effort, making its nominations to the same fourteen boroughs. The nominees included three privy councillors (Sir Julius Caesar, Sir Richard Weston, and Sir John Suckling), and six (Crofts, Thomas Carey, Walter, Trevor, Crane, and Sir Richard Smyth) of the prince's officers. Two others, Miles and Sir John Hobart, were sons of the prince's chancellor, Sir Henry Hobart. Of the fifteen men nominated by the duchy, including Suckling's replacement, Sir Francis Cottington, the prince's secretary, eleven were outsiders. That should hardly surprise; the duchy had customarily recommended strangers to its Cornish boroughs.[73] Five boroughs (Bossiney, East Looe, Saltash, Fowey, and Launceston) elected their nominees without apparent trouble. Camelford, which returned Cottington in Suckling's place, and Lostwithiel, which elected Sir John Hobart in his brother's stead, also showed no resistance to the duchy. The story, however, was different at Helston and St. Ives. Despite the additional pressure of Sir Edward Conway, Helston would have nothing to do with Sir Thomas Crew, although it did return another duchy nominee, Thomas Carey. Perhaps Carey's Cornish ties were responsible. St. Ives, too, showed surprising resistance. Privy Councillor Sir Julius Caesar failed there, although his Cornish connections, the Killigrews, probably backed him, and another influential Cornishman, Arthur Harris, certainly did. Harris was upset: he blamed Caesar's defeat on "the absence of some of my friends of the town of St. Ives at the time of the election," and well Harris might. Caesar lost the place by one vote. Two duchy auditors, Thomas Gawen, chosen at Bossiney, and William Hockmore, again returned for St. Mawes, could be credited to the duchy's patronage column. But even with their inclusion, the duchy still won only ten places, a sharp and surprising reduction from its 1621 level. What had happened? Since there is no hard evidence to tell the tale, speculation will have to suffice. Grampound chose two locally influential squires over Carey, who was a courtier with Cornish connections. Liskeard and St. Ives, though, may have reacted against the duchy's customary practice of nominating outsiders, for they both returned members of significant neighboring families. These three elections might reflect the opposition aroused in Cornwall by the duchy's comprehensive campaign, for one Cornishman, Arthur Harris, complained that "the prince's letters I think have disappointed many, for few towns were left unsolicited by him." Plymouth continued its successful resistance and remained loyal to its corporation's members, but at Newport, Launceston, and West Looe, the duchy's troubles were different. They came under the patronage of great aristocrats, the duke of Buckingham and the earl of Pembroke. Their intervention in 1624 was at the duchy's expense and could have cost the duchy a place at each borough. The sharp decline was possibly caused by two differing developments: a loyalty to local gentry aroused by heavy duchy interference in behalf of outsiders and aristocratic intervention.[74]

In its three elections (1614–24) the duchy gathered 36 places in seventeen Cornish boroughs.[75] The prince, however, did not restrict his electioneering to those boroughs under his authority as duke of Cornwall. In 1621 he also nominated candidates, through his council, at Bewdley and Chester. Bewdley Manor had been granted to Henry, prince of Wales, and at his death passed to Charles, who held it until 1623. Bewdley could not avoid such a presence, and the election of privy councillor and diplomatist Sir Thomas Edmonds in 1621 was the result.[76] Charles had historic links to Chester, explicit in his title as earl of Chester, and also held rights to the fee farm of the city; but as the election of 1621 proved, Chester had little interest in historic or economic rights. It refused Charles's candidates, preferring instead, in a hotly contested election, its own.

The Prince's Council nominated two candidates for Chester, Sir Henry Cary, a courtier and controller of the royal household, and Sir Thomas Edmondes. To put even more pressure on Chester's corporation, the lord president of the Council of the Marches of Wales, William Compton, earl of Northampton, wrote the city, at the prince's request, in support of Cary. Candidates with substantial claims on Chester's affection were also abundant. Thomas Savage, a near neighbor and member of a prominent Chester family, nominated his brother John and also supported Sir John Bingley's candidacy. Bingley had served Chester twice before and, although a native of the city, had made his career in the Exchequer. Tradition dictated that Chester choose its recorder, in 1621 Edward Whitby, who had been joined with Bingley in the last parliament. Whitby's family had long been influential and active in city affairs; his father had been Chester's mayor, and another kinsman served as sheriff. Through marriage he had allied himself with another prestigious Chester family, the

Gamulls. The corporation was in a vexing position. It had accepted both outside nominations and was, as well, confronted by three other locally important candidates.

Chester had jealously preserved its electoral freedom in both previous elections. Surrender now, explicit in the choice of Cary and Edmondes, could destroy its hardy independence. The law provided a glimmer of hope. The city fathers informed the Prince's Council that Cary was ineligible to serve for Chester since he was not a freeman. The corporation's fears were greatly relieved when, shortly after taking this courageous legal stand, they discovered that Cary was already chosen elsewhere. The way seemed clear to appease both their powerful patron, the Prince's Council, and custom: Chester would elect Edmondes and Whitby. All would be well.

But Edmondes, too, was not a freeman of Chester. His election—indeed, his candidacy—was illegal. The corporation, though, was determined to ignore that unhappy technicality, but the resourceful Whitby was not. In 1619 Whitby and the mayor had engaged in an awesome battle that led to a tumultuous assembly meeting, the jailing of a common councilman, and the suspension of another. Whitby had even been briefly suspended as recorder, but by the end of that summer, all was settled, or so Chester's citizens thought. Whitby, however, was biding his time, and the 1621 election provided the opportunity for his revenge. He also, perhaps inadvertently, saved Chester's election independence.

Whitby gulled the corporation completely. He had, like his corporation brethren, made no objection to Edmondes. But while the corporation espoused Edmondes, Whitby stealthily worked among the citizenry, raising objections against Edmondes and gathering support for John Ratcliffe, an alderman and former mayor. The whole plot exploded in the corporation's face on election day, Christmas, 1620. After the mayor had nominated Edmondes to the assembled citizens, Whitby detonated his bombshell. Edmondes could not stand, Whitby claimed; since he was a nonresident and no freeman, he was ineligible to be elected! Ratcliffe, however, was most eligible; he was clearly the better choice. The corporation was helpless. The crowd was strongly behind Ratcliffe. Whitby had done his work well. The mayor claimed that the corporation was forced to give way to avoid a tumult. He may have been right; there was no doubt of Ratcliffe's popularity and support. Whitby gained his revenge and maintained Chester's election independence.[77]

The Prince's Council, however, had far more ambitious election schemes in 1624. In addition to its nominations through the Duchy of

Cornwall, it also made recommendations to thirteen other boroughs that involved its nomination of fifteen candidates. Little wonder that Charles's council ordered that its three messengers, carrying "sundry [electoral] letters into sundry parts of their kingdom" were to receive £10 each for their pains.[78]

Even though he controlled Bewdley manor, the prince made doubly sure of Bewdley's place by directing the earl of Northampton (who had been similarly employed by the prince at Chester in 1621) to make certain that Bewdley choose Ralph Clare, of the Prince's Chamber, as its member. Clare's nomination was a happy union of local and royal influence, since Clare held the lease on Bewdley manor from the crown and resided in the town when in Worcestershire. Given all these reasons, it is hardly surprising that Bewdley elected Clare.[79] Charles held the honors of Eye and Clare in Suffolk, which provided the foundations for his council's nomination of Francis Finch at Eye and Sir Francis Cottington at Bury St. Edmunds. Finch easily won election at Eye, but trouble developed at Bury. Cottington, as events would prove, would have the hardest time in finding a place. Indeed, his plight even attracted the attention of the famous London gossip John Chamberlain, who reported that although "the Prince has written to Bury and one or two places more for Sir Fran. Cottington and yet he is not provided." His record as a wandering candidate was hard to beat: he was nominated at Chester, Warwick, Bury St. Edmunds, and, at last with success, for Camelford, much, no doubt, to his relief! The reason, though, for his troubles at Bury are obscure. He was nominated there on 7 January, but within a week another letter had to be sent. Mallowes, Bury's steward, had assured the council of the town's willingness to choose Cottington, but he also pointed out that Bury already "purposed to make choice of Sir Thomas Jermyn," its usual member, for one place. The council assured Mallowes of the prince's esteem for Jermyn and urged Bury to elect them both. But something went wrong. Cottington, ready to rush off to Bury to take its freeman's oath, never got the chance. Bury returned Jermyn and Anthony Crofts, of an influential Suffolk family, instead. Perhaps Bury took Charles's approval of Jermyn as tantamount to a royal recommendation for Jermyn and decided that one such nominee was enough; perhaps it rebelled against the choice of any outsider, no matter who his patron happened to be. Jermyn, of nearby Rushbrooke, and Crofts might have simply refused to give way for Cottington. There is the chance, too, that news of Cottington's election at Camelford might have reached the council, which then could have informed Bury, allowing Crofts to join with Jermyn in the election.[80]

Poor Cottington. His chances at Chester were practically nil; its election in 1621 sealed the fate of any outside nominee, and in 1624 it was loyal to its enterprising recorder, Whitby, and John Savage, who was chosen more because of his family's Chester influence than because his brother was in the prince's service. Warwick, too, where Charles held the manor, elected representatives of Warwickshire families, Francis Lucy and Sir Edward Conway, junior, son of the principal secretary, Sir Edward Conway. At least Warwick's choice of Conway would satisfy the court; his county connections helped, but the backing of Fulke Greville, Baron Brooke, was probably decisive.[81]

Sampson Hopkins, one of Coventry's members in 1621, had established quite a reputation for himself within court circles for his outspoken criticism of the court. Lord Brooke wondered why Hopkins "was always so cross and violent in Parliament against the King's affairs," and, when planning for the elections of 1624, it may have been Hopkins's past performance that contributed to the prince's decision to nominate Sir Thomas Edmondes at Coventry. Brooke, well before the election, had hoped for Sampson's reformation, through the persuasion of his father, Sir Richard Hopkins, serjeant-at-law. But Sir Richard was not interested in converting his son, at least not yet. Indeed, he had complaints of his own: two judges, junior to him, had been promoted ahead of him to the Bench, but he promised that he would straighten out his son, along with "several others of his friends who went in the House of Commons as peevishly as his son did." Whether Sir Richard, the ambitious yet frustrated serjeant, could have stopped his son's mouth will never be known; Sampson was never again returned for Coventry. Apparently, he was not even a candidate in 1624, but Edmondes, possibly because of Hopkins's past actions, was.

Edmondes's chances at Coventry looked good. Shortly after his nomination, he was made a freeman of the town without any apparent trouble. His election seemed assured, but it became a three-way battle. Henry Harwell, alderman, mercer, and former mayor, and the great legal giant, Sir Edward Coke, Coventry's recorder, entered the race. Coke now seemed to be a clear opponent of the king, so much so that he had almost been shipped into exile in Ireland to keep him out of the forthcoming parliament! Coke's views were more attractive to Coventry than Edmondes's court reputation; the great judge and alderman Harwell were elected.[82]

Although the court may have made other nominations at Coventry, it was never a factor in its election history. Sir Edward Coke's position as recorder explains the choice of his son in 1614 and his own elections in 1624 and 1625, and the other burgesses for the borough through 1626 were local men from the town. In 1628, however, Coventry's frustrated and rebellious freemen overthrew the corporation's nominees and returned, instead, two neighboring squires. The court had no role to play at either Chester or Coventry.[83]

Charles also held the honor, lordship, castle, and forest of Knaresborough, the manor and town of Aldborough, the borough of Boroughbridge, the manor of Beverley, and the honor of Pontefract, properties and rights he intended to put to good use in the forthcoming election. In February, John Cartwright, the feodary of Pontefract honor, was ordered "to make known unto the Mayor & Bailiffs or other chief officers of the boroughs" whom the prince expected his Yorkshire towns to elect. Of his first five candidates, only Sir Henry Holcroft, nominated at Pontefract, and Sir Henry Vane, recommended to Beverley, were returned. Aldborough rejected William Peasley in favor of two Yorkshiremen, Christopher Wandesford of Kirklington and its legal agent, John Carvile. Boroughbridge turned down Charles's nominee, Sir Edmund Verney, of Charles's Privy Chamber, in favor of Sir Ferdinando Fairfax and a possible candidate of the Duchy of Lancaster, Sir Philip Mainwaring. Boroughbridge evidently decided that one stranger, Mainwaring, was enough. Knaresborough, too, remained loyal to traditional friends: it rejected Sir Arthur Mainwaring in favor of Sir Henry Slingsby of Scriven and Sir Richard Hutton of Goldsborough, neighbors of the borough. Charles, despite his holdings, discovered that Yorkshire's influential gentry were more powerful than his nominees, strangers to the north.[84]

Pontefract accepted the prince's candidate, Holcroft, who complicated matters by deciding to serve for Stockbridge, instead. The prince promptly nominated Robert Mynne to fill Holcroft's place. In the second election, three candidates vied for the borough's remaining burgess-ship: Mynne, Sir Richard Beaumont, and the town's legal adviser, Sir John Jackson, a close friend of Sir Thomas Wentworth, who had been chiefly responsible for the restoration of Pontefract as a parliamentary borough. The contest quickly became a bitter struggle between Beaumont and Jackson. The mayor and some of the aldermen favored Jackson and, it was claimed, recruited a number of recusants, brought them into Pontefract, and made them burgesses so as to ensure Jackson's triumph. Not content with that, on election day the mayor and his followers refused to let any of Beaumont's friends enter Mote Hall, the site of the election. The sheriff, apparently determined to avoid trouble at all costs, made a double return of both Jackson and Beaumont, washing his hands of the whole affair and inviting the House of Commons to make the final judgment. Beaumont's followers, as might be expected, petitioned the House, and the election was overturned since no poll was taken nor was there any clear understanding of just who was eligible to vote. As the House so often did, it solved the latter question by ordering that all the inhabitants, householders and residents alike, should have a voice. Finally, after all this fuss, Jackson was again elected. Beaumont, an inveterate gambler, lost as usual. Mynne played no role at all; Pontefract, after accepting Holcroft, ignored Mynne altogether.[85] Only little Beverley accepted the prince's candidates without protest, possibly because it did not want to endanger its chances of a new charter. It obediently elected Vane, and, when he chose to sit for Carlisle, it dutifully returned Charles's second nominee, Sir Henry Carey, the eldest son of Lord Leppington, later created (1626) earl of Monmouth. Carey had already served for Camelford, with the prince's support through the Duchy of Cornwall, in 1621.[86]

At St. Albans, the Prince's Council found itself involved with Francis Bacon, viscount St. Albans, and William Cecil, second earl of Salisbury. First, the prince nominated John Maynard, but, when he was placed elsewhere, his council recommended Sir Thomas Edmondes and urged both Bacon and Salisbury to back him with all their power. Bacon's efforts were not enough, and Salisbury ignored the council's plea. He nominated Sir John Luke, and Edmondes lost the election. Salisbury must not have endeared himself to the prince for his refusal to abandon Luke. Sir Arthur Capel, junior, a Hertfordshire resident, took the other place. Maynard, a favorite of Buckingham's, was chosen at Chippenham, probably through the influence of the Bayntun family. Maynard's sister had married Sir Edward Bayntun of Broham, Wiltshire, who held among his substantial county properties lands in and near Chippenham.[87]

The prince's election plans even included the restoration of Hertford as a parliamentary borough. In the whole of Elizabeth's reign and that of her first two Stuart successors, Hertford's restoration was unique, coming not as the result of local pressures but as the consequences of court intervention. Although a part of the Duchy of Lancaster, the manor and castle had been leased to the prince in 1609; and it was his council that initiated Hertford's restoration as a parliamentary borough, urging the town to "prepare a petition for reviving the said privilege this parliament and send it up unto us." The Prince's Council promised all its support for Hertford; indeed, it would do so without charge. But there was, after all, a price for Hertford, as it soon discovered. The council nominated, for

Hertford's eventual election, Sir John Hobart and Christopher Vernon, the prince's "officer in his Majesty's Exchequer." Hobart, however, was chosen at Loswithiel, and Vernon's employment, the council claimed, precluded his attendance in parliament. In their place it nominated Sir William Harrington, the prince's steward at Hertford, "a near neighbour unto you."[88] Lord Keeper Williams also intervened, asking the great local patron, William, earl of Salisbury, to support William Wynn, one of the lord keeper's servants. Salisbury refused; he was "already engaged for William Ashton, an old servant and annuitant of his father." Many of Hertford's citizens also pressured the earl, asking him to back Thomas Fanshawe of Ware Park, Hertfordshire, for one of the borough's burgess-ships. Salisbury, keeping a keen eye on his own favor in Hertford, promised that he would refuse to nominate anyone that might contend with Fanshawe for a place. When Hertford finally held its election, Harrington received the least support of any of the candidates. Ashton won the first seat with 103 votes, followed by Willows, a borough burgess, with 58, and Harrington with 42. In the poll for the second place, the mayor (who had voted for Ashton before) cast his voice for Harrington, but influenced hardly anyone else to support the prince's nominee. Fanshawe easily won with 101 voices. Willows again was second, and Harrington finished a poor third with 48 votes.[89] As so often happened at other boroughs where the Prince's Council intervened, local interests proved too strong for the council to overcome. It was humiliating. Hertford's parliamentary privileges had been restored, thanks to the Prince's Council's diligence, yet its candidate was summarily rejected. Obviously, the council's price was too high for Hertford to pay; its attempt to secure a safe borough for its candidates had backfired.

The Prince's Council was not a very successful election agent. Its story, though, and that of the Duchy of Cornwall, too, is a useful one: it offers positive testimony of a unique early Stuart development: the electioneering of the central government. No official, like Sir Humphrey May or Edward Lord Zouch, was involved in the electoral process; the court, itself, through the prince's officers, was responsible. In 1621 it intervened at Chester and Bewdley; in 1624 it was far more ambitious: it nominated fifteen candidates at thirteen boroughs but with scant success. Only Eye, Bewdley, Beverley, and, in its first election, Pontefract, accepted the prince's nominees. And Pontefract, in its second election, ignored the prince's candidate. Explanations for such failures are not hard to find. Of the fifteen candidates, only two, Clare and Harrington, had any link with their prospective boroughs; and, as Harrington's defeat showed, that might not even be enough. Ten boroughs, if we add Pontefract, preferred local men to outsiders, an indication that the influence of a neighboring squire was far harder to resist than that of a distant court. The story of the Prince's Council illustrates a court agency's electioneering and its problems: the antagonism that the nomination of outsiders aroused and the strength of the local gentry that combined to make it difficult, if not impossible, to place such candidates in borough elections. Parochial interests were too powerful, the strength of the county community too great, even for the prestige of the prince and his council to overcome.[90]

## 4. The Council of the North and Elections, 1614–1628

As James's first election showed, the lord president of the council, Edmund, Baron Sheffield, was an energetic election patron. Unfortunately, his influence in 1614 and that of his successor as lord president, Emanuel, Lord Scrope, in the elections of 1621–28, is difficult, if not impossible, to assess with accuracy. Evidence is sadly lacking; of the boroughs that the council's electioneering might affect, only York, Scarborough, and Hull possess manuscript sources that permit investigation of their electoral history, and they are incomplete. Furthermore, the lord presidents were members of Yorkshire's nobility, which raises the question of patronage responsibility. If a Sheffield or Scrope nomination was successful, was it because of their own prestige or their influence as lord president? Finally, many of those elected were Yorkshire's leading gentry and, as such, often served on the Council of the North. It was as much a part of their lives as leaders of county society as their employment in the office of sheriff, deputy lieutenant, or justice of the peace. But that hardly means that the council's influence was predominant in their election; their own prestige and connections explained their choice. Service on the council was, for most of them, simply recognition of their Yorkshire status.[91]

Sheffield and the council were, as in 1604, active patrons in 1614. Positive evidence can only be found for Scarborough but it seems likely that Yorkshire, Ripon, Aldborough, Beverley, Hedon, Thirsk, and Richmond were subjected to council intervention. Given Sheffield's enthusiastic backing for Sir John Savile in 1604, it is probable that the council once again lent its support to the return of Sir John and his partner, Sir Thomas Wentworth, for the county. Sheffield wrote to Scarborough's corporation to reserve a place, "the like courtesy having been often afforded to my predecessors heretofore." He wanted Scarborough to send him a blank return at York, explaining that as "the usual course held with other noblemen who obtain the like from corporations in countries where they have command." Sheffield's intervention paid off; Scarborough returned his nominee, Mr. Edward Smith, and William Conyers, a lawyer like Smith, whose father was a borough bailiff. A third candidate, Sir John Suckling, the courtier and royal official, was rejected, despite the support he received from Sir Henry Griffiths of Burton Agnes.[92]

Hedon's election also showed sure signs of council success. It elected Sheffield's son, William, and an outsider, Clement Coke, a son of the famous jurist Sir Edward Coke. Thirsk's choice of a courtier, Sir Robert Yaxley, may have been the result of council persuasion, which might also explain Ripon's return of Sir Thomas Vavasour, knight marshal of the Household. Vavasour's election is a perfect example of the difficulties of assessing election patronage. Although of a Yorkshire family, he spent most of his time in London and served as a justice of the peace for Kent in 1608. Boroughbridge, presumably because of the earl of Salisbury's intervention, had elected him in 1609, and he was, in 1614, also chosen for Horsham, thanks to the earl of Arundel's support. Given his preferences for the court and the south, it seems very likely that his choice at Ripon can only be explained through the council's patronage. Beverley's election of an outsider, William Towse, was another example of likely council success. Towse regularly served for Colchester in the next four parliaments after becoming its town clerk in 1618. He lacked any connection with Yorkshire, and his promotion to serjeant-at-law after his loyal labors in the Parliament of 1614 testified to the crown's favor. Sir Richard Williamson, steward of East Retford and a master of requests, may have owed his choice at Richmond to council backing, and the same may be said for Aldborough's election of one John Wethered in 1614. Wethered may have been a kinsman of George Wethered, who served as an examiner of causes for the Council of the North. Sir Thomas Wentworth, before the Yorkshire election of 1621, wrote to George Wethered, urging him to "move him [my lord—probably Scrope, the lord president] thoroughly to deal with Sir Henry Constable and Sir Thomas Fairfax of Gilling" to further Wentworth's (and Calvert's) cause. Two years later, Wentworth recommended a "Mr. Wetheridd" to Cranfield, the lord treasurer, for a post as collector of the king's revenue. Another Wethered, Francis, served as "surveyor of his Majesty's Stables" between 1626 and 1639. Given George Wethered's position and the family's apparent lack of influence in Yorkshire affairs, it is probable that John Wethered's election for Aldborough was due to council intervention.[93] Sheffield, as council president, was a fairly successful electioneer. In the first two elections of James's reign, as many as twenty places could be credited to such intervention.

Before James's third election, the Council of the North had a new president, Emanuel, Lord Scrope, who was named to replace Sheffield in 1619. Scrope's appointment was, for many Yorkshiremen, further evidence of the increasingly pro-Catholic policies being pursued by the court. Sheffield had favored coercion, a hard line, against recusants; Scrope, a supposed Papist himself, did not. Indeed, his religious sympathies were so suspect that Sir Thomas Hoby bitterly complained to the Commons in 1625 of the increase in Yorkshire recusancy, implying that Scrope was to blame. Scrope "came to be regarded as a protector of the Catholic community north of the Trent"; and, in a county in which the Catholic question had always been important and potentially divisive, the issue could only grow in significance as the allegedly pro-Catholic policies of the Stuarts became more apparent. And there were enough signs of such a policy: Charles's courtships involved Europe's two great Catholic powers; the penal laws had been relaxed; and Scrope had been made lord president, a clear example of the court's attitude for many Yorkshiremen. The decline of the council's electoral influence begins with Scrope's administration. It is intriguing to speculate on just what effect the appointment of a suspected Papist had on the council's patronage; it does not appear to have been salutory.[94] In 1621 its nominees may have been returned at Scarborough and Boroughbridge, and Sir William Alford, had he chosen to serve for Scarborough in 1625, would have owed his place to Scrope's support. Only Richmond, in 1628, returned a council nominee, and in 1624 and 1626 there is nothing to suggest that the council enjoyed any electoral success whatever. But though the impact of Scrope's religious sympathies on the council's record can only remain an intriguing speculation, the strength of Yorkshire's gentry can be readily revealed through a summary of borough electoral patterns between 1621 and 1628.

Boroughbridge, Aldborough, and Ripon, in Elizabeth's reign and during Sheffield's administration, had frequently been influenced by the Council of the North. Their stories, though, change between 1621 and 1628. Ripon's electoral tale was that of Sir Thomas Hoby and Sir William Mallory, who controlled its representation. Hoby was chief seneschal of Ripon manor, a church appointment, from 1616 to 1629. To explain his success by that alone seems dangerous, but it could be done. He lived at Hackness, near Scarborough; his neighborly influence led to his election there in 1604. But after becoming chief seneschal at Ripon, he was returned there for the next five parliaments, 1621–28.

His own family prestige and the support of the archbishops probably explain Ripon's constant favor. Mallory's family, on the other hand, were near and influential neighbors. Although part of their lands were held of the archbishop and members of the family occasionally served as stewards of Ripon for him, their own prestige accounted for their election predominance. Sir William Mallory was returned in 1621, 1624, 1625, and 1628; a kinsman by marriage, Thomas Best, was elected at Ripon in 1626.[95]

Yorkshire's squirearchy controlled Aldborough's elections with one possible exception, the election of Henry Darley in 1628. Darley, of Buttercrambe, may have been nominated by one of Sheffields's (then earl of Mulgrave) sons, Sir William Sheffield, who had tried, unsuccessfully as it turned out, to place him at Scarborough in the same election. In 1621 Wentworth suggested to Sir Henry Savile, who was anxiously seeking a burgess-ship, that he "try your ancient power with them of Aldborough," where Savile had served before (1604, 1614). But there is nothing to suggest that Wentworth went any further and sought the aid of Lord Scrope or Calvert in Savile's behalf at Aldborough as he did at Richmond. Savile's "ancient power" failed him; Aldborough returned two other Yorkshiremen, Christopher Wandesford and John Carvile, the town's legal representative in London.[96] Boroughbridge's election of George Wethered in 1621 was the only sign of probable council interference in its elections since, save for possible Duchy of Lancaster intervention for Philip Mainwaring (1624–26), it, too, had surrendered to neighboring squires, especially Sir Ferdinando Fairfax of Denton (1614–28); but the other two men it elected, George Marshall (1614) and Francis Neville (1628), had Yorkshire ties, which explained their choice.[97]

Two other boroughs, Thirsk and Beverley, also escaped the council's influence after 1614. With the exception of the choice of Sir William Sheffield in 1624 and Henry Stanley in 1625, the Belasyse family controlled Thirsk's returns. Sheffield was presumably the nominee of his father, Lord Sheffield, the former lord president, and Stanley's election apparently reflected the will of the owner of the Thirsk manor, William Stanley, the earl of Derby. Lord Scrope nominated one of Beverley's burgesses (1625, 1626, 1628), Sir William Alford, at Scarborough in 1625, but his elections for Beverley were due to his own influence; he lived only four miles from the town, at Meaux Abbey. Save for the successful intervention of the Prince's Council in 1624, Beverley was under the control of country squires, particularly the Hothams.[98]

The Council of the North had very little success at Richmond. At Wentworth's request both Calvert and Lord Scrope tried to place Sir Henry Savile there in 1621, but "Sir Tho. Wharton's predominant power with our Aldermen seconded with earnest solicitation of other the burgesses and an undertaking to free the town from all check of my Lo: President and Mr. Secretary Calvert" cost Savile the place. Scrope succeeded, however, in 1628 when Richmond returned his secretary, James Howells, who was later employed by Wentworth in Ireland and held a variety of court posts. Richmond was crown property. Lord Scrope was its bailiff, steward, and constable of its castle, yet the power of the Bowes family, who resided at Aske, three miles from Richmond, was so great that the 1628 election was the only one in which Scrope's influence was felt.[99]

Scarborough's elections in 1621, 1624, and 1625 attracted the council's attention, although with mixed results. Sir Richard Cholmley, chosen in 1621, probably owed his election to his kinsman, Lord Scrope, since despite Cholmley's Yorkshire connections, it was his first parliamentary appearance. The council tried to repeat its success in 1624 when two council members, Sir George Ellis and Sir Thomas Tildesley, who was the king's attorney for the county Palatine of Lancaster and vice chancellor of the Duchy of Lancaster, nominated solicitor Richard Osbaldeston of York and London. Osbaldeston was a cousin of Ellis, who urged his friends at Scarborough to support Osbaldeston's candidacy. It was all for nothing since, despite his county ties and council support, Osbaldeston was not elected. Lord Scrope recommended Sir William Alford in 1625, promising the bailiffs that Alford would serve "without any charge to you." The bailiffs accepted, reporting their "friendly intentions . . . towards me [Alford] for a burgesses's place"; but since he had already been chosen at Beverley, Alford turned Scarborough down but promised to tell Lord Scrope of its "forwardness to satisfy his desire." Scarborough's 1625 election was not without other complications since Lord Sheffield was also involved. Indeed, Sheffield even won the port's promise to defer its election until he could name his nominee. Scrope was worried and upset; he could not understand why the port preferred Sheffield's request since he was "more able to do a courtesy for the town." Scrope's fears were groundless; Alford could have served for Scarborough, and Sheffield's eventual nominee, Sir Edward Waterhouse, was refused.[100] Although Scarborough continued in 1626 and 1628 to attract numerous and influential patrons for its burgess-ships, nothing indicates that the Council of the North ever tried to influence either election. Scarborough remained loyal to Hugh Cholmley in 1626 and joined him with another neighbor, Steven Hutchinson of Wykeham Abbey, who had "ever deemed myself a member of the town as being a freeman amongst you." In 1628 Buckingham, whose bid for both Scarborough's places in 1626 had failed, was probably behind the return of the customs farmer, John Harrison, and Sheffield, now earl of Mulgrave, saw to Sir William Constable's choice.[101]

In Yorkshire elections Scrope and the council played some part, at least in 1621 and 1625, but it was hardly the decisive role Sheffield and the council performed in 1604. Sir Thomas Wentworth sought and won Scrope's aid in 1621 and even urged Scrope to "show himself for you [Sir George Calvert, on election day] in the Castle Yard" to ensure Calvert "of fair carriage in the choice." The lord president of the Council of the North, after all, was still "the most powerful nobleman north of Trent," and, as such, Wentworth paid considerable attention to Scrope's influence in the heated Yorkshire election of 1621. Sir Thomas Fairfax, in 1625, also turned to Scrope for help, complaining to him of the "scandalous and seducing letters" employed by the Saviles in the county election. There can be no doubt, though, that the Council of the North, especially from 1621 onward, had little impact on either county or borough elections.[102]

What explanations might be offered to account for the council's demise as an election patron? As was the case elsewhere—the Duchy of Lancaster, for example—much depended on the reputation and place-seeking enthusiasm of the lord president. Sheffield scored higher on both counts than Scrope. Indeed, as has been briefly noted, Sheffield, earl of Mulgrave from 1626, remained an active, although not always successful, patron, even after his replacement as lord president. Scrope's religious sympathies aroused misgivings, and, although it is impossible to judge just what precise effect it had on the council's patronage, it may have contributed to the near disappearance of its electoral influence. But, in all probability, the major reason was the competition for places provided by Yorkshire's squirearchy. And it proved to be too much for the Council of the North. Richmond's 1621 election provided a case in point. It was decided by Sir Thomas Wharton, whose promise "to free the town from all check of my Lo: President and Mr. Secretary Calvert" proved decisive. Wharton's promise, more than anything else, tells the story. The Whartons, Slingsbys, Bensons, Wentworths, Hildyards, Hothams, and Bowes, to name but a few, had captured Yorkshire's county and borough representation.[103]

## 5. The Council of the Marches of Wales and Elections, 1614–1628

In 1617 Edward Lord Zouch was succeeded by William Lord Compton as president of the Council of the Marches of Wales. Zouch and Compton (earl of Northampton from 1618) enjoyed little success as electioneers from 1614 to 1628; indeed, of all the crown's agencies, the Council of the Marches was the least effective The competition from the powerful earl of Pembroke and his Welsh relatives and from the proud Welsh gentry was too great. The council had practically no Elizabethan influence. In 1604 Zouch and the council could claim credit for one place at Shrewsbury, a success the council never repeated. Ludlow was the council's headquarters, and although its 1604 election showed no trace of intervention, from 1614 to 1628 one of its burgesses was either a council official or nominee.

Ludlow's story in Elizabeth's reign was one of proud and determined independence, a tradition it maintained in 1604 and again in 1609, when it refused the nominees of both the earl of Salisbury and Lord Eure. In 1614 it bade fair to continue its custom, returning Robert Berry and Sir Henry Townshend. Berry, a bailiff and porter of the castle, had served Ludlow in six previous parliaments, and Townshend, although a member of the council and justice of Chester, had been Ludlow's recorder since 1577. Richard Tomlyns, who had been born in Ludlow, was refused since he was not a burgess. Ludlow's corporation had again staunchly opposed the choice of any outsider, even one born in the borough. During the election the corporation restated its determination that its burgesses "shall be elected out of the 12 and 25, councillors and capital burgesses of this town" and chose Townshend "one of the company of the 25 common councillors" in order to maintain its pledge. Townshend responded with a suitable gift and went off, with Berry, to Westminster, where trouble erupted over Berry's return.

Berry's election was overthrown by the House of Commons since he had returned himself a burgess, something the House would not allow. Ludlow's independence ended in its bye-election to replace Berry. It returned one Robert Lloyd, a "sewer to the Queen's Most Excellent Majesty" who was admitted freeman "gratis" and chosen, as the corporation minute book succinctly put it, "for good causes." The council had intervened; Lloyd was a stranger in Ludlow's terms but he would serve without pay, "any former order heretofore made to the contrary notwithstanding for this time and parliament only." So much for Ludlow's brave resolutions; its independence, so resolutely defended in the past, was gone. It would not be won back.[104]

Ludlow elected one of its own and a council nominee from 1621 to 1628. The local member was a London resident, Richard Tomlyns, who had taken pains to be admitted a member of the corporation and then, in the 1621 election, probably assured his return by promising to serve without pay. He also pointed out "that long since I had a purpose out of my poor estate to do some good for the town. It may be in part while I live, but sure after my decease." He made good on his promise since, in 1650, the town found itself mixed up in a legal fight over Tomlyns' charitable bequest to his birthplace. The council's nominee in 1621 was the lord president's son, Spencer Lord Compton. The return violated Ludlow's standing orders, but the orders were "for this time only void. And the same orders forever hereafter shall stand in their full force and efficiency as they did before time." No doubt the corporation's conscience was soothed by this pious hope. Ralph Goodwin and Tomlyns served together from 1624 to 1628, although Tomlyns ran into some trouble in 1624. Rumour claimed he was "inclinable to Popery, and will (if he be chosen) expect or sue for his charges of attendance in Parliament." The corporation hotly and successfully denied the claims; Goodwin and Tomlyns were chosen, and the corporation's orders were again declared "for this time only made void." Goodwin, although a resident, was a career official in the Council of Wales. He first served as an examiner in the court of the Marches and later became deputy secretary and clerk of the council, a post he held for sixteen years. Goodwin and Tomlyns always served without pay, perhaps the most important factor in explaining Ludlow's surprising fall from grace as an independent borough. But Ludlow enjoyed one distinction: it became the only borough where the Council of the Marches of Wales enjoyed electoral influence.[105]

In Wales the council had little, if any, electoral authority. The fiercely competitive Welsh gentry battled each other for parliamentary places, although, in central and south Wales, the earl of Pembroke and his kinsmen enjoyed a dominant electoral influence. If a locally significant landowner was frustrated in his search for a knightship of a shire, he turned, and with a vengeance, to the boroughs; and there were not enough to go around, or so it must have seemed. A. H. Dodd was right in defining Welsh election struggles as microcosms of "the wars and diplomatic manoeuvres to maintain the balance of power in Europe."![106] There was no room for the Council of Wales in such a faction-ridden election arena, and its lack of influence shows, perhaps better than anything else, the rugged independence and bitter individualism of Welsh politics.

Perhaps the absence of council influence was best illustrated during the hard-fought battle for Caernarvonshire's places in 1621 between the Wynns of Gwydir and the Griffiths of Cefnamlwch. Apparently, neither side sought the aid of the lord president of the council, although he did intervene. The zealous electioneering of Lewis Bayly, bishop of Bangor, whose enthusiasm for the Wynns was more than a man of God should show, or so Northampton seemingly believed, won the bishop a strongly worded caution from the lord president. Indeed, Bayly's ardor had gotten him into so much trouble that Lord Chancellor Bacon had seen a petition protesting the bishop's electoral efforts; the same petition was perhaps resting on Northampton's desk as he wrote. The sheriff of Caernarvonshire had brought Northampton a copy of it. The contest threatened to become so volatile that Northampton kept the king and the Privy Council abreast of developments and warned the sheriff and justices of Caernarvonshire that if "factious persons be suffered to carry weapons in the town when the said election shall be, that blood and breach of his Majesty's peace may ensue therein if great care be not had to prevent the same." The only armed men must be, Northampton ordered, the Sheriff and his servants "in livery"; and if anyone else bore arms, they would answer for it to the Council of Wales. The council's sole function, it seemed, was to maintain the king's peace and prevent the factions from attacking each other. Its election patronage was not involved.[107]

By 1622 there was evidence of Northampton's favor for John Griffith, which may account for the Wynn' earnest solicitation of Sir James Whitelocke's support for their candidates in the 1624 elections. Whitelocke, an active member of the Council of the Marches of Wales, was at such odds with the lord president, Northampton, that he was finally transferred to the King's Bench in 1624. Maybe one source of disagreement was the Wynn-Griffith feud, but, at any rate, it was to Whitelocke the Wynns turned, not to the lord president. They advised their friend, Sir Roger Mostyn" to "procure Sir James Whitelocke's letter to the justices of the peace of their county [Anglesey] in the behalf of [his son] Jack Mostyn" for the election. Sir Roger finally agreed, and although Whitelocke's response is not certainly known, John Mostyn was returned for Anglesey in 1624.

Northampton and the council played no apparent role. Whitelocke's intervention was personal and clearly not council business. Perhaps the Wynns, and the Mostyns too, were out of favor with Northampton; perhaps, too, the council's influence simply was not great enough to be an electoral factor.[108]

Sir Peter Mutton and Sir Edward Littleton, judges on the North Wales circuit, won the Wynns backing for the county and borough elections in Caernarvonshire in 1626 but not because they had the support of Northampton or the Council of Wales. They had, however, the influence of Bishop Bayly and the lord keeper, John Williams, behind them, but their own prestige and office was more important. Sir William Thomas emphasized their power in consultations with Sir John Wynn. If Wynn, Thomas, and their allies failed to back Mutton and Littleton, they could "withdraw their favours for the assizes from that place that did oppose them"; furthermore, they could have their revenge, through their office, against "such particular persons as will not cleave to their side." The council and its lord president were not mentioned in any of the surviving election correspondence.[109]

The Welsh gentry and, to some extent, the earl of Pembroke and his family, held the election power that counted in Wales. However, if membership in the Council of Wales was counted as the major reason for electoral success, then the council would have had an incredible patronage record. But to say that is folly. Early Stuart government, like its immediate successor, lacked the resources, and perhaps the will, to organize and maintain an expensive body of servants and officials to staff its agencies, maintain its peace, and man its military. Instead, it relied upon the loyalty and service of its squirearchy to perform many of the functions a civil service or corps of professional administrators would otherwise undertake. The offices of sheriff, deputy lieutenant, and justice of the peace were hardly staffed by bureaucrats; they were filled by country gentlemen who undertook, by dint of their economic situation, marriage ties, birth, and, perhaps most of all, their well-developed social instinct — their determination to make their mark within county society — to fulfill those administrative and judicial functions. The crown, to mark such status and achievement, rewarded them with places on the Council of the North or the Council of the Marches of Wales, signifying both its favor and their standing within the county community. It was this influence, prestige, and connection that most often brought local gentry to Westminster to parliament, the most prestigious sign of a local squire's position in society. The Councils of Wales and the North greatly depended on local men of influence and stature who dominated the election scene by reason of their importance and not because of their council service.[110] A council position did not detract from a man's parliamentary prospects, but it did not make his election certain or even more likely. It was, more often than not, simply a mark of his own achievements, a reward for loyal, unpaid service rendered to a distant court. Ludlow was a borough for the Council of the Marches of Wales; it was the only one. Welsh and Shropshire families, be they on the council or not, dominated the elections.

### 6. The Privy Council and Elections, 1614–1628

No discussion of court electioneering would be complete without a summary of the Privy Council's role. Its electioneering outside the capital was negligible; its intervention in the Essex election of 1628, discussed elsewhere, is the only certain example. In 1614 the council was probably behind the return of Sir Humphrey May for Westminster, James Button for Bewdley, and London's choice of its recorder, Sir Henry Montagu. Montagu was not, however, returned without opposition; at first the city refused him because "he is the King's serjeant." A compromise was worked out between the court and the city, and Montagu was finally elected. Succeeding recorders, Sir Robert Heath (1621) and Sir Heneage Finch (1624–26), were returned without any known difficulty. In 1628, though, the story abruptly changed; the outrage aroused by the forced loan cost Finch his accustomed place. London's voters were "very unruly, not only passing by the Recorder and others but disgracing them with public outcries." Finch was refused "with great disgrace" because he had "relation to whom [the crown] they do not affect." London, like neighboring Westminster, preferred two known opponents of the court, James Bunce, an alderman "lately in prison for the loan," and Henry Waller, one of Sir John Eliot's friends. London's traditional election of its crown-appointed recorder was over.[111]

Middlesex may have also been under the Privy Council's influence before Buckingham became its lord lieutenant in 1622. In 1614 four men were candidates at Middlesex: the council's likely nominees, Sir Julius Caesar and Thomas Lake, Sir Walter Cope, and Sir Francis Darcy. Cope withdrew, presumably because of crown pressure and the promise of a Stockbridge burgess-ship; and although Darcy also stepped down, he apparently refused to follow the crown's wish that he publicly support Caesar and Lake. On election day one of Darcy's servants did his best to stir up trouble by announcing that Darcy's candidature had been blocked by the king and urging his master's followers "to give their voices to Master Chancellor [Caesar], and for the second place to do as God should put in their minds." Lake, however, was still returned, although the servant's action indicated that an appeal to anti-courtier sentiments was considered a useful electoral tactic, an attitude that the furious Privy Council's actions, in having Darcy's man "committed and his master called in question for the message," endorsed.[112] Darcy had his revenge in 1621. Caesar and Sir Thomas Edmonds "made all the means they could to have been knights of the shire for Middlesex" but to no avail. The freeholders, believing "they could not have access to such great persons as Privy Councillors," preferred their neighbors, Darcy and Sir Gilbert Gerrard, instead. The 1621 election was the last sign of council intervention in Middlesex. Altogether, the council's nominees probably took five places in 1614 and one place, at London, in each succeeding election until 1628, when even London turned down its candidate.[113]

## Summary: The Court as an Election Patron

The table below indicates the certain, probable, and possible electoral patronage of the court for the elections of 1604–28.

ELECTION INVOLVEMENT

| Patron | 1604 | 1614 | 1621 | 1624 | 1625 | 1626 | 1628 |
|---|---|---|---|---|---|---|---|
| D. Cornwall | — | 10 | 15 | 15 | — | — | — |
| D. Lancaster | 8 | 9 | 10 | 13 | 10 | 10 | 8 |
| Prince's C. | — | — | 2 | 13 | — | — | — |
| C. North | 7 | 8 | 4 | 1 | 2 | — | 1 |
| C. M. Wales | 1 | 1 | 1 | 1 | 1 | 1 | 1 |
| Privy C. | 3 | 4 | 2 | 1 | 1 | 1 | 2 |
| Ld. Wd. | 7 | 7 | 7 | 7 | 7 | 7 | 7 |
| Totals | 26 | 39 | 41 | 51 | 21 | 19 | 19 |

Places won, or possibly or probably won, through court intervention

| | | | | | | | |
|---|---|---|---|---|---|---|---|
| D. Cornwall | — | 12 | 14 | 10 | — | — | — |
| D. Lancaster | 9 | 10 | 11 | 16 | 12 | 12 | 9 |
| Prince's C. | — | — | 1 | 4 | — | — | — |
| C. North | 9 | 10 | 2 | — | — | — | 1 |
| C. M. Wales | 1 | 1 | 1 | 1 | 1 | 1 | 1 |
| Privy C. | 2 | 5 | 1 | 1 | 1 | 1 | — |
| Ld. Wd. | 7 | 10 | 10 | 10 | 8 | 5 | 6 |
| Totals | 28 | 48 | 40 | 42 | 22 | 19 | 17 |

On average, in each election from 1604 through 1628, the court intervened in 31 elections and secured 31 places. Its "vintage" years for electoral intervention were in 1614 (39), 1621 (41), and 1624 (51) when it gained more places (48 in 1614, 40 in 1621, and 42 in 1624) than it did in any other election. And although the figures given in many cases are tentative at best, its dependence on the Duchy of Cornwall and the Prince's Council is clearly illustrated by the higher figures attained in both categories when the prince's agencies were electoral patrons. Without such help the court's electioneering was practically negligible. Its intervention peaked in 1624, when it was probably involved in 51 elections, or nearly 20 percent of all elections held, whereas in 1614 its agencies can be credited with capturing as many as 48 places, or 10.3 percent of all places available in that election.[114] Patronage in Cornwall after 1624, became the province of the local gentry and aristocratic patrons like the earl of Pembroke and the duke of Buckingham. But the patronage possibilities for the court were clearly not forgotten since, with the birth of an heir and the reestablishment of the Prince's Council, the electoral interference of that council and the duchy was a significant part of the court's campaign in the 1640 elections.

A combination of factors merged to make Bacon's suggestions for court electioneering much less effective than might have been expected. The power of the local gentry and their determination to retain their grip on elections was too much for the court's agencies to overcome. Indeed, the court's interference probably stimulated neighborhood loyalties to an even higher pitch, especially when a local candidate was challenged by a stranger; and the court's candidates were usually strangers. Of the 276 court nominees that can be identified from 1604 to 1628, 177, or 64.1 percent, were outsiders. When that problem was mixed with the growing animosity court policy aroused within the county community, it became all the more difficult to challenge local electoral influence. The court's agencies could not, as the elections indicate, truly compete with the power of the neighboring gentry for places at Westminster. The gentry's ambition and prestige brought them offices as justices of the peace, deputy lieutenants or sheriffs; they would not allow the highest prize, a place at Westminster, to escape them.[115]

1. C. Ross, *Edward IV* (London, 1974), pp. 342–45; S. E. Lehmberg, *The Reformation Parliament, 1529–1536*, pp. 13, 169–70, and his *The Later Parliaments of Henry VIII, 1536–1547* (Cambridge, 1977), pp. 3–7, 9, 41–47, 49–50; Neale, *Elizabethan House of Commons*, pp. 233–45, 282–300. There is certain evidence of court electioneering for the Parliaments of 1621, 1624, and the Short and Long Parliaments of 1640, and it seems most probable that the elections to the Addled Parliament of 1614 received similar attention.

2. See sections 1–3 below.

3. More to Winwood, 29 Oct. 1611, *HMC Buccleuch*, 1:101–2; Neville's advice to James I, 1612, P.R.O., St. P. Dom. 14/74:44; Moir, *Addled Parliament*, pp. 12–15, 17–20; Bacon to the King, 31 May 1612, Spedding, *Bacon*, 4:279–80; Willson, *Privy Councillors*, pp. 132–37; Prestwich, *Cranfield*, p. 138.

4. Spedding, *Bacon*, 4:365–73; Prestwich, *Cranfield*, pp. 138–40; Willson, *Privy Councillors*, pp. 134–35.

5. James was probably quite willing to intervene in elections. He had created new Irish boroughs *en masse* before the Irish Parliament of 1613 to ensure a Protestant majority and also actively intervened in Scottish parliamentary elections (Willson, *James VI & I*, pp. 314, 328; Lake to an Unnamed Nobleman, 19 Feb. 1614, BM Cottonian MSS, Titus F. iv, f. 337, in Nichols, *Progresses*, 2:755). The figures are taken from Appendix Two.

6. Chamberlain to Carleton, 3 Mar., 14 Apr., 12, 19 May, 1614, McClure, ed., *Chamberlain's Letters*, 1:515–16, 526, 528, and P.R.O., St. P. Dom. 14/77:26; Throckmorton to

Trumbull, 1 Apr. 1614, *HMC Downshire*, 4:363; Moir, *Addled Parliament*, pp. 108, 109; Willson, *Privy Councillors*, pp. 142–46; *HMC Hastings*, 4:232–33, 240; BM Cottonian MSS, Titus F. iv, fols. 351–352v; Notestein, et al., eds., *Commons Debates, 1621*, 7:634; Holles to Lord Norrice, 28 Apr. 1614, *HMC Portland*, 9:27–28; Wentworth to Wm. Wentworth, 5 Apr. 1614, Sheffield City Library, Wentworth Woodhouse MSS, 21(7).

7. Spedding, *Bacon*, 5:194–207; Minutes of the Council Meeting of 28 Sept. 1615, P.R.O., St. P. Dom. 14/81:115; Willson, *Privy Councillors*, pp. 35–40; Prestwich, *Cranfield*, pp. 138–40, 151.

8. Their original draft of the 1603 proclamation summoning parliament called for the election of "free men of the cities, boroughs, or places for which they shall be chosen" or, at least, county residents.

9. Spedding, *Bacon*, 7:114–17, 123, 127–28; *CSPV, 1619–1621*, p. 440; Buckingham to Bacon, 19 Oct. 1620, BM Harleian MSS 7,000, f. 27; "Proclamation of 6 Nov. 1620," P.R.O., St. P. Dom. 14/187:86; Rymer, *Foedera*, 17:270–71; Chamberlain to Carleton, 9 Nov. 1620, Nichols, *Progresses*, 4:628; Birch, *Court and Times of James I*, 2:214.

10. Chamberlain to Carleton, 4 Nov. 1620, P.R.O., St. P. Dom. 14/117:59, in McClure, ed., *Chamberlain's Letters*, 2:325, Nichols, *Progresses*, 4:628, and Birch, *Court and Times of James I*, 2:211; "Proclamation of 6 Nov. 1620", P.R.O., St. P. Dom. 14/187:86; in Rymer, *Foedera*, 17:270–71.

11. Bacon to Buckingham, 16 Dec. 1620, Bodleian Library, Tanner MSS 290, f. 43, in Spedding, *Bacon*, 7:152; Spedding, *Bacon*, 7:155; Locke to Carleton, 16 Dec. 1620, P.R.O., St. P. Dom. 14/118:30; *CSPV 1619–1621*, pp. 479, 563; *CSPV 1621–1623*, p. 438; Willson, *Privy Councillors*, pp. 60–61, 160–61; Prestwich, *Cranfield*, pp. 433–35; *Cabala Sive Scrinia Sacra: Mysteries of State and Government in Letters of Illustrious Persons*, pp. 90–91; J. Hacket, *Scrinia reserata: A Memorial . . . of John Williams, D.D.*, pt. 1, p. 137.

12. Rymer, *Foedera*, 17:531; More to Nicholas, 25 Dec. 1623, P.R.O., St. P. Dom. 14/156:1; Locke to Carleton, 26 Dec. 1623, P.R.O., St. P. Dom. 14/156:3; *Acts of the Privy Council*, 39:157–58; Chamberlain to Carleton, 3, 31 Jan. 1624, in McClure, ed., *Chamberlain's Letters*, 2:536, 543; Willson, *Privy Councillors*, p. 166; *CSPV 1623–1625*, pp. 182–83, 192, 196, 201, 211, 216–17; Earl of Kellie to the Earl of Mar, 5 Feb. 1624, *HMC Mar and Kellie*, supplementary report, 2:191.

13. Paul to Conway, 24 Oct. 1625, P.R.O., St. P. Dom. 16/8:34; North to the Earl of Leicester, 4 Nov. 1625, in A. Collins, ed., *Letters and Memorials of State*, 2:365–66; Ingram to Wentworth, 7 Nov. 1625, Nov. 1625, in W. Knowler, ed., *Strafford's Letters*, 1:28–29; Sheriff's list of 10 Nov. 1625, List of Sheriffs, 1626?, P.R.O., St. P. Dom. 16/9:43, 43:16; Rudyerd to Nethersole, 23 Nov. 1625, P.R.O., St. P. Dom. 16/10:16; Gardiner, *Hist. of England*, 6:33–34.

14. Hacket, *Scrinia reserata*, 2:4; Willson, *Privy Councillors*, pp. 168–69; Gardiner, *Hist. of England*, 5:320.

15. They would not be reconstituted until after the birth of Charles's first son in May 1629.

16. Buckingham, in the elections of 1625–28, attempted, it seems, to extend his influence into thirteen boroughs that had, before 1625, been subjected to the influence of the Prince's Council or Duchy of Cornwall. Twelve of the boroughs were in Cornwall, one in Suffolk.

17. Neale, *Elizabethan House of Commons*, p. 241.

18. See Appendix Two for a tabulation, by election and agency, of the number of outsiders nominated by the lord warden and the crown's agencies.

19. This discussion of the electoral influence of the lord wardens is based upon Gruenfelder, "The Lord Wardens and Elections, 1604–1628."

20. Northampton placed one nominee at each port in 1604 and, in the five bye-elections following through 1610, he placed at least four, and possibly five, more nominees.

21. Gruenfelder, "The Lord Wardens and Elections, 1604–1628," pp. 3–7.

22. Northampton's patronage has been defined as court patronage since he owed his office as lord warden to the crown. There is nothing to indicate that his nominees were subjected to the same scrutiny by the court as Zouch's were in 1621. Zouch was a known antagonist of Buckingham and the duke's pro-Spanish policies; indeed, the very fact that his nominees were reviewed by the crown indicated the growth of a more political climate at the court. It is also noteworthy that, in 1624, when the court was apparently united (save for the reluctant James) on a strong anti-Spanish line, Zouch's candidates apparently escaped a similar review.

23. Gruenfelder, "The Lord Wardens and Elections, 1604–1628," pp. 7–8; BM ADD MSS 29, 622, f. 113; Hull, ed., *The White and Black Books of the Cinque Ports*, pp. xxxi, 409.

24. For a more detailed discussion, see Gruenfelder, "The Lord Wardens and Elections, pp. 8–9, and sources cited therein.

25. Gruenfelder, "The Lord Wardens and Elections, 1604–1628," pp. 9, 15.

26. Ibid., pp. 10, 12–13; Collins to Zouch, 6 Dec. 1620, P.R.O., St. P. Dom. 14/118:9. Sir Alexander Temple, the frustrated candidate at Winchelsea in 1624, was accused by the mayor of "Popish Recusancy" and of being "allied to the Arch-Recusants of England." And, if that was not enough, the mayor also tried to juggle voting qualifications in order to deny Temple's supporters the vote (East Sussex RO, Winchelsea Borough MSS 55, Court Book 1597–1627, fols. 280, 280v, 283v; Buckingham to the Mayor of Winchelsea, 30 Jan. 1624, the same to Temple, 5 Feb. 1624, the same to Eversfield, 6 Feb. 1624, BM ADD MSS 37, 818, fols. 145v, 146, 147v, 148; *Commons Journals*, 1:677, 726).

27. Gruenfelder, "The Lord Wardens and Elections, 1604–1628," pp. 10–12; Hirst, *Representative of the People?*, pp. 81, 88, 101, 133, 134, app. 2, pp. 207–9.

28. Gruenfelder, "The Lord Wardens and Elections," pp. 13–15; Hirst, *Representative of the People?*, pp. 81, 133, app. 2, pp. 201–3. The quarrel between Mainwaring, Buckingham, and Zouch also probably explains why Emanuel Gifford, by 1624 a client of Buckingham's, failed to receive Zouch's backing in his bid for a place at Rye (Zouch to the Mayor and Jurats of Rye, 12 Jan. 1624, Angell to the same, 16 Jan. 1624, East Sussex RO, Rye Corp. MSS 47/98, 28:5, 7).

29. Hirst, *Representative of the People?*, pp. 11, 66, 67–68, 73, 75.

30. Gruenfelder, "The Lord Wardens and Elections, 1604–1628," p. 16.

31. Ibid., pp. 15–17, 19–21. Hythe's freemen apparently gained the franchise, in part at least, through Buckingham's intervention. They had been informed spectators in the 1624 election but in 1625 won the franchise, possibly because the corporation wanted their support for its refusal of Buckingham's second nominee. It is also notable that once they had the vote, Hythe never returned a Buckingham nominee again (Hirst, *Representative of the People?*, p. 53).

32. Gruenfelder, "The Lord Wardens and Elections, 1604–1628," pp. 16, 17–20; Hirst, *Representative of the People?*, app. 2, pp. 201–3.

33. Gruenfelder, "The Lord Wardens and Elections, 1604–1628," pp. 15–16, 18–21; Hirst, *Representative of the People?*, app. 2, pp. 207–9.

34. Willson, *Privy Councillors*, p. 79.

35. Gruenfelder, "The Lord Wardens and Elections, 1604–1628," pp. 15–22.

36. Buckingham's nominees, both certain and probable, secured but nineteen places in three elections (1625–28), whereas Zouch, in two elections, (1621–24) probably saw his candidates win twenty places. The earl of Northampton, in two elections (1604, 1614) may have won seventeen places for his likely candidates. These figures are taken from Appendix Two.

37. "Sir Thomas Parry," *DNB*, 15:385; Moir, *Addled Parliament*, pp. 10, 46; Chamberlain to Carleton, 18 July 1612, 12 May 1614, in Birch, *Court and Times of James I*, 1:187, 310; Willson, *Privy Councillors*, p. 83.

38. *Commons Journal*, 1:477, 478–79, 480–81, 502; *HMC Portland*, 9:132; *HMC De L'Isle and Dudley*, 5:175; Spedding, *Bacon*, 5:52; Notestein et al., eds., *Commons Debates*, 7:635, 637; Winwood to Carleton, 10 May 1614, P.R.O., Venice Correspondence, St. P. Dom. 99/16:20; Chamberlain to Carleton, 17 Mar., 12 May 1614, P.R.O., St. P. Dom. 14/76:49, 77:22; More to Trumbull, 12 May 1614, *HMC Downshire*, 4:400–401; Neale, *Elizabethan House of Commons*, pp. 226, 227, 231–32; Moir, *Addled Parliament*, p. 45; "Sir Thomas Parry," *DNB* 15:385; Keeler, *Long Parliament*, pp. 376–78; W. Harry Rylands, ed., *Visitations of Hampshire*, Harleian Soc. (London, 1913), p. 193. Ironically enough, Gifford was the duchy's steward for Somborne Hundred, Stockbridge Borough and Manor of the Duchy's courts in Hampshire! His local influence, however, was great enough to practically guarantee him a place for Stockbridge; he served the borough 1621–28 (Somerville, *Office-Holders in the Duchy and County Palatine of Lancaster*, p. 221).

39. Parry nominated Leigh after discovering Felton would not be able to serve. Moir, *Addled Parliament*, pp. 43–44; Nichols, *Hist. Leicestershire*, vol. 2, pt. 1, pp. 341, 425; Leicester Museum, Dept. of Archives, City of Leicester MSS, Hall Book 1587–1708, BR/II/1/3:398; Parry to the Mayor and Burgesses of Leicester, 21 Feb., Heyrick to the same, 26 Feb., Earl of Huntingdon to the same, 4 Mar., Mayor and Burgesses of Leicester to Harvey, 7 Mar., Harvey to the Mayor of Leicester, 11 Mar., the Mayor and Burgesses of Leicester to the Earl of Huntingdon, 14 Mar., the same to Parry, 16 Mar., 1614, Leicester Museum, Dept. of Archives, City of Leicester MSS BR II/13/3, 3v, 4, 4v, 5, 5v, 6, 6v, 7, 7v, 8, 8v, 9; Thompson, *Hist. Leicester*, pp. 326–27, 344; "Henry Rich, first Earl of Holland," *DNB*, 16:997–1000, "Francis Leigh first Earl of Chichester," *DNB*, 11:875–76, which contains information about his father Sir Francis Leigh, chosen at Leicester in 1614; "Sir William Hericke or Herrick," *DNB*, 9:694–95.

40. "Sir Henry Slingsby," *DNB*, 18:375–77; Keeler, *Long Parliament*, pp. 53–54, 75, 107–8, 172–73; Bean, *Northern Counties*, p. 884; Moir, *Addled Parliament*, pp. 45–46; Neale, *Elizabethan House of Commons*, p. 229; Pape, *Newcastle-under-Lyme*, pp. 136–37; Sperling, *Hodson's Hist. of the Borough of Sudbury*, pp. 45, 92; Williams, *Parl. Hist. Wales*, pp. 134, 135; Pink and Beaven, *Members of Parl. for Lancashire*, pp. 115–18, 148–51, 185–87. Ireland, of Bewsey, Warrington, was the king's counsel of the duchy and vice-chamberlain of Chester; Somerville, *Office-Holders in the Duchy and County Palatine of Lancaster*, pp. 21, 54, 67, 150–51, 154, 156, 158.

41. Prestwich, *Cranfield*, pp. 256–57, 296, Willson, *Privy Councillors*, pp. 66, 94–95, 98, 177, 195, 199–200; Zagorin, *Court and Country*, p. 59; "Sir Humphrey May," *DNB*, 13:140–41.

42. Savile Radcliffe to Sir Richard Beaumont, 16 Dec. 1620, in Weeks, *Clitheroe in the Seventeenth Century*, 2:224–26; J. J. Cartwright, *Chapters in Yorkshire History*, pp. 204–6, W. D. Macray, ed., *Beaumont Papers*, pp. 45–46.

43. Pink and Beaven, *Members of Parl. for Lancashire*, pp. 115–18, 148–51; Black, *Parl. Hist. Isle of Wight*, pp. 11–13, 32–33; Keeler, *Long Parliament*, pp. 171–73, 185, 336; "John Selden," *DNB*, 17:1150–62; Nichols, *Progresses*, 3:404 & n, 4:982 & n; Rylands, ed., *The Visitation of Buckinghamshire*, p. 21; Neale, *Elizabethan House of Commons*, p. 225; Somerville, *Office-Holders in the Duchy and County Palatine of Lancaster*, pp. xvii, i, 21, 66–67, 94, 126, 191, 207.

44. S. Radcliffe to Beaumont, 16, 30 Dec. 1620, Cartwright, *Chapters in Yorkshire History*, pp. 204–6; Macray, ed., *Beaumont Papers*, pp. 45–46; Weeks, *Clitheroe in the Seventeenth Century*, 2:224–27, 294; Pink and Beaven, *Members of Parliament for Lancashire*, pp. 70, 251–52; Keeler, *Long Parliament*, pp. 92, 208, 236; *VCH Lancashire*, 4:327 & n; May to the Bailiffs and Burgesses of Clitheroe, 9 Apr. 1625, *HMC Kenyon*, p. 31; "Sir Christopher Hatton," *DNB*, 9:162–63; Somerville, *Office-Holders in the Duchy and County Palatine of Lancaster*, pp. 67, 70, 192, 237.

45. Pink and Beaven, *Members of Parl. for Lancashire*, pp. 223–25; Sinclair, *Hist. Wigan*, 1:193–96; Keeler, *Long Parliament*, pp. 171–72; Gleason, *JP's*, p. 180; *VCH Lancashire*, 4:72; Neale, *Elizabethan House of Commons*, p. 225; Black, *Parl. Hist. Isle of Wight*, pp.

11–13, 32–33. Somerville, *Office-Holders in the Duchy and County Palatine of Lancaster*, p. 54; Hirst, *Representative of the People?*, pp. 114–15.

46. Keeler, *Long Parliament*, pp. 53–54, 155–56, 277, 347–48; Pink and Beaven, *Members of Parl. for Lancashire*, pp. 185–87; Chandler, *Liverpool under James I*, pp. 1–2, 12, 13, 38–39, 241; McClure, ed., *Chamberlain's Letters*, 1:230 & n; Stone *Aristocracy*, p. 108; *CSPD 1623–25*, pp. 324, 327, 328; *CSPD 1628–29*, p. 425; "James Stanley, seventh Earl of Derby," *DNB*, 28:958–60; "Henry Jermyn, first Earl of St. Albans," *DNB*, 10:779–781; Muir, *Hist. Liverpool*, p. 111; Baines, *Hist. Liverpool*, pp. 294–95, 300; *VCH Lancashire*, 4:17, 19–20. Somerville, *Office-Holders in the Duchy and County Palatine of Lancaster*, pp. 54, 94.

47. Pink and Beaven, *Members of Parl. for Lancashire*, pp. 278–79; Neale, *Elizabethan House of Commons*, pp. 189–90; *VCH Lancashire*, 4:88, 135, 168; 6:468 & n, 540, 543; *VCH Berkshire*, 3:258; Somerville, *Office-Holders in the Duchy and County Palatine of Lancaster*, pp. 94, 100; *CSPD 1603–1610*, p. 615; *CSPD 1619–1623*, pp. 497, 499; *CSPD 1627–1628*, p. 587; *CSPD 1625–1649*, p. 12; Nichols, *Progresses*, 3:761; at Edmondes's death George Gerrard described him to Edward Viscount Conway as a "drunken beast," and suggests that Sir Thomas "may be glad he is rid of him" (*CSPD 1635*, p. 385).

48. Neale, *Elizabethan House of Commons*, pp. 224–26.

49. Mayor of Leicester to the Earl of Huntingdon, 17 Nov. 1620, *HMC Hastings*, 4:203; "Sir Richard Moryson," *DNB*, 13:1071; *VCH Leicestershire*, 4:353; G. E. Aylmer, *King's Servants*, pp. 286–87; Stone, "The Electoral Influence of the Second Earl of Salisbury, 1614–68," pp. 392–93; De Villiers, "Parliamentary Boroughs Restored by the House of Commons, 1625–41," p. 192; Cussans, *Hist. Hertfordshire*, 1:54, 94, 104, 263.

50. Huntingdon to the Mayor and Brethren of Leicester, 31 Dec. 1620, Mayor and Corporation of Leicester to Huntingdon, 4 Jan. 1621, *HMC Hastings*, 4:204; Mayor and Corporation of Leicester to ?, n. d.; the copy of Morison's oath, n. d.; Mayor of Leicester to Huntingdon, n. d.; undated MS reporting Leicester's decision about the countess of Devonshire's nominee; Mayor of Leicester to Huntingdon, 16 Dec. 1620, the same to Harvey, 16 Dec. 1620, Leicester Museum, Dept. of Archives, City of Leicester MSS, Hall Papers Bound, 1620–23, BR II/18/14:8, 10, 14, 20, 21: Thompson, *Hist. Leicester*, pp. 346–47.

51. Leicester City Museums, Dept. of Archives, City of Leicester MSS, Hall Book 1578–1708, BR/II/1/3:448; Nichols, *Hist. Leicestershire*, vol. 2, pt. 1, p. 425; "Sir William Hericke or Herrick," *DNB*, 9:694–95. After Sir William's defeat in the 1614 election, his brother Robert urged him, should he want to serve for Leicester in the future, to "speak to Mr. Chancellor to write but two lines to our town, that you may be one; it will be as sure as any act of parliament" (Nichols, *Hist. Leicestershire*, vol. 2, pt. 1, p. 341.

52. May to the Earl of Huntingdon, 4 Jan., Huntingdon to the Mayor and Burgesses of Leicester, 9, 15 Jan., May to Huntingdon, 21 Jan. 1624, *HMC Hastings*, 4:63, *VCH Leicestershire*, 4:60, 5:11; Nichols, *Hist. Leicestershire*, vol. 2, pt. 1, p. 426; Thompson, *Hist. Leicester*, p. 349; Mayor of Leicester to Bale, Sheriff of Leicestershire, 10? Jan., Meeting of the Common Hall of Leicester, 16 Jan., Mayor of Leicester? to May, ? Jan., Mayor of Leicester to the Earl of Huntingdon, 12, 16 Jan., election indenture of 16 Jan., May to the Mayor and Corporation of Leicester 20 Jan. 1624, Leicester City Museum, Dept. of Archives, City of Leicester MSS, Hall Papers Bound, 1623–25, BR/18/15:274, 279, 281–84, 286; Hall Book 1578–1708, BR/II/1/3:470; "Sir Humphrey May," *DNB*, 13:140–41.

53. May to the Mayor and Corporation of Leicester, 2 Apr., Haselrige to the Mayor of Leicester, 19 Apr., the Common Hall meeting held 3 May for choice of burgesses, the election indenture for 3 May, Mayor of Leicester to Sir Geo. Hastings, the same to May, 3 May 1625, Leicester City Museum, Dept. of Archives, City of Leicester MSS, Hall Papers Bound, 1623–25, BR II/18/15:557, 559–61, 563, 564; Hall Book, 1587–1708, BR/II/1/3:484; Thompson, *Hist. Leicester*, p. 350; "Sir Arthur Hesilrige or Haselrig," *DNB*, 9:743–47; Keeler, *Long Parliament*, p. 213; Nichols, *Hist. Leicestershire*, vol. 2, pt. 1, p. 426.

54. May to the Mayor of Leicester, 10 July, Common Hall meeting of 22 July, election indenture of 22 July, Mayor of Leicester to May, 23 July 1625, Leicester City Museum, Dept. of Archives, City of Leicester MSS, Hall Papers Bound, 1623–25, BR/II/18/15:597, 598, 600, 601; Thompson, *Hist. Leicester*, p. 351; Keeler, *Long Parliament*, p. 236. Jermyn was a kinsman of May, accounting for his elections at Leicester in 1625, Lancaster in 1626, and Clitheroe in 1628.

55. Earl of Huntingdon to the Mayor, Bailiff, and Burgesses of Leicester, 12 Jan. 1626, *HMC Hastings*, 2:68; Common Hall meeting of 13 Jan., Mayor of Leicester to May, 14 Jan., the same to Sir Geo. Hastings, n. d., probably 1626, Common Hall meeting of Feb. 1628, Leicester City Museum, Dept. of Archives, City of Leicester MSS, Hall Papers Bound, 1625–28, BR II/18/16:7, 53, 54, 243; Hall Book 1587–1708, BR/II/1/3:492; Nichols, *Hist. Leicestershire*, vol. 2, pt. 1, p. 426; Thompson, *Hist. Leicester*, pp. 352, 354; Cokayne, *Peerage*, 2:232.

56. Neale, *Elizabethan House of Commons*, p. 227. For Whitehead, see Keeler, *Long Parliament*, pp. 391–92; Gifford married into the powerful Hampshire family of Wallop (McClure, ed., *Chamberlain's Letters*, 1:159, 196 & n); he lived at King's Somborne, Hampshire, where James I was a guest (Nichols, *Progresses*, 1:112, 250, 253); he also served as keeper for the Forest of Roche in 1627, was a commissioner for the sale of crown lands in Hampshire, and served as a deputy-lieutenant in the county (*CSPD 1627–28*, pp. 38, 60, 460, 513; *VCH Hampshire*, 4:445, 470, 471, 472 & n, 516, 522); Prince's Council to the Feodary of Pontefract Honour, 1 Jan. 1624, Duchy of Cornwall RO, "Burgesses for Parliament 1623–24," f. 34; Wentworth to Clifford, 23 Jan. 1624, Cartwright, *Chapters in Yorkshire History*, pp. 214–15; for Ayloffe, Badger, and Holcroft, see Nichols, *Progresses*, 1:118 & n, 471, 2:24, 108, 3:177, 246, 465, 761; McClure, ed., *Chamberlain's Letters*, 2:14, 56, 129, 282, 617; *CSPD 1603–10*, p. 190; *CSPD 1619–23*, pp. 65, 324, 497, 499, *CSPD 1623–25*, p. 509; *CPSD 1627–28*, p. 587; *CSPD 1629–31*, p. 316; *CSPD 1634–35*, p. 398; *CSPD 1635*, p. 553; *CSPD 1625–49*, p. 12; *Commons Journal*, 1:759, gives the results of the disputed Stockbridge election of 1624 in which Holcroft and Gifford were elected and their return was upheld.

57. Neale, *Elizabethan House of Commons*, p. 227; Williams, *Parl. Hist. Wales*, pp. 134, 135.

58. Neale, *Elizabethan House of Commons*, pp. 225, 229; *CSPD 1619–23*, p. 492; *CSPD 1623–25*, p. 54; *CSPD 1628–29*, pp. 506–7; "Sir Philip Mainwaring," *DNB*, 12:792; Ormerod, *Hist. Cheshire*, 1:482–83; Lawson-Tancred, *Records of a Yorkshire Manor*, pp. 374–76; Lawson-Tancred, "Parliamentary History of Aldborough and Boroughbridge," pp. 329, 359; Cokayne, *Peerage*, 6:63; "Ferdinando Fairfax," *DNB*, 6:996–97; Keeler, *Long Parliament*, pp. 171–72. John Ferne, chosen in 1604, was a secretary of the Council of the North; he died and was replaced in 1609 by Sir Thomas Vavasour, who probably owed his election to that council. The same was probably true of the return of George Wethered in 1621 for Boroughbridge. Philip Mainwaring's success in finding a place under Wentworth also aided the family situation for his brother, Edmund Mainwaring, was appointed to the Council of the North in 1629 (Reid, *Council of the North*, app. 2, p. 498).

59. Pape, *Newcastle-under-Lyme*, pp. 132–43; "Sir John Davis," *DNB*, 5:590–94; *CSPD 1619–1623*, p. 370; *CSPD 1625–26*, pp. 28, 132, 566; "Sir Thomas Glemham," *DNB*, 7:305–6; McClure, ed., *Chamberlain's Letters*, 1:227; Keeler, *Long Parliament*, pp. 63, 241–42, 250; Zagorin, *Court and Country*, pp. 93–94; Cokayne, *Peerage*, 3:285–86, 4:381–82; Wedgwood, *Parl. Hist. Staffordshire*, 1:409, 2:8, 12, 15–16, 20, 24–25, 28–29, 33, 47–48, 50, 54; V. F. Snow, *Essex the Rebel*, p. 84. A contested election in 1624 led to an enlargement of the borough's franchise, a decision that may have contributed to the end of the duchy's influence since, after that election, the borough's places became the property of its neighboring squires. It came under the patronage, however, of the earl of Essex in both 1640 elections (Snow, *Essex the Rebel*, pp. 199, 225–26, 238–39). For a discussion of the local problems that plagued the borough, see Hirst, *Representative of the People?* app. 2, p. 204.

60. Neale, *Elizabethan House of Commons*, pp. 226, 228; C. G. Grimwood and S. A. Kay, *History of Sudbury*, p. 108; Moir, *Addled Parliament*, p. 46; "Sir Nathaniel Barnardiston," *DNB*, 2:1162–64; Keeler, *Long Parliament*, pp. 96–97, 145–46, 178–79, 208, 261–62; 330; McClure, ed., *Chamberlain's Letters*, 2:149 & n; Hobart to Crane, 23 Nov. 1620, Bodleian Library, Tanner MSS 290, f. 54; Prince's Council to the Feodary of the Honor of Pontefract, 1 Jan. 1624, Duchy of Cornwall RO, "Burgesses for Parliament 1623–1624," f. 34; *CSPD 1603–10*, p. 648; *CSPD 1611–18*, pp. 44, 324, 385; *CSPD 1627–28*, pp. 485, 523; *CSPD 1628–29*, p. 387; *CSPD 1631–33*, p. 570; *CSPD 1625–49*, p. 503; Sir Arthur was a brother of Sir Henry Mainwaring, Zouch's troublesome lieutenant at Dover Castle, (*CSPD 1619–23*, p. 572); *Burke's Extinct Peerages*, p. 257; "Sir Christopher Hatton," *DNB*, 4:162–63; *VCH Huntingdonshire*, 2:14, 23–28.

61. Neale, *Elizabethan House of Commons*, pp. 228–29; *OR* 1:452, 459, 464; Keeler, *Long Parliament*, pp. 57, 150–51; *VCH Northamptonshire*, 3:268; Cokayne, *Peerage*, 3:341–42; Lawson-Tancred, *Records of a Yorkshire Manor*, pp. 374–76; despite Lawson-Tancred's assertion that most of the members were "nominees of the Crown," in his "Parliamentary History of Aldborough and Boroughbridge," p. 326, a glance at the returns of its members shows the importance of Yorkshire interests. In fact, his own study of its membership confirms that very point ("Parliamentary History of Aldborough and Boroughbridge," p. 359); Bean, *Northern Counties*, p. 716. There was competition, too, among the Yorkshire leadership for Aldborough's places. Sir Henry Savile, returned in both 1604 and 1614, lost out in 1621 (Pepper to Savile, 8 Jan. 1621, BM Harleian MSS 7,000, f. 41, in Cartwright, *Chapters in Yorkshire History*, pp. 203–4; K. Sharpe, *Sir Robert Cotton 1586–1631*, p. 176.

62. Neale, *Elizabethan House of Commons*, pp. 226–32.

63. For a table indicating the duchy's record in each election, see Appendix Two.

64. M. Coate, *Cornwall in the Great Civil War, 1642–1660*, pp. 5, 14–15, 17–18; Neale, *Elizabethan House of Commons*, p. 213.

65. Kenny, "Parliamentary Influence of Charles Howard, Earl of Nottingham, 1536–1624," p. 231; Keeler, *Long Parliament*, pp. 97, 365, 370–71; "Sir Robert Naunton," *DNB*, 14:126–29; "Sir Francis Crane," *DNB*, 5:9–10; "Sir Henry Vane the elder," *DNB*, 20:113–16; "Sir Francis Barnham," *DNB*, 1:1184; Duchy of Cornwall RO, "Letters and Patents, 1620–1621," f. 39v; "Burgesses for Parliament 1623–1624," f. 33v; "Sir Robert Killigrew," *DNB*, 11:110–11.

66. Courtney, *Parl. Repr. Cornwall*, pp. 325–27, 363–64; *CSPD 1603–1610*, p. 121; *CSPD 1625–1626*, p. 67; Cokayne, *Peerage*, 8:160; Somerville, *Office-Holders in the Duchy and County Palatine of Lancaster*, p. 224.

67. Moir, *Addled Parliament*, p. 48; Courtney, *Parl. Repr. Cornwall*, pp. 63–64, 84–85, 130–32, 148–50, 209–12, 301–4; "Sir Ranulphe Crew or Crewe," *DNB*, 5:81–82; "Sir Robert Phelips," *DNB*, 15:1030–31; Sir Edw. Phelips to Sir Robt. Phelips, 28 Mar. 1614, Somersetshire RO, Phelips MSS, vol. 2, fols. 14, 14v: E. Farnham, "The Somersetshire Election of 1614," p. 588.

68. Courtney, *Parl. Repr. Cornwall*, pp. 84–85, 230–32, 251–53; M. Coate, "The Vyvyan family of Trelowarren," pp. 115–16; Keeler, *Long Parliament*, p. 374.

69. The Prince's Council to Roscarrock, 1 Dec. 1620, Duchy of Cornwall RO, "Letters and Patents, 1620–1621," f. 39v. The boroughs listed were Lostwithiel, Camelford, Bossiney, St. Ives, East Looe, West Looe, Fowey, Helston, Launceston, Newport, Grampound, Saltash, Liskeard, and Plymouth.

70. "Sir John Walter," *DNB*, 20:704–5; "Sir Edward Coke," *DNB*, 4:685–700; "Lionel Cranfield, Earl of Middlesex," *DNB*, 5:14–16; "William Noy or Noye," *DNB*, 14:698–700; "Sir Robert Naunton," *DNB*, 14:126–29; "Sir Fulke Greville, first Baron Brooke," *DNB*, 8:602–86; "Sir Henry Vane the elder," *DNB*, 20:113–16; "Oliver Cromwell," *DNB*, 5:155–86; "Sir Henry Finch," *DNB*, 7:12–13; "Sir Thomas Trevor," *DNB*, 19:1155; *VCH Huntingdonshire*, 2:14–15, 124, 136; Neale, *Elizabethan House of Commons*, p. 50; Keeler, *Long Parliament*, p. 365; Moir, *Addled Parliament*, p. 148; Cokayne, *Peerage*,

1:247–48, 5:331–32; Nichols, *Progresses*, 3:671; *CSPD 1625–1626*, p. 161; Prestwich, *Cranfield*, pp. 117, 125; "Sir Robert Carey, first Earl of Monmouth," *DNB*, 3:984–85.

71. Naunton was returned for Cambridge University *OR*, 1:450–55.

72. Sir Robert Killigrew was probably responsible for Penryn's return of two courtiers, Sir Francis Crane and Robert Jermyn. Crane had served the borough before, thanks to Killigrew's influence, and Jermyn's mother was a Killigrew (Courtney, *Parl. Repr. Cornwall*, pp. 17–18, 84–85, 114–16, 148–50, 168–69, 230–32, 342–44; Cokayne, *Peerage*, 7:194–95); "Sir Heneage Finch," *DNB*, 7:7–8; "Sir Henry Carey, second Earl of Monmouth," *DNB*, 3:979–80; Keeler, *Long Parliament*, pp. 369–70; Baines, *The History of the County Palatine and Duchy of Lancaster*, ed. J. Croston, 4:200; Reid, *Council of the North*, app. 2, p. 498. The probability that Sir Thomas Smyth had the duchy's backing is increased by the favor James I showed him during the dispute within the Virginia Company in the 1620s (A. Brown, *Genesis of the U.S.*, 2:1015).

73. Prince's Council to Roscarrock, 1 Jan. 1624, Duchy of Cornwall RO, "Burgesses for Parliament, 1623–1624," fols. 33, 33v; "Sir Henry Hobart," *DNB*, 9:924–25; "Sir Francis Crane," *DNB*, 5:9–10.

74. Rowe, "The Influence of the Earls of Pembroke on Parliamentary Elections, 1625–41," p. 250; H. Hulme, *Eliot*, pp. 42–43; Zagorin, *Court and Country*, p. 98; Harris to Verney, 25 Jan. 1624, P.R.O., St. P. Dom. 14/158:47; Conway's Letter Book, 6 Jan. 1624, P.R.O., St. P. Dom. 14/214; Courtney, *Parl. Repr. Cornwall*, passim; "Francis Cottington, Baron Cottington," *DNB*, 4:1218–21; "Sir John Walter," *DNB*, 20:704–5; "Sir Francis Crane," *DNB*, 5:9–10; "William Noy or Noye," *DNB*, 14:698–700; "Sir Julius Caesar," *DNB*, 3:656–59; "Sir John Glanville the younger," *DNB*, 7:1291–92; Worth, ed., *Hist. Plymouth*, pp. 162–63; *A Complete Parochial History of the County of Cornwall*, 4 vols. (London and Truro, 1867–72), 1:133, 137; W. T. Lawrence, *Parl. Hist. Cornwall*, p. 285; Keeler, *Long Parliament*, p. 163; "John Mohun, first Baron Mohun," *DNB*, 13:555–56; J. Allen, *Hist. of the Borough of Liskeard*, pp. 311–12, 462–63.

75. For the number of places the Duchy of Cornwall secured in each election, see Appendix Two.

76. *VCH Worcestershire*, 4:308, 309, 311; P. Styles, "The Corporation of Bewdley under the Later Stuarts," p. 94; "Sir Thomas Edmondes," *DNB*, 6:391–93. The Privy Council had probably intervened at Bewdley in 1614.

77. For a detailed account of the election contest, see Gruenfelder, "The Parliamentary Election at Chester, 1621," pp. 35–44, and for a discussion of the local problems that vexed Chester's corporation and commons and contributed to the contest in 1621, see Hirst, *Representative of the People?*, p. 49, app. 2, pp. 197–98.

78. Prince's Council to Newton, the Prince's Treasurer or Receiver General, 1 Jan. 1624, Duchy of Cornwall RO, "Burgesses for Parliament 1623–1624," f. 36v; the Prince's Council to Ireland, Vice-Chamberlain of Chester, the same to Stapleton and Chamberlain, for Edmondes's election at Coventry, the same to Mallett, Deputy Steward of the Manor of Warwick, the same to William, Earl of Northampton, the same to Cartwright, Feodary of the Honor of Pontefract, the same to Mr. Clerk or Mr. Gray, for Finch's election at Eye, all dated 1 Jan. 1624, Duchy of Cornwall RO, "Burgesses for Parliament, 1623–1624," fols. 34, 34v, 35; Prince's Council to Mallowes, Steward of Bury St. Edmunds, 7, 14 Jan., the same to Viscount St. Albans, 31 Jan., the same to Cartwright, 20 Feb., the same to the Mayor and Burgesses of Beverley, 23 Feb., the same to the Mayor and Burgesses of Hertford, 9 Feb., 7 Feb., 24 Apr. 1624, Duchy of Cornwall RO, "Burgesses for Parliament, 1623–1624," fols. 34v–40; Prince's Council to the Mayor and Burgesses of Hertford, 9 Feb., 24 Apr. 1624, Hertfordshire RO, Borough of Hertford Corporation Records, vol. 23, fols. 10, 11.

79. Prince's Council to William, Earl of Northampton, 1 Jan. 1624, Duchy of Cornwall RO, "Burgesses for Parliament 1623–1624," f. 35; "Sir Ralph Clare," *DNB*, 4:388–89.

80. Prince's Council to "Mr. Clerk or Mr. Graye touching the election of Francis Finch . . . one of the burgesses for . . . Eye," 1 Jan. 1624, Duchy of Cornwall RO, "Burgesses

for Parliament 1623–1624," fols. 35, 35v, 36; Chamberlain to Carleton, 31 Jan. 1624, P.R.O., St. P. Dom. 14/158:72, in McClure, ed., *Chamberlain's Letters*, 2:543: Keeler, *Long Parliament*, pp. 64, 234–35; Cokayne, *Peerage*, 2:426–27; Burke's *Extinct Peerage*, p. 149; Coppinger, *Suffolk Manors*, 1:267, 272, 273, 346, 381, 404, 412, 4:207, 6:248, 7:102.

81. Prince's Council to Ireland, Vice Chamberlain of Chester, the same to Mallett, Deputy Steward of the Manor of Warwick, 1 Jan. 1624, Duchy of Cornwall RO, "Burgesses for Parliament, 1623–1624," f. 34v; Gruenfelder, "The Parliamentary Election at Chester, 1621," pp. 35–44; Cokayne, *Peerage*, 2:345; 7:60; Ormerod, *Hist. Cheshire*, 2:716; Warwickshire RO, Warwick Borough MSS, Minute Book 1610–1662, W. 21/6, f. 83; Keeler, *Long Parliament*, pp. 69, 259–60; *VCH Warwickshire*, 8:496–97; "Edward Conway, first Viscount Conway," *DNB*, 4:975–76.

82. Greville to Secretary Conway, Dec. 1621, P.R.O., St. P. Dom. 16/522:88. This letter was misdated as December 1625; but since Hopkins only served in parliament in 1614 and 1621, it can hardly be of that date and is for 1621; Prince's Council to Stapleton and Chamberlain, "touching the election of Sir Thomas Edmondes . . . for . . . Coventry," 1 Jan. 1624, Duchy of Cornwall RO, "Burgesses for Parliament 1623–1624," f. 34v; Coventry City RO, A. 14, Council Book A, 1557–1640, f. 268; T. W. Whitley, *Parliamentary Representation of the City of Coventry*, pp. 72–73; *VCH Warwickshire*, 8:249–50; Chamberlain to Carleton, 17 Jan. 1624, P.R.O., St. P. Dom. 14/158:33, in McClure, ed., *Chamberlain's Letters*, 2:540, and Birch, *Court and Times of James I*, 2:447–48, Willson, *Privy Councillors*, p. 166.

83. Keeler, *Long Parliament*, pp. 68, 316; Whitley, *Parl. Repr. Coventry*, pp. 64–65, 68–69, 70, 72–76; *VCH Warwickshire*, 8:249–250; City of Coventry RO, Coventry Borough MSS, A 14, Council Book A 1557–1640, fols. 201v, 202; William Purefoy and Richard Green, chosen in 1628, were both Warwickshire gentry ("William Purefoy," *DNB*, 16:490). Coventry's early seventeenth-century history was marred by a simmering dispute, essentially economic in origin, between its freemen and the increasingly elitist corporation, which erupted in the election of 1628 (Hirst, *Representative of the People?*, pp. 46–47, 51–52, 56, 136).

84. Prince's Council to Cartwright, Feodary of the Honor of Pontefract, 1 Jan. 1624, Duchy of Cornwall RO, "Burgesses for Parliament, 1623–1624," f. 34; Batho, ed., *The Household Papers of Henry Percy, Ninth Earl of Northumberland 1564–1632*, app. 3, p. 150; Lawson-Tancred, *Records of a Yorkshire Manor*, pp. 374–76; Lawson-Tancred, "Parliamentary History of Aldborough and Boroughbridge," pp. 329, 359; Cliffe, *The Yorkshire Gentry*, pp. 154–55, 323; "Christopher Wandesford," *DNB*, 20:742–44; "Sir Philip Mainwaring," *DNB*, 6:996–97; "Sir Henry Slingsby," *DNB*, 18:375; Bean, *Northern Counties*, pp. 884, 904.

85. Prince's Council to Cartwright, 1 Jan., 20 Feb., 1624, Duchy of Cornwall RO, "Burgesses for Parliament, 1623–1624," fols. 34, 39; Wentworth to Beaumont, the same to Lord Clifford, 18, 23 Jan., 1624, Sheffield City Library, Wentworth-Woodhouse MSS 2(123–24), (125–26), the letter to Clifford is in Knowler, ed., *Strafford's Letters*, 1:19; Cartwright, *Chapters in Yorkshire History*, pp. 214–15; Bean, *Northern Counties*, pp. 963, 988; G. Fox, *Hist. Pontefract*, p. 61; Cliffe, *The Yorkshire Gentry*, p. 126; *Commons Journal*, 1:714, 745, 751, 797–98; "Thomas Wentworth, first Earl of Strafford," *DNB*, 20:1179–94; A. J. Fletcher, "Sir Thomas Wentworth and the Restoration of Pontefract as a Parliamentary Borough," pp. 88–97. For Wentworth's influence at Pontefract, see Gruenfelder, "The Electoral Patronage of Sir Thomas Wentworth, Earl of Strafford, 1614–1640," pp. 564, 568–69, 573. I should like to thank the Trustees of the Fitzwilliam (Wentworth) Estates and the Director of the Sheffield City Libraries for their courtesy in allowing me to use the Wentworth Woodhouse MSS.

86. Prince's Council to Cartwright, Feodary of the Honor of Pontefract, 1 Jan., the same to the Mayor and Burgesses of Beverley, 23 Feb. 1624, Duchy of Cornwall RO, "Burgesses for Parliament, 1623–1624," fols. 34, 39v; Bean, *Northern Counties*, pp. 740, 758; "Sir Henry Vane the elder," *DNB*, 20:113–16; Cokayne, *Peerage*, 5:332; Courtney, *Parl. Repr. Cornwall*, pp. 84–85, 168–69, 186–88, 342–44. Sir Henry Carey's return for

Beverley may have been helped, too, by his connection to the Wharton family of Easby, Yorkshire (Cokayne, *Peerage*, 8:125–26).

87. The Prince's Council to Francis, Viscount St. Albans, with a "like letter" to the Earl of Salisbury, 31 Jan. 1624, Duchy of Cornwall RO, "Burgesses for Parliament 1623–1624," f. 37; Stone, "The Electoral Influence of the Second Earl of Salisbury," pp. 389–91; Cussans, *Hist. Hertfordshire*, 3:356, 358; Capel was the son of Sir Arthur Capel of Hertfordshire; Nichols, *Progresses*, 1:111 & n; McClure, ed., *Chamberlain's Letters*, 2:249 & n; "Sir John Maynard," *DNB*, 13:155–57; Morant, *Hist. Essex*, 2:432; Keeler, *Long Parliament*, pp. 101–2; Goldney, ed., *Chippenham*, p. xviii; W. C. Metcalfe, ed., *The Visitations of Essex*, 2 pts., Harleian Soc. (London, 1878–79), pt. ii, p. 595.

88. Neale, *Elizabethan House of Commons*, pp. 141–46; De Villiers, "Parliamentary Boroughs Restored by the House of Commons, 1621–1641," pp. 175–202; Prince's Council to the Mayor and Burgesses of Hertford, 9 Feb. ?, Feb., 24 Apr. 1624, Duchy of Cornwall RO, "Burgesses for Parliament 1623–1624," fols. 37v, 38v, 40; same to the same, 9 Feb., 24 Apr. 1624, Hertfordshire RO, Borough of Hertford Corporation Records, vol. 23,fols, 10, 11; *VCH Hertfordshire*, 2:27, 3:502; Cussans, *Hist. Hertfordshire*, 2:54; Stone, "The Electoral Influence of the Second Earl of Salisbury, 1614–68," p. 391; *HMC MSS of Lincoln. Bury St. Edmund's and Great Grimsby Corporation*, p. 162.

89. Stone, "The Electoral Influence of the Second Earl of Salisbury, 1614–68," pp. 392–93; De Villiers, "Parliamentary Boroughs Restored by the House of Commons, 1621–41," p. 192; Keeler, *Long Parliament*, p. 172; "Sir Thomas Fanshawe, first Viscount Fanshawe of Dromore," *DNB*, 6:1054; Hertfordshire RO, Borough of Hertford Corporation Records, vol. 23, fols, 13, 13v, 14. Hirst's suggestion that an alliance between Salisbury and "unofficial Prince's Council influence secured victory for Ashton and Fanshawe" seems quite wrong. The Prince's Council nominated Harrington; Salisbury supported Ashton and only promised to do nothing that would deny Fanshawe a place. If the council wanted Fanshawe returned, then why would it nominate another? (Hirst, *Representative of the People?*, p. 128).

90. The election of 1624 was the last for the Prince's Council and the Duchy of Cornwall under the prince's officers. It would not be back as an electoral agent until the 1640 elections. Charles's heir was not born until May 1630 and probably was not declared Prince of Wales and earl of Chester until 1638, if not later. The Prince's Council that made the nominations discussed above was dissolved. The Cornish boroughs were, of course, still not free of patronage: the duke of Buckingham and the earl of Pembroke stepped into its place.

91. Cliffe, *Yorkshire Gentry*, pp. 3, 30; the list of council members and officials can be found in Reid, *Council of the North*, app. 2, pp. 489–90, 494–98.

92. Sheffield to the Bailiff and Burgesses of Scarborough, 14 Feb., 7 Mar., Griffiths to the Bailiffs and Burgesses of Scarborough, 6 Mar., Hickson to Thompson and Lacy, 28 Mar. 1614, Scarborough Borough MSS, General Letters B. 1., 1597–1642; Cliffe, *Yorkshire Gentry*, p. 104; Reid, *Council of the North*, app. 2, p. 497; "Sir John Suckling," *DNB*, 19:141; Gleason, *JP's*, pp. 173, 175, 177; Baker, *Hist. Scarborough*, pp. 176, 250, 283–84. For a more detailed review of Yorkshire borough elections, see Gruenfelder, "Yorkshire Borough Elections, 1603–1640." For Sir Thomas Wentworth's electoral influence in Yorkshire's county and borough elections, see Gruenfelder, "The Electoral Patronage of Sir Thomas Wentworth, Earl of Strafford, 1614–1640."

93. Harrison, ed., *Ripon Millenary Record*, pt. 2, pp. xiii–xiv; Willson, *Privy Councillors*, p. 108; Cokayne, *Peerage*, 3:307–8; Carrol, "The Parliamentary Representation of Yorkshire, 1625–1660," pp. 68–71, 85–86; Moir, *Addled Parliament*, pp. 47, 148; Morant, *Hist. Essex*, 2:507, 574, 575; G. Rickwood, "Members of Parliament for Colchester," pp. 195–96; W. C. Metcalfe, ed., *Visitations of Essex*, pt. 1, p. 505; Bean, *Northern Counties*, pp. 812, 1001, 1023, 1081; Gleason, *JP's*, pp. 126, 129, 231–32; Wentworth to "George Weatheridde Esqr.," 8 Dec. 1620, Sheffield City Library, Wentworth-Woodhouse MSS, 2(60); Wentworth to the Earl of Middlesex, 5 June 1623, in Knowler, ed., *Strafford's Letters*, 1:16;

*CSPD 1603–1610*, p. 511; *CSPD 1611–1618*, p. 386; *CSPD 1625–1626*, p. 565; *CSPD 1638–1639*, p. 460; *CSPD 1639–1640*, p. 89; Wethered's possible kinsman, George, was Lord Scrope's secretary by 1620–21. Notestein et al., eds., *Commons Debates 1621*, 2:418, 420, 3:382, 387, 405–6; 4:404; 5:194, 394, 6:184. Brown, *Genesis of the U.S.*, pp. 545, 1065.

94. M. Havran, *The Catholics in Caroline England*, pp. 64, 94–95; Cliffe, *Yorkshire Gentry*, passim, but especially pp. 174, 200, 201–2, 243, 285–86, 295, 297.

95. Harrison, ed., *Ripon Millenary Record*, pt. 2, pp. xiii–xiv; Keeler, *Long Parliament*, pp. 75, 265–66; Neale, *Elizabethan House of Commons*, pp. 228–30; Cliffe, *Yorkshire Gentry*, pp. 88, 274, 285, 291. Hoby's antagonism toward Scrope and his loss of favor in 1626 may well indicate his own position of strength at Ripon, which continued to return him as one of its burgesses; Bean, *Northern Counties*, pp. 1037–38; Gleason, *JP's*, pp. 37–41, 75, 101, 111, 230, 233–35, 237.

96. Keeler, *Long Parliament*, pp. 74, 82, 153–54, 348–49; Cliffe, *Yorkshire Gentry*, p. 272; Darley's views and connections would hardly have recommended him to the Council of the North; Nichols, *Progresses*, 3:272 & n; W. Sheffield to the Bailiffs of Scarborough, 17 Jan. 1628, Scarborough Borough MSS, B. 1., General Letters, 1597–1642; Pepper to Savile, 8 Jan. 1621, BM Harleian MSS 7,000, f. 41, in Cartwright, *Chapters in Yorkshire History*, pp. 203–4. It is doubtful that Wentworth had anything to do with Wandesford's return. Their close friendship developed after the 1621 parliament and the death of Wentworth's wife, Margaret, in 1622; Cokayne, *Peerage*, 7:263. C. V. Wedgwood, *Strafford*, pp. 46–47; Wentworth to Sir H. Savile, 28 Nov. 1620, Sheffield City Library, Wentworth-Woodhouse MSS, 2(54), in Knowler, ed., *Strafford's Letters*, 1:8–9; see also Cartwright, *Chapters in Yorkshire History*, pp. 198–99; Burke, *Extinct Peerages*, p. 570; "Christopher Wandesford," *DNB*, 20:742–44; Lawson-Tancred, *Records of a Yorkshire Manor*, pp. 10–11, 374–76; Carvill, returned by Aldborough in 1621, 1624, 1625, and 1626, had been in the service of the earl of Northumberland (Batho, ed., *The Household Papers of Henry Percy, Ninth Earl of Northumberland, 1564–1632*, app. 3, p. 150). Carvill was of Nun Monkton, near Knaresborough, and had married the daughter of another county resident, Robert Kaye of Woodsome. Richard Aldborough, elected for the borough in 1625 and 1626, owed his place to his father, Arthur, who lived at Ellingthorpe Hall, Aldborough, and who bought the manor from the crown in 1629. Wandesford served again in 1624, and Robert Stapleton, elected in 1628, also owed his choice to his county influence. His religious views would hardly have been attractive to the council.

97. Lawson-Tancred, *Records of a Yorkshire Manor*, pp. 374–76; "Ferdinando Fairfax, second baron Fairfax of Cameron," *DNB*, 6:996–97; Bean, *Northern Counties*, p. 769; Cliffe, *Yorkshire Gentry*, pp. 53, 97.

98. McClure, ed., *Chamberlain's Letters*, 2:129, 610; Nichols, *Progresses*, 3:465; *CSPD 1625–1626*, p. 41; Keeler, *Long Parliament*, pp. 74, 75, 103–4, 134–35, 222–23; Bean, *Northern Counties*, pp. 740, 756, 761–62, 1087, 1088–89, 1091, 1093, 1094–95; Cliffe, *Yorkshire Gentry*, pp. 75, 91, 100, 289, 291, 292–93, 295, 298; *VCH Yorkshire North Riding*, 2:61, 63; A. M. W. Stirling, *The Hothams*, 1:20, 26; "Sir John Hotham," *DNB*, 9:1302–4; J. Dennett, ed., *Beverley Borough Records, 1575–1821*, p. xv; Lord Scrope to the Bailiffs of Scarborough, 14 Apr. 1625, Scarborough Borough MSS B. 1., General Letters 1597–1642. Alford's career in the county earned him the support of both Scrope and the court.

99. Wentworth to Sir H. Savile, 28 Nov. 1620, Sheffield City Library, Wentworth-Woodhouse MSS, 2(54); Pepper to Sir H. Savile, 8 Jan. 1621, BM Harleian MSS 7,000, f. 41, in Cartwright, *Chapters in Yorkshire History*, pp. 203–4; Bean, *Northern Counties*, p. 1016; Porritt, *Unreformed House of Commons*, 1:263–64; "James Howell," *DNB*, 10:109–14; *VCH Yorkshire, North Riding*, 1:11. Wharton's influence at Richmond was very short-lived; he died, aged 34, in April 1622 (Cokayne, *Peerage*, 8:125–26).

100. Cliffe, *Yorkshire Gentry*, 2:237; R. T. Gaskin, "The Cholmleys of Whitby," pp. 430–31, although Gaskin makes it 1624, when Hugh Cholmley, Sir Richard's son, served for Scarborough; Keeler, *Long Parliament*, pp. 134–35. William Conyers, elected from 1614 to 1624, was the son of a bailiff of Scarborough, and Sir Richard Cholmley's growing

influence at the port explained the election of his son, Hugh, in 1624–26. William Thompson, returned in 1625, owed his choice to the influence of John Ramsay, the earl of Holderness, and his own local connections. Scarborough attracted the attentions, too, in 1625 of Sir Edward Coke, who nominated himself, and the candidacy of Sir Guildford Slingsby, "controller of his Majesty's ships," probably had the backing both of his brother, Sir Henry Slingsby of Scriven, and the lord admiral, the duke of Buckingham. Another Yorkshireman, Richard Darley, also tried to place his son, Henry, at Scarborough. Tildesley and Ellis to the Bailiffs and Burgesses of Scarborough, 16 Jan. 1624, Bailiffs of Scarborough to Wm. Conyers, 26 Jan. 1624, R. Cholmley to the Bailiffs and Burgesses of Scarborough, 27 Jan. 1624, Lord Scrope to the Bailiffs, 14 Apr. 1625, Wm. Alford to the same, 6 May 1625, Bailey to Peacock, 21 Apr. 1625, Gargrave to Peacock and Ford, Bailiffs of Scarborough, 7 Apr. 1625, 1 May 1625, Sir Edw. Coke to the same, 25 Apr. 1625, Darley to the same, 1 May 1625, Sir R. Cholmley to the Bailiffs, 15 Apr. 1625, Wm. Thompson to Mr. Christopher Thompson, 25 Apr. 1625, Scarborough Borough MSS, General Letters, B. 1., 1597–1642; "Sir Hugh Cholmley," *DNB*, 4:268–69; Sir H. Cholmley, *The Memoirs of Sir Hugh Cholmley*, p. 25; *VCH Yorkshire, The North Riding*, 2:542, 556; Earl of Holderness to the Bailiffs of Scarborough, 4 Apr. 1625, in Baker, *Hist. Scarborough*, pp. 224–25; Baker also printed some of the other letters about the 1625 election, pp. 224–27; Carrol, "Parl. Repr. Yorkshire 1625–1660," pp. 51, 65–66; Cliffe, *Yorkshire Gentry*, pp. 87, 90, 100, 125, 164, 272; Cokayne, *Peerage*, 4:238.

101. Richard Darley's son Henry, in spite of the help of influential friends in 1626 and 1628, never won a place, nor did Thomas Alured, another local candidate, who tried in 1628. Duke of Buckingham to the Bailiffs of Scarborough, 6 Jan. 1626, Wm. Thompson to Jo. Ferrar, Bailiff, 8 Jan. 1626, Hutchinson to Ferrar and Peacock, Bailiffs, 16 Jan. 1626, Fox to Peacock and Ford, Sir. H. Cholmley to the Bailiffs 17 Jan. 1628, Harrison to the Bailiffs, Aldermen, and Burgesses of Scarborough, 31 Jan. 1628, Sir Wm. Constable to Fish and Wm. Conyers, Bailiffs of Scarborough, 1 Feb. 1628, the Earl of Mulgrave to the Bailiffs of Scarborough, 2 Feb. 1628, L. Alured to the same, 9 Feb. 1628, Scarborough Borough MSS, General Letters, B. 1., 1597–1642; Keeler, *Long Parliament*, pp. 153–54, 205–6; Cliffe, *Yorkshire Gentry*, pp. 16, 53, 338, 353; *VCH Yorkshire, North Riding*, 2:427, 499, 500; Baker, *Hist. Scarborough*, p. 227.

102. Pepper to Savile, 8 Jan. 1621, BM Harleian MSS 7,000, f. 41, in Cartwright, *Chapters in Yorkshire History*, pp. 203–4; Gooder, *Parl. Repr. Yorkshire*, pp. 126–28; Wentworth to Calvert, 5 Dec. 1620, the same to Lord Scrope, to Geo. Wethered, to Lascells, all 8 Dec. 1620, Sheffield City Library, Wentworth-Woodhouse MSS, 2(55-56), 2(60), 2(62), 2(63); the Wentworth to Calvert letter is in Knowler, ed., *Strafford's Letters*, 1:10; Sir T. Fairfax to the Lord President of the Council of the North, Lord Scrope, n.d. 1625, G. W. Johnson, ed., *The Fairfax Correspondence*, 1:5–7; it is also in Cartwright, *Chapters in Yorkshire History*, pp. 215–16.

103. York was under the steady control of its own corporation, and Knaresborough, once free of the Duchy of Lancaster's influence, was a gentry borough, dominated by the Hutton, Benson, and Slingsby families. Pontefract, restored to parliamentary representation in 1621, was, save for the prince's brief success in 1624, another safe borough for Yorkshire's gentry, particularly Sir Thomas Wentworth and his friends, who took the majority of its places from 1621 to 1628. Neale, *Elizabethan House of Commons*, pp. 190–92; Keeler, *Long Parliament*, pp. 75, 85–86, 107–8; "Sir Henry Slingsby," *DNB*, 18:375–77; Bean, *Northern Counties*, pp. 784, 824, 831, 904, 963; Cliffe, *Yorkshire Gentry*, pp. 103, 119, 126, 138, 146, 254, 283, 323, 356; De Villiers, "The Parliamentary Boroughs Restored by the House of Commons, 1625–41," pp. 186–187; Carrol, "Parl. Repr. Yorkshire, 1625–1660," pp. 49, 88; Cartwright, *Chapters in Yorkshire Hist.*, pp. 214–15; Wentworth to Lord Clifford, 23 Jan. 1624, Wentworth to Jackson, 6 Apr., Wentworth to the Mayor of Pontefract, spring? 1625, Beaumont to Wentworth, 9 June 1625, in Knowler, ed., *Stafford's Letters*, 1:25–27; the same letters are in the Wentworth-Woodhouse, MSS, Sheffield City Library, 20(254), and in Knowler, ed., *Strafford's Letters*, 1:30; Jackson to

Wentworth, 5 Feb. 1628, Bodleian Library, Firth MSS b. 2., f. 191a; Mayor of Pontefract to Wentworth, 6 May 1628, Wentworth Woodhouse MSS, Sheffield City Library, 12(31).

104. Neale, *Elizabethan House of Commons*, pp. 163–64; H. T. Weyman, "Members of Parliament for Ludlow," pp. 3–4, 16, 18–19; *Commons Journal*, 1:463; *HMC De L'Isle and Dudley*, 5:174; Shropshire County RO, Ludlow Corporation Minute Book, 1590–1648, 356/2/1, fols. 103v, 104.

105. Weyman, "Members of Parliament for Ludlow," pp. 20–25; Shropshire RO, Ludlow Corp. Minute Book 1590–1648, 356/2/1, fols. 131, 142, 150, 157v; Keeler, *Long Parliament*, pp. 190–91; Cokayne, *Peerage*, 6:71–72; "Spencer Compton, second Earl of Northampton," *DNB*, 4:905–6.

106. Dodd, *Studies in Stuart Wales*, pp. 178–79, 184–86, and "Wales's Parliamentary Apprenticeship," pp. 67–69, 70–72; Lloyd, *The Gentry of south-west Wales*, pp. 94, 111–12, 116, 130–32.

107. Owen Wynn to Sir Jo. Wynn, 11 Nov. 1620, Sir Rich. Wynn to Sir Jo. Wynn, 20 Dec. 1620, Compton, Earl of Northampton, to Bayly, Bishop of Bangor, n.d. Dec., 1620, Bayly to Owen Wynn, 24 Dec. 1620, NLW, Wynn MSS, (9057E), 918, 931, 934, 995; Northampton, Whitelock, and Townshend to the Sheriff and Justices of the Peace of Caernarvonshire, n.d. 1620, *HMC Rye and Hereford MSS*, 260. The document can be dated properly by remembering that Townshend, who signed it, died in 1621, which meant that the admoniton was aimed at the election of 1621 and not succeeding contests; Keeler, *Long Parliament*, pp. 79, 197, 402–3; Dodd, *Studies in Stuart Wales*, pp. 179–80, 188–89, and "Wales's Parliamentary Apprenticeship," pp. 42–43.

108. "Sir James Whitelocke," *DNB*, 21:117–19; Wm. Wynn to Sir Jo. Wynn, 6 Mar. 1622, Owen Wynn to the same, 12 May 1622, the same to the same, 14 June 1622, 2 Dec. 1623, Mostyn to Sir Jo. Wynn, 5, 8 Jan. 1624, Sir Wm. Thomas to Sir Jo. Wynn, 21 Jan. 1624, NLW, Wynn MSS (9058E), 1011, 1018, 1025; Keeler, *Long Parliament*, p. 281.

109. Sir Jo. Wynn to Sir Thos. Littleton, 6 Apr. 1625, Sir Wm. Thomas to Sir Jo. Wynn, 7 Apr. 1625, Sir Edw. Littleton to Sir Wm. Thomas, 12 Apr. 1625, Sir Jo. Wynn to Sir Wm. Thomas, 14 Apr. 1625, the same to Mutton, 14 Apr. 1625, Sir Wm. Thomas to Sir Jo. Wynn, 14 Apr. 1625, Mostyn to the same, 15 Apr. 1625, Mutton to the same, 16 Apr. 1625, Sir Jo. Wynn to Mutton, 17 Apr. 1625, Mutton to Sir Jo. Wynn, 18 Apr. 1625, NLW, Wynn MSS (9060E), 1314, 1316, 1318, 1320–22, 1324–25, 1328–30; Williams, *Parl. Hist. Wales*, p. 66; "Sir Edward Littleton, first Baron Littleton," *DNB*, 11:1245–47; A. H. Dodd, "Wales in the Parliaments of Charles I," pt. 1, 1625–29, p. 18.

110. Dodd, *Studies in Stuart Wales*, p. 59; Reid, *Council of the North*, app. 2, pp. 496–98.

111. "Sir Humphrey May," *DNB*, 13:140–41; Williams *Parl. Hist. Worcestershire*, p. 163; *VCH Worcestershire*, 4:309; A. Beaven, *The Aldermen of the City of London*, 1:276, 290; "Sir Heneage Finch," *DNB*, 7:7–8; "Sir Robert Heath," *DNB*, 9:346–49; Chamberlain to Carleton, 3 Mar. 1614, P.R.O., St. P. Dom. 14/76:39, in McClure, ed., *Chamberlain's Letters*, 1:515–16, and Birch, *Court and Times of James I*, 1:301–2; Zagorin, *Court and Country*, p. 143; Mead to Stuteville, 1 Mar. 1628, BM Harleian MSS 390, f. 350b; Beaulieu to Puckering, 27 Feb. 1628, BM Harleian MSS 7010, f. 75; Thomas Herbert? to Thos., Ld. Fairfax, 24 Feb. 1628, in Johnson, ed., *The Fairfax Correspondence*, 1:89–90, also in *HMC Hodgkin*, p. 44. London's municipal elections were, in the late 1620s, unruly affairs; and, as Hirst points out, the London parliamentary election in 1628 was also "matched by a municipal election challenge" that could "represent at least in part a spill-over from the municipal upheaval." London, like so many other cities and boroughs, was plagued by friction between its governing body and its citizenry (Hirst, *Representative of the People?*, pp. 48, 54–55, 109, 136, 142–43). Moir suggests that London only gave way to Montagu's election in 1614 because the crown abandoned its plan to have another London M.P., Sir Thomas Lowe, as Speaker of the House. The city would not, he argues, have "both its knights spokesmen of the Crown." (*Addled Parliament*, pp. 41–42); Marsham to Trumbull, 4 Mar. 1614, *HMC Downshire*, 4:325. Bewdley manor, held by Princes Henry and

Charles, was a court-controlled borough that was restored to the parliamentary franchise by the crown in 1605 with an electorate of thirteen. The first earl of Salisbury was probably behind its choice of Richard Young, Zouch's nominee at Dover in 1621 and 1624, in 1605, and the Prince's Council placed its candidates there in 1621 and 1624. Plumb, "The Growth of the Electorate in England from 1600 to 1715," p. 99 and n; Williams, *Parl. Hist. Worcestershire*, pp. 163–65.

112. Moir, *Addled Parliament*, p. 31; Chamberlain to Carleton, 3, 17 Mar. 1614, P.R.O., St. P. Dom. 14/76:39, 49, in McClure, ed., *Chamberlain's Letters*, 1:515–16, 517–19; "Sir Julius Caesar," *DNB*, 3:656–59; "Sir Thomas Lake," *DNB*, 11:417–19.

113. Locke to Carleton, 16 Dec. 1620, P.R.O. St. P. Dom. 14/118:30; Gerrard to Robt. Cotton, 16 Dec. 1620, BM Cottonian MSS, Julius C. III, f. 176; Sir Ch. Montague to Sir Edw. Montagu, 13 Dec. 1620, *HMC Buccleuch and Queensberry*, 1:255–56; Prestwich, *Cranfield*, pp. 289–90; Keeler, *Long Parliament*, pp. 185–86. Edmondes, refused by Middlesex in 1621, found a place at Bewdley, thanks to the Prince's Council, and Caesar, presumably with the help of Maldon's steward, the courtier Sir Henry Mildmay, was returned for that Essex borough. Maldon's Bailiffs to Sir Julius Caesar, n.d. January 1621?, Essex RO, D/B 3/3/392/67; Keeler, *Long Parliament*, p. 274. It is very doubtful that either Poole or Gatton, as Moir has suggested, came under Privy Council influence in 1614. Aristocratic patronage dominated Poole's Elizabethan elections, and, from 1603–1640, its returns seem to have been the province of its neighboring squirearchy (Moir, *Addled Parliament*, p. 49; Neale, *Elizabethan House of Commons*, pp. 197, 200, 211, 243). Gatton's manor lords, the Copleys, were recusants, something that kept them in constant hot water and ended their electoral control over the borough. Burghley intervened in 1584, and the council, through Sir Francis Walsingham, was involved in Gatton's 1586 election; but after that, it is more probable that Surrey's premier courtier-aristocrat, Lord Howard of Effingham, later the earl of Nottingham, was, along with Surrey's gentry, the more powerful electoral influence. The first earl was probably behind Sir John Brooke's return in 1614, and his successor as earl of Nottingham presumably saw to Gatton's choice of his kinsman, Sir Charles Howard, in 1625–28 and the election of the speaker designate for the Parliament of 1625, Sir Thomas Crew. Samuel Owfield had purchased a country estate at Gatton in 1624 and apparently gained control over one of the borough's seats. He served for Gatton in 1624, 1626, 1628, and 1640. However, he was elected at Midhurst, thanks it seems to Viscount Montague's patronage in 1625. He could have had a Gatton seat, but his election for Midhurst opened the way for Crew's return at Gatton, an election that suggests the Howard influence since Owfield's place at Midhurst was at the expense of a Hampshire courtier, Sir Walter Tichborne, who was returned, instead, for the earl of Suffolk's borough, Wootton Bassett in Wiltshire. The Copleys, however, were nothing if not determined; as late as 1628, Copley's return of Sir Jerome Weston and Sir Thomas Lake was refused by the House of Commons. Moir, *Addled Parliament*, p. 49; Neale, *Elizabethan House of Commons*, pp. 184–89; Brayley, *Hist. Surrey*, 4:89, 90; Manning and Bray, *Hist. Surrey*, 2:227, 231, 233–34; *VCH Surrey*, 3:196, 198–99 and n; Keeler, *Long Parliament*, pp. 65, 109–10, 116–17, 219–92; *Commons Journal*, 1:875; Ruigh, *Parliament of 1624*, pp. 98–100 and notes.

114. These figures are based on those shown in Appendix One. In 1614 the court was probably involved in 39 elections for its return of 48 places, whereas in 1624, when it intervened in 51 elections, it only gained 42 places, perhaps a suggestion that its electioneering was affected by the excitements that marked the elections of 1624 (Hirst, *Representative of the People?*, pp. 139–40).

115. For a detailed account of outsiders nominated by the various court agencies in each election, see Appendix Two.

# FOUR

## Aristocratic Patronage, 1614–1628

### 1. The Great Patrons

The electioneering of the aristocracy, of peers like Leicester, Essex, Huntingdon, or Norfolk, forms an essential part of the Elizabethan electoral story. Doubts, however, have been raised about the continuing importance of the peerage as electoral patrons in the reigns of Elizabeth's immediate successors. As territorial holdings shrank and political issues of a constitutional, economic, and religious nature became increasingly significant, the argument goes, the electoral influence of the aristocrat, and especially one with strong court connections, became increasingly precarious. It is a persuasive interpretation that becomes all the more interesting when it is recalled that between 1603 and 1628 "the peerage was given well over a million pounds' worth of crown lands and rents, which was perhaps as much as a quarter of all royal estates in 1603," and, as Professor Stone has estimated, assuming a possible population of around five million in 1630, "there were about twenty-five peers per million people," a figure that, with one exception, was "the highest ratio ever reached." Given that great increase in numbers, however, it does seem possible that aristocratic patronage would continue to play a prominent role in early Stuart elections.[1]

This chapter attempts to evaluate the electioneering of the early Stuart nobility from 1614 through 1628. It is divided into two sections, the first assessing the influence of the great patrons and the second discussing what is called the "Middle Rank" of aristocratic patronage, the influence of locally prestigious peers like the earls of Hertford, Salisbury, Warwick, or Rutland. The patronage of the earls of Pembroke and Arundel and the duke of Buckingham made them the three most significant aristocratic patrons between 1614 and 1628. Their stories illustrate the varied foundations of electoral influence. And, as a matter of convenience, the earl of Montgomery, Pembroke's brother, and the other Howards — Northampton, Berkshire, Nottingham, Suffolk — are also discussed. Only through such an evaluation can any appreciation of aristocratic patronage be obtained and the argument, that such influence was in decline, be tested.[2]

William Herbert, third earl of Pembroke, was the greatest electoral patron. In the elections from 1614 through 1628, his nominees may have taken as many as 98 places through his intervention in some 88 elections! His power rested on the solid foundations of land and great office. His nominees included kinsmen like Sir Edward Herbert, elected for Montgomery (1621), and Downton (1625–28), his stewards William Kent, returned for Devizes (1614), and Sir Thomas Morgan, one of Wilton's burgesses (1614–28), or his secretaries, John Thoroughgood, returned for Shaftesbury (1624–28) and Derby (1626), and Michael Oldisworth, one of Old Sarum's members (1624–28). Friends and clients like Sir John Stradling, chosen at St. Germans (1624), Old Sarum (1625), and Glamorganshire (1626), or Sir Benjamin Rudyerd, who served for Portsmouth (1621–25), Old Sarum (1626), and Downton (1628), were not forgotton; they owed their electoral careers to Pembroke's patronage.

Pembroke was a formidable officeholder. In 1604 James appointed him warden of the stannaries and lord lieutenant of Cornwall; in 1609 he became the captain of Portsmouth, and two years later he joined the Privy Council. That was just the beginning for, before James's death in 1625, Pembroke was also appointed as lord chamberlain (1615–25) and made chancellor of the University of Oxford (1617). He succeeded the earl of Hertford as lord lieutenant of Somersetshire and Wiltshire in 1621. Charles confirmed him in his offices in 1625 and advanced him to the post of lord steward in 1626. Pembroke's marriage, in 1604, linked him to the powerful Derbyshire influence of the Shrewsbury-Cavendish connection and contributed to Derby's decision to select him as its high steward in 1617.[3]

Pembroke and his family were great landowners in western England and in southern and central Wales. Wiltshire's elections showed his hand, as did borough contests at Wilton (his residence), Downton, Old Sarum, Shaftesbury, and Cardiff, where his manorial rights gave him a powerful voice. However, Salisbury, only a few miles from his home, rejected his patronage, as its firm refusal of his nominee in 1626 demonstrated. Pembroke and his friend the earl of Hertford saw to Wiltshire's 1625 election of Hertford's kinsman Sir Francis Seymour and Sir Henry Ley. Seymour probably enjoyed similar support in the county contests of 1621 and 1628, and it is possible that in 1624 Pembroke's influence might have contributed to the county's choice of one of Buckingham's friends, Sir John St. John, whose Wiltshire influence was hardly enough to warrant his choice. Prince Charles had, in late 1623, done his utmost to reconcile Pembroke and the royal favorite, Buckingham, and St. John's rather surprising return may have been a byproduct of the prince's good offices.[4]

It is likely that, from 1614 through 1628, Downton returned at least one Pembroke nominee in each election; and in 1625, 1626, and 1628, both its members were probably his candidates. Wilton's elections were even more under his control. It was the earl's home, and its returns showed it. His power was so complete that he could order the mayor to "send me up a blank, that therein I may insert the name of such one of my friends as I shall think fit"; and this after already nominating his steward, Sir Thomas Morgan, for one of its places. Sir John Evelyn, returned with Morgan in 1626, was presumably Pembroke's second nominee. Wilton gave up eleven, possibly all twelve, of its places to Pembroke's candidates. Morgan served in all six parliaments and was joined by the earl's friend Sir Robert Sidney in 1614, his kinsman Sir Percy Herbert in 1624, and Sir William Herbert in 1625 and 1628. With that record of predominance, it is hard to imagine that Sir Thomas Tracy's choice in 1621 was not due at least to Pembroke's tacit agreement. But with or without Tracy, Wilton was Pembroke's pocket borough.[5]

Old Sarum, perhaps the most famous — or possibly infamous — of all parliamentary boroughs, was so supine that its favors were the cause of a battle between two competing patrons, the second earl of Salisbury and Pembroke! Robert Cecil, the first earl of Salisbury, held the castle of Old Sarum at his death in 1612. Pembroke, however, was the tenant of the manor of Old Sarum, a position he employed to probably win both places for his nominees in 1604 and 1614. However, the second earl of Salisbury, who may have leased "the castle site and sporting rights," was determined to have his way over Old Sarum's elections. His bid for influence failed in 1614, but he did manage to place a candidate at Old Sarum in both 1621 and 1624. Pembroke was furious at Salisbury's challenge and, in 1621, took Salisbury to task for his interference, plainly telling him "in these elections of Burgesses I can not conceive how your Lordship can claim any right, the nominating of them depending only upon their own choice, and swayed by their affection," a perhaps surprising thing to say, coming from as veteran a patron as Pembroke! But what really galled Pembroke was that Salisbury's triumph violated Pembroke's traditional power: "The dwellers of that borough have ever since my memory showed their respect to my father and myself in choosing those whom we have recommended unto them." He was sarcastic, too; he could not understand why Salisbury, "having the Castle or rather the stones," should try to assert his authority. Salisbury fought back; in 1624 he brought in the leasehold interest and started Chancery proceedings to secure clear control. But his efforts were of little avail. Pembroke's nominees, Michael Oldisworth and Sir John Stradling, took both places in 1625 and again in 1626, when Sir Benjamin Rudyerd joined Oldisworth. Salisbury and Pembroke split the representation in 1628 when Oldisworth was elected along with Salisbury's receiver-general, Christopher Keightley. Pembroke had by far the better of Old Sarum's elections: his candidates took nine places, Salisbury's three. As for Old Sarum, its elections from 1614 through 1628 did nothing to change its image as a "rotten" borough.[6]

The manor of Shaftesbury had become part of the Pembroke patrimony in 1553, but William, the third earl, only came into its possession in September 1621; his mother had held it prior to her death. This made no difference in its elections. In 1614 Henry Croke was probably his nominee; Sir Simeon Steward, of Cambridge University, who replaced Sir Miles Sandys at Shaftesbury, also enjoyed Pembroke's support. Shaftesbury chose another outsider and possible Pembroke nominee, Sir William Beecher, in 1621 and matched him with one of its own, Thomas Sheppard. But their election was of short duration. Beecher preferred to sit for Leominster, and Sheppard made an apparently unhappy speech that led to his expulsion from the House; Pembroke's relative, Percy Herbert, took one of the vacant places. Pembroke's secretary, John Thoroughgood, was returned from 1624 to 1628, and when in 1626 he chose to serve for Derby instead, another Pembroke nominee nimbly stepped into his place, Buckingham's violent antagonist, Samuel Turner. Shaftesbury was not totally under the earl's power; he can only be credited with seven of its twelve places, but it is still enough to place the borough in Pembroke's sphere of influence — a safe seat for each election.[7]

Although it is true that Pembroke's influence, and that of his kinsmen, did not reach "beyond mid-Wales" into the north, his family's power in Glamorgan, Montgomery, and Monmouthshire is impressive. The list of M.P.'s for Cardiff and Glamorganshire is a roll call of Pembroke's clients, kinsmen, and friends. William Price, whom we have met as a Pembroke nominee for Old Sarum in 1614, served for Glamorganshire in 1621 and then, thanks to his Welsh connections and Pembroke's support, was returned from 1624 through 1626 for Cardiff. Cardiff had elected another possible Pembroke nominee in 1614, Matthew Davies, and William Herbert owed his election in 1621 to "the Countess of Pembroke [who] out of her honorable disposition toward me" wrote "her bailiffs and townsmen of Cardiff that they should make choice of me for their burgess." Lewis Morgan, the son of Pembroke's steward, Sir Thomas Morgan (Wilton's M.P. 1614–28), filled Cardiff's place in 1628. Glamorganshire's story was similar. By the elections of 1624, another courtier with Welsh ties, Sir Robert

Mansell, had become a client of the earl's; his election for Glamorganshire in 1624, 1625, and 1628 was the result. In 1626 the county returned another Welshman who was part of Pembroke's group, Sir John Stradling. Glamorganshire was, for Stradling, the end of a Pembroke-sponsored parliamentary career: he had previously served for St. Germans (1624) and Old Sarum (1625). Of the twelve places for Glamorganshire and Cardiff, eleven were Pembroke's. The county and borough elected seven men between 1614 and 1628; to some degree six of them owed their parliamentary service to Pembroke's patronage.[8]

This was not the end of the Herbert influence in Wales. The Herberts of Cherbury, kinsmen to the earl, completely dominated Montgomeryshire's returns from 1614 through 1628. Sir William Herbert was returned for the county in all six parliaments, preferring it to Wilton, which also elected him in 1625 and 1628. Sir John Danvers, who became Oxford University's favorite member, was chosen at Montgomery in 1614; his marriage tied him to the Herberts of Montgomery Castle. His successor in 1621 was Sir Edward Herbert of Aston; he would be elected for Downton in 1625–28 and end his career at Old Sarum in the 1640s. The poet George Herbert served for Montgomery in 1624 and 1625; he was Lord Herbert of Cherbury's brother and married the daughter of Charles Danvers of Wiltshire, a kinsman to Montgomery's member in 1614. In 1626 the borough returned another brother, Sir Henry Herbert, who had served with Sir Robert Cecil in the French negotiations of 1598 and who was, during James's reign, master of the revels. Given Montgomery's election record from 1614 through 1626, it is probable that Richard Lloyd (1628) was a nominee of, or at least acceptable to, the Herberts. But since there is no direct connection, Lloyd is not included among the Herberts' successes. Even without him, the results are impressive testimony to their influence, and since both Sir William and Sir Edward Herbert were also chosen in Pembroke's English constituencies, the results in Montgomeryshire can fairly be added to the patronage picture of the earl of Pembroke. The county and borough had twelve places; the Herberts captured eleven. Montgomeryshire belonged to them. Two of Pembroke's nominees at Wilton also served for Monmouthshire. A Welshman, Sir Edmund Morgan (Wilton, 1601), was returned for the county in 1621 as was Robert, Lord Lisle (Wilton, 1614), who took a Monmouthshire place in 1624 and 1625. Pembroke's other nominee in the county was another relative, William Herbert, chosen in 1626.[9]

Pembroke's offices also provided him with opportunities for patronage that he quickly seized. His post as Derby's high steward and his connections to the Cavendish family probably explained the election of

Sir Edward Leech of Cardens, Cheshire, and London, a master in chancery who was returned for Derby 1621–25 and Derbyshire in 1628. Leech had begun his royal service with the Duchy of Cornwall (thanks to Pembroke?), and the earl employed one of Leech's kinsman, John Leech, as his secretary. John Leech visited America in 1621 when Pembroke wanted some firsthand knowledge of the Virginia colony. John Thoroughgood's election for Derby in 1626 was a sure sign of Pembroke's support, and the town's choice of another outsider, Philip Mainwaring in 1628, one of Arundel's nominees at Steyning in 1624, may have also been Pembroke's work. Portsmouth, where Pembroke served as governor from 1609, also granted him a place from 1621 through 1626. Sir Benjamin Rudyerd, who never left the shelter of a Pembroke borough, was elected in 1621, 1624, and 1625. Pembroke's control of one place was so secure that Rudyerd could write, in February 1626: "I am not yet certain that I am of the Parliament [he would be, serving for Old Sarum], having delivered my usual place of Portsmouth to my brother Harrington Lieutenant there, who desired it of me so late, that all my Lord's letters were sent out before." Harrington was returned, but since he was also elected at Hertford and preferred it to Portsmouth, another Pembroke nominee, Sir James Fullerton, stepped into Harrington's place. In 1628, though, the story changed. Thanks to their reconciliation, Pembroke turned over his influence at Portsmouth to the duke of Buckingham, who saw to the ports' election of Owen Jennings and William Towerson.[10]

Traces of Pembroke's patronage as Oxford University's chancellor are hard to find, but given his electoral enthusiasm and the precedent of his predecessor's 1614 interference, Pembroke's intervention is highly probable. He was presumably behind the choice of Clement Edmondes, clerk of the Privy Council, in 1621; and when Edmondes's colleague, Sir John Bennett, was expelled from the House of Commons for bribery, Pembroke probably nominated Sir John Danvers to replace him. Danvers had married into the Herbert family and had served for the family borough of Montgomery (1614). In 1624 Pembroke's influence may have secured one place, and in 1625 and 1626 Pembroke probably joined his friend and frequent ally George Abbot, archbishop of Canterbury, in nominating Sir Thomas Edmondes. They succeeded in 1625 but in 1626 ran afoul of an electoral rebellion led by the junior bachelors and masters who backed Sir Francis Stuart. Their petition against Edmondes's return was accepted by the House of Commons, and in the following election, Stuart won. Stuart, oddly enough, was Pembroke's nominee at Liskeard, but the scholars' revolt apparently foiled Pembroke's plan to place both Edmondes and Stuart, his allies against Buckingham in 1626. Pembroke nominated two men in 1628. His first nominee, Sir Henry Marten, was a man the university both knew and admired; Pembroke promised Marten would serve without charge. However, his second candidate, his secretary, Michael Oldisworth, was refused. By 1628 one nominee was all the university's electorate would stand. But despite growing resistance, Pembroke still had employed his office as university chancellor to electoral advantage.[11]

As lord warden of the stannaries and lord lieutenant, Pembroke could have been expected to play a considerable role in Cornwall's elections. But he faced stiff competition from the local gentry, the Duchy of Cornwall (under the Prince's direction), and, after 1624, from the duke of Buckingham. Pembroke was probably behind Lostwithiel's choice of Edward Leech in 1614, and his interest in the Virginia Company might have been the reason behind Callington's 1621 return of the earl of Southamptom's fifteen-year-old (!) son. In 1624 possibly four places can be credited to Pembroke's influence. William Coryton, a Cornish squire who was Pembroke's vice-warden and deputy lieutenant, was returned for Cornwall, and the choice of his clients, Sir John Stradling at St. Germans and George Mynne by West Looe, was further evidence of the earl's successful intervention. He may also have placed a candidate at Fowey. In Charles's first election, only Coryton's return for Liskeard and the choice of his dependent Sir James Fullerton at St. Mawes, was Pembroke's work. However, in 1626 the story changed. By election time the Pembroke-Buckingham alliance had collapsed, and Pembroke spared no effort in finding places for prospective antagonists of the duke. He had, as Buckingham's western agent Sir James Bagg admitted, the "means of placing divers burgesses; and most readily by the solicitation of William Coryton." Coryton had allegedly admitted that he had "delivered to his Lordship [Pembroke] the burgess-ship of Lostwithiel for Sir Robert Mansell," a statement born out by the indenture since Mansell's name was inserted in a different hand on the document. And that was not all. Pembroke's secretary, Thoroughgood, had urged Coryton to find places for "Sir Francis Stuart, Sir Robert Mansell, Sir Clipsby Crew, and Mr. William Murray." Bagg could not remember the name of the fifth candidate, but it must have been Sir Benjamin Rudyerd, usually chosen at Portsmouth (1621–25), who appeared as one of three candidates in a hotly contested Grampound election, which he won, although he preferred another Pembroke borough, Old Sarum. If Bagg was right, and he probably was, Coryton did his work well. Mansell, thanks to the blank indenture, served for Lostwithiel, Crew for Callington, Murray at Fowey, and Stuart, an outspoken critic of Buckingham, for Liskeard. Coryton won one of Cornwall's places. Had Rudyerd remained at Grampound, it would have given Pembroke a total of six Cornish places in 1626. Before the next election, however, Buckingham had patched up his relationship with Pembroke, arranging a marriage alliance with Pembroke's heir, the son of his brother the earl of Montgomery, and seeing to Pembroke's new post as lord steward. Buckingham had listened to the advice of his clients, like Sir John Hippisley, who had urged him "to get my Lord Steward [Pembroke] to make such as shall comply with the king's occasions and not to make Sir Thomas Lake and Doctor Turner and such like that" members of the impending parliament. Pembroke, though, did not abandon all his friends. Coryton was elected for Cornwall, Murray for East Looe, and Stuart at Liskeard.[12]

Pembroke's success as an election patron was remarkable for any period; it exceeded anything known about an Elizabethan aristocrat's patronage and provides a powerful criticism of the suggested decay of aristocratic influence. It was recognized by Pembroke's contemporaries; in 1625, when Sir Dudley Carleton sought a place in parliament, it was suggested that he try "my Lord Chamberlain [Pembroke]." In 1628 Hippisley's suggestions to Buckingham afforded a similar glimpse of Pembroke's election power. And no wonder; Pembroke's influence was the greatest of the early seventeenth century, and the court knew it, from the great Buckingham down to the courtier Sir Dudley Carleton.[13] Pembroke, however, was not the only patron in the family, and before leaving the Herberts, his brother's patronage should be reviewed.

. Pembroke's younger brother, Philip, earl of Montgomery from 1605, enjoyed modest electoral success. His rise was assured by James's esteem and affection; his patronage was based on royal rewards. He was granted the captaincy of Queenborough Castle, which, custom indicated, included nomination rights for one of the town's burgessships. But Montgomery, between 1614–1628, turned the town into his pocket borough, settling for one place in 1614, 1625, and 1628 and taking both in 1621, 1624, and 1626. Sir Roger Palmer, the Kentish courtier, was his favorite client; he served for Queenborough in 1614 and again from 1624 to 1628. Montgomery's preeminence did not go unchallenged, although the competition, in 1621, came from another peer, Kent's lord lieutenant, the duke of Lennox, who unsuccessfully tried to place "Richard Hadsor, Esqr., . . . one of his Majesty's Learned Counsel" for Ireland. Montgomery had no trouble in 1624; and although he promised the corporation that its double choice of his clients would not "prejudice you in your future elections," there can be no doubt that the earl's interests already exceeded his predecessor's acknowledged nomination rights.

Queenborough, however, took Montgomery at his word, for in 1625 it resisted his attempt to nominate both burgesses; one was enough. The earl was not at all happy about this surprising turn of events. Palmer was elected, but the town's refusal of Robert Pooley was "indiscreet and uncivil." Queenborough had chosen Sir Edward Hales, a Kentish squire, but even the fact that the election was over did not deter the furious Montgomery. He claimed that Hales was ready "to waive acceptance of that burgess-ship, which you would inforce upon him; if in his room you choose not the said Mr. Pooley, . . . I shall construe it as a neglect and scorn doubled upon me." His letter ended on an ominous note: he was Queenborough's "friend according to your behavior to me in this and in the future." It is not clear if Queenborough buckled under this blast; Hales is listed in the *Official Return* as one of its burgesses, but in the same year Queenborough won a new charter thanks to Montgomery's help. If Hales was eased out in Pooley's favor, nothing survives to tell the tale; perhaps, too, Queenborough promised its angry patron all future subservience and Montgomery dropped the matter.[14] Montgomery's men took both places in 1626, but in the next election, the earl settled for one. Of Queenborough's twelve places, nine were taken by his nominees; four of the six men who served for the town were his servants or clients. Queenborough was the election property of the earl of Montgomery, captain of its castle.[15]

Montgomery was appointed lord lieutenant of Kent in 1625 and promptly intervened in that county's election. He urged Rochester's corporation to rally support for Buckingham's successful candidate, Sir Albertus Morton, and Mildmay Fane, Lord Burghersh. The earl also intervened at Canterbury, winning a seat there for John Fisher in 1625 and nominating his servant James Palmer in 1626. The 1626 election was a bitter battle, involving some of Canterbury's ministers of the "popular" side—against Palmer—and the corporation, which backed him with a campaign featuring threats, slander, the sheriff's contumacy, alehouse electioneering, and ineligible voters. With the corporation's steadfast, if questionable, assistance, Palmer won the burgess-ship.[16]

Woodstock, Oxfordshire, was far different than Queenborough for Montgomery. Although he was the steward of the royal manors and keeper of both the house and park, Woodstock resolutely fought off his place-hunting. He tried in 1614 without result, and if he made nominations in the next three elections, he was just as unsuccessful. However, with the election of Edmund Taverner in 1626 and 1628, Montgomery finally had his way. Taverner, a courtier, was a secretary of his brother, the earl of Pembroke, and after Pembroke died in 1630, he entered Montgomery's service. Woodstock customarily preferred to choose its recorders or the nominees of its steward, Sir Thomas Spencer.[17]

Montgomery was much the junior partner in the family electoral firm, as befitted a younger man who had to rely for his patronage solely on the offices he won from a grateful king. Altogether, from 1614 to 1628, he was probably involved in twelve elections in behalf of candidates who may have secured thirteen places, a far cry from his older brother's patronage record. As noted earlier, Pembroke probably intervened in as many as eighty-eight elections with a likely return, for his servants, clients, and kinsmen, of some ninety-eight places. His most active election, it seems likely, was in 1626; he was probably involved in nineteen elections in behalf of candidates who can be credited with twenty places.[18] Pembroke and Montgomery were not the only place-hunting aristocrats, nor was Pembroke the only great patron. The Howard family, too, was an electioneering lot, and its influence deserves investigation.

The most influential of the Howards was Thomas, earl of Arundel and Surrey, privy councillor and earl marshal by 1621. His influence can be found in elections in Suffolk, Surrey, Northumberland, Sussex, and Norfolk, where, in addition to some county electoral success, his nominees also found burgess-ships at Castle Rising and Thetford. In Sussex, Arundel, Bramber, Horsham, Shoreham, and Chichester came, in varying degrees, under his influence between 1614 and 1628. Arundel's returns clearly illustrated his domination, and at Chichester, where he was high steward from 1618, he shared electoral patronage with its powerful neighbors at Petworth, the Percys. In 1625 Arundel's letters of recommendation for Shoreham, Chichester, and Arundel were delivered by his servant Humphrey Haggett to Lady Arundel's steward, "Mr. Spiller," no doubt Sir Henry Spiller. Spiller, who had already been elected for Arundel in 1614, 1621, and 1624, was again dutifully chosen by the borough. Other likely nominees of the earl included Lionel Cranfield, elected in 1621 and his son, Henry Howard, Lord Maltravers, chosen in 1628. Only once, in 1626, did Arundel's elections show no apparent trace of the earl's influence. All told, his patronage accounted for a minimum of six of the borough's twelve places. At Chichester his intervention probably accounted for its choice of Sir Edward Cecil (1621), Sir Thomas Edmondes (1624), and his servant Humphrey Haggett (1625, 1626). Shoreham, however, escaped the Howard grasp. Arundel's kinsman, the earl of Nottingham, had placed nominees there in five elections between 1586 and 1614, but Arundel had almost no success. Sir John Leeds, the Sussex courtier, had been chosen at Bramber, where Arundel was lord of the manor, in 1614; his return at Shoreham in 1621 may have been the earl's work. But his bid in 1625 certainly failed. Shoreham elected a resident, William Marlott, who owned malthouses in the town, and a neighboring squire, Anthony Stapley, who lived at Patcham, Sussex. Their return illustrated Shoreham's changing electoral pattern: it had become a safe borough for the Sussex squirearchy.[19]

Horsham's elections, however, testified to Arundel's successful patronage. In 1614 the choice of Sir Thomas Vavasour, an outsider and courtier, was possibly Arundel's work, and in 1621 it is likely that another outsider, Thomas Cornwallis, owed his Horsham seat to the earl's intervention. Arundel's secretary, John Borough, was returned from 1624 to 1626; he was, thanks to Arundel, appointed Mowbray Herald in 1623. Dudley North, another stranger to Horsham, won a place in 1628, completing the roster of likely Arundel electoral clients.[20] The earl, however, did not do so well at Steyning, where evidence of his intervention survives. His nominees, "Mr. Philip Mainwaring and Mr. William Gardiner," were turned down in both 1621 and 1624, although, on the latter occasion, he even promised the borough "they shall not require any parliament wages." Arundel's influence was unable, it appears, to compete with that of the Percys, whose residence was but twelve miles away from Steyning and whose steward, Sir Edward Francis, represented the borough in every parliament from 1614 to 1626. The remainder of the borough's members were, in all likelihood, the nominees of neither nobleman.[21]

Norfolk and two of its boroughs, Castle Rising and Thetford, were occasionally subjected to Arundel's patronage. He was a great Norfolk property owner and the county's lord lieutenant, but despite these advantages, he hardly dominated county elections. As Derek Hirst has pointed out, the combination of Norfolk's large electorate and its politically sophisticated gentry often meant contested elections. Gentry agreement, freeholder disagreement, and suspicion about the motives and influence behind the candidacy of Arundel's county agent, Sir Thomas Holland of Quidenham and Wortwell Hall, Norfolk, led to an exciting contest in 1624. Holland's candidacy aroused considerable suspicion among the freeholders and some of the gentry, too, perhaps, "the best suspecting Sir Tho: (Holland) for his patron's sake." Some even claimed that Holland would "rather serve his Lord [Arundel] in the county than in parliament"; but in spite of much turmoil, an abortive and confused poll, and a resulting petition, Holland's election was confirmed by the Commons. The bitterness of the struggle was echoed by the House itself; it had to take a division, rare indeed in election cases, before accepting Holland's return. It was not without significance that Thetford's member, Drew Drury, spoke strongly in Holland's behalf during the debate. His kinsman Sir Robert Drury had sought, through Sir Robert Cotton, the electoral aid of both the earls of Arundel and Northampton in 1614, and Drew Drury's return for Thetford in 1624 was probably Arundel's work and explained Drury's defense of Holland's election. It is likely, too, that Drew Drury (Norfolk 1621) and Sir Anthony Drury (Norfolk 1625) had Arundel's help.[22]

Thetford's elections from 1621 through 1628 show Arundel's hand. His deceased kinsman, Northampton, had placed a nominee at Thetford in 1614, and Arundel was able, in the succeeding elections, to sustain the Howard influence. The choices of Sir Thomas Holland (1621) and Drew Drury (1624) can be credited to the earl's account. Firm evidence reveals his intervention in 1625 when Thetford's corporation informed Sir Robert Cotton that, although he was a "a stranger unto us, yet upon the commendation of the right honorable the Earl of Arundel our most worthy lord," they would willingly choose him as one of their burgesses. Sir John Hobart, a courtier and Norfolk gentleman, probably had Arundel's support in 1626, and in the next election, the earl nominated Sir Henry Spiller, his frequent candidate at Arundel borough. Spiller, however, preferred to serve for Middlesex, which aroused the hopes of the Gawdy family for the suddenly vacant burgess-ship. It was thought that Framlingham Gawdy, then serving as Norfolk's sheriff, might "easily prevail with them [Thetford] to choose Sir Charles Gawdy . . . which my Lord of Arundel can be no means take ill from them of the town since their intentions were to have gratified his Lordship in choosing Sir Henry Spiller." The Gawdys, however, sadly underestimated Arundel's power and efficiency: he substituted Sir Henry Vane, a courtier and royal official, in Spiller's place.[23]

Castle Rising was another borough that sometimes listened to Arundel. He nominated "R. S. and J. W." successfully in 1621; the initials stand for Robert Spiller, Sir Henry's son, and John Wilson, presumably another Arundel dependent. The evidence for their nomination is contained in a misdated letter at the Public Record Office, one of three "form" letters prepared by Arundel before the 1624 election for, among other boroughs, Castle Rising. In 1624 Spiller was again nominated, along with "A. D.," who might have been Anthony Drury of Besthorpe. Whoever A. D. happened to be, he was not returned; Arundel had to be satisfied with Spiller's choice. Sir Robert Cotton's election in 1628 marks the only other certain sign of Arundel's influence. Thomas Bancroft, returned by Castle Rising from 1624 to 1628, had been an Exchequer official who had purchased the manor of Santon from Arundel in 1623. His parliamentary career began immediately after his land purchase, a somewhat surprising event in a county like Norfolk, where the gentry were anxious place-hunters. His sudden parliamentary success can possibly be explained by Arundel's support. If that is so, then Arundel's nominees took eight of Castle Rising's twelve places, a better record than he achieved at Thetford, where he had to settle for five of its twelve burgess-ships. His competition, the influential Norfolk squirearchy, were a hardy and determined lot.[24]

Three widely scattered boroughs—Aldeburgh, Suffolk; Reigate, Surrey; and Morpeth, Northumberland—complete Arundel's patronage story. At Reigate, Arundel succeeded in placing "T. G. [Sir Thos. Glemham] upon my nomination" in 1621, but his nomination of "R. Co. [Robert Cotton?]" in 1624 was refused, and, with that denial, Arundel's influence came to an end. Reigate, though, remained in the Howard family orbit: the second earl of Nottingham and his stepmother continued to exercise a determining voice in its elections. Arundel had better luck with Aldeburgh. In the second of the form letters he prepared for the elections of 1624, he pointed out that at the last parliament" upon my recommendation and nomination you did readily and freely make choice of Sir Hen: Glemham Knt. [his successful nominee in 1614 at Aldeburgh] and Mr. C. Gl. [Charles Glemham] for your burgesses." He nominated them again, stressing that they "shall willingly serve you at their own charge." Aldeburgh chose the Glemhams in 1621, but in 1624 Arundel's plans went wrong: neither was returned. But he was not discouraged; perhaps his letter had simply been late in 1624. He was behind the election of Sir Thomas and Charles Glemham in 1625, and in 1626 Aldeburgh chose Sir Thomas Glemham and William Mason, possibly one of Arundel's servants. The Glemhams had strong Suffolk connections and were related to the Sackvilles, earls of Dorset. Charles Glemham was in Arundel's employ in 1614 and later held a variety of minor court appointments. He served as captain of Sandown Castle, Kent, until his death and was interested in matters of overseas trade, gaining a commission in 1622 to travel to the lands of the "Great Mongul"; and three years later, he was involved, at the king's request, in the affairs of the Levant company. He also sought Buckingham's support in his hopes for a post in the king's Household. Sir Henry Glemham, in contrast, seemed to confine himself to Suffolk affairs. Seven of Aldeburgh's twelve places, from 1614 to 1628, were taken by Arundel's nominee's; he had certainly succeeded in keeping the borough loyal to the Howard family.[25] Morpeth's manor lord was the Catholic Lord William Howard of Naworth, brother to the earl of Suffolk and uncle to the earl of Arundel. From Morpeth's returns it seems clear that Lord William frequently put Morpeth's burgess-ships at the disposal of his kinsmen. Arundel's success at Morpeth was a result of such generosity and explained the election of Sir Thomas Reynell (1624–28) of Devonshire and Lalam, Middlesex, whose wife was the daughter of Arundel's dependent, Sir Henry Spiller. Thomas Cotton, chosen in 1625, was Lord William Howard's son-in-law; he was also the son of Arundel's friend Sir Robert Bruce Cotton, whom Arundel placed, in the same election, at Thetford. Morpeth's burgess-ships were, to all intents and purposes, a family preserve; Arundel and Suffolk's clients filled eight of its twelve places from 1614 to 1628. Suffolk's contribution will be dealt with later; Arundel, it seems, can be safely credited with four places at his uncle's borough.[26]

Arundel's intervention in as many as forty-four elections, with a likely harvest of forty-five places, made him the most successful of the Howards and, behind Pembroke and Buckingham, the most energetic place-hunter in England. His achievement was all the more noteworthy when it is remembered that he did it without the aid of any great office that could bring him the ready prospect of election patronage.[27]

Henry Howard, earl of Northampton, had been the most prolific electoral patron among the Howards in 1604; he was again in 1614. His strength rested on the usual foundations of land and office, and he used them well. As we have seen, he employed his position as lord warden of the Cinque Ports to good effect, gathering a harvest of ten places in the ports alone. At Cambridge University, where he was chancellor, he placed Sir Miles Sandys. Sandys's victory was won through the assistance of the sheriff and the loyalty of the university community, who, in a quarrelsome election, managed to overcome the determination of the vice chancellor and the heads of the colleges to keep control of the university's elections in their own hands. Northampton also asked Dartmouth and Totness for one place, but at each borough the stubborn opposition of the corporations and competition from Sir George Carey, who had his own nominees to place, proved too much for Northampton to overcome. At least at Dartmouth, Carey failed too.[28]

Success marked Northampton's other efforts. He was lord of the manor at Bishop's Castle, which elected his candidate, Thomas Hitchcock, a London barrister who promised, as an added inducement, "to serve without fees for the town." At Strafford, where he was high steward, his successful nominee was Thomas Gibbs, and Portsmouth returned his secretary, John Griffith. In Norfolk, Thetford was committed "to the commandments of my Lord of Northampton" and elected Sir William Twysden of East Peckham, Kent; Castle Rising's choice of Thomas Bing and Great Yarmouth's election of Sir Theophilus Finch may also have been at his request. Northampton might have tried to capture a place at Eye since Sir Charles Cornwallis, who gained a certain fame for his participation in the breaking of the Addled Parliament, intended to serve in that parliament and set off for Eye, where he had hopes of being elected. Did he have a letter from Northampton in his behalf? If so, he never mentioned it; but he did admit that he had given to "two gentlemen recommended unto me by Dr. Sharpe letters recommendatory from the Earl of Northampton for two burgess-ships." One was for Hitchcock (Bishop's Castle), but he never identified the second and leaves us wondering if there was another borough within the earl's grasp. Eye's election was finished when Cornwallis arrived; Sir Robert Drury, who had sought Northampton's help at Thetford, had been chosen. Perhaps the earl placed him at Eye? It is, at least, a possibility.[29] Northampton's patronage, including his intervention as lord warden, accounted for eighteen places in seventeen elections, a very strong showing, indeed.[30] It was his last; he died shortly after the dissolution of the Parliament of 1614.

Although he never ventured into Essex or its borough elections again, after 1604–10, Thomas Howard, earl of Suffolk, still managed to find electoral influence elsewhere. Most of his patronage was the result of his second marriage into the Knyvett family of Charlton, Wiltshire, where Suffolk built a grand house at Charlton Park. His wife's estates were close to Malmesbury, on the edge of Charlton Park, and within about a twelve-mile radius of Charlton, Suffolk could cast his eye on the elections at Calne, Cricklade, and Wootton Bassett. From the returns of those boroughs from 1614 through 1628, it seems pretty clear that Suffolk and, later, one of his sons by Catherine Knyvett, Thomas Howard, Viscount Andover (1622) and earl of Berkshire (1626), did just that.[31]

In 1614 Suffolk intervened in the Norfolk election and at Ipswich and Dunwich, with little success. His plans for Norfolk's election went badly awry, thanks to the sheriff's chicanery. Sir Henry Rich, one of James's favorites, went forth "confidently into Norfolk with my Lord Chamberlain's [Suffolk] warrant and letters" and, no doubt, with the knowledge that all the Howard tenants had been mustered in his behalf. The sheriff, however, was more loyal to the local candidates, Sir Henry Bedingfield and Sir Hamon le Strange; when it became obvious that Rich had the greater number of freeholders at the shire court, held as usual at Norwich, the sheriff's deputy, following a prearranged plan, abruptly moved the county court some twenty miles to Swaffham, where, surprisingly enough, the sheriff was ready to hold the election. Only a few freeholders, loyal to Bedingfield and le Strange, were present; they were, as might be expected, declared elected by the scheming sheriff. Suffolk's nominee, Rich, was neatly undone. Despite some protests the election was not overturned, but Rich found a place, thanks to the earl of Huntingdon, at Leicester. Ipswich, where Suffolk was high steward, refused one of his sons a place (although it generously paid his messenger twenty shillings); but the earl had better luck at Dunwich, where he successfully nominated "one Henry Dade esquire."[32]

Suffolk probably collaborated with his brother, Lord William Howard of Naworth, to see to the election of two candidates at Morpeth, Suffolk's servant Sir Arnold Herbert and a Wiltshire squire, Sir William Burton, "a Howard family agent" who was later employed by Suffolk in the scandalous Essex-Howard divorce. In Wiltshire, Suffolk did reasonably well. His son, Sir Thomas Howard, was elected for Wiltshire; another of his clients, Sir Roger Dallison, served for Malmesbury, and at Cricklade his influence probably accounted for the choice of one of the earl of Northampton's associates, Sir Thomas Monson (Northampton's nominee at Castle Rising in 1604) and Sir Carey Reynell, a relative by marriage of Sir Henry Spiller, one of the earl of Arundel's dependents.[33] In 1614 Suffolk intervened in seven elections and, thanks chiefly to his Wiltshire connections, apparently placed seven nominees. Except for occasional help from his brother Lord William, his electoral energies were, from 1621 until his death in early June 1626, confined to his Wiltshire boroughs although his son, Sir Thomas (earl of Berkshire in 1626) may have successfully backed a former employee of his father, Sir William Button, in Wiltshire's 1628 election. They probably had a decisive voice in the elections at Cricklade, Wootton Bassett, and Malmesbury, and to a much lesser extent, at Calne. Suffolk's predominance at Cricklade was obvious: its return of his sons, Sir Thomas Howard (1621) and Sir William Howard (1624–26), was a positive sign of Suffolk's intervention as was, in all likelihood, the choice, again, of Sir Carey Reynell (1621) and Lord Percy's servant, Edward Dowse (1625). The election of Sir Edward Howard, son of the earl of Nottingham's brother, by Calne (1624, 1625) was another probable sign of Suffolk's patronage. Marriage connections could have been responsible for the return of other burgesses at Wootton Bassett and Malmesbury. Suffolk's daughter, Elizabeth, married William Knollys, Viscount Wallingford and earl of Banbury; that link might explain the choice of two Berkshire residents, Richard Harrison (1621) and Sir Robert Hyde (1625), at Wootton Bassett, and another marriage connection, between Suffolk's son Sir Thomas and a daughter of the earl of Exeter, was probably behind the election of Thomas Hatton, a relative to Exeter by marriage, at Malmesbury (1624, 1625). Sir John Banks, elected at Wootton Bassett in 1624, may have been a Suffolk nominee; that is the possible explanation for his return for Morpeth, a borough under Suffolk's brother's control, in 1626 and 1628. Suffolk was probably also behind Morpeth's bye-election return of his former servant, Sir Arnold Herbert, in 1625; and Sir Thomas Lake, a loyal Howard dependent in James's court, was his successful candidate for Wootton Bassett in 1626. Indeed, the stream of outsiders, courtiers, and royal officials returned by Malmesbury and Wootton Bassett may be best explained by the patronage of their near neighbor, the earl of Suffolk and, after 1626, his son, the earl of Berkshire.[34] Together, their patronage may have accounted for 35 places in 27 elections from 1614 through 1628.

In contrast to his successes in the election of 1604, the aging lord admiral, Charles Howard, earl of Nottingham, played little part in the elections of 1614–24. Indeed, it is doubtful that he intervened at all in 1624 since it was his wife's patronage that was so much a part of Blechingley's contested election. In 1614, however, Nottingham probably placed Thomas Trevor at Newport and a naval official in his service, Sir Robert Mansell, at both Harwich and Carmarthenshire, where Mansell's family links were strong. His second son and eventual heir, Sir Charles Howard, found a place at Shoreham. Blechingley chose two of his likely candidates, Sir John Trevor and Nottingham's relative Charles Howard of Lingfield; and Gatton's return of the courtier Sir John Brooke was probably an additional sign of his influence. Reigate, where the earl was manor lord and maintained his principal residence, elected his nephew Sir Edward Howard and Sir John Suckling, connected by marriage to Lionel Cranfield, farmer of Nottingham's "patent to license the sale of wines." In the next election, that of 1621, Nottingham's patronage almost disappeared. He probably saw to the choice of Henry Lovell at Blechingley and Robert Lewis at Reigate. Lewis may have been linked to the earl of Holderness who, like Nottingham's son, had married a daughter of Sir William Cokayne. And, with that negligible showing, it seems that the lord admiral's patronage disappears from the early Stuart scene.

Nottingham's wife, who shortly after his death married Sir William Monson, later viscount Monson of Castlemaine, and Nottingham's son and successor as earl, tried to keep some of the family's electoral patronage alive. Nottingham's wife was certainly active; in 1624 she "commanded Sir M. [Miles] Fleetwood and Mr. Lovell for burgesses" at Blechingly in what became a wild election, involving allegations of bribery, threats of punitive action against the townsmen, and a certain politically inclined vicar, Harris, who even attacked the Committee of Privileges in a Sunday sermon. Lovell, despite Lady Howard's backing, found himself in the Tower and Harris had to beg the House of Commons for its pardon. She probably, also in 1624, saw to the choice of Robert Lewis once again for Reigate. In 1625 the only signs of possible influence were Reigate's return of Sir Roger James, the Howard tenant at Reigate Castle, Gatton's choice of Sir Charles Howard, the lord admiral's son by his second wife, who kept his Gatton seat in 1626 and 1628, and Sir Thomas Crew, the crown's nominee for Speaker of the House in the Parliament of 1625. Lovell was returned again at Blechingley in 1626, and Monson served for Reigate, where he was followed, in 1628, by Charles Cokayne, kinsman by marriage to the second earl of Nottingham. Those few returns from 1625 through 1628 were the only probable signs of the patronage of the second earl of Nottingham and his stepmother. To sum it up, the Nottingham connection probably intervened in eighteen elections and may have secured as many as twenty-two places, only six more than the first earl had won in 1604.[35]

The Howards' electoral influence was truly substantial. In the elections of 1614–28, the Howard connection probably intervened in 96 elections, and the men who had their backing may have secured as many as 110 places.[36]

Except for Arundel, the Howard patronage depended heavily on great office, as Northampton's record in 1614 clearly showed. Thanks to his offices as lord warden and chancellor of Cambridge University, he was, of all the Howards, the most successful patron in any one election. By 1614 Nottingham's declining court influence was apparent, even in the election results, and, without any substantial territorial base, neither his wife nor son could play an important electoral role. In 1619 Suffolk lost his post as lord treasurer, and though his wife's rapacity might have led to the charges of embezzlement that brought him crashing down, her properties provided the foundation for whatever electoral influence he would have following the abrupt end of his court career. But of them all, Arundel's patronage was the most significant. It was exclusively the result of his greatness as a landholder. Unlike the other great patrons, Pembroke and Buckingham, Arundel never held any great office that afforded him the opportunity to gather burgess-ships for his friends and dependents. His patronage was that of the great landowner, and, given that limitation, his success was substantial indeed.

Buckingham's electoral patronage, unlike that of Pembroke and Arundel, was founded almost entirely on office—on the rewards his grateful Stuart patrons heaped upon his willing shoulders. In a rise to favor without parallel in early Stuart annals, his influence soon became all-embracing; and his acquisition of offices, great and small, was almost dazzling. He became lord admiral in 1619 and lord warden of the Cinque Ports in 1624. He was appointed lord lieutenant of Buckinghamshire (1616), Kent (1620), and Middlesex (1622). He was high steward of Westminster (1622) and Windsor (1625) and became (1626) chancellor of Cambridge University. All of these offices provided him with patronage, and though little evidence has survived to testify to it, there can be no doubt of his electoral interest. As early as 1621 his support was sought for a "Burgesses's place," and similar requests were made throughout his career. When events took an increasingly dim turn for Buckingham, as in 1625 or 1628, his friends stressed the necessity of careful electoral planning. He paid some heed to their worries and urgings; in February 1628, only a few weeks before parliament began, he was in London "negotiating and working with all his might, so that the members returned for the Lower House may be on his side." Although the evidence of his intervention is disappointingly meager, it is still necessary to attempt a tentative review of the electoral patronage of the greatest of the early Stuart favorites, George Villiers, duke of Buckingham.[37]

Almost every office Buckingham held was a source of possible electoral patronage.[38] As we have already seen, his intervention as lord warden of he Cinque Ports accounted for nineteen places from 1625 through 1628, and there can be little doubt that he also tried to use his position as lord admiral to advantage. Following Sir John Suckling's refusal of a burgess-ship for Hull in 1624, Buckingham nominated Emmanuel Gifford, a stranger to the port, to take Suckling's place; but in spite of Suckling's reluctant help, Hull turned Gifford down. He may have been behind the unsuccessful attempt of Sir Guildford Slingsby, a navy official, to serve for Scarborough in 1624; and in 1626 Scarborough refused his request to elect two outsiders, Sir John Brooke and William Turner. The port probably gave way in 1628 when it returned John Harrison, the customs farmer, who nominated himself. Harrison had launched his career under the guidance of Sir

John Wolstenholme of Nostell Priory, but his influence alone could not account for Harrison's choice. Buckingham's backing as lord admiral was probably decisive. A Lincolnshire squire, Sir Clement Cottrell, returned for both Grantham and Boston in 1624, may well have had Buckingham's backing at the latter. Cottrell, vice-admiral for Lincolnshire, managed to secure a grant of £5,000 "as [the] King's gift" in July 1628 and was described by Chamberlain as "a creature of the Lord of Buckingham" as early as 1619. Buckingham may also have urged Harwich to choose an outsider, Sir Edmund Sawyer, a revenue auditor in the Exchequer, in 1625. Sawyer's return was probably another result of the temporary alliance between Buckingham and the earl of Warwick in the Essex election, the likely result of the duke's courtship of the "popular party." Portsmouth gave up its places to Buckingham's nominees in 1628, fulfilling a pledge Buckingham's secretary at the admiralty, Sir Edward Nicholas, had received that Portsmouth's corporation "shall think ourselves happy to grant his grace's request." Sir Allen Apsley, lieutenant of the Tower, who had wanted Buckingham's aid for Hythe in 1625, sought it again in 1628 when he appealed for a place at Rochester—potentially amenable to Buckingham's influence as Lord Admiral—"or some other where I may not miss." If Buckingham tried to meet Apsley's plea, his effort was in vain; Apsley was not returned. Given Buckingham's appetite for patronage, it is possible that he made other attempts as lord admiral to gather places for his servants and friends, but the evidence simply does not survive.[39]

Although Buckingham was not Cambridge University's chancellor until after the elections of 1626, it is quite likely that his influence was felt earlier. The university's returns of his clients (all secretaries of state) Sir Robert Naunton in 1621 and 1624, Sir Albertus Morton in 1625, and Sir John Coke in 1626, were probable signs of his successful patronage. Buckingham's first election as chancellor came in 1628 and was confused by the actions of his own secretary, Robert Mason, who apparently believed he would be Buckingham's nominee. Mason repeatedly pestered Nicholas about his nomination; his anxiety can only be explained by his assumption that he was to be one of Buckingham's candidates, if not the only one. Perhaps Buckingham had intimated his intention to nominate his secretary to Cambridge's scholars in the hope that they would make Mason their own choice, allowing the duke to suggest Sir John Coke as his candidate, and thereby securing both places. If this was Buckingham's intention, it seems likely that once he discovered that it was either Coke or Mason, Mason was abandoned in favor of the more valuable and experienced secretary. Cambridge University was not daunted by its new chancellor; one nominee was enough.[40]

Buckingham's lord lieutenancies were of little electoral value. Buckinghamshire's elections apparently escaped his attention altogether, and there is not much evidence to indicate his influence in Middlesex elections. His other lieutenancy, for Kent, was of such brief duration (31 May to 8 June) that it obviously cannot explain his zealous electioneering in Kent. His offices, as lord warden and lord admiral, were probably behind his active intervention. In 1624 Buckingham nominated Sir John Hippisley for Middlesex, perhaps in an effort to deny the choice of Sir John Suckling, a brother-in-law of his opponent, Cranfield, the earl of Middlesex and lord treasurer. A local favorite, Sir Gilbert Gerrard, also sought a place, as did Sir John Franklin, a Middlesex resident and Buckingham's nominee for Rye in 1625. Gerrard easily carried one place, and Hippisley had apparently won the second; "but upon examination many of his followers were from the stable, and mint men or *monnoyeurs* brought by the lieutenant of the Tower [Sir Allan Apsley], which would not be admitted for freeholders." Suckling was awarded the seat. In 1625 Buckingham's candidate for Rye, Sir John Franklin, was returned for Middlesex, presumably with the duke's blessing. And with Franklin's election, all traces of Buckingham's patronage disappears from the Middlesex story.[41]

Buckingham took an active interest in Kent's elections. In 1624 the prince and Buckingham helped to prevent Sir Edwyn Sandys's Irish appointment, and, since Sandys had "made his peace with promise of all manner of conformity," Buckingham may well have supported him in Kent's election. A contest developed since Sir Nicholas Tufton and Sir Dudley Digges had the field to themselves until Sandys's sudden appearance. It was a defamatory campaign; Tufton was accused of being a Papist, and Digges was assailed as a royalist. Sandys won the election in questionable circumstances since, although absent on election day, he "carried it [from Digges], either in truth and number of voices or by partiality of the sheriff as is pretended." There is, however, no doubt of Buckingham's involvement in the county's election in 1625. He ordered the mayor of Rochester to gather "all your friends and tenants being freeholders and particularly all such freeholders at or about Rochester or Chatham as have any relation to me or my office of Admiral, . . . to assist in the election of Mr. Secretary Morton." Buckingham also rallied an impressive collection of peers in Morton's behalf: the earls of Montgomery (newly appointed Kent's lord lieutenant), Dorset, and Westmorland (who purchased his peerage through Buckingham) all campaigned for Morton's return. And with all that support in addition to his local ties, it is hardly surprising that Morton was elected. Buckingham also supported Sandys, but his aristocratic allies went their own ways when it came to Morton's running mate. Sir Edward Dering, an influential squire of Surrenden, Kent, must have been badly perplexed when his neighbor at Knole, the earl of Dorset, urged him to back Sandys and Westmorland pressed him to support his son, Mildmay Fane, Lord Burghersh, for the other knight-ship. Montgomery, too, backed Burghersh. Sandys was refused and had to settle for a place at Penryn, thanks to its election master, Sir Robert Killigrew. The election provided a remarkable picture of aristocratic electioneering. Dorset and Westmorland relied on their long-standing Kentish connections for influence, and Montgomery and Buckingham counted on their offices to carry the necessary electoral weight. In Sandys's case, however, the backing of Buckingham and Dorset was not good enough. Perhaps Sir Edwyn's action — or, rather, lack of it — in the previous parliament was too much for their influence to overcome.[42] Buckingham supported Sandys for Kent again in 1626; his agent in the Cinque Ports, Sir John Hippisley, urged him to "send to all those of the navy to be there for Sir Edwyn tomorrow, I do not think he will carry it, otherwise I think you might bring him in the ports." Hippisley's pessimistic forecast of Sandys's chances for a knightship was correct, and, as in 1625, Sandys had to content himself with a Penryn place. Sandys may have been the victim of Kent's sophisticated electorate — or at least the sophisticated leaders of that electorate — who had noted Sandys's extravagant support for supply, an enthusiasm that led him to support taxation before any "bargaining" over grievances had been attempted by the House of Commons. The duke was not put off by these setbacks; he tried again in 1628 and may have backed Sir Edward Dering, whose mother-in-law was the duke's relative, and Sir Thomas Finch. Sandys urged their election, while Nicholas, Lord Tufton, assured Dering that "the Duke desires much to engage as many friends as he can" for his candidates. Sandys was Buckingham's choice for Sandwich; the Sandys-Buckingham axis lends credence to Buckingham's presumed support of Finch and Dering. If so, Buckingham had to be content with one place; Finch won, Dering lost.[43] Buckingham's nominees for Kent had county connections, which should have helped them in the shire's elections. But that was not always true, as Buckingham discovered; Kent's squirearchy still had a great deal to say about the county's elections. Of Kent's eight places in the elections of 1624–28, it is likely that Buckingham played a role in the choice of two candidates (Morton, Sandys) and possibly a third (Finch) in 1628. Sandys failed twice, in 1625 and 1626; Dering lost in 1628. Even with those defeats, however, Buckingham's influence was a significant part of Kent's electoral story.

Buckingham was the constable of Windsor Castle and High Steward of the borough, offices he presumably employed to win as many as four places for his nominees in the town's elections from 1624 to 1628. He may have supported Sir Edmunds Sawyer's candidacy in 1624 and, in the next election, unsuccessfully nominated "Sir William Russell the treasurer of his Majesty's navy." Buckingham may have been rebuffed, but it is more likely that Russell was simply unable to serve since he was chosen, without apparent opposition, in 1626. In 1625 Sir Robert Bennett and Sir William Hewett were returned. Both were courtiers, and it is quite possible that Bennett, surveyor of the works of the castle, had Buckingham's backing; he was in the duke's service. Sir William Beecher, long one of Buckingham's clients, was elected in 1628.[44]

Thanks to the dean of Westminster, Bishop John Williams, there is much less guesswork involved in assessing Buckingham's patronage at Westminster. Sir Robert Cotton, casting about for a burgess-ship in 1628, sought out Williams and inquired about his chances at Westminster. The good dean's reply made clear Westminster's election customs. Williams admitted that he nominated one burgess but "none other, than was recommended unto me by my Lord of Buckingham, our High Steward." The other place was controlled by the borough corporation or vestry, "and if they pitch upon anyone of the 12 burgesses, they are like that little God Terminus, that will not be removed from their opinions." Westminster's returns bear witness to the truth of Williams's remarks. From 1621 through 1625 Buckingham's half brother, Sir Edward Villiers, was chosen; and in 1626 one of the duke's clients, Sir Robert Pye, was elected. In 1628, however, Westminster's electoral history was abruptly reversed, much to the surprise and chagrin of both the duke and the vestry. Buckingham's nominee, Sir Robert Pye, was overthrown — as were the vestry's candidates — in a tumultuous election that lasted three full days and, among other things, provoked some enthusiastic rhyming; for when Pye's followers would shout "A Pye, A Pye, A Pye," the adverse party would cry "A Pudding, A Pudding" and others, "A Lie, A Lie, A Lie." It was all very exciting and ended in a sharp defeat for Buckingham and the borough's corporation. "Bradshaw, a brewer & Morris, a grocer [candidates of the popular faction], carried it from him [Pye] by above 1,000 voices." Mann and Hayward, the vestry's candidates and former M.P.'s for the town, also went down to ignominious defeat since "they had discontented their neighbours in urging the payment of the loan." At one stroke the popular party, outraged by the loan, had reversed Westminster's electoral history. It was, however, Buckingham's sole defeat; until 1628 he had successfully placed one member for the town in every election from 1621 through 1626.[45]

Buckingham's manorial holdings gave him influence at Buckingham and Leominster. The manor of Whaddon, Buckinghamshire, went to the duke as early as 1616, and its location, near to Buckingham borough, gave the duke a burgess-ship there. The election of Richard Oliver in 1621, 1624, 1625, and 1628 was Buckingham's work. Oliver was in his employment as early as November 1621 and, by 1628, was the duke's "receiver." He served for Tiverton in 1626, where Nicholas knew that Buckingham's friend, "Mr. Drake [John Drake of Ash, Devonshire], the choice pillar of our county . . . told me of a burgess-ship for Tiverton for a gen[tlemen] you wrote for, which accordingly was affected." Oliver was Buckingham's man at Tiverton when Drake, elected for the county, relinquished his borough place in Oliver's favor. Oliver's usual place at Buckingham was taken by another likely nominee of the duke, Sir John Smith or Smythe. In 1620 Buckingham received the manor of Leominster, which gave him a voice in that borough's elections that he probably employed to place Sir William Beecher (his nominee at Windsor in 1628) in 1621 and 1624. Beecher's elections, however, are the last indication of Buckingham's patronage at Leominster.[46]

Cornwall's boroughs, as the first earl of Salisbury, Pembroke, and the Duchy of Cornwall had realized, were prone to listen to the blandishments of electoral patrons, and Buckingham knew it, too. He was well aware of the duchy's success, and, with the Prince's Council no longer able to give the duchy a lead, Buckingham stepped in, clearly determined not to let such opportunities slip away from his and the court's grasp. His action was completely in keeping with his unique status, for, as in everything from foreign policy to the sale of peerages, Buckingham's influence predominated. It is hardly surprising that, from 1625 through 1628, he became the court's electoral agent; and with the Cornish boroughs added to the Cinque Ports as the foundations of his influence, Buckingham became, for three elections, the greatest patron of them all. He probably helped his clients, Eliot at Newport and Bagg at West Looe, in 1624. Sir Miles Fleetwood, who also looked to Buckingham as his patron and proved his loyalty by the vehemence of his attacks on Buckingham's enemy, Lord Treasurer Middlesex in the Parliament of 1624, may have also owned his return for Launceston to the duke. However, it was in the next election that

Buckingham, taking the place of the defunct Prince's Council and duchy, made his electoral presence known. His intervention may have harvested as many as nine burgess-ships in nine elections. He presumably backed three former duchy nominees, Sir Francis Cottington (Bossiney), Sir Richard Weston (Callington), and Sir Henry Vane (Lostwithiel). His client, Sir Henry Hungate, was returned for Camelford, where his Cornish connections must have helped, and his western agent, Sir James Bagg, found a seat at East Looe. Buckingham's influence probably also explained the returns of John Wolstenholme, son of the customs farmer Sir John Wolstenholme, at West Looe, Nathaniel Tomkins at St. Mawes, and Londoner Sir William Parkhurst at St. Ives. He may have also supported Eliot's successful bid for a place at Newport.[47] Buckingham's success in 1625 was never repeated; faction at court and the growing discontent of 1627–28 eroded his Cornish influence.

The bitter quarrel between Pembroke and Buckingham that erupted in 1625 had its results in the Cornish borough elections of 1626. Pembroke used his post as lord warden of the stannaries to place five clients, including two who took burgess-ships Buckingham's dependents had won at Callington and Lostwithiel in 1625. Trouble also developed over Sir Henry Hungate's election for Newport, where he battled an influential Cornishman, Thomas Gewen, a duchy employee, and one Mr. Thomas Williams, junior, who enjoyed the support of "the inhabitants and freeholders." The impending clash over the franchise failed to materialize, however, for Williams "deserted the cause"—under pressure, perhaps?—and Gewen and Hungate were finally allowed to serve by the House of Commons. Eliot, still loyal to Buckingham, won a place at St. Germans, where his own influence was substantial, but Buckingham was probably responsible for the choice of Bagg at East Looe, William Carr at St. Mawes, and West Looe's election of Wolstenholme and John Rudhall of Herefordshire, whose brother-in-law was one of Buckingham's favorite clients, Sir Walter Pye.[48]

The shadow of the forced loan fell over Buckingham's Cornish patronage in 1628. His influence can be traced in only five elections. His western agent, Bagg, won a burgess-ship at Plympton Earl (where Buckingham had probably controlled a place in 1624) and found a place for Cottington at Saltash. Bagg also secured "two blanks, one for Looe, the other for Probus [Grampound?], in which you may (if you so please) appoint Mr. Packer, Captain Heydon, or Sir Robert Pye, as Mr. Mohun besought you." There was opposition at Saltash, but Bagg was equal to it; he put pressure on the mayor, who, he admitted, "deserves exceeding well" since he had given Cottington the burgess-ship against the "opposition of Sir Richard Buller their Recorder and divers others." The mayor had even claimed, perhaps in an effort to overawe Buller and his friends, that he was "the Duke's servant." Buller was no mean opponent; he lived near Saltash and represented a family of power and influence both there and in the county. He was, by 1627, an outspoken critic of the court. Given the tense atmosphere that often prevailed in the elections of 1628, Buller might have linked local feelings against the return of a stranger to anti-court sentiment. Cottington, an outsider, courtier, and nominee of Buckingham, was the perfect target for such a campaign. Newport's confusing contest, which was marked by a franchise dispute, may have been another example of such an election. Buckingham's probable nominees, the outsiders Sir John Wolstenholme and John Herne, were challenged by Buckingham's former friend and now bitter enemy, Sir John Eliot, who backed a local opponent of the loan, Nicholas Trefusis. Five separate returns were made (three by the town's officials, the "vianders"), and each claimed a different franchise. One "viander" made two returns, matching Trefusis, who clearly won one place, with Killigrew on one and joining him with Piers Edgcombe on the other. The other "viander," perhaps more fearful of Buckingham, returned Wolstenholme and Herne. Eliot attacked the results in the House; the Committee of Privileges investigated the mess, and its recommendation, for the seating of Trefusis and Edgcombe, opponents of the court, represented a clear defeat for the duke. He had, however, some success elsewhere. Packer was chosen at West Looe, Pye served for Grampound, and Sir Robert Carr, chosen at Preston through the Duchy of Lancaster's influence, and at Lostwithiel, was possibly another Buckingham nominee. Carr, who preferred Preston, was replaced by another courtier with links to Buckingham, Sir Thomas Badger.[49] Buckingham's patronage in Cornwall steadily declined after 1625. His dispute with Pembroke hurt his efforts in 1626, and in 1628 opposition to royal policy, and especially the forced loan, brought his influence to its lowest ebb. The growing dispute between the court, which Buckingham personified, and the country was making its mark.

Buckingham's other electioneering was opportunistic in nature, scattered about the realm, and often relied upon the influence of locally powerful friends or clients. He lent his support to his Dorset-shire friend, Sir Richard Strode, at Bridport in 1626; and, presumably because of Strode's local influence, also nominated his former candidate at Hythe in 1625, the diplomatist Edward Clarke. Strode easily won, "being a man who we well known [*sic*], and did incline to make choice of him before"; but Clarke's candidacy was another matter since, as the corporation explained, they had already agreed to elect Sir Lewis Dyve, one of their members in 1625. Dyve must have been known to Buckingham; he had been with Prince Charles and the duke in Madrid in 1623. And this is where Dyve's troubles with the Duke began. His mother's second husband was the earl of Bristol, Buckingham's enemy, who had served as ambassador to Spain and who had his own view of the sorry plots and schemes involved in the Spanish marriage negotiations. Little wonder, then, that Buckingham backed a petition to the House of Commons protesting Dyve's election. Bridport's bailiff was accused of holding a "corrupt election," and when Strode was "pressed to name who was so chosen," he named Dyve. Dyve treated the charge with contempt and urged the House to investigate the complaint. Dyve knew his fellow members; the House did not even bother to refer the issue to the Committee of Privileges and threw out the petition. One can only speculate that Strode's attachment to Buckingham may have prejudiced the House.[50]

Buckingham's other patronage is harder to trace. He was involved in the Essex election of 1625 with Thomas Darcy, viscount Colchester, as his ally. Herefordshire's return of Sir Walter Pye in 1626 and 1628 may have been, partially at least, through Buckingham's help; he could rely upon the aid of a powerful Herefordshire friend, Sir John Scudamore, viscount Scudamore, who was "especially attached to Buckingham." Pye's colleague in 1626 was Sir Robert Harley, who had married the daughter of another Buckingham client, Sir Edward, baron Conway, secretary of state. Given Harley's tangles with other influential Herefordshire families — the Coningsbys, Crofts, and Sampson Eure, an attorney of the Council of the Marches — Buckingham's possible assistance in Harley's elections for Herefordshire (1624, 1626) may have been invaluable. Harley's return for Evesham in 1628 was Conway's work. It is interesting, too, to notice that Harley's troubles at the mint began only after Buckingham's death. The duke might also have helped in John Rudhall's Herefordshire election in 1625; Rudhall had married into the Pye family and was probably one of Buckingham's Cornish nominees in 1626.[51]

Since Buckingham took over the Duchy of Cornwall's patronage after 1624, it is possible that he succeeded the Prince's Council at Eye and Bury St. Edmunds as well. Both boroughs had been targets for the prince's nominees in 1624, and Eye's return of Francis Finch, the council nominee in 1624, from 1625 to 1628 and Bury St. Edmund's election of Buckingham's servant Emmanuel Gifford in 1626 strongly suggest Buckingham's intervention. The influential Suffolk courtiers Sir Roger North and the Jermyns must have helped, too.[52] Finally, it is possible that Buckingham backed Richard Graham's election at Carlisle in 1626 and 1628. Graham, with strong Cumberland connections of his own, had made his career with the duke at court, accompanying him and the prince to Spain in 1623 and serving as Buckingham's master of the horse. Graham's local influence might have been enough to win him the burgess-ships, although it may be significant that he made his first appearance in parliament in 1626, when Buckingham was doing his best to find whatever support he could. Buckingham, like the first earl of Salisbury before him, sometimes used the patronage of others to place his nominees. The power of the Mores of Loseley probably explained the election at Guildford in 1626 of Buckingham's appointee as solicitor general, Sir Richard Shelton, who also served on the duke's personal council. Edward Savage, one of the duke's "gentlemen ushers" who later became one of the king's "gentlemen of his Privy Chamber," was elected at Midhurst in 1628, thanks, it seems, to the patronage of the Catholic aristocrat viscount Montague, who usually controlled one Midhurst burgess-ship.[53] But even after discounting such elections as part of Buckingham's direct patronage, the results of his electioneering are impressive, indeed. Counting his influence as lord warden, Buckingham, in five elections (1621–28), may have intervened in as many as ninety-five elections in which those he nominated or supported probably secured eighty-seven places.[54]

After intervening in four elections for four places in 1621, Buckingham became an important patron in 1624. In that election his involvement can probably be found in sixteen elections; those he backed secured a possible fourteen places. In the elections of 1625–28, however, Buckingham became the most influential patron in the realm chiefly because of his acquisition of nearly all the court's patronage. He was lord warden of the Cinque Ports and, in addition, took over much of the patronage formerly exercised by the Duchy of Cornwall and the Prince's Council. Only the Duchy of Lancaster escaped his attention. His grasp on the levers of court electoral patronage was nearly total. In 1625 his influence probably secured twenty-six places in twenty-six elections. He was, it seems, involved in twenty-four elections for twenty-two places in 1626, and in 1628 he may have intervened in twenty-five elections for twenty-one places.[55]

Buckingham's success was remarkable for another reason. Unlike Pembroke and Arundel, his patronage was founded almost entirely on the fruits of office, on the influence he won as the greatest courtier-aristocrat of early Stuart history. Buckingham's electioneering, and the foundation upon which it rested, closely parallels that wielded by James's first great adviser, the first earl of Salisbury. Only the elections at Leominster and Buckingham, where his property holdings provided the basis of his influence, were exceptions; and that land was another of the rewards his grateful monarchs showered upon him.

The great patrons, Buckingham, Pembroke, and Arundel, were enthusiastic place-hunters. Their stories readily exemplify the sources of such power. Buckingham's was primarily the product of office, Pembroke's success depended on a combination of landed influence and office, and Arundel's was almost entirely founded on his territorial holdings and local connections. The tables below reflect the different foundations of their electoral influence. The first table indicates the electoral impact of territorial influence, local connections, and borough office. In each column, the figure to the left is the number of elections Arundel, Buckingham, or Pembroke were probably involved in, the number at the right shows the total of places probably secured in each election. The second table indicates the importance, for their electioneering, of great office.[56]

| | 1614 | 1621 | 1624 | 1625 | 1626 | 1628 | Totals |
|---|---|---|---|---|---|---|---|
| Arundel | 4–4 | 9–11 | 9–6 | 8–8 | 6–7 | 5–6 | 41–42 |
| Buckingham | ... | 2–2 | 5–5 | 4–3 | 6–7 | 6–6 | 23–23 |
| Pembroke | 9–12 | 10–10 | 10–12 | 10–14 | 11–12 | 9 11 | 59 71 |
| Totals | 13–16 | 21–23 | 24–23 | 22–25 | 23–26 | 20–23 | 123–136 |

| | 1614 | 1621 | 1624 | 1625 | 1626 | 1628 | Totals |
|---|---|---|---|---|---|---|---|
| Arundel | 0–0 | 1–1 | 1–1 | 1–1 | 0–0 | 0–0 | 3–3 |
| Buckingham | ... | 2–2 | 11–9 | 22–23 | 18–15 | 19–15 | 72–64 |
| Pembroke | 1–1 | 4–3 | 6–6 | 5–5 | 8–8 | 5–4 | 29–27 |
| Totals | 1–1 | 7–6 | 18–16 | 28–29 | 26–23 | 24–19 | 104–94 |
| Totals, both tables | 14–17 | 28–29 | 42–39 | 50–54 | 49–49 | 44–42 | 227–230 |

Arundel, Buckingham, and Pembroke intervened in approximately eleven percent of all elections in 1621 and, by the elections of 1625–26, had raised that figure to almost one in every five, or nearly twenty percent. And although their involvement declined somewhat in 1628 to approximately seventeen percent, it remained at a substantial level, indeed. Their nominees or those that they supported, again in approximate terms, took nearly seven percent of all places available in 1621, a percentage that increased to eight percent in 1624 and peaked in 1625 and 1626 at between ten and eleven percent of parliament's places. It declined slightly, to about nine percent in 1628, but, even with that small reduction, their joint success is a singular comment on the electoral influence of the peerage. They were the great patrons; they were not, however, alone in their electioneering. Many other aristocrats were also busily at work in elections from 1614 through 1628, and, though such men's individual patronage came nowhere near that of the great patrons, the cumulative effect of their efforts made a strong impression on elections. Before any account, therefore, of aristocratic patronage can be considered complete, the work of the "middle rank" of noble patronage must be explored.

## 2. The Middle Rank of Patronage, 1614–1628

Arundel, Buckingham, and Pembroke stood at the apex of the pyramid of electoral patronage. Below them were the noblemen whose landholdings, borough stewardships, and lord lieutenancies gave them electoral domination within their own bailiwicks. These aristocrats, the earls of Essex, Salisbury, Hertford, and Banbury, to mention only a few, can be described as men of the "middle rank." Their influence usually accounted for four or five places in an election, and though as individuals they hardly ranked with a Pembroke, the cumulative effect of their intervention was large enough to illustrate further the scope of aristocratic influence.

Rotherfield Greys or Greys, Oxfordshire, was the principal seat of William Lord Knollys, viscount Wallingford (1616), and earl of Banbury (1626). He was lord lieutenant of Berkshire and Oxfordshire and high steward of Abingdon, Wallingford, Reading, Oxford, and Banbury; and such offices, coupled with his broad acres and connections, enabled him to become an important election figure in Berkshire and in four of the five boroughs. Only at little Banbury did his electoral influence leave no trace. Knollys had almost complete control of Abingdon's returns. His nephew Sir Robert Knollys, son of his brother Richard, served there in 1614, 1624, 1625, and 1626. Nephew Robert did not stop with Abingdon, either; his uncle's influence and his own Berkshire holdings brought him a knightship for Berkshire in 1621, and Knollys secured a place for him at Wallingford in 1628. Wallingford granted its high steward one place, and Knollys used it to place Sir William [?] Reynolds in 1614, and in 1621 the borough returned Samuel Dunch, "chosen by the right honorable the Lo: Viscount Wallingford our High Steward." Knollys was also the constable of the castle and steward of its honor, the reversion of which went to his brother-in-law Sir Thomas Howard, one of Suffolk's sons, in 1609. This connection possibly explained the choice of Sir Edward Howard in 1624, presumably at Knollys's insistence; indeed, Sir Thomas Howard, later earl of

Berkshire, eventually replaced Knollys as high steward at both Wallingford and Oxford. Sir Anthony Forrest was probably Knollys's choice in 1625–26; nephew Robert served there in 1628. All in all, Knollys controlled one place in each election at Wallingford, a record he maintained at Reading as well.[57]

Reading's elections in 1614 and 1621 passed off quietly enough. The town dutifully returned another of Knollys's nephews, Sir Robert Knollys, the oldest son of his brother Sir Francis. However, before the next election, that of 1624, the smooth relationship between Reading and its high steward was in ruins. Reading was employing John Saunders as its legal adviser, which put at risk the position of Knollys's client as the town's steward, Sir Edward Clarke. Indeed, in 1623 Reading "insulted" Knollys by firing Clarke in favor of Saunders. The furious Knollys forced Reading to restore Clarke's fees and eventually to reappoint Clarke as its steward. Knollys, determined to assert his "injured" authority and exact revenge, countered by nominating, in 1624, two of his nephews, Sir Robert (Reading, 1614, 1621) and his younger brother Sir Francis Knollys, junior, in an obvious bid to deny Saunders a burgess-ship and bring the corporation to heel. The election, however, brought Knollys to heel! Reading chose Sir Francis Knollys, junior, and Saunders; Sir Robert Knollys finished a poor third. Knollys acknowledged his defeat in 1625 when he recommended Sir Francis once more and wisely, as Reading's election proved, left the second place "to your election, presuming you will make choice of Mr. Saunders." The town's choice of Saunders and Sir Francis fulfilled Knollys's gloomy but realistic expectation. Sir Francis Knollys, junior, and Saunders were returned again in 1626 and 1628, although Knollys probably tried for both places. Sir Robert Knollys failed again in 1626, and his nominee, the stranger Sir John Brooke, whom Knollys had placed at Oxford in 1621, was refused in 1628. That might have been the last straw for Knollys; he quit as high steward two years later, although his advancing age must have also been a factor. Knollys had overestimated his influence at Reading, for, as its elections from 1614 through 1628 indicated, one nominee was its limit.[58]

At Banbury, despite his position as high steward, Knollys was without electoral influence. The borough's representation belonged to the Copes of Hanwell, Oxfordshire, who dominated its elections from 1572 through 1624, although Knollys's successor as high steward, William Fiennes, viscount Saye and Sele, successfully intervened in 1625. Knollys did a little better at Oxford, where, in 1614, he probably placed Sir John Ashley, a courtier from Kent. In 1621 Knollys apparently found an Oxford burgess-ship for a Lincolnshire courtier, Sir John

Brooke; but the election, which may also have involved Buckingham, resulted in a petition to the House of Commons. The town corporation had presented Brooke and Sir Francis Blundell, one of Buckingham's clients, to the "rest of the commons who were not admitted into the Court-Hall, they all [the commons] named Mr. Wentworth of Lincoln's Inn, their Recorder" to serve with Brooke. Wentworth, returned by Oxford in 1604 and 1614, had recently assisted the commons in their quarrel with the corporation over the town charter and municipal voting rights and was probably the victim of the corporation's revenge. When the House of Commons discovered that Wentworth had 100 more voices than Blundell among the commonalty, its reaction was predictably in favor of the wider franchise. Blundell's election was refused; Brooke and Wentworth were seated. Following that decision, all traces of Knollys's influence at Oxford disappeared. Broader franchises could make customary patronage difficult, if not impossible, to maintain; that might explain the end of Knollys's electioneering at Oxford.[59]

Knollys's influence was greatest at Abingdon, Reading, and Wallingford, weaker at Oxford, and nonexistent at Banbury. Sir Francis Knollys, his brother, was returned for Berkshire in 1625; his nephew had served for the county in 1621. Both held considerable Berkshire property; both probably could have won election on their own; but it certainly helped to have a member of the family who was, respectively, a baron, viscount, and earl. Knollys can be credited with as many as twenty places between 1614 and 1628. His best years were in 1614, 1621, and 1625, when his intervention in four elections probably accounted for four places. His worst election was 1628; only two places, won in a like number of elections, can be credited to his account. In 1624 and 1626, his nominees or kinsmen took three places as a result of his intervention. His electioneering was a typical example of what an aristocrat of the "middle rank" could do.

The county elections in Essex and, to a lesser extent, those for Harwich and Maldon showed the influence of the powerful Rich family, earls of Warwick from 1618. Two county elections, in 1625 and 1628, were noteworthy in themselves. The 1625 election was a good example of the fruits of the short-lived alliance between Buckingham and the country "party", whereas the struggle that developed in 1628 was an excellent illustration of the growing conflict between the court and county. It also brought the Privy Council, for the second time in the reign of the early Stuarts, into the county as an election participant.

The domination of the Rich family becomes clear when the candiates and evidence are examined, even in a most cursory way. But it was hardly an unchallenged domination, as the bitter battle in 1604 had indicated and as the election of 1628 reaffirmed.[60] In 1614 the election went quietly enough: the county chose two of its own, Sir Richard Weston, later the earl of Portland and son of an Essex gentleman, Sir Jerome Weston of Skreens, Roxwell, Essex, and Sir Robert Rich, in 1619 second earl of Warwick. His family, the county's greatest land-owners, was the center of a network of alliances, based upon marriage and religious and political attitudes, that dominated county life and contributed, in no small way, to the growth of the country or reform group not just in Essex but in neighboring counties and beyond. In 1621, as in 1624–28, the Warwick influence continued to be felt. Sir Francis Barrington was returned together with a county gentleman, Sir John Dean. Barrington was a prominent member of Warwick's group and a consistent opponent of the court from 1618. Dean's son, al-though linked to the Gorings of Sussex — a courtier connection — by marriage, soon attached himself to the Warwick faction as well and, like the Grimstons, Barringtons, Mashams, and Sir Thomas Cheeke, became an active member. Barrington served again for Essex in 1624, along with Cheeke, whose wife was the sister of the second earl. In James's last three parliaments, Essex had elected four men who were either tied by blood, marriage, or a similarity of views to the Rich family. And there seems to have been no opposition.[61]

The 1625 election was a product of the alliance between court (Buck-ingham) and country (Warwick). Thomas Darcy, viscount Colchester, was the first patron to make his wishes known. He urged the bailiffs of Colchester to see to it "that the voices of your freeholders" at the county election "be cast upon Sir Francis Barrington and Sir Thomas Cheeke." He stressed that his recommendation was "at the request of my Lord of Buckingham"; but, within twenty-four hours, Colchester's bailiffs must have been dismayed by Warwick's instructions that re-quired them to inform all his "friends and neighbours the freeholders" that he planned to support Barrington and Sir Arthur Harris! The differing instructions were not, however, signs of impending faction but only of confusion. Viscount Colchester was soon busy trying to correct the situation. He first released the bailiffs from any promise of support for Cheeke and once more emphasized Buckingham's en-thusiasm for Barrington. Colchester was, though, clearly an agent for others, since he was soon back at his desk again, this time urging them at Warwick's request to back Barrington and Harris. Cheeke, the cause of it all, must have told Warwick that he could have a place in the west, at Beeralston. Given the heavy artillery backing them, Barrington and Harris were easily elected.[62]

The 1626 election was a tranquil affair. Barrington was returned with Sir Harbottle Grimston, who was making his first appearance for the county. Barrington would have had Warwick's support, and, since in 1628 Grimston enjoyed the earl's full backing, it is practically certain that Warwick aided his quest for a knight-ship. The next election (1628) was, however, an altogether different affair.[63]

Rumors of the impending court and country clash first appeared early in February, on the same day (the ninth) that viscount Colchester, now Earl Rivers, urged Colchester's bailiffs to back Sir Richard Weston, the courtier, royal official, and former knight for Essex, should "he stand for it." Rivers was unaware of what was going on, but, for that matter, so was Warwick, whose letter to Colchester supporting Barrington and Sir Harbottle Grimston, reached the town some three weeks after Rivers had written and only one week before the election. Warwick had, it seems, expected no trouble for his friends although, when he finally discovered what was occurring in Essex, he rushed into action to prevent their defeat.[64]

Two Essex justices, Sir Thomas Wiseman and Sir William Maxey, had asked the constable of the hundreds "to bring as many freeholders" as possible to the election at Chelmsford, "there to give their votes with two such knights of the shire as the major part of the justices of the peace should nominate." Since Weston never stood, they must have been planning to choose two court candidates, the privy councillor Sir Thomas Edmondes and Sir Thomas Fanshawe, both strangers to Essex. Early in February, it was reported that they "had privately procured the writ for Essex and the Sheriff to come to Stratford but the country having intelligence from London came in so fast that they durst not trust them and so were dismissed without doing anything." If that was true, and other accounts only modify the story, it looks as if Edmondes and Fanshawe, backed by Wiseman and Maxey, may have planned a snap election; but when that scheme collapsed, the two justices stepped in and tried to gather a following that would bring victory to the two courtiers. Grimston and Barrington discovered the scheme when the constable of Tendring hundred showed them the letter from Wiseman and Maxey. They promptly told Warwick, who stopped at nothing to save the situation. Warwick and his allies carried out a number of temporary land sales "for some two days, some three or four days, to poor men that had no freehold lands nor copyhold at all" to enable them to give their voices in the election for Barrington and Grimston; and that, coupled no doubt with a vigorous canvass, saved the day. The county responded in great numbers to Warwick's campaigning, for although estimates of the number of freeholders who flocked to Chelmsford vary from 10,000 to 15,000, it was still far more than the 1,000 to 1,200 that turned up at Stratford Layton to support Barrington and Grimston, who, with that kind of backing, easily carried the election.

Wiseman and Maxey soon found themselves in London facing the Privy Council. The council had every reason to be upset with the two justices, for the letter they had sent to the constables placed responsibility for their action squarely with the Privy Council. The letter that so mobilized the county's passions stated: "We [the justices] have received a command from the King's Majesty and the Lords of his Highness's privy council" to be at the election "where we shall further understand his Majesty's pleasure touching the election." No wonder the uproar ensued; no wonder, too, that it was complained of as a "thing that never was done before" and that Barrington and Grimston wanted it shown in parliament "as an unparalleled violation of the subject's liberty." If the council had been behind Edmondes and Fanshawe, and it is certainly possible, its coup had to succeed to avoid such repercussions. But the coup failed and left Wiseman and Maxey holding the bag. Wiseman was committed to the Fleet to think it over; Maxey, after being ordered to bring the offending letter to the board, was directed to hold himself in readiness to meet the council again. Even the Venetian ambassador found the election noteworthy enough to include in his dispatches. Although it may be impossible to know if the council was involved, as some believed, it is just as difficult to believe that two Essex justices would take the really remarkable gamble of preparing a letter with that claim — a command from the king and Privy Council — on their own authority. It simply seems too risky. Although responsibility cannot be assessed, what is clear is that Warwick, once news of the plot was out, quickly rallied the county behind Barrington and Grimston and, by fair means or foul, carried the day.[65]

Warwick's kinsmen and friends were also returned for Harwich, Maldon, and, to a lesser extent, Colchester. At Harwich, in 1621, the second earl nominated his brother-in-law, Cheeke, for the earl was gracious enough to thank the mayor "& the rest of your brethren" for Cheeke's election. Although that is the only direct evidence of Warwick's influence at Harwich, the port's returns provide ample testimony of his family's patronage. Sir Harbottle Grimston was chosen in 1614, and Sir Nathaniel Rich was elected in 1624, 1626, and 1628. Harwich's choice in 1625 of Sir Edmund Sawyer, a revenue auditor in the Exchequer, may have been another result of Buckingham's brief alliance with the country.[66] At Maldon, Warwick shared the borough's patronage with its high steward, Sir Henry Mildmay, master of the king's jewels. The earl's nominee for the county in 1625, Sir Arthur Harris, was chosen at Maldon in 1624, 1625, and 1628; and when he decided to serve for Essex in 1625, his replacement, Sir William Masham of Otes, High Laver, Essex, probably enjoyed Warwick's support. Masham, whose views were similar to those of the earl, was no stranger to Maldon; he had won election there in 1624 and would do so again in 1626. Indeed, Masham's choice in 1626 may have represented a double victory for Warwick since Masham's partner was the ubiquitous Sir Thomas Cheeke. There was some competition for Maldon's places. The master of the rolls, Sir Julius Caesar, had won a place in 1621, but when he tried again in 1625, Maldon refused him, preferring instead Harris and its steward Mildmay.[67]

Colchester's returns show almost no trace of Warwick's intervention. Only its election of Sir Harbottle Grimston (1626) and of Sir Thomas Cheeke (1628) and Sir William Masham (who replaced Edward Alford in 1628) can possibly be credited to the earl's account. Its contested election in 1628, however, may have helped the earl to establish his influence. The corporation held its customary meeting and chose Cheeke and Edward Alford, an outsider from Sussex, who had been one of the corporation's choices for parliament from 1604 to 1625. Alford, who had not sought the place, was delighted. He had been returned for Steyning, "which is near to me," but promised Colchester's corporation he would "never leave you till you leave me." Alford's departure, however, was near at hand, for even as the corporation made their return, "in a lower room, the common sort of burgesses in general elected Sir Tho. Cheeke and Sir Wm. Masham." The freemen petitioned the House of Commons, and the narrow franchise was overthrown; so, too, was Alford's election. The freemen may have found an ally in Warwick, who had seen to the appointment of his younger brother, the earl of Holland, as Colchester's recorder in 1627 and who was also intervening in the town's clerical affairs. It is also noteworthy that, in the 1625 election, the corporation, which had favored the choice of Sir Henry Hobart's son, had been forced to back down when the subject was broached to the "multitude." The commonalty's intervention in the election of 1628 was, it seems, not wholly unprecedented. Alford's connections to the corporation were, no doubt, fatal to his chances in the 1628 election, which, at the same time, fairly set Colchester within Warwick's electoral orbit.[68]

The earls of Warwick were the commanding figures in Essex elections. It must also be admitted, however, that most of their nominees were men who might well have won election on their own. Nevertheless, the second earl did nominate Barrington, Harris, Cheeke, and

Grimston for parliament; and given their mutual beliefs and those of Sir William Masham, another prominent county figure, it seems clear that the second earl, whose electioneering covered the parliaments of 1621–28, and his predecessor played a predominant role in the borough and county elections. Altogether, the earls of Warwick probably accounted for twenty-three places in seventeen county and borough elections from 1614 through 1628. That does not include the return of Christopher Harris, a kinsman of Sir Arthur, at Harwich from 1624 through 1628; but even without him, it is still an impressive testimonial to the predominance that the Riches, earls of Warwick, enjoyed in Essex.

The earl of Huntingdon's power at Leicester has already been discussed; his influence in the county was equally as great and was challenged seriously only once, in 1621. Then difficulties arose, a petition resulted, and the House of Commons found itself coping with a very sticky problem, indeed. The earl expected both places and nominated Sir George Hastings, his successful candidate in 1614, and Sir Henry Hastings. His tenants and freeholders were dutifully rounded up and, just as dutifully, mustered themselves on election day and cast their 1,200 voices for the earl's nominee. But then, almost unbelievably, the sheriff, Sir Alexander Cave, balked, took legal advice, and declared that Sir George was a nonresident and, therefore, ineligible for election. Cave announced that Sir Thomas Beaumont, Buckingham's cousin, was well elected. Despite the efforts of Buckingham, who tried to get Sir George to drop the whole thing, Sir George Hastings was not to be denied and off went his petition to the House of Commons. The problem was a mare's nest. The allegation that Hastings was a nonresident was very dangerous since, if accepted, most members had no business at Westminster. Counsel appeared for both sides, and the various statutes defining eligibility were trotted out, explored, reviewed, analyzed, and probed. The lawyers and precedent-searchers had a marvelous time. But the nightmare lurked in the background, and Sir Lawrence Hyde, one of Beaumont's counsel, summed it up well: "he never knew any put out of this House for non-residency; for so the better part of the house should be put off." Pragmatism won out: Beaumont was rejected, Sir George Hastings judged well elected, the earl had his way, and the members settled back, fears of their ineligibility removed. Poor Cave, though, was still in hot water: Beaumont threatened him with legal action, but the House granted him its protection.[69]

Cave's actions, perhaps encouraged by some of the county's gentry tired of Huntingdon's domination, may have forced the earl to settle for the election of Sir Henry Hastings in 1624. Huntingdon, however, was up to his old tricks in 1625 when he nominated his brother Sir George again, and "at my coming home you shall know who I desire should be the other knight of the shire." His try for both places failed. Sir Wolstan Dixie, a kinsman of the Beaumonts, was returned; he was hardly a Huntingdon nominee. Indeed, Sir George Hastings missed a knight-ship as well. Huntingdon placed him at Leicester, possibly to avoid trouble over the residency issue, and, instead, saw to the county's election of his son and heir, Ferdinando, Lord Hastings. The earl settled for one county place in the next two elections; Sir Henry Hastings (1626) and Ferdinando, Lord Hastings (1628), carried the Huntingdon colors to Westminster. Thanks, however, to Cave's surprising action in 1621 and the opposition of Leicestershire's gentry, the earl never established a claim to both the county's knight-ships.[70]

Rutlandshire's elections also showed the impact of the earl's patronage. He had been appointed lord lieutenant of the county in 1614, and, probably because of that office, became active in its elections, nominating in an undated letter, "Sir William Bulstrode and Sir Guy Palmer [Palmes] as knights of the shire." Palmes and Bulstrode served for Rutland in 1624, 1625, and 1628. Both might have won their places without Huntingdon's aid, although Palmes, of Ashwell, Rutland, and Northamptonshire, had been a prospective nominee of the lord warden in 1621, a possible sign that his electoral prospects were not all that secure. If that is true, then Huntingdon's support was valuable indeed. Considering the earl's enthusiastic electioneering in Leicestershire, where it was founded on land and office, it is difficult to imagine that he showed any reluctance to employ his position as lord lieutenant of Rutlandshire for the same purpose. In every election from 1614 through 1628, Huntingdon's influence accounted for at least three places for his family and friends; and in 1625 and 1628, his patronage can be credited with four. In Leicestershire his interference won twelve county and borough places; add Rutlandshire's election of Palmes (1614–25, 1628) and Bulstrode (1624–28) to that count and it reaches a total of twenty-one for the Huntingdon interest.[71]

William Cecil, second earl of Salisbury, enjoyed almost total control over Hertfordshire elections; his nominees took eleven, and possibly all twelve, of the county's places between 1614 and 1628. That he nominated county gentry undoubtedly helped maintain his domination, but, nevertheless, the evidence of his intervention provides a story of success. Sir Henry Carey, who had served in 1614, best expressed Salisbury's power when he wrote the earl in 1621 that "having made my first desire known to your lordship to be a knight for this Parliament and relied on your lordship's assistance, I have been silent to everybody else"; he now intended to seek other supporters and hoped Salisbury would "afford me your defence and the continuance of your favour for the place." He need not have worried; Salisbury backed him, along with Sir Charles Morison, and both were elected. The tale was repeated, with William Lytton joining Morison, in 1624. The earl ordered his bailiffs to see that the freeholders knew of his desire that they "give their voices first for Sir Charles Morrison and next for Mr. William Lytton." His power was successfully mobilized for his nominees, Sir John Boteler (1625, 1626), Mr. John Boteler (1625), and Sir Thomas Dacres (1626). Although evidence is lacking for 1628, the choice of his previous candidates, Sir Thomas Dacres and Sir William Lytton, signifies his continuing and, indeed, overwhelming influence over Hertfordshire. Salisbury's power in county contests was impressive; few of his fellow peers could match it.

When Sir Francis Bacon fell from power in 1621, his patronage over St. Albans passed to Salisbury; and between 1624 and 1628, the earl supported or approved of men who filled six of its seats. His domination was such that, in 1625, the corporation sent a message to the earl "to talk with him about the Burgesses for the Parliament for our Town." Messengers passed back and forth, and finally, after negotiations, the town apparently managed to get Salisbury to rest "contended to have but one" place. Sir John Luke, elected in both 1624 and 1625, was Salisbury's probable nominee. However, in 1625 Luke served with one of Salisbury's former county candidates, Sir Charles Morison. If the corporation was bent on controlling one place, it made certain — by returning Morison — that it would not offend the earl. In 1626 Morison served again, no doubt with Salisbury's blessing. St. Albans joined him with an outsider, Sir Edward Goring. Despite Salisbury's apparent promise to settle for only one nominee, it looks very much like his friends took both places at St. Albans in 1625–26. At least Morison was a thoughtful candidate: he sent a buck to the corporation following the election. In 1628 the borough regained its rights to elect one member (Sir John Jennings) and left the other nomination (Robert Kirkham) to Salisbury. Hertford, restored at the prince's behest in 1624, also came under the earl's influence, no doubt to the chagrin of the prince and his council. In 1624 and 1625, Salisbury placed an old servant of his father, William Ashton, and in 1628 he probably controlled one seat. Except for 1626, when Salisbury was apparently rebuffed, he kept his grip on one of Hertford's burgessships; and, presumably to make his influence certain, he bought the manor and Castle of Hertford for £253 in 1627. Counting the three Hertford places that the earl's nominees captured, Salisbury controlled twenty places in Hertfordshire. Indeed, given Sir Ralph Coningsby's connections to the Boteler family, it may well be that Salisbury lent his voice to Coningsby's return for Hertfordshire in 1614 with Carey. If so, then he may have won a surprising twenty-one places in Hertfordshire's elections alone. Salisbury was also involved in a few Wiltshire borough contests. He was ready to try his luck at Chippenham in 1614, and, as we have already noted, his feud with the earl of Pembroke over Old Sarum's burgess-ships did not prevent Salisbury's clients from taking a place there in 1621, 1624, and 1628.[72]

Salisbury's patronage can be traced in twenty elections that probably secured for his nominees, from 1614 through 1628, twenty-four places. Salisbury's patronage stands as a telling example of what great office could mean to a patron. The second earl managed in six elections to secure as many places as his father, James's great adviser and lord treasurer, might capture in one!

Pembroke was not the only patron to be reckoned with in western England. The Seymours, earls of Hertford, were also influential; and the returns for Wiltshire, Great Bedwin, Marlborough, and Ludgershall frequently revealed their success. The Hertford connection, thanks to the marriage of William Seymour to the earl of Essex's sister in 1617, ties in with the patronage exercised by Essex in Staffordshire as well. It can be traced by following the election career of the Kirtons, Sir James and his nephew, Edward, of Castle Cary, Somersetshire. The Seymours owned Castle Cary, and the Kirtons were agents of the family. Sir James was M.P. for Ludgershall, and his nephew's parliamentary career was based on Seymour patronage and on Essex's influence since Edward Kirton made his first appearance for parliament from Newcastle-under-Lyme in 1621. He followed that with burgess-ships for Ludgershall (1624), Marlborough (1625, 1626), and Great Bedwin (1628), thanks to Hertford's patronage or connections. At Great Bedwin the Seymour influence probably accounted for eight of the borough's twelve places from 1614 through 1628. Sir Giles Mompesson, who had county connections, was returned twice (1614, 1621), and acted as a creditor of the family. William Cholmley (1624, 1625) had connections in Yorkshire and London but not, save for the Seymours, in Wiltshire. He was "the foreign opposer general of the exchequer" whose ties with Great Bedwin are obscure, to say the least. Another outsider, the courtier Sir John Brooke (1625), and the great lawyer John Selden (1626) were also likely Seymour nominees. In 1628, in addition to Kirton, the Seymour's patronage probably accounted for the borough's choice of Sir John Trevor. By then he was linked with Pembroke, and given the connections between Pembroke and Hertford and their similarity of views, Trevor, usually elected for Welsh boroughs, had probably been shifted into a secure seat at Great Bedwin. Ludgershall's elections also have the Seymour imprint. James Kirton (1614) and Edward Kirton (1624) were surely Seymour nominees, and the elections of Sir Robert Pye (1625) and Sir William Walter (1626) probably were other examples of the Essex-Hertford link. Pye's brother was the earl of Essex's western agent, and Walter was chosen in 1628 for Litchfield, where Essex might have enjoyed some influence. Ludgershall's 1626 election was a confused affair; in addition to Walter, a Wiltshireman, Sir Thomas Jay, and Robert Mason, a Hampshire gentleman, were all involved. The only evidence of trouble is found in a terse entry in the Commons Journal: Walter's election was declared "good" but Mason and Jay were refused.[73] Fourteen of the borough's twenty-six electors had voted for Jay, and Mason had fourteen voices; but the whole dispute revolved around the vote of "one Bishop." John Selden's election for Ludgershall (1628) was probably through Hertford's patronage. As Ludgershall's returns showed, Hertford could usually count on having one burgess-ship in each election at his disposal. At Marlborough we are on surer ground; the Seymour influence probably accounted for eleven of the borough's twelve places. Sir William Seymour, Lord Beauchamp (1621), and his son, Sir Francis Seymour (1624, 1628), later Baron Seymour of Trowbridge, and Edward Kirton (1625, 1626) were all returned through the Seymour influence.[74] Sir Francis lived in Marlborough from time to time; he owned the manor, and, given that power, it is inconceivable that the town's legal adviser, Richard Digges, could not have been a Seymour nominee. Digges served for Marlborough nine times! Only Sir Francis Popham, returned in 1614, might have secured his own election, and even that is a gamble. Marlborough was a pocket borough for the Seymours.

The Seymours' electioneering was not confined to boroughs. In 1614 Hertford lent his support to Sir Robert Phelips's unsuccessful campaign in Somersetshire, and in 1621 the old earl—he was in his eighties by 1620—tried to employ his influence and office, as Somersetshire's lord lieutenant, to win a knight-ship for his nephew, Edward Lord Beauchamp. The county's leaders, including John Poulett, John Stawell, John Horner, William Walrond, and Robert Hopton (himself a candidate), would have none of it. They were firmly committed to the choice of Sir John Portman and Hopton and emphasized "that the place of knight for the shire, do properly belong unto the

gent[lemen] inhabiting in the country." Faced by such resolute opposition, Hertford probably gave up his Somersetshire plans for Lord
Beauchamp since Hopton and Portman were returned, and nothing
indicates that it was a contested election. In Wiltshire, though, the
Seymours influence counted for more. The respect that influence
earned, when linked as it was to Pembroke's, was clearly revealed by
Sir Henry Ley in 1625 when he informed another prospective candidate for a Wiltshire place, Sir Thomas Thynne, that he had "received
yesterday a letter from London that my Lord of Pembroke and my
Lord of Hertford have taken order that all their voices go first for Sir
Francis Seymour, and the other for me, if I shall join with him, which
appointment and agreement of their Lordships I dare not dissent
from." Little wonder that Sir Francis Seymour was chosen a knight
for Wiltshire in 1621, 1625, and 1628, and that Ley, too, was returned
in 1625. It is, of course, possible that such intervention may have
occurred in every Wiltshire election from 1614 through 1628, but
without more positive evidence, such patronage cannot be credited to
the Pembroke-Hertford alliance.[75] The Seymours, although limited
through their lack of great office, were still energetic and successful
election patrons. Between 1614 and 1628, the Seymours, earls of
Hertford, probably accounted for twenty-seven places in twenty-two
elections. They had clearly employed their local influence to good
effect.

The earls of Rutland and Exeter enjoyed important electoral influence in Lincolnshire. Together they probably accounted for twenty-
six places, Rutland securing seventeen and the earls of Exeter nine.
Thomas Cecil, first earl of Exeter, followed in his father's, Lord Burghley's, footsteps at Stamford. His estate was only a few miles outside
the town, and his influence controlled at least one place in Stamford's
elections. His second son, Sir Richard Cecil, was returned in 1614
with an outsider, John Jay, and in 1621 served again, this time with
another kinsman, John Wingfield. Courtier Sir George Goring, of
Sussex and London, probably owed his election at Stamford in 1624
to William, the second earl of Exeter; and when Goring chose Sussex
instead, it is possible that John St. Amand, who also served in 1625,
was an Exeter nominee. Exeter possibly backed Sir Bryan Palmes at
Stamford in 1626, and in 1628 his influence may have accounted for
both places. Sir Thomas Hatton had married Exeter's niece; Edward
Bash, a Rutland nominee for Lincoln in 1614, had probably found his
Stamford place through Rutland's suggestion to Exeter. Such requests could work both ways. John Wingfield, returned for Grantham
in 1621, was a kinsman of Exeter who, it seems likely, requested

Rutland's aid for his Grantham elections. The first earl of Exeter also tried his hand in Boston's election of 1621. His first bid was refused on the grounds that the corporation had decided to choose "two of its own freeman," but the port's choice of Sir Thomas Cheeke of Essex, possibly at the earl of Lincoln's request, apparently ended Boston's resolve. Cheeke, though, preferred to serve for Harwich, leaving the way open for Exeter, who tried again, but to no avail. Boston would have nothing to do with his candidates.[76]

Rutland's influence was the stronger in Lincolnshire; in 1621 his brother, George Manners, ordered that if the shire election was not yet over, "then be notice given to all my neighbour . . . that I shall desire their companies at Lincoln . . . for choosing the knights of the shire." If it was already past, he wanted the corporation of Grantham notified that he expected one of its places. His postscript, alas, explains the lack of evidence for the Manners' electioneering; "Show my letter to no man," he wrote, "but burn it." The shire election had not yet occurred, and Sir George, no doubt assisted by his brother, was elected in 1621 as he had been in 1614. But the Rutland influence was under fire, partially because of suspicions about the earl's religion—he was presented as a Papist in the Parliament of 1624 by another powerful Lincolnshire gentleman, Sir Thomas Grantham— and his own preference for the court and its policies was bound to get him into trouble in a county where the leading gentry viewed the policies of James and Charles I with antipathy, to say the least. Indeed, Sir George Manners, after his victories in 1614 and 1621, never served for Lincolnshire again, possible evidence of the antagonism aroused by the earl's career and the decline in the family's election fortunes. It is just possible that the return of Sir Nicholas Saunderson in 1625 might have been the last evidence of Rutland's patronage; Saunderson's own influence was substantial, but his son married into the Manners family.[77]

Great Grimsby, Grantham, and Lincoln showed traces of Rutland's electioneering. Rutland's kinsman Henry Pelham, who served under Rutland as Grantham's deputy recorder and who became the earl's adviser, was elected at Grimsby from 1621 to 1628. Although Pelham had county connections of his own, his principal residence was in London, at Gray's Inn, and his ties to Rutland make him a likely nominee. Grantham's returns also reflected the earl's intervention. The borough returned two outsiders in 1614, probably at Rutland's request. Sir George Reynell was a Devonshire courtier and gentleman pensioner of King James, and Richard Tufton was a relative of the earl's second wife. Sir George Manners found sanctuary there in 1624 and 1625, and John Wingfield, kinsman to the earls of Exeter, was returned in 1621 and 1626. Rutland's hand can also be seen in Lincoln's elections, but he was forced to share his influence with the county's leading squires, who ended his participation by 1625. Only the elections of Edward Bash (1614) and Sir Lewis Watson of Northamptonshire (1621, 1624), who married the eighth earl of Rutland's sister, marked Rutland's influence at Lincoln. And, following Watson's choice in 1624, further evidence of the Earl's patronage disappears from the city's returns.[78] Lincolnshire's squirearchy was the force to be reckoned with in the county's political life, as the rather low totals for Rutland and the Exeters indicate. Together they may have accounted for twenty-six places—still not a bad showing, given the powerful competition of Lincolnshire's gentry.

In Cumberland and Westmorland, the Cliffords, earls of Cumberland were influential electoral patrons. Henry, Lord Clifford and eventual fifth earl of Cumberland, served for Westmorland in 1614 and 1621, and at Appleby his power was great enough to guarantee his sister's husband, Sir Thomas Wentworth, a place should his bid for a Yorkshire seat in 1621 fail. Clifford played a role, too, in Yorkshire, lending his prestige and, more importantly, his tenants to Wentworth's election campaigns over the years. Appleby was Clifford's borough. He was probably behind its return of Sir George Savile, whose primary influence was in Yorkshire, and the courtier and royal official Sir Henry Wotton in 1614. Other outsiders who must have enjoyed Clifford's support included Sir Arthur Ingram, Wentworth's friend and ally, who was chosen at Appleby in 1621 and 1624, and two other notable Yorkshiremen, Sir John Hotham, elected in 1625, and Sir William Slingsby, returned in 1626. Thomas Hughes benefited from his daughter's marriage into the Clifford family: he was elected at Appleby from 1621 to 1624. Another marriage connection, between Clifford and the daughter of the first earl of Salisbury, probably explains Appleby's return of William Ashton, a servant of Salisbury, in 1626 and 1628. Altogether, Clifford's patronage accounted for eleven of Appleby's twelve places between 1614 and 1628.[79] At Carlisle, Clifford placed his kinsman George Butler in 1614 and 1621, and was probably behind its return in 1614 of Nathaniel Tomkins, later a clerk of the Queen's Council and a frequent nominee of Lord Arundell of Wardour at Christchurch. Sir Henry Vane's returns for Carlisle (1621–26) was also the likely result of Clifford's intervention. Like Tomkins he was a royal official and courtier without connection to Carlisle save for his elections. Clifford probably secured seven of the city's places from 1614 through 1628, and, adding those to his achievements in Westmorland and Appleby, the Cumberland-Clifford patronage can be credited with twenty places, evidence of the family's territorial influence in the north.[80]

These peers, examples of what can be called the "middle rank" of aristocratic patronage, had, in a cumulative sense, a surprising impact on the elections of 1614–28. Their influence varied from that of the earls of Exeter, who can be credited with just nine places in seven elections, to that of the earls of Hertford, who were probably involved in twenty-two elections for a probable twenty-seven places from 1614 through 1628. The second earl of Salisbury (twenty elections, twenty-four places), the earl of Banbury (twenty elections, twenty places), and Lord Clifford (nineteen elections, twenty places) were also, in a local sense, effective electoral patrons. As a group, these peers probably intervened in as many as 142 elections and secured, or helped to secure, for their friends, servants, clients, and kinsmen, 161 places.[81] These peers represent the second, and most typical, group within the aristocratic patronage structure. They exercised whatever influence they had through their territorial strength, family connections, local offices, lord lieutenancies, and high stewardships.[82] Their story shows that great patronage was chiefly a product of great office. None of them enjoyed the royal favor that could offer, among its rewards, the patronage of a lord warden of the Cinque Ports or of an influential office in the Duchy of Cornwall or Lancaster. However, peers of this "second" rank still had an impressive electoral significance. Salisbury, Clifford, and the others discussed could be expected to intervene, on the average, in twenty-three elections and were probably involved in the return of about twenty-seven members to each parliament from 1614 through 1628. Their influence is only a sample of the patronage wielded by the peerage as a whole and its aristocrats of the cloth, the great churchmen.

It is likely, too, that had more evidence survived, the amount of aristocratic influence would be even greater. One example will suffice. Hertfordshire's returns would probably lead a historian to assume that it was a gentry county; its knights of the shire were from its leading families; their influence alone, based on marriage alliances, family ties, and land, could account for their election. That picture, of course, is wrong, as Professor Stone's essay on the second earl of Salisbury's electioneering reveals. It was Salisbury, not Hertfordshire's gentry, who made that county's election history from 1614 through 1628.[83] Perhaps, with additional evidence, counties like

Warwickshire, Dorsetshire, and Lancashire might have similar election histories. However, even without it, it is clear that the power of the peerage was a great force in early Stuart elections.

In the elections of 1604–28, England's peerage intervened in almost 43 percent of all elections held; and their nominees, or those that they either supported or probably supported, secured 27 percent of the places available in parliament.[84] That aristocratic patronage was so important should come as no surprise. England was still a structured society with carefully delineated lines of power and authority based on rank, office, and land. Although the private armies were gone, clients, dependents, and servants remained, drawn to the peer through hopes of advancement and reward. Personal dependence still obtained: careers could be decided, for better or worse, on the strength of such connections. A place in parliament could be considered as payment for faithful services or as a mark of continuing favor. Thomas Hesilrige wanted a burgess-ship for his son, who was, he claimed, "desirous to become a scholar in the best school of Christendom." How many clients or servants of Pembroke felt that way cannot be ascertained, but their election, through their patron's influence, was probably evidence—in their own eyes—of Pembroke's favor and esteem. Such patronage hardly harmed Pembroke's reputation; it cannot be doubted that electoral influence was a significant symbol of prestige and power in a pushing and socially aware society. There were, of course, more mundane reasons for such electioneering. Private bills might need attention and support, favors could be repaid with burgess-ships, and an aristocrat's interest might require assistance in the House of Commons. The motives, furthermore, of the place-seeking squire and the aristocratic electioneer were not that different. Parliamentary elections recognized status, and to be able to influence an event as important as an election was a clear mark of social and political greatness.[85]

Aristocratic intervention, in terms of places won, increased substantially in 1614; and that, coupled with the court's first electioneering effort, makes the loud outcries of the Addled Parliament against undertaking and influence more understandable. Aristocratic involvement, both in terms of elections attempted and places secured, or probably secured, increased in 1624, peaked in 1625, showed a slight decline in 1626, and fell off considerably, in terms of places won, in 1628. However, the electoral intervention of the nobility in 1628 did not show a corresponding reduction.[86] It seems clear that after 1625 the electoral success of the peerage began to decline, but what is not clear is why.

It is possible that aristocratic patronage may have been assuming a more "political" aspect. The increase in intervention noted in 1624–25 may have been the result of a consensus among the politically powerful: the Buckingham-Pembroke alliance provides an example. And it could have had some impact on elections. In 1625 Buckingham and Warwick were allies in the Essex election. Their association may be a reflection of the new and more popular thrust of royal policy toward Spain. John Preston, perhaps the most politically minded of reformist divines, basked in the favor of Buckingham and Charles; all things, even the reform of the church at home, seemed possible. That consensus, however, began to break up in 1626 and was shattered by 1628. Buckingham's schemes were in ruins; privy seal loans, voluntary gifts, and the forced loan, seen by many of the county community as an attack on property, were recent memories in the elections of 1628. And since the court and aristocracy were socially, politically, and economically linked, the county community's growing opposition to Stuart policy may have accounted for the reduction in aristocratic electoral influence.

The gradual erosion in aristocratic electoral success may also have been caused by the increasing opposition of the county community, the local squirearchy, who themselves were determined to serve in parliament. Indeed, the almost constant concern shown in the House of Commons for electoral reform indicates both the power of aristocratic intervention and the awareness of the members of the Commons that such influence was detrimental to their own prospects. In almost every parliament from 1604 to 1640, election reform bills were introduced, and nearly every one contained clauses designed to eliminate undue influence in elections.[87] That the House of Commons was so concerned with free elections may well be the strongest evidence of the power of patronage in early Stuart elections.

1. Neale, *Elizabethan House of Commons*, passim; Stone, *Crisis of the Aristrocacy*, pp. 97–115, 121, 258–63, 493.

2. Stone, *Crisis of the Aristocracy*, pp. 258–63.

3. Cokayne, *Peerage*, 6:218–19; R. Simpson, *A Collection of Fragments . . . of the Hist. and Antiquities of Derby*, p. 94; Moir, *Addled Parliament*, p. 49.

4. Ruigh, *Parliament of 1624*, pp. 36, 75, 127 & n, 264–65; "Francis Seymour, first Baron Seymour of Trowbridge," *DNB* 17:1244–56; Keeler, *Long Parliament*, pp. 337–38; Prestwich, *Cranfield*, pp. 433–34; Willson, *Privy Councillors*, pp. 164–67; Salisbury Corp. MSS, General Entry Book, D/34, Ledger C. f. 323v.

5. Probable Pembroke candidates at Downtown were Sir Clipsby Crew (1624, 1625), his kinsman Edward Herbert (1625, 1626, 1628), and Sir Benjamin Rudyerd (1628). It is

also quite likely that Downtown's election of the Hampshire squire Herbert Doddington in 1626 was Pembroke's work, and it is more likely that Doddington's replacement (he preferred to sit for Lymington, Hampshire), William Trumbull, the diplomatist, had Pembroke's support. It is also possible that the Raleighs, Sir Carew and Gilbert, were supported by the earl in their Downton elections in 1614 and 1621. Wilton's bye-elections in 1621 (Sir Henry Neville for the deceased Tracy) and 1628 (Robert Pooley for Sir William Herbert, who preferred Montgomeryshire) also probably reflected Pembroke's influence. Pooley was a frequent nominee of Pembroke's brother, the earl of Montgomery, at Queenborough; Keeler, *Long Parliament*, pp. 45, 70–72; Hoare, *Wiltshire*, 2:73; 3:18–19; Bagg to Buckingham, Mar. 1626, P.R.O., St. P. Dom. 16/523:77, in *Notes and Queries*, 4th ser., 10(1872): 325–26; Rowe, "The Influence of the Earls of Pembroke on Parliamentary Elections, 1625–1641," pp. 244–45; Moir, *Addled Parliament*, p. 48; the command, issued by Pembroke to Wilton's mayor, is cited in Stone, "The Electoral Influence of the Second Earl of Salisbury," p. 395; *VCH Wiltshire*, 5:117; "William Trumbull," *DNB*, 19:1191–92; *VCH Hampshire*, 4:562, 606, 610. Trumbull had been introduced at court by Sir Thomas Edmondes, whose elections for Oxford University probably had Pembroke's backing.

6. Moir, *Addled Parliament*, pp. 48–49; the quotations used above are from Stone, "The Electoral Influence of the Second Earl of Salisbury, 1614–68," upon which most of the discussion is based; Rowe, "The Influence of the Earls of Pembroke on Parliamentary Elections," pp. 243, 244; *VCH Wiltshire*, 6:65, 66; Keeler, *Long Parliament*, pp. 71, 290; "Michael Oldisworth," *DNB*, 14:1007–8; "Sir John Stradling," *DNB*, 19:15–16; Stone *Family and Fortune*, pp. 130–32. Pembroke's probable nominees were Edward Leech (1604), William Ravenscroft (1604, 1614), William Price (1614), Michael Oldisworth (1624–28), Sir John Stradling (1625), Sir Benjamin Rudyerd (1626), and, although Stone disagrees, George Mynne (1621), whose election for West Looe in 1624 was probably the result of Pembroke's Cornish patronage. Mynne was not a nominee of the Duchy of Cornwall, nor did Salisbury have any influence in Cornish boroughs. The second earl's successful candidates at Old Sarum were Thomas Brett (1621), Sir Arthur Ingram (1624), and Christopher Keightley (1628). Robert Cotton, who replaced Ingram in 1624, was also a likely nominee of Salisbury. T. Brett to Salisbury, 4 Nov. 1620, Sherfield to Salisbury, 20 Nov. 1620, Pembroke to Salisbury, 10 Dec. 1620, Keightley to (?Thomas) Hooper, May 1627 (?), *HMC Salisbury*, 22:135, 135–36, 136, 229.

7. Hutchins, *Hist. Dorset*, 3:17, 19; Bagg to Buckingham, Mar. 1626, P.R.O., St. P. Dom. 16/523:77, in *Notes and Queries*, 4th ser., 10 (1872): 325–26; Rowe, "The Influence of the Earls of Pembroke on Parliamentary Elections, 1625–1641," p. 243; Mayo, "Shaftesbury," p. 41; Keeler, *Long Parliament*, pp. 45, 367–68; "Samuel Turner," *DNB*, 19:1281; "Sir Simeon Steward," *DNB*, 18:1148; Moir, *Addled Parliament*, p. 38; W. D. Pink, *Notes and Queries for Somerset and Dorset*, pp. 90–91.

8. Williams, *Parl. Hist. Wales*, pp. 91, 97, 106; J. H. Matthews, ed., *Records of the County Borough of Cardiff*, 5:489–90; D. Mathew, "Wales and England in the Early Seventeenth Century," p. 39, is where the letter concerning William Herbert's election for Cardiff in 1621 is cited; Rowe, "The Influence of the Earls of Pembroke on Parliamentary Elections, 1625–41," pp. 245, 251; Lloyd, *Gentry of south-west Wales*, pp. 111–12; Dodd, *Studies in Stuart Wales*, pp. 181–82, 184–85, and his "Wales's Parliamentary Apprenticeship," pp. 35, 36, 60, (1944); 21, 22, 25, 26, 27, 36–37, 49 (1946).

9. Williams, *Parl. Hist. Wales*, pp. 122, 142–43, 148, 149; Keeler, *Long Parliament*, pp. 56, 80, 211, 212; Dodd, *Studies in Stuart Wales*, pp. 180–81, 184–85; and his "Wales Parliamentary Apprenticeship," pp. 43, 46, 62, 70–71, and his "Wales in the Parliaments of Charles I," pp. 21, 26, 27, 49; Rowe, "The Influence of the Earls of Pembroke on Parliamentary Elections, 1625–41," p. 245; "Sir Edward Herbert," *DNB*, 9:632–34; "Sir John Danvers," *DNB*, 5:490–91; "Robert Sidney, second Earl Leicester," *DNB*, 18:237–39. It is tempting to add Henry Wynn's elections for Merionethshire in 1624–25 to Pembroke's patronage list since, late in January 1624, Sir Richard Wynn urged his brother Henry to be sure to stand for that county, promising him that he would "have all the help the Herberts can

give." It is possible, of course, that Pembroke was involved, but it seems more likely that Wynn's allies were the Herberts of Dolguog and Berthddu, Montgomery, who, although kinsmen to the earl, probably were influential enough in their own right to assist Wynn without Pembroke's support. After all, Sir Edward Herbert, later Lord Herbert of Cherbury, had served for Merionetshire in 1604. And there is nothing in Sir Richard Wynn's letter that indicates Pembroke was taking an interest in Henry Wynn's candidacy (Sir Rich. Wynn to Henry Wynn, 31 Jan. 1624, NLW, Wynn, MSS (9059E), 1190).

10. Simpson, *Derby*, p. 94; Ormerod, *Hist. Cheshire*, 2:701; "John Leech," *DNB*, 32:387; Courtney, *Parl. Repr. Cornwall*, pp. 209–12; Moir, *Addled Parliament*, pp. 48, 193; Willson, *Privy Councillors*, pp. 201–2, 203 and n; "Sir Benjamin Rudyerd," *DNB*, 17:385–87; Keeler, *Long Parliament*, p. 329; Rowe, "The Influence of the Earls of Pembroke on Parliamentary Elections, 1625–1641," pp. 242–43, 251; Rudyerd to Nethersole, 3 Feb. 1626, P.R.O., St. P. Dom. 16/20:23. Nethersole was also seeking a place through Pembroke's influence, but, as Rudyerd had to tell him, "I moved my Lordship [Pembroke] for you, who will do what he can, but he is exceedingly straightened upon a double return you may haply [happily] be sped." But nothing came of it, and Nethersole was not a member of the 1626 Parliament; *VCH Hampshire and the Isle of Wight*, 3:189; R. East, ed., *Extracts from Records of Portsmouth*, p. 637; Hoare, *Wiltshire*, 5:addenda, Hundred of Mere, p. 2; Bagg to Buckingham, Mar. 1626, P.R.O., St. P. Dom. 16/523:77, in *Notes and Queries*, 4th ser., 10:325–26; HMC *Downshire*, 4:193, 198.

11. Ellesmere to Singleton, Vice-Chancellor of Oxford, 13 Mar. 1614, Bodleian Library, Tanner MSS 74, f. 34; Moir, *Addled Parliament*, p. 39; Rex, *University Representation in England 1604–1690*, pp. 48–49, 75–77, 88–89, 97, 99–104, 107, 108–10, 114–16, app. 4, 356–59; Willson, *Privy Councillors*, pp. 18, 76, 164, 167, 180, 183, 187; Williams, *Parl. Hist. Oxfordshire*, pp. 142–49; Notestein et al., eds., *Commons Debates 1621*, 2:302, 314; 3:28, 29, 31, 57; 5:339, 340, 341; 6:91; G. Roberts, ed., *The Diary of Walter Yonge*, p. 37; Dodd, *Studies in Stuart Wales*, pp. 180–81; A. A. Wood, *The History and Antiquities of the University of Oxford*, ed. J. Gutch, 1:356–57; *Commons Journal*, 1:826, 834, 837; Mead to Stuteville, 11 Mar. 1626, BM Harleian MSS 390, f. 25b; Chamberlain to Carleton, 7 Mar. 1626, P.R.O., St. P. Dom. 16/22:40, in McClure, ed., *Chamberlain's Letters*, 2:630–31, and Birch, *Court and Times of Charles I*, 1:84–85, and J. Heywood and T. Wright, eds., *Cambridge University Transactions*, 2:337–38; "Sir John Danvers," *DNB*, 5:490–91; "Sir Clement Edmondes, *DNB*, 6:389–91; "Sir Isaac Wake," *DNB*, 20:441–42; "Sir George Calvert, first Lord Baltimore," *DNB*, 3:721–24; "Sir Thomas Edmondes," *DNB*, 6:391–93; "Sir Henry Marten," *DNB*, 12:1146–48.

12. Courtney, *Parl. Repr. Cornwall*, pp. 84–85, 102–3, 114–16, 130–32, 186–88, 209–12, 251–53, 268–69, 283–86, 301–4, 392–97; Prestwich, *Cranfield*, pp. 433–34, 483; Zagorin, *Court and Country*, pp. 54, 61, 62, 110–11; Willson, *Privy Councillors*, pp. 149–50, 164, 166–67, 180, 183–87, 195–96, 201–2; Ruigh, *Parliament of 1624*, pp. 128–30; Rowe, "The Influence of the Earls of Pembroke on Parliamentary Elections, 1625–41," pp. 242–43, 244, 246–47, 250, 251; *Commons Journal*, 1:821; Keeler, *Long Parliament*, p. 143; "Sir John Stradling," *DNB*, 19:15–16; "William Coryton," *DNB*, 4:1186–87; "Sir William Murray, first Earl Dysert," *DNB*, 13:1304–5; Bagg to Buckingham, Mar. 1626, P.R.O., St. P. Dom. 16/523:77, in *Notes and Queries*, 4th ser., 10 (1872): 325–26; Hulme, *Eliot*, pp. 171–72; Hippisley to Buckingham, 2 Feb. 1628, P.R.O., St. P. Dom. 16/92:12. Bishop Williams had urged Buckingham to take the lord steward's post for himself, but, as part of the peace settlement with Pembroke, it went to the earl.

13. Nethersole to Carleton, 24 Apr. 1625, P.R.O., St. P. Dom. 16/1:83; Hippisley to Buckingham, 2 Feb. 1628, P.R.O., St. P. Dom. 16/92:12.

14. "Philip Herbert, Earl of Montgomery and fourth Earl of Pembroke," *DNB*, 9:659–63; Keeler, *Long Parliament*, pp. 200–201, 208–9, 293–94; Montgomery to the Mayor and Brethren of Queenborough, 6 Nov. 1620, the same to the same, 6 Jan. 1624, 25 Apr. 1625, Kent RO, Queenborough MSS, Qb/C1/30, 32, 33; the last two letters are in *Archaeologia Cantiana*, 22 (1897); p. 183; Lennox to the Mayor, Jurats, and Commons of Queen-

borough, 9? Nov. 1620, Kent RO, Queenborough MSS, Qb/C1/31: Rowe, "The Influence of the Earls of Pembroke on Parliamentary Elections, 1625–41," p. 243; *CSPD 1625–26*, p. 71.

15. Montgomery to the Mayor, Burgesses, and Commonalty of Queenborough, 31 Dec. 1625, Kent RO, Queenborough MSS, Qb/C1/34. Montgomery's nominees were Sir Roger Palmer (1614, 1624–28), James Palmer (1621), William Frowde (1621), and Robert Pooley (1624, 1625, and 1626).

16. Montgomery to the Mayor of Rochester, 20 Apr. 1625, *Gentlemen's Magazine*, vol. 68, pt. 1 (1798), pp. 116–17; "Mildmay Fane, second Earl Westmoreland," *DNB*, 6:1042–43; "Sir Albertus Morton," *DNB*, 13:1045; Scott MSS, 13–30, 33.

17. Bruce, ed., *Liber Famelicus*, pp. 40–41; Williams, *Parl. Hist. Oxfordshire*, pp. 199–201; Keeler, *Long Parliament*, p. 60; "Sir James Whitelocke," *DNB*, 21:117–19; Rowe, "The Influence of the Earls of Pembroke on Parliamentary Elections, 1625–41," p. 250.

18. Pembroke's electioneering totals, in addition to those for 1626, show an involvement in 10 elections for 13 places in 1614, 14 elections for 13 places in 1621, 16 elections for 18 places in 1624, 15 elections for 19 places in 1625 and, in 1628, 14 elections for 15 places. These figures are again, at best, tentative but are a very likely indication of his consistent electoral influence.

19. Keeler, *Long Parliament*, pp. 68, 83, 248, 267, 280, 349; "Anthony Stapley," *DNB*, 28:991–93; Kenny, "Parliamentary Influence of Charles Howard, Earl of Nottingham, 1536–1624," pp. 220, 221; Horsfield, *Hist. Sussex*, vol. 2, Cooper, app. 3, p. 55; Haggett to E. Edwards, 25 Apr. 1625, in B. E. Howells, ed., *A Calendar of Letters Relating to North Wales*, p. 218; Moir, *Addled Parliament*, p. 47. Sir John Leeds was expelled from the House of Commons in 1621, but Arundel's influence accounted for the choice of Inigo Jones as his replacement. Arundel's patronage also accounted for the return, by Arundel in a bye-election in 1621, of Sir Richard Weston, privy councillor and later earl of Portland and lord treasurer ("Sir Richard Weston, first Earl of Portland," *DNB*, 20:1275–78; *OR*, 1:453, 454). The contested election at Arundel in 1624 that led to an enlarged franchise did not break the earl's grip on the borough's elections, although his apparent bid to see his nominees secure both places was foiled. *Commons Journal*, 1:748; BM Harleian MSS 159, f. 98v; Nethersole to Carleton, 25 Mar. 1624, P.R.O., St. P. Dom. 14/161:36; Hirst, *Representative of the People?*, p. 132; K. Sharpe, "The Earl of Arundel, His Circle and the Opposition to the Duke of Buckingham, 1618–1628," in K. Sharpe, ed., *Faction & Parliament*, pp. 222–23.

20. Moir, *Addled Parliament*, pp. 47–48; "John Borough," *DNB*, 2:863–64; Keeler, *Long Parliament*, pp. 273–74, 286; "Dudley North, fourth Baron North," *DNB*, 14:596–97; Walter Rye, ed., *Visitation of Norfolk, 1563, 1613*, Harleian Soc. (London 1891), pp. 162, 207, 260; Horsfield, *Hist. Sussex*, vol. 2, Cooper, app. 3 p. 42.

21. Keeler, *Long Parliament*, pp. 82–83, 173–74; "Sir Thomas Shirley the younger," *DNB* 18:138–39; Cokayne, *Peerage*, 1:154; Arundel to the Mayor and Corporation of Steyning, n.d. 1624?, in Merewether and Stephens, *Hist. of Boroughs and Municipal Corporations*, 3:1513–14; it is also in Horsfield, *Hist. Sussex*, vol. 2, Cooper, app. 3, p. 56, and partially in W. Albery, *A Parliamentary History of Horsham, 1295–1885*, p. 16.

22. Sainty, *Lieutenants of Counties, 1585–1642*, p. 28; le Strange to Townsend, 13 Jan. 1624, Baker to the same, 26 Jan. 1624, le Strange to the same, 27 Jan. 1624, in H. W. Saunders, ed., *The Official Papers of Sir Nathaniel Bacon of Stiffkey, Norfolk, 1580–1620*, pp. 38–41; Keeler, *Long Parliament*, pp. 219–20; R. H. Mason, *History of Norfolk*, p. 251; R. Drury to Cotton, 14 Feb. 1614, BM Cottonian MSS, Jul. C. III, f. 160; *Commons Journal*, 1:749; BM ADD MSS 18,598, fols. 30v, 65v, 66. Sir Anthony Drury could have been Arundel's nominee "A.D." at Castle Rising in 1624 (Arundel to the Mayor and Inhabitants of Rising, 1624? [wrongly dated 1622], P.R.O., St. P. Dom. 14/135:42); Hirst, *Representative of the People?*, pp. 143, 144, 146; K. Sharpe, *Sir Robert Cotton 1586–1631*, pp. 114–28, 136–40, 143, 145, 156–59, 164, 168, 176, 184, 186, 190, 204–5, 206 & n. 42, 209.

23. Mayor and Corporation of Thetford to Sir Robt. Cotton, 25 Apr. 1625, BM Cottonian MSS Jul. C. III, f. 284; Ch. Gawdy to his brother Framlingham, High Sheriff for Norfolk, n.d. 1628 (three undated letters), BM ADD MSS 27, 395, fols. 188, 196, 197, 198; Stanhope to Framlingham Gawdy, 25 Feb. 1628, BM Egerton MSS, 2715, f. 240, in *HMC Gawdy*, p. 127; *OR* 1:476; "Sir Robert Bruce Cotton," *DNB*, 4:1233–40; Keeler, *Long Parliament*, pp. 184, 219–20, 281–82; "Framlingham Gawdy," *DNB*, 7:958; Blomefield, *History of Norfolk*, 1:410–11; Manship, *History of Great Yarmouth*, ed. C. R. Palmer, 1:414–16; Gleason, *JP's*, pp. 154, 158.

24. Bradfer-Lawrence, *Castle Rising*, pp. 60–61, 118; Blomefield, *Hist. Norfolk*, 1:474–75; 4:668; Rye, ed., *The Visitations of Norfolk, 1563–1613*, pp. 6, 142; Keeler, *Long Parliament*, p. 56; Arundel to the Mayor and Inhabitants of Rising, 1624? (wrongly dated 1622), P.R.O. St. P. Dom. 14/135:42; Nichols, *Progresses*, 3:774 & n; *CSPD 1623–1625*, pp. 54, 598.

25. Arundel to the Mayor of Reigate?, n.d. 1624, P.R.O., St. P. Dom. 14/135:42; "Sir William Monson, first Viscount Monson of Castlemaine," *DNB*, 13:649–50; Keeler, *Long Parliament*, pp. 65–66, 106–7, 275; *VCH Surrey*, 3:233, 235, 236–37; Brayley, *Hist. Surrey*, 4:30; Manning and Bray, *Hist. Surrey*, 1:278; Arundel to the Corporation of Aldeburgh, n.d. 1624, P.R.O., St. P. Dom. 14/135:42; "Sir Thomas Glemham," *DNB* 7:305–6; H. P. Clodd, *Aldeburgh, The History of an Ancient Borough*, pp. 21–23, 60; McClure, ed., *Chamberlain's Letters*, 1:227; *CSPD 1619–1623*, pp. 154, 370, 422; *CSPD 1631–1633*, pp. 138, 441; *CSPD 1625–1649*, p. 12; Charles Glemham, Arundel's servant, to Arundel, 17 Aug. 1614, *HMC Cowper*, 1:87.

26. Bishop's Castle, controlled by another of Suffolk's sons, Sir Robert Howard, followed a completely different course than Morpeth did. Sir Robert used it as his pocket borough, and none of its M.P.'s were clients of his kinsmen. Cokayne, *Peerage*, 1:153–54; 7:311; Hodgson, *A History of Northumberland*, pt. 2, vol. 2, pp. 379, 381, 517; Sir George J. Armytage, ed., *Middlesex Pedigrees*, Harleian Soc. (London, 1914), pp. 107–8; C. H. Hunter Blair, ed., "Members of Parliament for Morpeth," pp. 97, 98; Bean, *Northern Counties*, pp. 541–42, 556, 562; "Sir Thomas Cotton," *DNB*, 4:1238–39; *CSPD 1638–1639*, p. 476; Keeler, *Long Parliament*, p. 223; "Sir Robert Howard," *DNB* 10:58–59.

27. In 1614 Arundel's agents probably intervened, in his name, in 4 elections for 4 places. In 1621 and 1624 his involvement can be probably traced in 10 elections before each of those parliaments, which may have secured 12 places in 1621 and 7 in 1624. In 1625 he probably intervened in 9 elections for a likely 9 places, and in 1626 his intervention can be traced in 6 elections for 7 places. In 1628 Arundel was probably involved in 5 elections, which may have won 6 places for his nominees.

28. C. H. Cooper, *Annals of Cambridge*, 5 vols. (Cambridge, 1842–53), enlarged edition of vol. 5, ed. J. W. Cooper (Cambridge, 1908), pp. 348–52; *Proceedings of the Cambridge Arch. Soc.*, 1865–79, 3:203–9; Rex, *University Representation*, pp. 49, 51–52, 58–59, 63–65, 85; J. B. Mullinger, *The University of Cambridge*, 2:463–64; Moir, *Addled Parliament*, pp. 39–41; *VCH Cambridgeshire and the Isle of Ely*, 4:98, 149, 153; Nichols, *Progresses*, 1:116, 2:491; Stone, *Crisis of the Aristocracy*, p. 355; Northampton to the Mayor and Brethren of Totness, 20 Feb. 1614, Mayor and Masters of Totness to Northampton, 1 Mar. 1614, *HMC 3rd Report*, pp. 346–47; "Sir Nathaniel Rich," *DNB*, 16:1005; Carey to the Mayor of Dartmouth, 14 Feb. 1614, Northampton to the same, 20 Feb. 1614, Mayor of Dartmouth to Northampton, n.d. 1614, Devon RO, Dartmouth Borough Records, D. D. 61850 (S.M. 1420), Dartmouth Court Book, S.M. 1989, f. 20; H. A. Merewether and A. J. Stephens, *The History of the Boroughs and Municipal Corporations of the United Kingdom*, 2:982; *Reports and Trans. of the Devonshire Association* 43(1911): 367, 368.

29. Corporation of Bishop's Castle, First Minute Book of the Corporation, Northampton to the Bailiffs and Burgesses, 21 Oct. 1610, f. 4v (numbered from the back of the book and not in order with the remainder of the volume) fols. 53, 66, 73; *Trans. of the Shropshire Arch. and Natural Hist. Soc.*, 2d ser., 10 (1898): 40–43; Moir, *Addled Parliament*, p. 47; Drury to Cotton, 14 Feb. 1614, BM Cottonian MSS, Jul. C. III, f. 160; Gleason, *JP's*,

p. 132; Snow, *Essex the Rebel*, p. 77; Bradfer-Lawrence, *Castle Rising*, p. 118; Blomefield, *Hist. Norfolk*, 4:668; Sir Ch. Cornwallis to the King, 22 June 1614, P.R.O., St. P. Dom, 14/77:42, also found in BM Harleian MSS 1221, fols. 96b–99b, and in *HMC Hodgkin*, pp. 36–40; Borough of Great Yarmouth MSS, Great Yarmouth Assembly Book 1598–1625, C 19/5, f. 125.

30. Without his patronage figures as lord warden, Northampton was involved in ten elections in which the candidates he supported probably secured eight places, still a creditable figure.

31. Cokayne, *Peerage*, 1:343; 7:311.

32. Chamberlain to Carleton, 17 Mar. 1614, P.R.O., St. P. Dom. 14/76:49, in McClure, ed., *Chamberlain's Letters*, 1:517–19; Moir, *Addled Parliament*, pp. 34–35; "Henry Rich, first Earl of Holland," *DNB*, 16:997–1000; *Commons Journal*, 1:457; *HMC 4th Report*, app. 1, ii, 119; *HMC Various Collections*, 7:93. Dunwich Borough MSS, Suffolk Record Office, Ipswich Branch, Dunwich Borough Minute Book, 1595–1619, EE 6:1144/10, fols. 255, 256. I should also like to thank the county archivist for Suffolk, Mr. D. Charman, M.A., for his kind permission to use the Ipswich Assembly Book III, Book 5, 1620–44, f. 14v, in the custody of the Suffolk RO, and for the use of the Dunwich Borough MSS, Dunwich Borough Minute Book, 1595–1619, EE:1144/10, fols. 255, 256, also to be found at the Suffolk RO.

33. Hunter Blair, ed., "Members of Parliament for Morpeth," pp. 96–97; *CSPD 1611–1618*, p. 190; Prestwich, *Cranfield*, passim, esp. pp. 392–93; Armytage, ed., *Middlesex Pedigrees*, pp. 107–8; Moir, *Addled Parliament*, pp. 56, 59; "Sir Thomas Monson first Baronet," *DNB*, 13:645–46; T. R. Thomson, ed., *Materials for a History of Cricklade*, pp. 143–47; L. Stone, *Family and Fortune*, p. 280.

34. J. Foster, ed., *Alumni Oxonienses*, 4 vols. (Oxford, 1891–92), reprint, 4 vols. in 2 (1968), 2:782; Keeler, *Long Parliament*, pp. 158–59, 181–82, Nichols, *Progresses*, 1:465 & n; 3:253 & n, 254, 487, 923 & n; McClure, ed., *Chamberlain's Letters*, 1:14, 2:497, 544 & n; Aylmer, *King's Servants*, pp. 187–88, 191, 368; *CSPD 1611–1618*, pp. 123, 287; *CSPD 1619–1623*, pp. 79, 332, 602, 611, 612; *CSPD 1623–1625*, p. 109; *CSPD 1627–1628*, p. 106; *CSPD 1629–1631*, pp. 32, 342; *CSPD 1631–1633*, p. 240; *CSPD 1633–1634*, p. 23; *CSPD 1634–1635*, pp. 418, 592; *CSPD 1637–1638*, p. 239; *CSPD 1639–1640*, pp. 153, 161–62; Gleason, *JP's*, p. 56; "Sir Robert Howard," *DNB*, 10:58–59; J. W. Clay, ed., *Visitation of Cambridgeshire, 1575, 1619*, Harleian Soc. (London, 1897), p. 84; Thomson, ed., *Materials for a History of Cricklade*, pp. 143–47; "Sir Thomas Lake," *DNB*, 11:417–19; "Sir John Bankes," *DNB*, 1:1041–43; Bean, *Northern Counties*, p. 542; Hunter Blair, ed., "Members of Parliament for Morpeth," pp. 97, 98; Cokayne, *Peerage*, 1:231, 343, Stone, *Crisis of the Aristocracy*, p. 113. Suffolk's other probable nominees at Malmesbury were Sir Roger Dallison (1614), Sir Edward Wardour (1621–25), and Sir William Crofts (1626), and his other successful candidates at Wootton Bassett possibly were the outsiders Sir Rowland Egerton of Cheshire (1624), Sir Walter Tichborne of Hampshire (1625), and Sir John Franklin (1626), who, although he held Wiltshire properties, was of Willesden, Middlesex. Suffolk's son, the earl of Berkshire, was, in all likelihood, behind the return of Anthony Rous of Fatcham, Surrey, and Franklin for Wootton Bassett (1628), and Croft's election at Malmesbury (1628).

35. Kenny, "Parliamentary Influence of Charles Howard, Earl of Nottingham, 1536–1624," pp. 216, 217–23; *Commons Journal*, 1:677, 694, 695, 726, 745–46, 753–54, 779, 781; "Sir Robert Mansell," *DNB*, 12:973–74; "Sir John Suckling," *DNB*, 19:141; Keeler, *Long Parliament*, pp. 116–17, 178–79, 261–62, 275, 365; *VCH Surrey*, 2:295–96; 3:232, 525; 4:255–56; Brayley, *Hist. Surrey*, 3:326; 4:30; Manning and Bray, *Hist. Surrey*, 1:278; 2:295–96; Lambert, *Blechingley* 2:424–25; Gleason, *JP's*, p. 79; Cokayne, *Peerage*, 3:236; 4:238; 5:334; 6:105–6. Fleetwood, however, preferred to serve for Launceston rather than Blechingley, and his replacement was Edward Bysshe of Burstown, Surrey.

36. In 1614 Arundel, Northampton, Nottingham, and Suffolk probably intervened in 28 elections for 28 places (not including Northampton's totals as lord warden). Arundel,

Nottingham, and Suffolk were involved in 15 elections for 18 places in 1621, in 16 elections for 16 places in 1624, in 16 elections for 20 places in 1625, and in 13 elections for 15 places in 1626. In 1628 Arundel, Berkshire, and Nottingham were probably active in 11 elections for 13 places. As a matter of convenience, the totals for Nottingham included those of his wife and successor, the second earl.

37. Cokayne, *Peerage*, 2:65–66; Spedding, *Bacon*, 7:152, 155; *CSPV 1625–1626*, p. 464; *CSPV 1626–1628*, p. 605; Goodere to Buckingham, 20 Nov. 1620, P.R.O., St. P. Dom. 14/117:83; Alured to Sir Jo. Coke, Drake to the same, 26 Dec. 1625, *HMC Cowper*, 1:240, 242; Hippisley to Buckingham, 2 Feb. 1628, P.R.O., St. P. Dom. 16/92:12; Prestwich, *Cranfield*, pp. 432–34; Willson, *Privy Councillors*, pp. 160–61, 162–64, 166–67, 191, 195–96, 200–204.

38. Buckingham's influence as lord warden is included in this chapter to further illustrate his dependence upon great office as a foundation for his electoral patronage. His electoral record as lord warden, however, is included with that of the court, not the aristocracy, in the appendixes that indicate court and aristocratic intervention in the elections of 1604–40.

39. Pembroke, as captain of Portsmouth, usually controlled one of its places; and Buckingham's 1628 success, when his nominees William Towerson and Owen Jennings were elected, was probably one result of the reconciliation between Pembroke and the duke. Hull Corporation MSS, Bench Book 5, fols., 122, 123; Abbott, Archbishop of Canterbury, to Hull, 30 Jan. 1624, Hull Corporation Letters, L. 204; Bailey to Peacock, 21 Apr. 1624, Buckingham to the Bailiffs of Scarborough, 6 Jan. 1626, Harrison to the Bailiffs, Aldermen, and Burgesses of Scarborough, 31 Jan. 1628, Scarborough Borough MSS, General Letters, B. 1., 1597–1642; Apsley to Nicholas, 2 Feb. 1628, Holt to the same, 6 Feb. 1628, P.R.O., St. P. Dom. 16/92:18, 53; *CSPD 1625–1626*, p. 406; *CSPD 1628–1629*, pp. 205, 394; McClure, ed., *Chamberlain's Letters*, 2:275; Keeler, *Long Parliament*, pp. 205–6; Cliffe, *Yorkshire Gentry*, pp. 53, 353; C. Thompson, "The Origins of the Politics of the Parliamentary Middle Group," pp. 73–75, 77–78.

40. Rex, *University Representation*, pp. 97, 98, 103, 105, 106, 107–8, 113–14, 360; Naunton to Buckingham, n.d. 1621, Goodman, *The Court of King James*, 2:225–26; Naunton to Buckingham, 14 Jan. 1624, P.R.O., St. P. Dom. 14/158:30; "Sir Robert Naunton," *DNB*, 14:126–29; *CSPV 1625–1626*, pp. 380–81; "Sir John Coke," *DNB*, 4:700–702; "Sir Albertus Morton," *DNB*, 13:1045; Mead to Stuteville, n.d. 1625, Birch, *Court and Times of Charles I*, 1:5; Chamberlain to Carleton, 6 May 1625, P.R.O., St. P. Dom. 16/2:27, in ibid., 2:18–19, and McClure, ed., *Chamberlain's Letters*, 2:614–15; Mead to Stuteville, 21 Jan. 1626, 1 Mar. 1628, BM Harleian MSS 390, fols. 5, 350b; Heywood and Wright, eds., *Cambridge University Transactions*, 2:364; Mason to Nicholas, 3, 7 Mar. 1628, P.R.O., St. P. Dom. 16/95:23, 47; Beinbrigge to Coke, 13 Mar. 1628, *HMC Cowper*, 1:341; Porritt, *Unreformed House of Commons*, 1:101.

41. Sainty, *Lieutenants of Counties, 1585–1642*, p. 25; Keeler, *Long Parliament*, pp. 181–82, 215–16; Chamberlain to Carleton, 31 Jan. 1624, P.R.O., St. P. Dom. 14/158:72, in McClure, ed., *Chamberlain's Letters*, 2:543; *Commons Journal*, 1:783.

42. Willson, *Privy Councillors*, pp. 73, 166; Chamberlain to Carleton, 3, 17 Jan. 1624, in McClure, ed., *Chamberlain Letters*, 2:536, 540, also in Birch, *Court and Times of Charles I*, 2:443–44, 447–48; Buckingham to Jackson, Bingley, and Others, 10 Apr. 1625, BM ADD MSS 37, 819, fols. 11, 11v; Dorset to Dering, n.d. 1625, BM Stowe MSS 743, f. 64; Westmorland to Dering, 13 Apr. 1625, BM Stowe MSS 743, f. 60; Buckingham to the Mayor and Corporation of Sandwich?, 8 Apr. 1625, BM ADD MSS 37, 819 f. 11v; Montgomery to the Mayor of Rochester, 20 Apr. 1625, *Gentlemen's Magazine*, vol. 68, pt. 1 (1798), pp. 116–17; Sir Tho. Walsingham the younger to the Mayor of Rochester, 23 Apr. 1625, *Gentlemen's Magazine*, vol. 68, pt. 1 (1798), p. 117; Scott MSS, 39v; J. Cave-Brown, "Knights of the Shire for Kent," *Archaeologia Cantiana* 21 (1895): 230–32; Prestwich, *Cranfield*, pp. 432–34, 435; "Mildmay Fane, third Earl Westmorland," *DNB*, 6:1042–43; "Sir Albertus Morton," *DNB*, 13:1045; "Sir Edwyn Sandys," *DNB*, 17:775–79. Buckingham also failed in finding a place for Sandys's son at Sandwich in 1625.

43. Hippisley to Buckingham, 8, 14 Jan. 1626, P.R.O., St. P. Dom. 16/18:28, 60; Nicholas Lord Tufton to Dering, 31 Jan., Sandys to ?, 2 Feb. 1628, Kent RO, Dering MSS, U 350, C2/17, 18; Buckingham to the Mayor and Burgesses of Sandwich, 9 Feb. 1628, Kent RO, Sandwich Borough MSS, Sa/ZB2/74; Keeler, *Long Parliament*, pp. 155–56, 200–201; "Sir Edward Dering," *DNB*, 5:845–46; Hirst, *Representative of the People?*, pp. 174, 180.

44. Buckingham to the Mayor and Corporation of Windsor, 8 Apr. 1625, BM ADD MSS 37, 819, f. 11; Ryland, ed., *Visitations of Berkshire*, 1:70, 170, 262, 280; Nichols, *Progresses*, 2:100, 706; Aylmer, *King's Servants*, pp. 156, 157, 356; Prestwich, *Cranfield*, p. 560; McClure, ed., *Chamberlain's Letters*, 2:97, 505, 573 & n; *CSPD 1611–1618*, pp. 98, 192; *CSPD 1623–1625*, pp. 12, 187; "Sir William Russell," *DNB*, 49:479–80.

45. Although Westminster's other contested election in 1621 had no impact on Buckingham's nominee, it was an excellent example of how far the vestry would go to have their way. The disputed election grew out of the town's attempt to elect a replacement for the vestry's candidate, Edmund Doubleday, who died shortly after the first election. Williams, acting for the vestry, employed all kinds of chicanery to see to the return of William Mann, a member of the vestry and the "collector of his [Williams] rent." It was claimed by those opposing Mann's return that "no public notice" of the election was given and that "the inhabitants of the parishes of St. Martins in the Fields, St. Clement Danes and St. Marie Savoy," the "greatest part" of the town, were denied their voices. Private notice had been given the night before the election "to every particular house" in a parish known for its loyalty to Mann; and on election morning, "a great multitude" of "serving men, apprentices, women, children, watermen" and many others, allegedly ineligible voters all, appeared to vote for Mann. Requests for a poll to examine voter eligibility were ignored, and Williams ordered Mann returned despite loud protests. Although the election was examined by the House of Commons, the return of Mann was accepted. Perhaps, in some memories at least, the disputed election of 1621 was still remembered in 1628 when Mann was, once again, a vestry candidate! Locke to Carleton, 16 Dec. 1620, P.R.O., St. P. Dom. 14/118:30; *Commons Journal*, 1:529, 568–69; Notestein et al. eds., *Commons Debates 1621*, 2:126–27, 141–43, 256–57; 4:93–94, 106–7, 181–82; 5:14–15, 62–63, 485, 519; 6:4, 12, 354–55, 430–31; Trywhitt, ed., *Proceedings and Debates*, 1:82, 99, 211–13. I wish to thank Major James More-Molyneux, of Loseley Park, for his kind permission to quote from the Loseley MSS, which are on long loan at the Guildford Museum Muniment Room and, too, the archivist, Miss E. M. Dance, for her courtesy and help. Loseley MSS, Guildford Museum and Muniment Room, L. M. 1989, 10 Feb. 1621; "Sir Edward Villiers," *DNB* 20:324–25; Williams to Cotton, 12 Feb. 1628, BM Cottonian MSS, Jul. C. III, fols. 402, 402v; Keeler, *Long Parliament*, p. 317; "Sir Robert Pye," *DNB*, 15:514–15; Mead to Stuteville, 8 Mar. 1628, BM Harleian MSS 390, f. 358b, in Birch, *Court and Times of Charles I*, 1:327–28; Beaulieu to Puckering, 27 Feb. 1628, BM Harleian MSS 7010, f. 75. Mann did pretty well for both Williams and as a receiver of fines from the King's Bench. At his death, at about eighty years of age, his estate totaled about £16,000, not a bad figure at all. It cannot come as a surprise that there was some antagonism aroused in 1608 over his apparent zeal in seeking out and collecting the fines! *CSPD 1603–1610*, pp, 397, 422, 425; *CSPD 1580–1625*, p. 515; *CSPD 1639–1640*, p. 146.

46. The Sir John Smith or Smythe who served for Buckingham in 1626 may have been the son of Sir Richard Smythe or Smith of Leeds Castle, Kent, who married, in 1617, "one Franklin's daughter of Middlesex," possibly the daughter of Buckingham's nominee at Rye in 1625, Sir John Franklin. Sir Richard Smythe's post, as receiver general of the Duchy of Cornwall, may account too for the election of Sir John Smith or Smythe at Michael in 1625–26, Chamberlain to Carleton, 15 Mar. 1617, in McClure, ed., *Chamberlain's Letters*, 2:62; Nichols, *Progresses*, 3:252 & n, 443; Hasted, *Kent*, 5:486; 8:340; *VCH Buckinghamshire*, 3:437, 439; Lipscombe, *Buckinghamshire*, 2:490, 496; *CSPD 1619–1623*, p. 307; *CSPD 1623–1625*, p. 385; *CSPD 1627–1628*, pp. 261, 581; Southcott to [Nicholas], 17 Apr. 1626, P.R.O., St. P. Dom. 16/25:11; Drake to Nicholas, 7 Oct. 1626?,

P.R.O., St. P. Dom. 16/37:52, in J. Forster, *Sir John Eliot*, 2:34; F. T. Colby, ed., *Visitation of Devonshire 1620*, Harleian Soc. (London, 1872), pp. 17, 94, 95. James Tomkins, M.P. at Leominster from 1624 to 1628, won election thanks to his county interests; and Sir Edward Littleton, chosen from 1625 to 1628, probably owed his place to his family's influence in Herefordshire and North Wales. He succeeded his father as chief justice of North Wales in 1621. Buckingham might have approved of his election for Leominster in 1625–26, but, following Littleton's attack on the duke in the Parliament of 1626, it is doubtful that Buckingham would continue to approve of Littleton's election. Littleton's case, though, may parallel Eliot's. Eliot probably had Buckingham's backing in 1625 and 1626, before his views became all too obvious to his erstwhile patron. Keeler, *Long Parliament*, p. 362; "Sir Edward Littleton, Baron Littleton," *DNB*, 11:1245–47; McClure, ed., *Chamberlain's Letters*, 2:97, 505, 573 & n; G. F. Townsend, *The Town and Borough of Leominster*, p. 90; W. R. Williams, *Parl. Hist. Herefordshire*, pp. 125–27; J. J. Stocker, "Pedigree of Smythe of Ostenhanger, Kent; of Smythe of Bidborough and Sutton-At-Home, Kent; and of the Smythes, Viscounts Strangford, of Dormore, Ireland," pp. 76–78.

47. Hulme, *Eliot*, pp. 42–43, 75; Zagorin, *Court and Country*, p. 98; "Sir John Wolstenholme," *DNB*, 21:815; "Sir John Eliot," *DNB*, 6:604–7; Courtney, *Parl. Repr. Cornwall*, pp. 63–64, 84–85, 114–16, 130–32, 209–12, 268–69, 325–27, 342–44, 375–79; Lawrence, *Parl. Hist. Cornwall*, p. 246. A double return was made for Lostwithiel. Vane's name was on the second return, the first including the names of Kendall, the borough's recorder, and Sir Reginald Mohun, member of an influential Cornish and Devonshire family. Burke, *Extinct Peerages*, p. 353; Cokayne, *Peerage*, 5:322–23; *CSPD 1627–1628*, pp. 340, 592; *CSPD 1629–1631*, p. 506. Bodmin's election of Robert Caesar and Henry Jermyn in 1625 and of Sir Richard Weston and Jermyn again, in 1626, was probably due to the influence of the courtier Sir Robert Killigrew. Jermyn's mother was Catherine Killigrew, sister to Sir Robert. It is possible, of course, that Bodmin's returns in 1625 and 1626 reflected Killigrew's willingness to accept the suggestions of the duke of Buckingham. Courtney, *Parl. Repr. Cornwall*, pp. 230–32; "Sir Robert Killigrew," *DNB*, 11:110–11; Keeler, *Long Parliament*, pp. 234–35, 239.

48. Hulme, *Eliot*, pp. 62–104; Willson, *Privy Councillors*, pp. 149–50, 164, 166–67, 180, 183–87; Prestwich, *Cranfield*, pp. 433–34; Zagorin, *Court and Country*, pp. 54, 62; *Commons Journal*, 1:837; Courtney, *Parl. Repr. Cornwall*, pp. 84–85, 114–16, 130–32, 230–32, 375–79; Williams, *Parl. Hist. Herefordshire*, p. 45; "Sir Walter Pye," *DNB*, 15:514. Camelford's return of the earl of Dorset's servants Edward Lindsay (1626) and Evans Edwards (1628) was probably due to the influence of Sir John Trevor, a friend of the first earl, whose marriage to a Trevanion gave him strong Cornish connections, Howells, ed., *A Calendar of Letters Relating to North Wales*, pp. 24, 25 & n; "Sir John Trevor," *DNB*, 19:1148; Keeler, *Long Parliament*, pp. 365–66; *CSPD 1603–1610*, p. 564, *CSPD 1628–1629*, pp. 586, 595.

49. Willson, *Privy Councillors*, pp. 195–96, 201–2; Prestwich, *Cranfield*, p. 434; Zagorin, *Court and Country*, p. 61; Bagg to Buckingham, 17 Mar., 6 Apr. 1628, P.R.O., St. P. Dom. 16/96:36, 16/100:47. Probus, mentioned by Bagg, did not return burgesses to parliament; however, he could have meant Grampound, which did return Buckingham's client, Sir Robert Pye. Keeler, *Long Parliament*, pp. 40, 121–22, 163–64; Courtney, *Parl. Repr. Cornwall*, pp. 130–32, 148–50, 186–88, 209–12, 375–79; McClure, ed., *Chamberlain's Letters*, 2:14, 56, 129, 282. Badger accompanied Buckingham to France in 1625 and, in March of that year, received a pension of £300 yearly. He was still receiving a court-paid fee and annuity in 1635, totaling £260. He also served, through the Duchy of Lancaster's patronage, for Stockbridge in 1625 and 1626. Chamberlain to Carleton, 15 May 1625, in *Chamberlain's Letters*, 2:617; Nichols, *Progresses*, 1:471; 2:24, 108; 3:177, 246, 465; *CSPD 1603–1610*, p. 190; *CSPD 1619–1623*, p. 324; *CSPD 1623–1625*, p. 509; *CSPD 1635*, p. 553; Hulme, *Eliot*, pp. 181–83; J. Waylen, *Launceston, Past and Present*, pp. 137–40; *Commons Journal*, 1:874, 883; *Parochial History of Cornwall*, 3:389, 395; "Sir William Killigrew," *DNB*, 11:116–17. John Jacob, elected at Plympton Earl in 1624, was

probably Buckingham's nominee; he was, from 1627 to 1637, an official of the admiralty in the Cinque Ports (Keeler, *Long Parliament*, p. 231 n. 15; Hirst, *Representative of the People?*, pp. 61–62).

50. After the election, Dyve presented the borough with "one silver salt cellar" which would "forever, to serve to stand up their tables at their court dinners and feasts." That, and the £5 apparently offered for the town's poor, was what Strode was complaining about; it does seem, however, a small enough price to pay for electoral victory. Dyve did not serve for Bridport again, making his last appearance, probably under the earl of Bristol's colors, for Weymouth in 1628. Gardiner, *Hist. of England*, 6:92–98; Willson, *Privy Councillors*, pp. 181, 194; the Bailiffs and Inhabitants of Bridport to the Duke of Buckingham, 28 Jan. 1626, P.R.O., St. P. Dom. 16/19:69; Hutchins, *Hist. of Dorset*, 2:12; H. G. Tibutt, ed., *The Life and Letters of Sir Lewis Dyve*, 1599–1669, pp. 8–9; *Commons Journal*, 1:820, 822–23; "Sir Lewis Dyve," *DNB*, 6:301–2; Edward Clark," *DNB*, 4:420; Keeler, *Long Parliament*, p. 44; Hirst, *Representative of the People?*, p. 119.

51. Willson, *Privy Councillors*, p. 156 & n; Salter, ed., *Oxford Council Acts*, p. 297; *Commons Journal*, 1:514, 515, 817, 819, 820; Viscount Colchester to the Bailiffs of Colchester, 28, 30 Apr. 1625, Essex RO, Morant MSS, vol. 43, pp. 55, 59, 63; Keeler, *Long Parliament*, pp. 203, 317; "Sir Robert Harley," *DNB*, 8:1282–83; "Sir Walter Pye," *DNB*, 15:514; Williams, *Parl. Hist. Wales*, pp. 22–23, 178–79; Williams, *The History of Radnorshire*, pp. 89–90; "John Scudamore, first Viscount Scudamore," *DNB*, 17:1092–95; *VCH Herefordshire*, 1:387; Williams, *Parl. Hist. Herefordshire*, pp. 44–46; Aylmer, *King's Servants*, pp. 308–13, 372–79; Cokayne, *Peerage*, 2:345.

52. Keeler, *Long Parliament*, pp. 64, 236, 286–87. The Jermyns probably supported Bury St. Edmund's return of Sir William Harvey of Ickworth, Suffolk, in 1628. The Jermyns, like Harvey, twice elected at Preston, had frequently enjoyed the support of the Duchy of Lancaster.

53. Keeler, *Long Parliament*, p. 67; "Sir Richard Shelton, Shelton or Shilton," *DNB*, 28:43–44; R. Ferguson, *A History of Cumberland*, pp. 170–71; J. Nicholson and R. Burn, *The History and Antiquities of Westmorland and Cumberland*, 2:465–66, 467. Sir Robert Pye's elections at Bath in 1621 and 1624 were probably due to the influence of Pye's son-in-law, Sir Edward Phelips, and not Buckingham (T. G. Barnes, *Somerset, 1625–1640*, pp. 26, 28).

54. His totals, without his record in the Cinque Ports, are still those of a great patron, as his likely intervention in 74 elections in behalf of candidates who probably secured 68 places, indicates.

55. Subtracting his results in the Ports, the figures for 1625 are 19 elections for 18 places, for 1626, 17 elections and 17 places, and, for 1628, 18 elections and 15 places.

56. This table reflects Buckingham's probable success as lord warden, lord admiral, chancellor of Cambridge University, constable of Windsor Castle, and as lord lieutenant of Middlesex. It also includes his apparent record in the boroughs formerly linked to the Prince's Council or the Duchy of Cornwall. For Pembroke it is a record of his likely electioneering as warden of the stannaries and lord lieutenant of Cornwall, lord lieutenant of Wiltshire, chancellor of the University of Oxford, and captain of Portsmouth. Arundel, although lord lieutenant of six counties, enjoyed electoral influence in only one, Norfolk, and that is shown in the second table.

57. Moir, *Addled Parliament*, p. 49; A. Beesley, *The History of Banbury*, p. 266; Neale, *Elizabethan House of Commons*, pp. 166–67; J. K. Hedges, *History of Wallingford*, 2:112, 113, 116, 120, 200; Keeler, *Long Parliament*, pp. 33–34; Aspinall, ed., *Parliament through Seven Centuries*, p. 48; A. C. Baker, *Historic Abingdon*, pp. 70, 71; "Sir Robert Knollys," Berkshire RO, D/EP/7/80, film no. 11; Cokayne, *Peerage*, 1:229, 231; Burke, *Extinct Peerages*, pp. 294–95; Wallingford Minute Book, 1507–1683, Berkshire RO, W/ACA i, fols. 98v, 105; J. Foster, *Alumni Oxonienses*, vol. 1, pt. 2, pp. 864, 865.

58. The polls for Reading's burgess-ships were for Sir Francis Knollys, junior, 21, Saunders, 16, and Sir Robert Knollys, 9, in 1624. In 1626 Saunders had 19 votes, Sir

Francis 16, and Sir Robert 4. Saunders garnered 20, Sir Francis 19, and Brooke none in 1628. Baker, *Historic Abingdon*, pp. 71–72; Aspinal, ed., *Parl. through Seven Centuries*, pp. 46, 48, 49–50, 107; J. M. Guilding, ed., *Reading Records*, 2:92, 103, 110, 115, 116, 133, 166, 168–69, 230–31, 270–71, 273, 384–87; Visct. Wallingford to the Mayor and Jurats of Reading?, 8 Apr. 1625, Berkshire RO, Borough of Reading MSS. HMC LIV, HMC 13. *HMC Duke of Leeds* et al., 183, 221; *VCH·Berkshire*, 4:545; Keeler, *Long Parliament*, pp. 244–45; Foster, *Alumni Oxonienses*, vol. 1, pt. 2, pp. 864, 865.

59. Beesley, *Hist. Banbury*, pp. 261–62, 265, 266, 281–82; Williams, *Parl. Hist. Oxfordshire*, pp. 49–50, 113, 115, 177–78, "Sir Anthony Cope," *DNB*, 4:1091; Neale, *Elizabethan House of Commons*, pp. 166–67; Keeler, *Long Parliament*, pp. 116–17, 387–88; "Thomas Wentworth," *DNB*, 20:1178–79; H. E. Salter, ed., *Oxford Council Acts, 1583–1626*, pp. 232, 294–97, 323; Notestein et al., eds., *Commons Debates*, 1621, 1:28–29, 68; 2:47–49, 107; 4:32–34; 5:444–45, 477; 6:361, 446; *Commons Journal*, 1:514, 515. For the local quarrel that complicated Oxford's election, see Hirst, *Representative of the People?*, app. 2, p. 205.

60. See pages 156–57 below.

61. "Sir Robert Rich, Earl of Warwick," *DNB*, 16:1014–19; Cokayne, *Peerage*, 8:65–66; Moir, *Addled Parliament*, pp. 31, 38; Keeler, *Long Parliament*, pp. 46, 97–99, 132–33; "Sir Richard Weston, first Earl of Portland," *DNB*, 20:1275–78; Wright, *Hist. Essex*, 1:491, 492; Morant, *Hist. Essex*, 2:278.

62. Viscount Colchester to the Bailiffs of Colchester, 28, 30 Apr. 1625, the Earl of Warwick to the same, 29 Apr. 1625, Essex RO, Morant MSS, vol. 43, pp. 55, 59, 63, 83; Cokayne, *Peerage*, 2:327; Morant, *Hist. Essex*, 1:254, 315, 322, 336, 342, 355, 356, 362, 371; 2:54. Sir Arthur Harris, a considerable Essex landowner, held some of his properties from the earl of Warwick. I would like to take this opportunity to thank Mr. F. G. Emmison, M.B.E., F.S.A., F.R. Hist. S., formerly the Essex county archivist, for his many kindnesses, courtesies, and invaluable assistance during my visits to the Essex County Record Office. Cheeke owed his place at Beeralston to his brother-in-law, Lord Mountjoy (Ruigh, *Parliament of 1624*, p. 67 & n). James F. Maclear, "Puritan Relations with Buckingham," pp. 111–32; Thompson, "The Origins of the Politics of the Parliamentary Middle Group," pp. 73–75, 77–78.

63. Keeler, *Long Parliament*, pp. 198–99.

64. Mead to Stuteville, 9 Feb. 1628, BM Harleian MSS 390, f. 324b; Rivers to the Bailiffs of Colchester, 9 Feb. 1628, Warwick to the same, 28 Feb. 1628, Essex RO, Morant MSS, vol. 43, pp. 67, 85.

65. Cayworth to Lord Montagu, 7 Feb. 1628, Northamptonshire RO, Montagu MSS, V. 70, in *HMC Buccleuch and Queensberry*, 3:323–24; Beaulieu to Puckering, 20 Feb. 1628, in Birch, *Court and Times of Charles I*, 1:323; Mead to Stuteville, 15, 22 Mar. 1628, BM Harleian MSS 390, fols. 361, 367b, in Birch, *Court and Times of Charles I*, 1:329, 333; Nuttall to Nicholas, 4 Mar. 1628, P.R.O., St. P. Dom. 16/95:35; Justices of Essex to the High Constables of the County, n.d. February 1628, P.R.O., St. P. Dom. 15/94:87; *Acts of the Privy Council*, 43:350, 352, 354, 358–59, 361; *CSPV, 1626–1628*, pp. 594, 605; *VCH Essex*, 2:244; 4:27; Wright, *Hist. Essex*, 1:197; Morant, *Hist. Essex*, 1:308, 357, 361; 2:176, 369, 536, 559, 563.

66. Warwick to the Mayor of Harwich, 21 Dec. 1620, Harwich Borough MSS, Bundle 109/1; Minute Book of the Council, Court of Common Council of Harwich, 1600–1644, B 98/3, fols. 26v, 37, 42, 42v, 43, from the manuscripts of the former Borough of Harwich, now held by the Harwich Town Council at Guildhall, Harwich, Essex; "Sir Nathaniel Rich," *DNB*, 16:1005, where he is linked to the Rich family as a probably illegitimate son of Richard, 1st baron Rich; Aylmer, *King's Servants*, pp. 156–57, 356; Prestwich, *Cranfield*, p. 560.

67. Keeler, *Long Parliament*, pp. 46, 268–69; "Sir Julius Caesar," *DNB*, 3:656–59; Bailiffs of Maldon to Caesar?, 10 or 13 Apr. 1625, BM ADD MSS 12,496, fol. 106; Memorandum of the 1625 Election at Maldon, Essex RO, D/B 3/3/392/53.

68. M. F. Keeler's suggestion that the Edward Alford who served for Steyning was the son of Colchester's former M. P. does not seem correct, since Colchester's Edward Alford remarked, in his letter to the corporation, that he had been elected for Steyning. Keeler, *Long Parliament*, pp. 82–83, 268–69; Rickwood, "Members of Parliament for Colchester," pp. 193–96; *Commons Journal*, 1:873, 876–77; BM ADD MSS 27, 878, fols. 70v-71; Borough of Colchester MSS, Borough Assembly Book 1620–46, fols. 44–45, 51v–52, 54, 68v, 69, 70, 73; Cheeke to the Bailiffs of Colchester, 8 Mar. 1628, Essex RO, Morant MSS, vol. 43, pp. 15, 17; Alford to the same, 17 Mar. 1628, Essex RO, Morant MSS, vol. 43, p. 8; W. Bruce Bannerman, ed., *Visitations of Sussex, 1530, 1633–1634*, Harleian Soc. (London, 1905), p. 206; Mereweather and Stephens, *Hist. Boroughs*, 2:1346; A. Fletcher, *County Community*, pp. 171–73, 232–33, 240. In 1626, when Sir Harbottle Grimston was also chosen for Essex, he was replaced at Colchester by another county gentleman, Sir Robert Quarles (Rickwood, "Members of Parliament for Colchester," pp. 195–96; Morant, *Hist. Essex*, 2:507, 574, 575). For a more complete discussion of Colchester's local problems, see Hirst, *Representative of the People?*, p. 134, app. 2, pp. 199–201.

69. Notestein, et al. eds., *Commons Debates, 1621*, 1:51; 2:49–52, 63, 94; 4:35–36, 40–41, 61, 68; 5:251–52, 445–46, 451, 474, 509–10; 6:360–61, 429–30, 445, 446–47, 449–50; Tyrwhitt, ed., *Proceedings and Debates, 1621*, 1:19–24, 33, 57; Buckingham to Sir Geo. Hastings, 23 Jan. 1621, *HMC Hastings*, 4:204; *VCH Leicestershire*, 2:107; *Commons Journals*, 1:511–12, 513, 515–16, 516–17, 523, 525–26.

70. *VCH Leicestershire*, 2:107; Huntingdon to Wright, 9 Apr. 1625, *HMC Hastings*, 2:67. There was further trouble in 1626 when Sir Henry petitioned the House against the sheriff's conduct. Hastings alleged that the sheriff was guilty of contempt, but what happened to cause the petition remains unknown (*Commons Journals*, 1:841, 844, 849, 854, 855).

71. Huntingdon to the Sheriff of Rutland, n.d. 1624? *HMC Hastings*, 2:64; Keeler, *Long Parliament*, pp. 294–95; Sainty, *Lieutenants of Counties 1585–1642*, pp. 26, 30.

72. Sir H. Carey to Salisbury, 7, 11 Dec. 1620, ? to (Richard) Storie, Jan. 1623/24?, the Bishop of Lincoln to Salisbury, 15 May 1624, Keighley to Conesbie, Apr. 1625, Salisbury to the Bishop of Lincoln, before May 1625, Keighley to ? Miles, 20 Jan. 1626, Pemberton to Salisbury, 6 Feb. 1628, *HMC Salisbury*, 22:136, 136–37, 188, 192, 205(2), 209–10, 241–42. In 1628 Hertford returned Salisbury's relative Sir Edward Howard, and when Howard was raised to the peerage, Sir Charles Morison, another Salisbury nominee, took his place. Morison died and was replaced by a third candidate who enjoyed Salisbury's backing, John Carey, Viscount Rochford, whose local prestige also must have contributed to his election. The discussion of Salisbury's influence is almost completely based on Lawrence Stone's excellent article, "The Electoral Influence of the Second Earl of Salisbury, 1614–68," and the documents cited above are from his essay. St. Albans Borough Records, Mayor's Accounts, nos. 161, 162, 164; C. Tufton to R. Wastfield, 20 Feb. 1614, Chippenham Borough MSS, Yelde Hall, no. 253; Stone, *Family and Fortune*, pp. 125, 129.

73. Mason still found a seat for parliament, serving for Christchurch, Hampshire.

74. Both of Marlborough's bye-elections also apparently reflect Hertford's successful patronage. In 1621, when Sir William Seymour was elevated to the peerage, he was replaced by Sir Walter Devereux whose choice was another example of the close relationship between Hertford and the Earl of Essex while, in 1628, the return of Henry Percy, the Earl of Northumberland's brother, was another likely indication of Hertford's influence.

75. Somersetshire RO, Phelips MSS, vol. 4, fols. 202, 202v; Horner et al. to the Earl of Hertford, 14 Dec. 1620, House of Commons Library Manuscript No. 19, in the custody of the House of Lords Record Office; Ley to Thynne, 14 Apr. 1625, cited in Ruigh, *Parliament of 1624*, p. 127 n. 56; Rich. and Hugh Cholmley to the Bailiffs of Scarborough, 12 Jan. 1628?, Scarborough Borough MSS, General Letters B. 1., 1597–1642; Keeler,

*Long Parliament*, pp. 70, 71, 116–17, 241–42, 303–4, 317, 336, 337–38, 365–66; *VCH Wiltshire*, 5:114, 115, 116, 121, 122, 126–27, 131–32; Hoare, *Wiltshire*, 2:85; Jas. Waylen, *A History of the Town of Marlborough* (London, 1854), pp. 142–43, 147; *CSPD 1639*, p. 276; *Commons Journal*, 1: 834; Snow, *Essex the Rebel*, pp. 84, 110, 199, 203; Dodd, "Wales's Parliamentary Apprenticeship," p. 54; Cokayne, *Peerage*, 4:224–25; "William Seymour, first Marquis and second Earl of Hertford, second Duke of Somerset," *DNB*, 17: 1271–73; "Henry Percy, Lord Percy of Alnwick," *DNB*, 15:588–89; "Francis Seymour, first Baron Seymour of Trowbridge," *DNB*, 18:1255–56; "Sir Robert Pye," *DNB*, 15:514–15; "Robert Mason," *DNB*, 19:1148. Two of Hertford's likely nominees, his agent Kirton and John Selden, were also elected at Ilchester in 1626. It is unlikely that their choice was further evidence of the Seymours' influence. Ilchester had provided Sir Richard Wynn a place in 1621, 1624, and 1625 through the intercession of the then lord keeper, Bishop Williams, who probably also backed Nathaniel Tomkins there in 1624. The borough's high steward, Sir Robert Phelips, was probably behind the choice of Kirton and Selden in 1626, offering a possible example of the country group's willingness to support candidates of similar views, for Phelips would have been sympathetic with Hertford's coolness toward the court. As for the influence of Bishop Williams earlier at Ilchester, Sir Richard Wynn, writing after his defeat in 1621 for Caernarvonshire, could still count on a burgess-ship since his "Mr. [Master] hearing I might miscarry in this business, has labored to get me a burgess-ship." Wynn's principal patron was Williams, and it must have been through the bishop's efforts that Sir Richard found himself a place at Ilchester. Sir Rich. Wynn to Sir Jo. Wynn, 25 Dec. 1620, NLW, Wynn MSS (9057E) 933.

76. Neale, *Elizabethan House of Commons*, p. 206; Drakard, *The History of Stamford*, pp. 138, 148, 153; "Sir Bryan Palmes," *DNB*, 15:170; Nevinson, *History of Stamford*, pp. 100–01; G. Burton, *Chronology of Stamford*, pp. 124, 169, 238; Stamford Borough MSS, Hall Books, vol. 3, 1461–1657, fols. 309, 332, 340, 343, 345; Aylmer, *King's Servants*, p. 368; *VCH Lincolnshire*, 2:287; Boston Corporation Assembly Book, vol. ii, 1608–38, fols. 146v, 147v, 148, 149v; W. B. Bannerman, ed., *Visitation of Surrey*, p. 155. John St. Amand was identified upon admission to Gray's Inn in March 1625 as one of Lord Keeper Williams's secretaries, but his returns from Stamford must have been at the request of the earl of Exeter, who controlled the borough's elections (J. Foster, ed., *The Register of Admissions to Gray's Inn, 1521–1889*, p. 176).

77. Sir Geo. Manners to Falcon, 3 Dec. 1620, *HMC Rutland*, 1: 457; Moir, *Addled Parliament*, p. 34; J. W. F. Hill, *Tudor and Stuart Lincoln*, pp. 113–21; Cokayne, *Peerage*, 2:188; Nichols, *Progresses*, 1:92 & n.

78. Keeler, *Long Parliament*, pp. 299–300; Neale, *Elizabethan House of Commons*, p. 314; *CSPD 1603–1610*, p. 139; Cokayne, *Peerage*, 6:384, 465; Nichols, *Progresses*, 1:213 & n; F. Turnor, *Collections for the Hist. of the Town and Soke of Grantham*, p. 57; "Sir Lewis Watson, first Baron Rockingham," *DNB*, 20:931–32; J. W. F. Hill, *Tudor and Stuart Lincoln*, p. 117. Rutland was also involved in the hotly fought Somersetshire election of 1614 in behalf of Sir Robert Phelips, and his wife, Cicely Tufton, also intervened in an election at Chippenham in 1614 (Somersetshire RO, Phelips MSS, vol. 4, fols. 202, 202v). For the Rutland influence at Lincoln in the sixteenth century, see J. W. F. Hill, *Tudor and Stuart Lincoln*, pp. 53, 54, 69, 70, 71, 73.

79. "Henry Clifford, fifth Earl of Cumberland," *DNB*, 4:520–21; Keeler, *Long Parliament*, p. 69; T. D. Whitaker, *A History of Richmondshire in the North Riding of the County of York*, 2:154; Cokayne, *Peerage*, 2:439–40; Cliffe, *Yorkshire Gentry*, p. 283; Nicolson and Burn, *The Hist. and Antiquities of the Counties of Westmorland and Cumberland*, 1:289, 308 ff.; Bean, *Northern Counties*, pp. 616, 638, 640. Sir Henry Wotton's return for Appleby in 1614 must have also been helped by his brother's marriage to Margaret, daughter of Philip, third Baron Wharton, whose wife was a daughter of the earl of Cumberland (Cokayne, *Peerage*, 7:204).

80. Clifford to the Mayor of Carlisle, 8 Dec. 1639, Carlisle City MSS Ca/2/120, f. 19; Keeler, *Long Parliament*, pp. 362, 370–71; Bean, *Northern Counties*, pp. 27, 49, 61–62; "Sir Henry Vane the elder," *DNB*, 20:113–16; S. Jefferson, *The History and Antiquities of Carlisle*, pp. 445, 447.

81. Clifford's involvement in Yorkshire's elections are included in the totals. The total for Rutland includes his wife's intervention at Chippenham in 1614 and the involvement of his tenants in Yorkshire's 1621 election, while, under the titles of Warwick, Hertford, and Exeter, the figures reflect the electioneering of the two earls of Hertford, Warwick, and Exeter. For Clifford's involvement in Yorkshire's elections, see Gruenfelder, "The Electoral Patronage of Sir Thomas Wentworth, Earl of Strafford, 1614–1640," pp. 559, 563, 564, 571.

82. Lord lieutenancies were held by all the peers discussed save the second earl of Hertford, who was not appointed to succeed the first earl as a lord lieutenant in Somersetshire and Wiltshire in 1621. The importance of the office as a source of electoral patronage, though, is impossible to determine. The peers discussed all enjoyed sufficient local influence and connection to support their electioneering. For example, Banbury was lord lieutenant of both Oxfordshire (1596–1632) and Berkshire (1596–1632). He had no discernible impact on Oxfordshire elections, and the influence he enjoyed in Berkshire was probably what he would have gained through his landholdings and county ties. The second earl of Warwick was a lord lieutenant in Essex for only a year (8 Sept. 1625–11 Sept. 1626), but the lack of office made no difference to his patronage. And, as has been shown, the second earl of Hertford's patronage remained substantial even though he was not appointed a lord lieutenant. In the case of the peers reviewed, it seems safe to say that a lord lieutenancy was recognition of their local preeminence and had little, if any, impact on their patronage (Sainty, *Lieutenants of Counties, 1585–1642*).

83. Stone, "The Electoral Influence of the Second Earl of Salisbury, 1614–68," pp. 385–86.

84. These are average figures and are based, as is much of the following discussion, on the tables detailing aristocratic electioneering in Appendix Two. The figures do not include the electoral influence of peers holding great court office, the lord wardens or lord presidents of the Councils of the Marches of Wales or the North, which are included in the tables illustrating court electoral influence in Appendix Two.

85. Hesilrige to the Mayor and Corporation of Leicester, 19 Apr. 1625, Leicester Museum, City of Leicester MSS, Hall Papers Bound 1623–25, BR II/18:15:560.

86. The nobility probably intervened in nearly 45 percent of all elections in 1624, 48 percent in 1625, almost 45 percent in 1626, and 43 percent in 1628. Its patronage may have secured as many as 27 percent of parliament's places in 1624, and slightly over 30 percent in 1625, and in 1626 it almost won 29 percent before it fell back to 25 percent in 1628. See Appendix Two.

87. Hirst, *Representative of the People?*, pp. 66, 67, 73, app. 7, pp. 229–31.

# FIVE

## The Elections of 1640

The elections for the Parliaments of 1640 have been rightly described as revealing "a new world when compared with their immediate predecessors."[1] More elections were contested than ever before; the atmosphere of excitement — indeed, even of passion — that often marked the elections was unique in the early seventeenth century. Sir Francis Windebank's remark, in late March 1640, that "the elections for Parliament have been very tumultary" was something of an understatement. That so much "sidings and faction" developed is understandable. Parliament had not met since March 1629, and in the intervening years of personal rule, royal policies seemed to emphasize the growing division of interest between the king and his subjects. By the spring of 1640, Charles's government was confronted with a revolution in Scotland and such opposition and discord at home that personal rule was doomed. Ship money collections nearly stopped and the king's finances were in danger of collapse. Antagonism against Laud's religious policy had reached such heights that Charles's shabby army had shown more enthusiasm for attacking offensive communion rails than in protecting the north from a Scottish invasion. The sudden dissolution of the Short Parliament only made the situation worse. London's summer was punctuated by further disturbances; Charles's personal intervention in the north failed, and in August twelve peers, representative of the very class that ought to have been most loyal to the king, outlined the opposition's grievances in a petition for another parliament. Charles finally gave way, and at his meeting of the Council of Peers at York on 24 September 1640, announced his intention of summoning parliament.[2]

Competition for places in both the 1640 parliaments was intense. Sir Edward Nicholas, clerk to the Privy Council and a court candidate, recognized that "there is very much labouring by divers to be parliament men," a situation that repeated itself in the fall elections, as Bulstrode Whitelock observed. The king and his advisers, well aware of the problems they faced, made that competition all the more intense by organizing and employing, as quickly as possible, the court's considerable electoral resources.[3] Indeed, the lord warden's letters of recommendation were on their way to the Cinque Ports within twenty-four hours of the king's decision to call the Short Parliament; the court acted with similar speed in the fall. Charles was urged to "treat with the Lord Chamberlain [the earl of Pembroke and Montgomery], and others that have Burgesses in their disposal, to reserve as many places as they can." The king went even further, directing "that his learned counsel, the Council in the Marches, the judges in Wales, the Queen's Council, the Prince's Council and Mr. Surveyor general should have notice that they should do their best endeavours to be of this ensuing parliament." The court had distinct electoral advantages. It could rely upon, as Windebank's letter suggested, the influence of the courtier aristocracy to supplement the electioneering of its own agencies, which went to work with a will.[4]

The Duchy of Cornwall made its most sweeping attempt in the spring elections when it nominated candidates for seventeen boroughs and may have intervened in one more, West Looe. On 9 December its officials notified the duchy's vice-warden, William Coryton, of its election plans. Every effort, Coryton was informed, must be made to secure the successful election of its nominees. No expenses should be spared; Coryton's "charges herein shall be fully allowed unto you." Weeks passed, however, before the duchy made its specific nominations; and when it finally did in late February, Coryton was again admonished to do everything in his power to promote the work. But despite all he could do, the busy and harassed Coryton's task of persuading Cornwall's gentry to do the duchy's bidding was a dismal failure. It managed to salvage something out of the wreck of its hopes, but not much. It was probably responsible for Sir Richard Wynn's election at Bodmin, and another courtier, Edward Read, may have taken the place of its original candidate for Camelford. That may also account for Fowey's choice of an outsider, Edwin Rich, and the return for St. Ives of Laud's secretary, William Dell, who had been refused by Canterbury. Coryton was returned for Grampound in what may have been another substitution; his own influence, however, was probably decisive. Anthony Mildmay of Essex may also have owed his choice at West Looe to duchy intervention. But even with those returns, the duchy's record was hardly impressive. Only one of its original candidates (Wynn) took a Cornish burgess-ship; of the sixteen boroughs on its original list, only three may have chosen duchy nominees. The duchy tried again in the fall, although, perhaps because of its spring failure, on a much reduced level. Coryton and his fellow officers were responsible for the nomination of only eight candidates. The results, though, were even worse than before: none were elected.[5]

Neither the Prince's Council nor the Queen's Council, making its first electoral appearance in 1640, enjoyed much success. The choice of Sir Henry Herbert, master of the revels, at Bewdley in the 1640 elections can be credited to the prince's intervention, which, however, failed at Chester in the spring and at Coventry, where it backed his attorney, Richard Lane, in both 1640 elections.[6] The Queen's Council made nominations "to the several burgess-towns within her jointure" with little success. Positive evidence survives to tell the story of its intervention at only three boroughs, Grantham, Carlisle, and Higham Ferrers. Grantham's corporation received a letter of recommendation "by the command of the Queen's most excellent Majesty touching the choosing of Burgesses" in the spring, but since the writ had not yet arrived, the corporation postponed any action on the royal request. The borough's return, however, of Henry Pelham and Sir Edward Bash, a chamberlain of the Exchequer, looks more like the work of the earls of Rutland and Lindsey than that of the Queen.[7]

Carlisle and Higham Ferrers refused her nominees outright. At Carlisle, where she owned the manor and castle, her council backed a Welshman, the courtier Henry Wynn; and when he was also nominated for Higham Ferrers, it urged the election of an Irish courtier, Arthur Jones. The queen also, albeit with some reluctance, backed Sir Richard Graham's election bid. Graham, formerly one of Buckingham's followers, had strong local connections; but perhaps because of his links with the court and the queen's support, he and Jones were rejected in favor of two of the town's neighbors. In the autumn her chancellor, Sir John Lambe, was probably her unsuccessful nominee. Higham Ferrer's spring election was marked by a bitter dispute between the corporation and the commonalty over voting rights, and the queen's nominee, Wynn, apparently failed to receive a vote. In the fall the queen and the chancellor of the duchy of Lancaster, Lord Newburgh, pressed Higham hard to win the return of Sir Thomas Strafford, a stranger who was "one of the gentlemen ushers of her Majesty's Privy Chamber," despite the objections of the queen's steward at Higham, Sir Christopher Hatton, who had been returned in the spring. Hatton warned Lambe that "the letter from your board cannot carry it" and sensibly urged, instead, that the queen back his candidacy since "the board can lose nothing by recommending one like to prevail." Hatton's warning was ignored just as, in the election,

Higham Ferrers ignored Strafford. Hatton was returned. Sir John Lambe, her chancellor, was refused by Cambridge University in the spring, although at Eye she may have been involved in the election of a young courtier, Sir Frederick Cornwallis of Bromehall, Suffolk, in the 1640 elections.[8]

The two councils, of the Marches of Wales and of the North, enjoyed mixed success as electoral agents in 1640. Despite Charles's hopes that "the Council of the Marches and the King's attorney and solicitors there" and "the judges of the Circuit in Wales" find places in the fall parliament, the Council of the Marches of Wales fared no better in the 1640 elections than it had in the past. It might have been responsible for the capture of four burgess-ships in 1640. The story, however, of the Council of the North was markedly different. Thomas Wentworth, earl of Strafford, was the lord president; his place-hunting zeal, his county prestige, his ties of family and friendship, and, no doubt, the tactics that had won him four Yorkshire elections in the past, reaped a substantial electoral harvest. Sixteen places, won in the elections of 1640, marked the Council of the North's greatest electoral success since 1614. They were not won, however, without opposition; furthermore, Strafford's influence was not always predominant. His nephew, Sir William Savile, won a Yorkshire place in the spring; but in the fall his nominees, Savile and Sir Richard Hutton, were refused. Indeed, the election grew so heated that the king "took out his army to exercise, to prevent trouble," but nothing Strafford could do saved his candidates. The sheriff, presumably at Strafford's request, even "adjourned the polling for knights of the shire to Pontefract," but Savile still "fell short of the number." Sir Ferdinando Fairfax and Henry Belasyse, both critics of Strafford, were elected. Fairfax had already won a previous victory over Strafford when Boroughbridge, a town he practically controlled, refused Strafford's nominee, Robert Read, in the spring. Scarborough accepted Strafford's first nominee, Sir Edward Osborne, the vice-president of the Council of the North, in the spring; but when Osborne decided to serve for York, it rejected his prospective replacement, George Butler. In the fall the port denied Strafford again. However, York, which had not accepted a nominee since 1601, probably gave up both places to Strafford's nominees in the spring. On election day the corporation was reminded of "the favours done by my Lord in the city" and chose Osborne along with a possible friend of the lord president, alderman Sir Roger Jacques. York changed its course in the autumn, though; for despite much "labouring for voices" and "a troublesome and disorderly election," it preferred two aldermen over Strafford's nominees, Osborne and its recorder, Sir Thomas Widdrington, who were "absolutely refused . . . because the Lord Lieutenant [Strafford] commended them and this done his Lo: P. being at York." For the first time in the early seventeenth century, the council's electioneering, under Strafford's energetic leadership, extended beyond Yorkshire's borders. Strafford's nominees captured three of Berwick-upon-Tweed's places in 1640, took another one at Morpeth for the Short Parliament, and, although refused in the spring, still managed to win a place at Newcastle-upon-Tyne the following autumn. In 1640 Strafford and the council were more successful in two elections than his predecessor, Lord Scrope, had been in five preceding elections.[9]

The Duchy of Lancaster, although under the direction of an active electioneer, Lord Barrett of Newburgh, could only match the Council of the North's successes. And for the duchy, that meant that its electoral record in 1640 was its worst since 1614. Six candidates stood in Wigan's 1640 elections, which were further enlivened by a bitter quarrel between the corporation and the commonalty over voting rights. The duchy probably backed the elections of Sir Orlando Bridgeman, whose local connections must have helped; but its other likely nominees, Simon Every in the spring and the outsider Sir Dudley Carleton in the autumn, each received only one vote. Preston and Clitheroe, traditionally part of the duchy's sphere of influence, apparently refused its nominees in 1640. At Lancaster it is probable that the customs farmer John Harrison (both 1640 elections) and Thomas Fanshawe (autumn 1640) owed their choice to the duchy, as did James, Lord Cranfield, eldest son of the earl of Middlesex (spring 1640) and the Welsh courtier, Sir Richard Wynn (autumn 1640), elected by Liverpool. Wynn was also chosen by Newton-in-Makersfield (spring 1640) along with another outsider, William Sherman of Lambeth; Newton returned a Kentish courtier, Sir Roger Palmer, for the Long Parliament. At Leicester the duchy won in the spring and lost in the autumn. Its 1640 nominee was "Simon Every, Esqr., Receiver General of his Majesty's Duchy of Lancaster," who was aided in his spring campaign by Leicester's neighbor and usual patron, the earl of Huntingdon. Every was returned along with the countess of Devonshire's candidate, Thomas Coke, secretary Coke's son. There were signs, however, of growing opposition to patronage, for Coke was Leicester's second choice. He was returned only after another candidate, the Puritan Roger Smith of Edmonton and "Gray's Inn, London," refused to take the freeman's oath. In the autumn the resistance centered on Every, and despite everything the mayor and some other leading members of the corporation could do, they were "overswayed with the greater part of voices"; and for the first time since 1621, the duchy's nominee was refused. The town elected the future regicide, Thomas, Lord Grey of Groby, the teen-aged son of Leicester's Puritan neighbor, the earl of Stamford. Coke, with the backing of the countess of Devonshire, was the town's other burgess in the Long Parliament. Monmouth's choice of William Watkins, a minor officeholder and resident of Westminster, in both elections and Newcastle-under-Lyme's return of Richard Lloyd (spring 1640), a courtier and lawyer, were the only other possible signs of the duchy's influence outside its Lancashire boroughs.[10]

No survey of the court's electioneering in 1640 would be complete without a brief review of the records of the lord wardens, Theophilus Howard, earl of Suffolk, who died in June 1640, and his successor, James Stuart, duke of Lennox. In the spring Suffolk was probably responsible for the return of only four nominees, and Lennox can be credited with the election of five for the Long Parliament. New Romney, which had refused the nominees of Buckingham (1626, 1628) and Suffolk (spring 1640,) finally gave way to a Lennox nominee in the autumn. Rye's spring election was noteworthy for a variety of reasons. Its past subservience, when mixed with the great interest in the forthcoming parliament, produced a harvest of nine candidates; and since six of them were either nominees of court officials or peers, it illustrates the court's intensive campaign. Indeed, four royal officials were active at Rye, either as patrons or nominees. Its election of the earl of Dorset's secretary, John White, and a Kentish squire, Sir John Colepeper, was a surprising defeat for the lord warden since it was the only time, from 1604 to 1640, that Rye had rejected his patronage. Local issues, which Colepeper stressed in his letters, probably decided his election. In the autumn, however, Rye probably chose one of the warden's candidates. Winchelsea, Hythe, and Hastings kept a place for the warden's nominees in 1640; but Sandwich, which returned one of Suffolk's candidates in the spring, refused Lennox in the fall. Dover, traditionally loyal to the warden in the past, chose two leading opponents of the court in both 1640 elections.[11]

Despite its most intensive electoral effort, the court's intervention can hardly be described as a success. Its agencies and the lord wardens interfered in fifty-four spring elections and thirty-eight in the fall. Its record, based only on actual nominations, is one of unrelieved disaster. In the spring it nominated thirty-eight candidates; twenty-seven were rejected. In the autumn elections, its nominees were even more harshly treated: of its twenty-two known candidates, only two were chosen. However, such figures are somewhat mitigated if the probable successes or failures, as at Clitheroe or Preston, are added. When that is done, the court's agencies and the lord wardens sought sixty-one places in the spring, winning thirty, and in the autumn elections backed forty-seven candidates for a return of twenty-three. In the elections of 1640, the court supported at least 108 candidates. Only fifty-three (49.0%) were chosen. The results would be even worse if it were possible to include the "List of such as are recommended to be burgesses" found in the State Papers. Only three of the twelve men named were elected, Edward Herbert at Old Sarum, Sampson Eure for Leominster, and Sir Orlando Bridgeman for Wigan. And of those three, only Bridgeman is included here since his election was probably the work of the Duchy of Lancaster. The others are impossible to include since, without knowing where they were candidates, it is impossible to guess what agency or aristocrat would have been responsible for their return. The other legal officials, in the Councils of the North and Marches of Wales, also apparently failed to find places. At a minimum, then, if the eight judges and nine men mentioned by the king as candidates who were not elected sought a place, the number of places wanted by the court would be raised from forty-seven in the autumn to at least sixty-four, making the scope of the court's defeat in the Long Parliament's elections even greater.[12]

Charles assumed, perhaps incorrectly, that other royal officials of noble rank would do their electoral duty. The lord chamberlain, the earl of Pembroke and Montgomery, was expected to employ his patronage in behalf of the crown, an assumption Charles also probably made about his lord admiral, the earl of Northumberland, and other peers like the earls of Arundel, Huntingdon, and Dorset as well as the great churchmen, like Laud of Canterbury and Neile of York. Another group of peers, however, including the earls of Warwick and Essex, Viscount Saye and Sele, and Lord Brooke, to mention only a few, threw their electoral weight into the balance against the court. The patronage of the aristocracy was a significant part of the 1640 elections, although, and this should not be forgotten, it reached its lowest points in terms of intervention and success in those elections.[13] Its significance, however, was not new or unique; what was different was the influence of the opposition peers or reformers. That is not to say, however, that there had not been aristocratic faction before. From James's reign onward, vague groupings could be discerned at court that favored or opposed parliament, that encouraged a more bellicose attitude toward Spain or favored a more lenient policy toward recusants while, at the same time, another faction was urging a more thorough protestant reformation of the church. A major division, for example, apparently occurred over the Petition of Right in 1628.[14]

The reform group grew out of opposition, often expressed in parliament, to Stuart religious, foreign, and financial policy. Some reformers were John Preston's friends; others had heard him and like-minded ministers preach. These men, whose leaders were religious reformers and staunchly anti-Catholic, had been, save for a brief anti-Spanish alliance, Buckingham's constant critics, had led resistance to the Privy Seal and Forced Loans, and were responsible for the Petition of Right. Parliament had been a platform for the expression of their views, and without it they were nearly helpless. Ship money, potentially a permanent tax that could prevent future parliaments, may have stirred them to the activity the Venetian ambassador reported in late 1636 when he claimed that "many of the leading men of the realm" were urging a parliament to alleviate alleged grievances. Henry Danvers, earl of Danby, and Robert Rich, earl of Warwick, had candid, if futile, interviews with Charles pleading for a parliament. At the same time, secret meetings were apparently taking place, possibly at Sir William Lytton's home in Hertfordshire, at Broughton Castle, Viscount Saye and Sele's residence, or at the Knightley home at Fawsley, Northamptonshire. The Scottish revolt was the opposition's opportunity; it gave them powerful allies with similar goals. In the increasingly anxious months of 1639 and 1640, the opposition's sympathies became more obvious, as Bulstrode Whitelock observed: "there was a strange spirit of disunion in the opinions and wishes of most men in these affairs, too many not only favouring but joining with and assisting the proceedings of the Scots Covenanters."[15]

The reform group's overt organizational structure centered on the Providence Island and Massachusetts companies, while London's Artillery Garden became another headquarters of its activity. Its greatest strength was its unity, founded on marriage ties, family connections, and commonly held religious views. The Puritan ministry in London and the countryside was ready to lend an eloquent voice to an election campaign. Leaders of the reform group, like the earl of Warwick, Viscount Saye and Sele, and Lord Brooke, had long been closely connected to leading Puritan clergy; Warwick and Brooke had provided both protection and pulpits to Puritan lecturers threatened by Laud's disciplinary zeal. The dissolution of the Short Parliament only intensified the work of the opposition. Many spent the summer of 1640 organizing county grievance petitions, urging the summons of another parliament, and protesting in louder and louder voices against the policies of the court.[16]

In the elections of 1640, it is possible to identify a minimum of thirteen peers who, by virtue of their actions and sympathies, were committed to reform.[17] And though their individual electoral importance varied widely, together they either nominated or backed seventy-two candidates in the elections, thirty-five in the spring and thirty-seven in the autumn. They were remarkably successful: only five men that enjoyed their support failed to win a place, three in the spring and two in the autumn. What is even more striking, however, is the unity of purpose that linked members of the reform group. Of the seventy-two candidates they backed, forty-six were men who continuously backed the parliamentary cause in the ensuing civil war. Another fourteen can be described as moderates; these were men who either had joined the king or sought political neutrality by 1644. Only six, one in the spring and five in the autumn, can be called royalists, and the remaining six, all candidates in the spring elections, cannot fit into any of these categories. The impact of commonly held religious beliefs, similar economic interests, and strong family connections provided the reform group with a cohesion and sense of purpose that it employed with excellent electoral effect.[18]

Elections in Essex showed the influence of a strong reform group. In the spring county election, a leader of the reformers, the Puritan earl of Warwick, employed his office as lord lieutenant to rally freeholders to the support of two well-known Essex gentlemen, both known critics of the court, Sir Thomas Barrington and Sir Harbottle Grimston. Warwick's reformist clergy were active spokesmen for the cause, and, despite a challenge from a royalist candidate, Barrington and Grimston carried the day. In the autumn Warwick saw to the choice of Sir William Masham, another locally known reformer, and his son Robert Lord Rich for the county. Warwick's influence probably played a strong part in securing ten places in Essex and its boroughs in the 1640 elections. The only other challenge to his domination was at Colchester, where his more volatile brother, the earl of Holland, who had been the town's recorder, tried his hand. He had come off second best in the spring election, but in the autumn he tried again. In fact, he was the first patron to notify the town of his hopes, urging the corporation to return his "good friend Sir Thomas Ingram." Unlike his more famous father, Sir Arthur Ingram, who had been Holland's nominee at Windsor in the spring, Sir Thomas was a royalist from Sheriff Hutton, Yorkshire. The earl of Warwick, who had placed Sir William Masham at Colchester in the spring, nominated Barrington, a county member in the Short Parliament. For Colchester it was an easy choice: it elected Barrington and its recorder, Harbottle Grimston, for, as the corporation explained to Holland, the town's concern over the "many impositions now laid upon trades" and the many "grievances that are now upon us" made it decide to choose "two gentlemen who are our neighbours" rather than Ingram, "a stranger, whose name was never heard of in these parts."[19]

In Warwickshire and Leicestershire, election contests were fought that developed on clear court versus country lines. Leicestershire's elections had traditionally been the preserve of the royalist Henry Hastings, earl of Huntingdon, whose influence came to an abrupt end in the elections of 1640.[20] In the spring Huntingdon nominated his son, Henry, and a Leicestershire royalist, Sir Henry Skipwith, confidently urging Leicester's corporation to "send your constables in their several wards to the freeholders to signify my desire unto them that as for my son in the first place so for Sir Henry in the second." Antagonism toward the court was, however, too great to be overcome, especially when it was harnessed by two resolute Puritan noblemen, Henry Grey, earl of Stamford, and Henry Lord Grey of Ruthin. They made the most of the county's discontent, for it returned Lord Grey of Ruthin and Sir Arthur Hesilrige, whose Puritan credentials were beyond question. Huntingdon's prestige was further shaken by the fall election, which was a quarrelsome affair; Sir Arthur Hesilrige was verbally abused, perhaps by one of the earl's friends on election day; but Huntingdon was powerless to change the outcome: Hesilrige and Lord Grey of Ruthin were reelected.[21]

Nothing had apparently disturbed Warwickshire's elections throughout the early Stuart years until, in 1640, another court and country clash abruptly shattered the county's tranquility. Robert Greville, Lord Brooke, a leader of the reform group, and Spencer Compton, the royalist earl of Northampton, fought it out for electoral supremacy. Northampton had one great advantage over Brooke: the county's sheriff was his firm ally. In the spring the sheriff traveled to London, got his hands on the election writ, and rushed back, hoping to hold a snap election to "elect the two knights that day, when it will not [be] possible for the 10th part of the freeholders to be present, by which means he may have a notable stroke in the election." Brooke and his allies must have discovered the plot since the choice of Sir Thomas Lucy and William Combes, known opponents of the court, was presumably their handiwork. Smarting from his defeat, Northampton went to work with a will in the fall, urging his wife to "be mindful about making James [his son] knight of the shire and [to] send to all those gentlemen of the country in whom I have an interest" for their support. He had already "sent to the shrieve and to Mr. Chamberlain of the court of wards" for their help. Brooke, meanwhile, was presumably canvassing for William Combes and another reformer, William Purefoy of Caldecote. On election day Northampton's alliance with the sheriff reaped its dividend. The sheriff shifted the location of the county court to discourage Purefoy's supporters, and, when that tactic apparently failed, broke off the poll. The election was a draw since Combes was chosen along with Northampton's son, returned through the sheriff's maneuvers. The House of Commons voided the return, but Northampton and the sheriff proved equal to the challenge of a second election. The earl's son and a Warwickshire royalist, Richard Shuckburgh, were elected despite the protests of Combes and his allies, who probably included Lord Brooke. [22]

Other peers, relying on their customary sources of influence, land, and office, were also active, although not always successful, patrons. Lord Keeper Finch, Cambridge's high steward, nominated candidates at both its 1640 elections as did the earl of Holland, who held a similar office at Windsor and Reading. Archbishop William Laud, who had recommended a candidate at his birthplace, Reading, in December 1639, was Oxford University's chancellor and probably saw to its election of Sir Francis Windebank in the spring and Sir Thomas Roe in the autumn. However, Laud and Kent's lord lieutenant, the earl of Pembroke and Montgomery, ran into serious trouble at Canterbury in the spring. The city's elections had long been plagued by a continuing battle between its dissident freemen and the corporation, rooted in the city's economic troubles. The quarrel surfaced again in the spring election, which was further complicated by an eruption of antipopery and anti-Laudianism. Little wonder, then, that despite the corporation's best efforts, Laud's secretary, William Dell, and the earl's nominee, Roger Palmer, formerly his candidate at Queenborough, were refused. Two locally known men, backed no doubt by the vociferous freemen and their supporters, won the election. On his own ground, the earl of Pembroke and Montgomery did very well. For example, he placed one candidate in each election at Salisbury and probably one candidate in each election at Shaftesbury, Old Sarum, and Downton and, in all likelihood, two in both the 1640 elections at Wilton. William Piers, bishop of Bath and Wells, however, failed to place his candidate at Wells, and the earl of Arundel was also often frustrated; even Aldeburgh, where he usually placed a nominee, apparently turned him down in the autumn. King's Lynn, too, denied Arundel a place. The earl of Dorset and the lord admiral, the earl of

Northumberland, failed at Great Yarmouth; Dorset's luck was no better at Lewes, either, where his and Lord Goring's nominees were flatly rejected. The chancellor of the Exchequer, Lord Cottington, was unable to place Windebank in Berkshire's spring election but received an unexpected bonus from Hindon when the town, in the spring, urged him "to nominate two such persons as you shall think fit" and Hindon would "most willingly choose them." Cottington did, and the election of the receiver general of the Court of Wards and Liveries, Sir Miles Fleetwood, and George Garrett was the result. Cottington was probably responsible for Hindon's fall returns as well.[23] Christchurch, long a pocket borough of Lord Arundell of Wardour, was a remarkable example of the zeal of electioneering aristocrats in 1640. It was flooded with nominees, partially because of the first Lord Arundell's death. Six different noblemen nominated twelve candidates at Christchurch! The borough, perhaps wearied by all this attention, rebelled. It returned, along with one of Lord Baltimore's nominees, a local man, Henry Tulse, to both 1640 parliaments. And that in itself was symptomatic of the troubles noblemen frequently ran into in 1640; Christchurch, like Great Yarmouth, Lewes, Reading, and Wells, for example, preferred their neighbors or residents to the outsiders so frequently recommended by the aristocracy.[24]

Great office was no guarantee of electoral success, as the lord admiral, Northumberland, discovered in 1640. Indeed, it was probably detrimental to his prospects since it linked him closely to the court. He may have intervened in as many as nineteen elections in 1640, thirteen in the spring and six in the autumn. Where his patronage was founded on his own property holdings or family influence, his nominees were never successfully challenged. His record, however, as lord admiral was quite a different story. As a great officeholder and apparent representative of the court, Northumberland intervened in fourteen elections in 1640; his nominees won only eight of a possible sixteen places. It seems plausible, indeed, to suggest that the clear difference in his electoral success may be explained by his reliance, as lord admiral, on office for electoral influence; and in the increasingly faction-ridden atmosphere of 1640, that was simply not good enough to overcome the animosity that a court connection could arouse among the local community.[25] As Bulstrode Whitelock observed in the autumn of 1640, "it was not a little strange to see what a spirit of opposition to the court proceedings was in the hearts and actions of most of the people." Sir Edward Dering, whose shifting attitudes perhaps offer the best testimony to the confusion felt by many in 1640 and beyond, was "absolutely resolved that in times so desperate I would contribute no help to any privy councillor or deputy lieutenant there standing [in Kent's spring election]."[26]

Such sympathies, encouraged by the gravity of the times, could harden even more when an outsider was nominated. Tewkesbury turned down the earl of Middlesex's inexperienced son twice in 1640 because, or so the corporation claimed in the spring, it was taking "an extraordinary care in elections at this time, when religion is so much concerned, and the good of the commonwealth never more."[27] Reading's 1640 elections were, perhaps, another example. In the spring the nominees of its high steward, the earl of Holland, and Archbishop William Laud, born at Reading and a generous benefactor to the town, ran into some trouble. Six of the corporation voted against Sir Edward Herbert and Sir John Berkeley because "a stranger . . . can be no friend to the town." Herbert and Berkeley were still elected, but when they chose to serve elsewhere, Reading returned two local men, Sir Francis Knollys senior and his son. Sir Robert Heath, another outsider and possibly Holland's candidate in the bye-elections, was ignored. In the autumn Reading reelected the Knollys, father and son, over another nominee of the earl of Holland. Animosity to outsiders, it seems, played at least some role in Reading's decision. All the men recommended by Laud and Holland—Herbert, Berkeley, Heath, and Sir James Thynne, Holland's son-in-law—were strangers. Similar sentiments may have been behind Cambridge's autumn election. There was no hint of trouble before the Short Parliament. The town, as usual, returned Thomas Meautys, the nominee of its high steward, Lord Keeper Finch. However, in the next election, when Finch tried to improve on his success and nominated Meautys and his brother, Sir Nathaniel Finch, Cambridge rebelled. It chose Oliver Cromwell, one of its members in the spring, and a common councillor, John Lowry, who became an active parliamentarian. Cambridge's decision was probably based on a combination of opposition to outsiders, local issues, and a fair touch of anti-court feeling.[28] A similar mixture marked the elections at Hastings and Sandwich as well. Edward Nicholas, the warden's candidate in the spring at Sandwich, was challenged on the grounds that he "lived at London." Neighbors to Sandwich (Sir Thomas Peyton and Edward Partridge) and Hastings (Nicholas Eversfield) enjoyed the hearty and, in the autumn, successful support of the commons partially, at least, because they were well known locally. The same explanation might account for Christchurch's surprising return of a local man, Henry Tulse, over the many strangers nominated by its crowd of prospective patrons.[29]

Patronage itself, especially when it involved the nomination of outsiders, provoked substantial, and often successful, resistance. The Duchy of Cornwall's electioneering was, perhaps, the best example. Fifteen men were listed as duchy nominees in the spring, and of those only one, Thomas Trevor, had any connection to Cornwall. The remainder were all strangers. So were all eight of the duchy's candidates in the autumn. Their rejection in the autumn was not, however, a sign of the court and country clash; six of the boroughs tried by the duchy — Liskeard, Grampound, Lostwithiel, Camelford, Helston, and Launceston — elected local royalists. However, of the sixty-one identified, or tentatively identified, as candidates of court agencies in the spring, forty were strangers, even to the county wherein their prospective boroughs were situated. In the autumn twenty-six of the forty-seven men backed by the crown were outsiders. Of these sixty-six "foreign" nominees, only twenty-seven were elected to the Parliaments of 1640. The return of local royalists in Cornwall strengthens the suggestion that the county community was resolved to elect its own. Indeed, the court's nomination of outsiders may have heightened the community's awareness of the court as an interventionist authority that had often ignored local interests. The returns for Wigan in the autumn, Carlisle, and Higham Ferrers provide additional examples. Wigan preferred Sir Orlando Bridgeman, whose Lancashire and Cheshire connections stood him in good stead; indeed, his uncle had twice been a Wigan M.P. An outsider, Sir Dudley Carleton, was not at all acceptable, as Wigan's polls showed. Carlisle preferred two neighbors, William Dalston and Richard Barwis, to the queen's nominees, Jones and Lambe, strangers to the town. The same story was repeated at Higham Ferrers, where, in spite of the sensible advice of Sir Christopher Hatton, the Queen's Council recommended, without success, the outsiders Henry Wynn and Sir Thomas Strafford.[30]

Candidates for the Parliaments of 1640 sought electoral victory in a variety of traditional ways. Clergymen were probably more involved than the limited evidence indicates since religious questions were important issues in 1640. Canvassing was heavy, a sign of hotly contested elections, and money played a significant role in 1640. The number of elections that involved entertainment expenditures was high, and, perhaps more ominously, the number of bribery cases in 1640 exceeded the total for all such elections from 1558 through 1628. Aristocratic, court, and clerical letters of recommendation were extensively employed; and though it is risky to read too much into the use of such tactics and strategems, it does seem safe to suppose that the candidates and their patrons, as perhaps never before, recognized the signal importance of the 1640 elections.[31]

The support of a patron remained the most popular way of seeking election. Charles I recognized it; so did a minor courtier like Robert Read. But few went so far as the Suffolk squire Sir Simonds D'Ewes, who, in his anxiety to serve in the Long Parliament, prepared and sent his own letter of recommendation to Henry, earl of Worcester, in the hope that the earl might find him a place. D'Ewes also turned to a neighboring friend, Sir Nathaniel Barnardiston, for help and, thanks to Barnardiston, was returned for Sudbury. Many other examples of similar requests for assistance, from either great noblemen or powerful local gentry, could be cited. Many boroughs, too, wanting to avoid any obligation to pay parliamentary wages, sought aristocratic or gentry patronage. Indeed, promises about wages were undoubtedly far more common than the evidence indicates since it was very unlikely that a patron, anxious to place his friend or nominee, would not offer such an inducement.[32]

There is no need here to detail again what were standard electoral tactics. Blanks were, no doubt, employed in both elections; indeed, in the Short Parliament, the House set up a committee to investigate that practice. Local offices were often used, as they had been before, to sway elections. John Sedley reminded Sir Edward Dering, during Kent's autumn election, to "have a care also of [the] sheriff" since "he abused us all the last time by his partiality," a warning any shire candidate had to heed, given the impact of a sheriff's "partiality" in Gloucestershire's spring election, in both of Warwickshire's 1640 contests, or Yorkshire's hotly fought autumn election. Suffolk's spring election was thrown into confusion through the actions of the sheriff's (Sir Simonds D'Ewes) underlings; the power of the Puritan justices of the peace in East Sussex contributed to the defeat of the earl of Dorset's and Lord Goring's nominees at Lewes in 1640 and justified Lord Keeper Finch's fears of justices who "carry things with a faction." Corporations, too, continued to play decisive roles in borough elections. Hindon, Chester, Tamworth, Sandwich, and Hastings provided ready examples in the spring: Northampton and Barnstaple, to mention but two, went through similar elections in the fall.[33]

Several corporations had trouble or, indeed, failed to see their recorders elected to the Parliaments of 1640. Salisbury's recorder, Robert Hyde, narrowly won a place in the city's disputed elections. Hyde, who had succeeded Salisbury's reformist recorder, Henry Sherfield, had opposed the program Sherfield and his friends devised for the relief of the city's pressing economic problems. He had also disagreed with the city in its quarrel with the Dean and Chapter. And when religious discord was added to the local grievances, the combination was almost fatal to Hyde's electoral prospects. During the heated spring election at Salisbury, it was claimed that "the Recorder of London was refused, & so was the Recorder of Excester, & divers others." London's recorder, Sir Thomas Gardiner, was refused in the 1640 elections, but that was nothing new. London had rejected its crown-appointed recorder before, in 1628. If Peter Ball, the queen's attorney general and Exeter's recorder, sought election there in 1640, the evidence does not survive. Ball had served for Tiverton in 1626 and 1628, and did so again in the spring. Exeter, unlike Salisbury, had not customarily elected its recorders to parliament. Nicholas Duck, chosen in 1624 and 1625, was the only recorder Exeter returned to any early Stuart parliament. Abingdon, Gloucester, York, and Oxford, however, did refuse their recorders.[34]

At Abingdon local issues and the competition Whitelock, the recorder, faced from a well-known and well-connected local squire, who effectively campaigned among the "vulgar," was too much for Whitelock and the corporation to overcome. William Lenthall, recorder at both Gloucester and Woodstock, lost both elections at Gloucester, probably because of the commonalty's opposition. Woodstock, with a smaller electorate (and perhaps because Lenthall was an Oxfordshire resident?), chose him for both parliaments. Sir Thomas Widdrington, York's recorder, lost the autumn election because of Strafford's backing; however, he was also Berwick's recorder, and, with Strafford's likely help, won a place there for the 1640 parliaments. The most surprising election, however, was at Oxford in the spring when, for the only time in the early seventeenth century, it refused to elect its recorder. John Whistler's defeat remains a mystery; the corporation listed him among its recommended candidates, but the commonalty, which had backed him before and would choose him in the autumn, turned him down. Perhaps, as Hirst suggests, it was simply a case of voter unpredictability.[35]

Most recorders, however, did not face the problems that Widdrington, Whitelock, Whistler, Lenthall, and Hyde confronted in 1640. Fifty boroughs returned their recorders in the elections of 1640, twenty-six in the spring and twenty-four in the autumn. Fifteen boroughs, including Grantham, which elected its deputy recorder, and Wenlock, which chose its recorder's son, sent their legal officers or their connections to both parliaments.[36] Recorders, like other candidates, could find their candidacies vexed by local grievances, stiff competition, or unpopular patrons. Religious problems and local complaints marked the Salisbury and Abingdon elections, and Gloucester's wide electorate and Strafford's support at York proved fatal to Lenthall and Widdrington. But then, neither Abingdon nor York had elected recorders to early Stuart parliaments; Gloucester had done so only in 1604. Canvassing, the solicitation of support from relatives, friends, freeholders, and tenants, was a time-honored strategem involving almost Byzantine diplomatic skill. The elections of 1640 were no exception; indeed, such canvassing, frequently caused by the prospect of faction, was common. Cautious soundings were made of county opinion; alliances were tentatively requested and firmly struck; anxiety over possible conflicts of loyalty was expressed again and again. The pens of a county's squirearchy must have been worn to the nub as the steady stream of letters pleading, exhorting, promising, and cajoling flooded from their desks as the search for voices went on, in some cases, right up to election morning. If a candidate dropped out, his voices were quickly snatched up by other hopefuls. Sir Thomas Hutchinson, an anxious Nottinghamshire candidate, hoped to gain "for the first place all those voices which you intended for Sir John Byron," who had given up the race. Kent's elections typified such electioneering. The county suffered from an abundance of candidates (there were six in the spring and almost as many in the fall) whose number dropped as their prospects evaporated in the negotiations and soundings that preceded election day. Kent's contests were further complicated by the involvement of the lord chamberlain, the earl of Pembroke and Montgomery, and by the possibility that ineligible voters might play an important role. That same question plagued Bedford's fall election, and in the spring an agent for Sir Walter Pye and Sir Robert Harley in the Herefordshire election circularized prospective voters with his interpretation of what were "admissible" qualifications for voting. Suffolk's elections, especially in the autumn, were marked — so D'Ewes, the county's sheriff, complained — by heavy canvassing because "my old acquaintance and allies are antagonists." Such mustering could backfire, too, as Gloucestershire's election showed. Sir Robert Cook's shrewdness almost undid the chances of the royalist Sir Robert Tracy. Tracy's friend, Lord Berkeley, had diligently raised 500 voices for Tracy; but before election day, Cooke informed Berkeley that since Tracy was unopposed, Berkeley "might (if he thought fit) spare both his own pains and prevent the attendance of his company." Berkeley agreed and discharged his followers, only to have Nathaniel Stephens, Cooke's ally and a fellow Puritan, gather up many of them against

Tracy. The scheme almost succeeded; only the trickery of Tracy's brother, the sheriff, saved his election![37]

Some campaigns, as in the spring for Gloucestershire or in Kent, London, Essex, and Northamptonshire, were enlivened by the zealous electioneering of the local clergy, who were persuasive campaign orators. In Northamptonshire, for example, Thomas Ball, the vicar of All Saints, Northampton, convinced the mayor of the town to support Sir Gilbert Pickering in the contested county election and urged other ministers to lend their voices to Pickering's campaign. Ball's tactics and zeal were rewarded: Pickering was returned. Candidates and their allies did not shy away from more abrasive tactics; threats and intimidation marked spring elections for Essex and East Grinstead and autumn contests for Northampton and Leicestershire. In Huntingdonshire's fall election, tempers frayed to such an extent that swords were drawn; weapons may have also been flourished in Suffolk's notable fall contest as well, and Maidstone's election dissolved into a near brawl. Great Marlow's election, too, for the Long Parliament came perilously close to riot and tumult; some trouble erupted in the second contest, but, as Bulstrode Whitelock smugly observed, quiet prevailed since his party, "being much the more numerous, kept the other in better awe."[38] These methods or strategems had been practiced before, although perhaps not as intensely. What did differ sharply from the past was the cost of electoral victory.

Sir George Stonehouse's expenditures for "beef, bacon and bag pudding" and for the drink "permitting as many of them as would be drunk at his charge" that helped him to win Abingdon's spring election was hardly a new tactic. Voters had often enjoyed the openhandedness of candidates anxious to serve at Westminster, and so it was in 1640. Spring elections at Knaresborough, Ludlow, and Essex, where Sir Thomas Barrington spent £42 2s. 6d., and the fall contests for Marlow, Kent, and Cambridgeshire were ones where food and drink were readily available. Candidates were, however, worried by the cost. One reason behind Bulstrode Whitelock's decision not to stand for Oxfordshire was his fear that it "would be the occasion of a very great expense to me"; and although Francis Read was eager to win a place in the Long Parliament, he admitted a contested election was out of the question: the "charge in preparing myself" would be "greater than I am fit to bear." Sir Edward Dering had similar fears in Kent's spring election, and his partner in the fall, Sir John Colepeper, who was hardly poor, tried to limit expenses as much as possible. And, as the expenses for the earl of Salisbury, Sir John Coke the younger, Sir Robert Harley, and Fitzwilliam Coningsby illustrate, there was every reason for such concern. Provision for entertainment had been made in Herefordshire's spring election, and if it was similar to the charges for the fall contest, then it is possible that Herefordshire's county elections were worth over £300 in expenses! In the fall, Harley and Coningsby, who were probably backed by many of the local gentry and the earl of Essex, still spent £155 9s. 6d., a tidy sum indeed. Herefordshire was still inexpensive, in comparison with Derbyshire and Hertfordshire. Sir John Coke the younger, in Derbyshire's fall election, spent over £300 on his supporters, and in Hertfordshire, a county customarily beholden to the earl of Salisbury in electoral matters, the earl paid out £350 2s. 6d. in the contested spring election alone. His expenses for both Hertford elections amounted to £119 7s. 2d., which meant that Salisbury, in three elections, spent almost £470. If Hertfordshire's autumn election was like the spring contest, his total election bill could have been over £800, a truly eighteenth-century sum. It may have cost Sir Christopher Hatton over £180, inclusive of his legal fees, to win his return for both Castle Rising and Higham Ferrers. Even uncontested elections could be costly affairs. Sir Thomas Pelham and Anthony Stapley spent £323 in the Sussex election of 1640, and they were unopposed.[39] Only one other election, for Kent in 1625, may have equaled such expenses. Little wonder then that candidates were concerned. And though it is true that such tactics were "in their infancy," the costs were already very substantial. Salisbury's expenditures for Hertford's elections alone were nearly three times the "total market value" (£42 10s.) of the annual crop of an "average" farmer. The owner of 1,000 sheep in East Anglia could expect a profit of between £120 and £140 per year for his investment and time; Salisbury spent almost four times the income of that sheep-owner in two elections. Indeed, Coke's costs in the Derbyshire election represented about one-fifth of the value of the goods John Hampden's father left at his death, and he has been described as a man of moderately wealthy means.[40] When costs are looked at in this fashion, it is not altogether correct to suggest that expenditure was on a "small scale." Indeed, given early Stuart incomes, it is clear that electoral expense was a factor worthy of serious consideration. The tensions of 1640 had, however, made some patrons and candidates determined to win an election regardless of the price. If their electoral opponents were equally resolute, a place in parliament was bound to be at a premium.

Similar anxiety over electoral victory may also explain the surprising increase in bribery cases. There were five in 1640, and though that may not seem to be a lot, it is still more than can be certainly identified since Elizabeth's accession. There may have been a sixth case, too, since Sir Samuel Rolle complained that he lost Beeralston's fall bye-election because of threats and "by money given," presumably to voters. But whether the "money given" was used for entertainment or bribes is impossible to tell. In other cases, however, there is no doubt. At Hastings, in the spring, bribery was part of Robert Read's successful bid to win a place, and both of Bramber's elections were marred by bribery. In the spring the courtier Sir John Suckling was accused of offering money "to the meaner sort" for votes. Suckling's antagonist, Sir Edward Bishop, who made the charge, emulated his opponent in Bramber's fall election when he offered a £10 bribe for a burgess-ship. In the fall election at East Looe, some £80 may have been used for bribes. Edward Pitt, fearful that his family's influence at Wareham might not be enough in its autumn election, tried similar tactics.[41] The likely increase in costs, the number of bribery cases, and the heavy canvassing and campaigning that marked the 1640 elections were further signs of the significance of the elections themselves.

1. Hirst, *Representative of the People?*, pp. 139–40, 147–50.

2. Windebank to Hopton, 27 Mar. 1640, O. Ogle et al., eds., *Calendar of the Clarendon State Papers*, 1:196; Holland to Gawdy, Nov. 1640, *HMC Gawdy*, p. 176.

3. Nicholas to Pennington, 12 Dec. 1639, P.R.O., St. P. Dom. 16/435:64; Poley to D'Ewes, n. d. 1640, BM Harleian MSS 383, f. 144; BM ADD MSS 35, 331, f. 74v; "Whitelock's Annals," BM ADD MSS 37, 343, fols. 206–7.

4. Suffolk to the Mayor and Jurats of Sandwich, 7 Dec. 1639, Kent RO, Sandwich Letter Book, Sa/C 1, f. 8; Suffolk to the Mayor and Jurats of Rye, 7 Dec. 1639, East Sussex RO, Rye Corp. MSS, 47/131, 39:2; Windebank to the King, 25 Sept., 4 Oct. 1640, *Clarendon State Papers*, 2:123, 127; Vane to Windebank, 27 Sept. 1640, P.R.O., St. P. Dom. 16/468:61, in P. Yorke, earl of Hardwicke, ed., *Miscellaneous State Papers*, 2:190; Bankes to Windebank, 12 Oct. 1640, P.R.O., St. P. Dom. 16/469:89; "List of such as are recommended to be burgesses," Sept. 1640? P.R.O., St. P. Dom. 16/468:36. The Prince's Council and the Duchy of Cornwall had disappeared as electoral patrons at Charles's accession in 1625, but with the birth of an heir, both were reconstituted; and in the elections of 1640, both agencies once again were actively engaged in the elections.

5. The duchy's nominees in the 1640 elections were William and Thomas Twysden, Sir Richard and Henry Wynn, Sir William Beecher, Sir Charles Harbord, Richard Lane, Sir Thomas Reynell, Philip Warwick, Sir Thomas Fotherley, John Ashburnham, Francis Palmes, Thomas Windebank, Thomas Trevor, Edward Nicholas, Sir Nicholas Selwyn, and Sir Dudley Carleton. Bossiney, Callington, East Looe, Grampound, Helston, Launceston, Lostwithiel, Michael, Newport, Penryn, St. Germans, St. Mawes, and Plymouth turned down its candidates in the spring, and Lostwithiel, Bossiney, Liskeard, Grampound, Camelford, Launceston, Helston, and Saltash denied them in the autumn. Duchy of Cornwall RO, Letters and Warrants, 1639–43, fols. 34, 44v–46,

66v–67v; List of Court Nominees, 1 Apr. 1640, P.R.O., St. P. Dom. 16/450:15; Coryton to Buller, 3 Mar. 1640, Hicks to Buller, 3 Mar. 1640, Cornwall RO, the MSS of Sir John G. Carew Pole, Bart., BO 20/63 and 73; Coate, *Cornwall*, pp. 5, 23–24; Canterbury Cathedral Archives, Canterbury City MSS, Burghmoot Book, A/C, 4, 1630–58, f. 151v. I should like to thank the Canterbury City Council for their gracious permission to cite Canterbury's borough manuscripts in this and subsequent notes.

6. The name of the Prince's Council's nominee at Chester is unknown. List of Government Candidates, 1 Apr. 1640, P.R.O., St. P. Dom. 16/450:15; Duchy of Cornwall RO, Letters and Warrants, 1639–43, fols. 56, 68; Keeler, *Long Parliament*, pp. 73, 211.

7. Tomkins to Lambe, 1 Oct. 1640, P.R.O., St. P. Dom. 16/469:11; Grantham Borough MSS, Court Minute Book I, 1633–1704, fols. 83–83v. The earl of Rutland had placed Bash at Grantham in 1614, and its other member, Pelham, was his kinsman and business adviser. Pelham was also employed by the earl of Lindsey as his business consultant (J.W.F. Hill, *Tudor and Stuart Lincoln*, p. 117; Keeler, *Long Parliament*, pp. 55, 299 300).

8. Hatton must have won substantial backing among the freemen of Higham Ferrers since it was due to his intervention that the franchise was finally extended; his heavy election expenses may have helped as well (Hirst, *Representative of the People?*, pp. 62, 119, 130–31, 135) Pontefract, also part of the queen's jointure, was under the electoral influence of Thomas Wentworth, earl of Strafford and lord president of the Council of the North. Henry Benson, elected at Knaresborough in 1640, was the queen's steward and bailiff, but his own influence was more significant in his election. His colleague Sir Henry Slingsby was another powerful Yorkshireman who customarily represented the town. Peter Ball, the queen's attorney, was returned at Tiverton in the spring, again thanks to his county connections; but despite Charles's concern that he be elected again, Ball was not returned. Tomkins to Lambe, 1 Oct. 1640, P.R.O., St. P. Dom. 16/469:11; "List of such as are recommended to be burgesses," Sept. 1640, P.R.O., St. P. Dom. 16/468:136; Graham to the Mayor of Carlisle, 30 Jan., 28 Feb. 1640, Carlisle City MSS, Ca/2/120. fols. 10, 22; Mayor and Corporation of Carlisle to Lord Clifford, 20 Jan. 1640, City of Carlisle MSS, Ca/2/120, f. 21; Wintour to the Mayor of Carlisle, 20 Feb. 1640, Carlisle City MSS, Ca/2/120, f. 17; Queen's Council to the Mayor and Corporation of Carlisle, 20 Mar. 1640, City of Carlisle MSS, Ca/2/120, f. 14; A. N. Groome, "Higham Ferrers Elections," p. 245; Northamptonshire RO, Finch Hatton MSS, 3467/1-3; 3468A and B; Lord Newburgh to the Mayor of Higham Ferrers, 28 Sept. 1640, Northamptonshire RO, Finch Hatton MSS 3451/3; Queen's Council to the same, 3 Oct. 1640, Northamptonshire RO, Finch Hatton MSS 3451/1; Hatton to Lambe, 12 Oct. 1640, Northamptonshire RO, Finch Hatton MSS 2375/1; the Corporation of Higham Ferrers to the Queen's Council and Lord Newburgh, n.d. November 1640, Northamptonshire RO, Finch Hatton MSS, 3469/2; Rex, *University Representation;* pp. 120–121; J. Crossley, ed., *The Diary and Correspondence of Dr. John Worthington*, 1:7; Keeler, *Long Parliament*, pp. 65, 75, 107–8, 142–43, 208, 211, 286–87, 340.

9. None of the eight Welsh circuit judges found a seat in the Long Parliament. In fact, only one of the men the king mentioned, William Morgan, his solicitor in the Marches of Wales, was elected in 1640 for Breconshire. In the spring the council might have been behind the return of a judge, Walter Rumsey, for Monmouthshire, and it was involved at Ludlow. The lord president of the Council of Wales, the earl of Bridgewater, failed to place his son-in-law, Sir Robert Napier; and the council's solicitor, Timothy Turneur or Turner, was also refused. Ludlow, however, did elect a veteran council officer, Ralph Goodwin, who had served for Ludlow before in the parliaments of 1614–28. "List of such as are recommended to be burgesses," Sept. 1640, P.R.O., St. P. Dom. 16/468:136; Bankes to Windebank, 12 Oct. 1640, P.R.O., St. P. Dom. 16/469:89; R. N. Kershaw, "The Elections for the Long Parliament, 1640," p. 49; Williams, *Parl. Hist. Wales*, p. 123; Martyn to Davies, 13 Jan. 1640, *HMC 3rd Report*, pp. 258–59; Brilliana Harley to Her Son Edward, 14 Mar. 1640, in Lewis, ed., *Letters of the Lady Brilliana Harley*, p. 58; Shropshire RO, Ludlow Corporation Minute Book 1590–1648, 356/2/1, fols 214, 216;

Weyman, "Members of Parliament for Ludlow," pp. 26–27; Keeler, *Long Parliament*, pp. 94–95, 190–91, 279–80, 284. For a more thorough discussion of Wentworth's influence in 1640, see Gruenfelder, "The Electoral Patronage of Sir Thomas Wentworth, Earl of Strafford, 1614–1640," and the sources cited therein.

10. For an analysis of Wigan's voting behavior in the spring and fall 1640 elections, see Hirst, *Representative of the People?*, pp. 119, 124–27, 191, 196; Keeler, *Long Parliament*, pp. 53–54, 68–69, 99–100, 115–16, 137–38, 152, 172–73, 195–96, 205–6, 248, 277, 323, 366, 381; Williams, *Parl. Hist. Wales*, p. 135; Sinclair, *History of Wigan*, 1:213–15, 221–23; 2:2–3, 10–11; Pape, *Newcastle Under Lyme*, pp. 143–44; Alex. Rigby to Geo. Rigby, 13, 23 Oct. 1640, *HMC Kenyon*, p. 58; Pink and Beaven, *Members of Parl. for Lancashire*, pp. 188, 225–26, 297–80, 447; Lancashire RO, Clitheroe Borough MSS, DDX/28/83. I should like to thank the Chief Executive of the Ribble Valley Borough Council for permission to use the Clitheroe Borough MSS. "Alexander Rigby," *DNB*, 16:1185–87; "Thomas Grey, Baron Grey of Groby," *DNB*, 8:649–50; Thompson, *History Leicester*, p. 359; *VCH Leicestershire*, 2:110, Nichols, *Hist. Leicestershire*, vol. 2, pt. 1, p. 427; Huntingdon to the Mayor and Burgesses of Leicester, 8 Feb. 1640, *HMC Hastings*, 4:218; Sir Jo. Coke the Younger to Sir Jo. Coke, 30 Mar. 1640, *HMC Cowper*, 2:252; Lord Newburgh to the Mayor and Corporation of Leicester, 19 Dec. 1639, Countess of Devonshire to the same, 20 Jan. 1640, Earl of Huntingdon to the same, 20 Jan. 1640, the same to the same, 8 Feb. 1640, the same to the same, 13 Feb. 1640, Roger Smith to the same, 27 Mar. 1640, the same to Sir Jo. Coke, 27 Mar. 1640, Countess of Devonshire to the same, 7 Apr. 1640, Leicester City Museums, Dept. of Archives, City of Leicester MSS, Hall Papers Bound 1637–40, BR II/18/21:548, 549, 550, 551, 552, 578, 584, 592; Meetings of the Common Hall of Leicester, Hall Papers Bound, 1637–40, BR II/18/21:579, 585, 591; City of Leicester MSS, Hall Book 1587–1708, BR/II/1/3:570, 578; Lord Newburgh to the Mayor and Corporation of Leicester, 29 Sept. 1640, Earl of Stamford to the same, 9 Oct. 1640, Countess of Devonshire to the same, 17, 31 Oct. 1640, Mayor and Corporation of Leicester to Lord Newburgh, 28 Nov. 1640, City of Leicester MSS, Hall Papers Bound 1640–45, BR/II/18/22: 3, 8, 9, 12, 16; Meeting of the Common Hall of Leicester, Hall Papers Bound 1640–45, BR/II/18/22:10; Angel to Sir Jo. Coke, 29 Sept. 1640, *HMC Cowper*, 2:261. Roger Smith's religious sympathies were similar to those of the earl of Stamford, but there is nothing in the abundant evidence for Leicester's 1640 elections to show that Smith owed his election to Stamford's patronage.

11. Dover returned Sir Edward Boys of Fedville, Kent, and Sir Peter Heyman of Somerfield in 1640 (Everitt, *The Community of Kent and the Great Rebellion, 1640–60*, pp. 74–75). Positive evidence of Suffolk's support for Sir Nicholas Crispe (Winchelsea), Robert Read (Hastings), and Sir John Manwood (Sandwich) has survived. He was also probably behind Hythe's election of John Wandesford. However, Suffolk failed to place Sir Edward Nicholas at Sandwich, and John Ashburnham withdrew from the Hastings election. Suffolk nominated his son, Thomas Howard, at Rye and then, for unknown reasons, shifted his support to Windebank's secretary, Robert Read, who was returned at Hastings. Read also had the backing of Sir John Manwood and Windebank at Rye, and the earl of Northumberland nominated Sir Nicholas Selwin for Rye. The earl of Dorset recommended his kinsman Sir John Sacksville and, when Sackville withdrew, replaced him with his secretary, White. Sir John Colepeper, Lawrence Ashburnham, Thomas Digges, and one W. Roberts, who claimed he had Suffolk's backing, were the other Rye candidates. In the fall Lennox was probably behind the return of Philip Warwick for New Romney, Crispe at Winchelsea, Sir John Jacob at Rye, and John Harvey, elected by Hythe. However, his bid for both places at Hythe failed. He also supported John Ashburnham at Hastings and could have also backed Robert Read's unsuccessful bid for a Hastings place, where Read had the support of the Privy Council. Lennox also tried, and failed, to secure a seat for Lord Grandison at Sandwich in the fall. Roberts to the Mayor and Jurats of Rye, 14 Dec. 1639, Suffolk to the same, 18 Dec. 1639, Ashburnham to the same, 18 Dec. 1639, Digges to the same, 24 Dec. 1639, Northumberland to the same, 31 Dec. 1639, Colepeper to the same, 8 Jan. 1640, East

Sussex RO, Rye Corporation MSS, 47/131, 39:3–8; Colepeper to the same, 13 Jan. 1640, East Sussex RO, Rye Corporation MSS, 47/132, 39:1; Suffolk to the same, 8 Feb. 1640, Manwood to the same, 26 Feb. 1640, earl of Dorset to the same, 28 Feb. 1640, Windebank to the same, 18 Mar. 1640, East Sussex RO, Rye Corp. MSS, 47/131, 39:10, 11, 13, 14; East Sussex RO, Winchelsea Borough MSS 58, Court Book 1628–91, f. 49v; Kent RO, New Romney Common Assembly Book, 1622–1701, NR/AC 2/f. 265; Hythe Borough Assembly Book 209, fols. 238, 240. I should like to thank the Hythe Town Council for its permission to use the Hythe Borough Assembly Books. *Lords Journal*, 4:549, 552–53; Wilks, *Barons of the Cinque Ports*, p, 80; J. B. Jones, *Annals of Dover*, p. 382; Manwood to the Mayor and Jurats of Sandwich, 24 Dec. 1639, Kent RO, Sandwich Borough MSS, Sa/ZB2/90. The lord admiral, Northumberland, may have made the first nomination of Sir Edward Nicholas for Sandwich, but Suffolk also supported Nicholas. Suffolk to the Mayor and Jurats of Sandwich, 17 Dec. 1639, Manwood to the same, 24 Dec. 1639, Northumberland to the same, 31 Dec. 1639, Kent RO, Sandwich Borough MSS, Letter Book, Sa/C1, fols. 12–13; Mayor and Jurats of Sandwich to the Earl of Suffolk, 13 Jan. 1640, P.R.O., St. P. Dom. 16/441:121; Hirst, *Representative of the People?*, app 2, pp. 208–9; Notes on Robert Read's candidature for Hastings, 10 Oct. 1640, P.R.O., St. P. Dom. 16/469:82; Read to the Mayor of Hastings, 11 Oct. 1640, P.R.O., St. P. Dom. 16/469:86 and enclosure i; Fran. Read to Robt. Read, 26 Oct. 1640, P.R.O., St. P. Dom. 16/470:68; Duke of Lennox to the Corporation of Sandwich?, 3 Oct. 1640, BM ADD ASS 33, 512, fol. 71, Jo. Ashburnham to Nicholas, 31 Mar. 1640, P.R.O., St. P. Dom. 16/449:44; "Deposition of Wm. Parker & John Jackson," 1 Apr. 1640, P.R.O., St. P. Dom 16/450:7; Keeler, *Long Parliament*, pp. 76–78, 89, 114–15, 147, 207–8, 231–32, 380, 390–91.

12. Given the urgency of the court's campaign, I have assumed that the Duchy of Lancaster nominated one man at each borough in 1640. The list "of such as are recommended to be burgesses" for September 1640 is in P.R.O., St. P. Dom. 16/468:136 and is referred to again, by attorney general Bankes in a letter of 12 Oct. 1640, to secretary Windebank, P.R.O., St. P. Dom. 16/469:89. Edward Herbert probably won his place at Old Sarum through the lord chamberlain, the earl of Pembroke and Montgomery, and Eure's return for Leominster was probably gained through his county influence.

13. Aristocratic intervention (which includes that of the great churchmen but not of those peers like the lord wardens of the Cinque Ports, whose patronage has already been discussed) can be traced in 104 of 260 elections in the spring (40.0%) and in 94 of 260 elections (36.1%) in the autumn. Such patronage probably accounted for no more than 118 of 487 identified places in the spring (24.2%) and 109 of 493 places (22.1%) in the autumn, the lowest totals for the early Stuart period. See Appendix Two.

14. For recent discussions of aristocratic division or faction and its effects, see Snow, *Essex the Rebel*, pp. 75–77, 102–5, 109–10, 117–18, 151–58, 163–64, 166, 168–77, 204–6; J. E. Farnell, "The Aristocracy and Leadership of Parliament in the English Civil Wars," pp. 79–86; J. S. Flemion, "The Struggle for the Petition of Right in the House of Lords: The Study of an Opposition Party Victory," pp. 193–210; M. Schwarz, "Viscount Saye and Sele, Lord Brooke and the Aristocratic Protest to the First Bishop's War," pp. 17–36.

15. *CSPV 1636–1639*, pp. 99, 110–11, 119, 121, 124–25, 136, 387, 418, 457, 506, 535–36, 558–59, 563; *CSPV 1640–1642*, p. 35; *Persecuto Undecima*, pp. 28–29; A. Kingston, *Herefordshire during the Great Civil War*, p. 28; Anthony Wood, *Athenae Oxonienses*, ed. P. Bliss, 3:546–47; "Whitelock's Annals," BM ADD MSS, 37, 343, fols. 199, 206; Temple to the Earl of Leicester, 4 Dec. 1638, 7 Feb. 1639, Earl of Northumberland to the Earl of Leicester, 10 Oct. 1639, 12 Dec. 1639, Collins, ed., *Letters and Memorials of State*, 2:579, 592, 612–13; Zagorin, *Court and Country*, pp. 42–49, 54–55, 58–66, 74–116, 170–81, 188–92, 197; Willson, *Privy Councillors*, pp. 136, 137, 140, 149, 153, 155, 164, 180–83, 188, 202; Prestwich, *Cranfield*, pp. 170–72, 216, 219, 423–55; C. Hill, *Puritanism and Revolution*, p. 240.

16. A. P. Newton, *The Colonising Activities of the English Puritans*, pp. 60–61, 65–67, 127–28, 240–47; J. H. Hexter, *The Reign of King Pym*, pp. 77–78; Pearl, *London and the*

*Outbreak of the Puritan Revolution*, pp. 160–68, 170–74; *Persecuto Undecima*, pp. 28–29; "A Letter from Mercurius Civicus to Mercurius Rusticus," by Samuel Butler, 1643, in Lord Somers, *A Collection of Scarce and Valuable Tracts*, ed. Walter Scott, 4:580–98; Keeler, *Long Parliament*, pp. 9, 68; Zagorin, *Court and Country*, pp. 100–102, 177–79; Gruenfelder, "The Elections to the Short Parliament, 1640," in Reinmuth, ed., *Early Stuart Studies*, pp. 218–19, 225–26, and sources cited therein; Vane to Windebank, 27 Sept. 1640, P.R.O., St. P. Dom. 16/468:61; Brograve to D'Ewes, 24 Sept. 1640, BM Harleian MSS 384, f. 86; Cliffe, *Yorkshire Gentry*, pp. 321–22. For an excellent example of the reformer's network of family connections and friendships founded on common religious and political views, see the ties between the various candidates in the Essex and Gloucestershire elections of 1640, Keeler, *Long Parliament*, pp. 46–47, 132–33, 136, 198–99, 268–69, 322–23, 350–51.

17. Not all thirteen were active patrons in both elections. Viscount Savile's influence can only be found in the spring election, and the earl of Stamford's intervention was apparently limited to one autumn election. The other peers, the earls of Essex, Hertford, Warwick, Bristol, Bolingbroke, Bedford, and Holland, Viscount Saye and Sele, and Lords Brooke, Paget, and Grey of Ruthin were engaged in both 1640 elections.

18. The elections reflecting the intervention of the reform peers were Warwickshire, Warwick, Lichfield, Newcastle-under Lyme, Staffordshire, Tamworth, Dorsetshire, Oxfordshire, Banbury, Leicestershire, Great Marlow, Essex, Colchester, Harwich, Tavistock, Totness, Milborne Port, Great Bedwin, Marlborough, Bedford, Bedfordshire, Windsor, Reading, and Cambridge University. In the spring Southwark and Wiltshire can be added, and in the Long Parliament elections, Leicester, Hertfordshire, and Maldon can be included. For the men returned, see Keeler, *Long Parliament*, passim, and subsequent references.

19. Gruenfelder, "The Election for Knights of the Shire for Essex in the Spring, 1640," pp. 143–46; PRO/PC/2, Entry for 17 Apr. 1640; Gruenfelder, "The Election to the Short Parliament, 1640," in Reinmuth, ed., *Early Stuart Studies*, pp. 210–11, 212, 227; C. Hill, *Economic Problems of the Church*, p. 56; Zagorin, *Court and Country*, p. 92; Colchester's election and that for the county, too, were complicated in the fall since Barrington, who had enjoyed Warwick's support for a county place in the spring, had been shifted, apparently by the earl, to Colchester. Warwick was backing Masham in Barrington's stead, and Barrington, it seems, had been somewhat nettled by the change in his fortunes. To prevent possible friction between Masham and Barrington, Warwick, his son Lord Rich, Masham, and Grimston urged Colchester to conduct its election as quickly as possible since, as Grimston put it, "if Sir Thomas Barrington be not provided for before the election for the county," Barrington might well challenge Masham's candidacy, causing "a competition which will occasion a great deal of trouble to the country and may engender discontent and breed a fraction where there is none, for Sir William Masham is so far engaged by my Lord of Warwick that he cannot decline the standing." Colchester's election of Barrington ended such fears. The potential quarrel over which "reformer" would stand for what place and the intervention of two reform peers at Colchester stands as an example that illustrates the impossibility of a nationally planned reform group electoral program. Holland to the Mayor and Commonalty of Colchester, 26 Sept. 1640, the Earl of Warwick to the same, 6 Oct. 1640, Masham to Grimston, 21 Oct. 1640, the Bailiffs of Colchester to the Earl of Holland, n.d. Oct. 1640, Essex RO, Morant MSS, vol. 43, pp. 35, 39, 51, 89; Grimston to the Mayor of Colchester, 20 Oct. 1640, Essex RO, Morant MSS, vol. 47, p. 76; Robert Lord Rich to Grimston, n.d. Oct.? 1640, Essex RO, Morant MSS, vol. 48, p. 53; Keeler, *Long Parliament*, pp. 46, 97–99, 229–30, 268–69, 322–23. Warwick was probably responsible for the elections of Sir William Masham at Colchester (spring 1640), Sir Thomas Cheek for Harwich (both elections 1640), Sir John Clotworthy at Maldon (fall 1640), and was behind the return of Masham (Essex, autumn 1640), Barrington (spring 1640, Essex, autumn 1640, Colchester), Sir Harbottle Grimston (Essex, spring 1640) and his son, Lord Rich (Essex, fall 1640). He was also, no doubt, involved in Harwich's choice of Sir Harbottle Grimston

(fall 1640). For a discussion of the local problems that plagued Colchester earlier in the century and affected its elections, see Hirst, *Representative of the People?*, app. 2, pp. 199–201.

20. Huntingdon's influence had secured at least one knight-ship in every county election from 1614 through 1628, and in 1621 his intervention accounted for both.

21. Huntingdon to the Mayor and Corporation of Leicester, 20 Jan., 13 Feb. 1640, Leicester City Museum, Dept. of Archives, Leicester City MSS, Hall Papers Bound 1637–40, BR II/21:550, 552; Withrings to Sir Jo. Coke, 3 Nov. 1640, Sir Jo. Coke the Younger to Sir Jo. Coke, 15 Nov. 1640, *HMC Cowper*, 2:262, 263; *VCH Leicestershire*, 2:110; Keeler, *Long Parliament*, pp. 54, 195, 213.

22. Newsletter of John, first Lord Scudamore, 28 Feb. 1640, BM ADD MSS 11,045, f. 96; Spencer, Earl of Northampton to His Wife, Countess Mary, 29 Sept. 1640, P.R.O., St. P. Dom. 16/468:87; Keeler, *Long Parliament*, pp. 68, 138–39, 259–60, 316, 338.

23. Cooper, *Annals of Cambridge*, 3:296–99, 303–5; Crossley, ed., *The Diary and Correspondence of Dr. John Worthington*, 1:8; Mullinger, *The University of Cambridge*, 3:147; Guilding, ed., *Reading Records*, 3:472, 475–76, 488–89, 492–93, 505, 506, 507; *HMC Duke of Leeds*, et al., p. 186; Aspinal, ed., *Parliament through Seven Centuries*, pp. 50–53, 108; H. R. Trevor-Roper, *Archbishop Laud*, pp. 384–85, 396; Rex, *University Representation in England*, pp. 120–21; Salisbury Corp. MSS, General Entry Book, D/34, Ledger C, f. 416; City of Wells MSS, Acts of the Corporation, 1635–41, fols. 139v, 140; Canterbury Borough MSS, Canterbury Cathedral Archives, Canterbury Burghmoot Book, A/C 4, 1630–58, fols. 151v, 152; Scott MSS, 3–7v, 13–31, 33–34; Hirst, *Representative of the People?*, pp. 56, 135, 148, 151; Northumberland to the Mayor and Corporation of Great Yarmouth, 10 Dec. 1639, Dorset to the Bailiffs of Great Yarmouth 10 Dec. 1639, 27 Feb. 1640, Bailiffs of Great Yarmouth to Dorset, 14 Dec. 1639, Palmer, *Hist. Great Yarmouth*, pp. 204–7; Burton to Bray, 27 Jan. 1639, P.R.O., St. P. Dom. 16/442:137; *Commons Journal*, 2:3; Suffolk Record Office, Ipswich Branch, Corp. of Aldeburgh Borough Letter Book, EE 1/01/1, f. 85, which can also be found in a copy in BM ADD MSS 41, 605, f. 112. I should like to thank the Suffolk Record Office for its kind permission to use the Aldeburgh Borough MSS. Borough of King's Lynn MSS, King's Lynn Hall Book, vol. 8, 1637–58, f. 65v; *HMC Southampton and King's Lynn*, p. 178; W. Richards, *The History of Lynn*, pp. 1198–99; Earl of Holland to the Mayor and Aldermen of Windsor, 9 Dec. 1639, *HMC Various Collections*, 8:53; Harrison to Windebank, 9 Dec. 1639, P.R.O., St. P. Dom. 16/447:63; Keeler, *Long Parliament*, pp. 33–34, 44–46, 52, 56, 57, 64, 67, 70–72, 97–99, 106–7, 111, 142, 178–79, 218–19, 220, 229–30, 243–44, 268–69, 292, 303, 320, 322–25, 349, 357–58, 361, 362, 395. Salisbury's acceptance of a nominee of the earl of Pembroke and Montgomery in the 1640 elections (it returned his secretary, Michael Oldisworth) marked the end of the independent electoral course the city had pursued in the early seventeenth century. In fact, it had not accepted a Pembroke nominee since 1572. However, the Puritan group that had dominated Salisbury's politics had suffered a severe blow when Salisbury's recorder, Henry Sherfield, died in 1634. His replacement, Robert Hyde, "had no sympathy" with Sherfield's ideals, worked closely "with the Dean and Chapter," and, in all likelihood probably supported the city's acceptance of Pembroke and Montgomery's nominee. It certainly seems that Salisbury's electoral independence was a product of its influential Puritan faction that dominated city government. P. Slack, "Poverty and Politics in Salisbury, 1597–1666," in P. Clark and P. Slack, eds., *Crisis and Order in English towns*, p. 191.

24. Lord Arundell's past influence over Christchurch was sought by his son and successor, the second Lord Arundell, and by another kinsman, William, as well as one of the first lord's sons-in-law, Cecil Lord Baltimore. Baltimore, because his nominees either took sick or preferred to contest other borough elections, made five nominations in the spring alone, with Sir Arnold Herbert finally winning a place, while the second Lord Arundell nominated two and the lord admiral, Northumberland, one. In the fall the story repeated itself, although with different patrons. The earl of Pembroke and Montgomery, acting, he claimed, with the consent of William Arundell, nominated

"the Lord Lisle and my cousin Henry Wroughton"; and Hampshire's lord lieutenants, the earl of Portland and the duke of Lennox, jointly recommended one William Lake. Baltimore successfully nominated "Matthew Davies of Shaftesbury." *VCH Hampshire*, 5:86–87, 92–93; Baltimore to the Mayor and Burgesses of Christchurch, 16, 18, 23 Dec. 1639, 25 Feb. 1640, 3 Mar. 1640, 29 Sept. 1640, Thos. Lord Arundell to the same, 16 Jan. 1640, Misham to the same, 10 Mar. 1640, Northumberland to the same, 10 Dec. 1639, Lennox and Portland to the same, n.d. 1640, Pembroke and Montgomery to the same, 20 Oct. 1640, Wm. Arundell to the same, 20 Oct. 1640, Jo. Kempe, Mayor of Christchurch, to Pembroke and Montgomery, 26 Oct. 1640, Christchurch Borough MSS; Keeler, *Long Parliament*, pp. 49, 154, 367. Baltimore's influence, since he was an Irish peer, is not included in the tabulations of aristocratic involvement in Appendix One.

25. Northumberland's "personal" influence accounted for his successes in both 1640 elections at Berwick and Northumberland; he also successfully supported a candidate in Chichester's spring election. However, as lord admiral, his intervention failed in the spring elections at Scarborough, Dover, Rye, Sandwich, Christchurch, and in both elections at Great Yarmouth. However, his candidates, or those he supported, won a place in each election for Yarmouth, Isle of Wight, and took three of Portsmouth's places in the 1640 elections. His intervention as lord admiral was also successful at Harwich in the spring and in both 1640 elections for Hull. Hull's return of Northumberland's nominee Sir Henry Vane may have been due more to Vane's father's influence at Hull than that of the earl, and it is likely that his candidate's failures at Christchurch and Rye can, to some extent at least, be attributed to the fierce aristocratic competition that developed over the two borough's burgess-ships. The rejection of his nominees cannot be explained, either, by the fact that many were often strangers to their prospective boroughs. Great Yarmouth's decisions may have been partially based on that, but Scarborough refused a Yorkshireman, Sir John Melton, in the spring, and Yarmouth, Isle of Wight, elected a stranger, Philip Lord Lisle, twice in 1640. Sir John Hippisley, although no stranger to Dover, was refused; Henry Percy, Northumberland's brother, and Sir Henry Vane, both strangers, were returned at Portsmouth and Hull as was another outsider, Sir John Jacobs, elected at Harwich in the spring. Northumberland to the Mayor and Jurats of Great Yarmouth, 10 Dec. 1639, Palmer, *Great Yarmouth*, p. 205; Northumberland to the Mayor and Burgess of Christchurch, 10 Dec. 1639, Pembroke and Montgomery to the Mayor and Aldermen of Christchurch, 20 Oct. 1640, Mayor of Christchurch to Pembroke and Montgomery, 26 Oct. 1640, Lord Arundell to the Mayor of Christchurch, 28 Oct. 1640, Christchurch Borough MSS; Northumberland to ?, Dover, 10 Dec. 1639, BM ADD MSS 18,016, f. 1v; Kempe to Dering, 29 Jan. 1640, Kent RO, Dering MSS, U 350, C2/73; Smith to Pennington, 30 Jan. 1640, P.R.O., St. P. Dom. 16/443:30; Northumberland to the Mayor and Burgesses of Kingston Upon Hull, 10 Dec. 1639, Stanewell, *Hull*, p. 195; Northumberland to the Mayor and Jurats of Rye, 31 Dec. 1639, East Sussex RO, Rye Corp. MSS, 47/131, 39:7; Northumberland to the Mayor and Burgesses of Sandwich, 31 Dec. 1639, Kent RO, Sandwich Letter Book, Sa/C 1, f. 12; Melton to the Bailiffs of Scarborough, Dec. 1639, Scarborough Borough MSS, General Letters B 1., 1597–1642; Popple to Vane, 21 Mar. 1640, P.R.O., St. P. Dom. 16/448:53; Batho, ed., *The Household Papers of Henry Percy, Ninth Earl of Northumberland*, pp. 43, 150–60; Keeler, *Long Parliament*, pp. 43, 49–50, 57, 58, 67, 74, 75, 77, 158–59, 174, 215–16, 272, 290, 303–4, 312, 335, 339, 371; "Sir John Fenwick or Fenwicke," *DNB*, 6:1193; "Sir John Melton," *DNB*, 12:1146–48; "Henry Percy, Lord Percy of Alnwick," *DNB*, 15:858–59; "Philip Sidney, third Earl of Leicester," *DNB*, 18:234–36. Northumberland's other nominees were Sir Henry Marten at Great Yarmouth in the spring (lost), Edward Nicholas for both Sandwich (lost) and Christchurch (lost), and Sir Nicholas Selwin or Selwyn for Rye (lost) in the spring. He was probably behind the return of his secretary Hugh Potter for Berwick in the spring and for Plympton Earl in a fall bye-election, an election that illustrated possible collaboration between Northumberland and the earl of Pembroke and Montgomery. Michael Oldisworth, originally elected for Plympton under Pembroke's banner, decided to serve for Salisbury, and Potter replaced him. Pembroke had also nominated Northumberland's nephew Philip Lord

Lisle at Christchurch, possibly as a form of electoral insurance should Lisle be refused at Yarmouth, Isle of Wight. Another of Northumberland's secretaries, Robert Scawen, served for Berwick in the fall following Potter's rejection, and Northumberland's servant Edward Dowse was returned for Chichester in the spring and took Henry Percy's place at Portsmouth in the fall. Sir John Fenwick, returned in the spring for Northumberland, probably had the earl's backing as well; in a later election, for the restored borough of Cockermouth, he probably had Northumberland's support.

26. "Whitelock's Annals," BM ADD MSS 37, 343, fols. 206–7; Bodleian Library, MS Top. Kent e. 6, 81; D. Hirst, "The Defection of Sir Edward Dering, 1640–1641."

27. Hill to the Earl of Middlesex, 15 Dec. 1639, Sackville MSS; Plevny and Hale, Bailiffs of Tewkesbury, to the Earl of Middlesex, 12 Oct. 1640, HMC, 4th Report, app. 1 and 2, p. 303.

28. Guilding, ed., Reading Records, 3:472, 475–76, 488–89, 492–93, 505, 506, 507; HMC Duke of Leeds, et al., p. 186; Aspinal, ed., Parliament through Seven Centuries, pp. 50–53, 108; Trevor-Roper, Archbishop Laud, pp. 384–85, 396; Cooper, Annals of Cambridge, 3:296–99, 303–5; Crossley, ed., The Diary and Correspondence of Dr. John Worthington, 1:8; Mullinger, The University of Cambridge, 3:147; Keeler, Long Parliament, pp. 34, 36, 243–44, 259; Hirst, Representative of the People?, pp. 53, 60, 203. Local problems, too, played a part in Reading's 1640 elections (ibid., pp. 58–59).

29. Gruenfelder, "The Election to the Short Parliament, 1640," in Reinmuth, ed., Early Stuart Studies, pp. 221–22, and sources cited therein; Notes Concerning Robert Read's Candidature for Hastings, 10 Oct. 1640, P.R.O., St. P. Dom. 16/469:82; Read to the Mayor of Hastings, 11 Oct. 1640, P.R.O., St. P. Dom. 16/469:86 and enclosure i; Hastings Borough MSS, Common Assembly Book C/A (a) 2, fol. 89; Duke of Lennox to the Mayor and Corporation of Sandwich?, 3 Oct. 1640, BM ADD MSS 33,512, fol. 71; Peyton to the Mayor, Jurats, and Commons of Sandwich, 19 Oct. 1640, the same to Colepeper, 25 Oct. 1640, BM ADD MSS 44,846, fols. 4–5; Keeler, Long Parliament, pp. 49, 467; Hirst, Representative of the People?, pp. 58, 59, 121, 135–36, 149, 151, app. 2, pp. 208–9.

30. Keeler, Long Parliament, pp. 37–40, 99–100, 115–16, 152; Gruenfelder, "The Election to the Short Parliament, 1640," in Reinmuth, ed., Early Stuart Studies, p. 222 and n.

31. Hirst, Representative of the People?, pp. 139–40, 147. For a table illustrating the electoral tactics employed in the elections of 1640, based on the evidence for 166 elections in that year, see Appendix Eight.

32. Other examples of candidates' interest in aristocratic support include the fall elections for Straffordshire and Hertfordshire, and similar gentry intervention was illustrated in elections for Thetford, Whitchurch, Callington, and East Looe; no doubt there were many more. Elections that involved inducements over parliamentary wages included those for Christchurch in both the spring and fall, Queenborough in the spring, Bishop's Castle for both the Short and Long Parliaments, and spring elections for Beverley and Windsor. Grimsby, Lincolnshire, required its members to prepare bonds promising that they would not demand payment for their services. Windebank to the King, 25 Sept., 4 Oct. 1640, Clarendon State Papers, 2:123, 127; Vane to Windebank, 27 Sept. 1640, P.R.O., St. P. Dom. 16/468:61; Webb to Read, 3 Sept. 1640, P.R.O., St. P. Dom. 16/468:119; Wrottesley to Devereux, 29 Sept. 1640, HMC 2nd Report, Appendix 1, 47; Harley and Coningsby to the Earl of Essex, 9 Oct. 1640, HMC Portland, 3:65; D'Ewes to the Earl of Worcester, 1 Oct. 1640, J. O. Halliwell, ed., Autobiography and Correspondence of Sir Simonds D'Ewes, 2:244–46; Barnardiston to D'Ewes, 5?, 30 Oct. 1640, BM Harleian MSS 384, fols. 64, 65; Framlingham Gawdy to the Mayor and Corporation of Thetford, 12 Oct. 1640, n.d. fall? 1640, BM ADD MSS 27, 396, fols. 166–68; his letter of 12 Oct. 1640 is in Mason, Hist. Norfolk, p. 279; Francis Read to Robt. Read, 28 Sept. 1640, P.R.O., St. P. Dom. 16/468:71, same to same, 3 Oct. 1640, P.R.O., St. P. Dom. 16/469:31, same to same, 18 Oct. 1640, P.R.O., St. P. Dom. 16/470:17; ? to Buller, 5 Oct. 1640, MSS of Sir John G. Carew Pole, Bart., Cornwall RO, BO 23/73;

Hicks to Francis Buller, 15, 16 Oct. 1640, MSS of Sir John G. Carew Pole, Bart., Cornwall RO, BO 20/73; Baltimore to the Mayor and Burgesses of Christchurch, 25 Feb. 3 Mar., 29 Sept. 1640, Christchurch Borough MSS; Harrison to the Mayor, Jurats, and Burgesses of Queenborough, 16 Mar. 1640, Kent RO, Queenborough Corporation MSS, Qb/C 1/37; Dennett, ed., *Beverely Borough Records, 1575–1821*, p. 102; *HMC Westmorland* et al., p. 403; Tighe and Davis, eds., *Annals of Windsor*, 2:144–45; Borough of Bishop's Castle MSS, 1st Minute Book of the Corporation, f. 199v; Election bonds of Mr. Gervase Holles and Sir Christopher Wray of 24 Mar. 1640, Borough of Grimsby MSS. I should like to thank the Great Grimsby Borough Council for its permission to use the borough's manuscripts.

33. Gruenfelder, "The Election to the Short Parliament, 1640," in Reinmuth, ed., *Early Stuart Studies*, pp. 210–13, 214–16, and sources cited therein; Gruenfelder, "The Spring Parliamentary Election at Hastings, 1640"; Gruenfelder, "The Election for Knights of the Shire of Essex in the Spring, 1640," p. 14; Rushworth, *Collections*, 3:986, 988, 4:38, 73, 88; Bodleian Library, MS Top. Kent e. 6, 87; Sedley to Dering, 21 Oct. 1640, BM Stowe MSS 184, f. 16; Raven, *Hist. Suffolk*, pp. 205–6; Halliwell, ed., *Autobiography of D'Ewes*, 2:246–49, 255; D'Ewes to Littleton, 10 Oct. 1640, BM Harleian MSS 286, f. 316; same to same, 14 Oct. 1640, BM Harleian MSS 374, f. 160; Bernardiston to D'Ewes, 30 Oct. 1640, BM Harleian MSS 384, f. 66; "Whitelock's Annals," BM ADD MSS 37, 343, f. 211; J. Gribble, *Memorials of Barnstaple*, pp. 346–50; Elliston to Baitson, 11 Oct. 1640, *HMC Various Collections*, 8:54; Petition of the freemen of Northampton, Oct. 1640, Northamptonshire RO, Finch Hatton MSS, FH 3501; Keeler, *Long Parliament*, pp. 38–39, 42, 64, 66, 76–77, 322–24, 349.

34. Salisbury's 1640 elections were noteworthy in another respect since its hitherto jealously guarded electoral independence vanished as well when it accepted a nominee of the earl of Pembroke and Montgomery in both its elections. Salisbury Corporation MSS, General Entry Book, D/34, Ledger C., f. 416; Searchers and Sealers of Leather Book, I/253, fols. 20v–21r; P. Slack, "An Election to the Short Parliament," pp. 110, 111–12, 114 (Slack also prints the document from the Searchers and Sealers of Leather Book noted above); Slack, "Poverty and Politics in Salisbury, 1597–1666," in P. Clark and P. Slack, eds., *Crisis and Order in English Towns, 1500–1700*, pp. 170–73, 181–91; Hirst, *Representative of the People?*, p. 72; *OR*, 1:457, 473, 469, 475, 481; Pearl, *London and the Outbreak of the Puritan Revolution*, pp. 66–67, 104, 112–13.

35. J. K. Gruenfelder, "The Spring, 1640, Parliamentary Election at Abingdon," pp. 41–47; Hirst, *Representative of the People?*, pp. 62, 80, 130, 134, 138, 147, app. 2, p. 205; Gruenfelder, "The Electoral Patronage of Sir Thomas Wentworth, Earl of Strafford, 1614–1640," p. 573; M. G. Hobson and H. E. Salter, eds., *Oxford Council Acts, 1626–1665* (1933), pp. 90–92; Keeler, *Long Parliament*, pp. 58, 60, 75–76, 387–88, 393–94. Lenthall, Speaker of the House, appealed to the Commons over the result of the autumn election at Gloucester, but nothing apparently came of his claim (Gruenfelder, "Gloucester's Parliamentary Elections, 1604–1640," pp. 57–58; Keeler, *Long Parliament*, pp. 47, 60, 250).

36. The boroughs that joined Grantham and Wenlock included Chipping Wycombe, Launceston, Derby, Barnstaple, Plympton Earl, Poole, Shaftesbury, Weymouth and Melcombe Regis, Colchester, Winchester, Boston, Great Yarmouth, and Chichester (Keeler, *Long Parliament*, pp. 34, 36, 39, 41–46, 50, 55, 57, 58, 60–62, 67, 70, 72, 73).

37. Gruenfelder, "The Election to the Short Parliament, 1640," in Reinmuth, ed., *Early Stuart Studies*, pp. 210–11, and sources cited therein; Everitt, *Kent and the Great Rebellion*, pp. 69–83, and sources cited therein; F. W. Jessup, *Sir Roger Twysden* (London, 1965), pp. 137–42, and sources cited therein; Boteler's petition against Luke's election for Bedford in the fall can be found in the Bedfordshire RO, TW 889, and the lists compiled, along with the poll for the election, are TW 890a, 890b, 891–94 (copyright in these documents remains with the owners, the heirs of the late Charles Trevor Wingfield, Esq.; I should like to thank the Bedfordshire County Record Office for allowing me to use them); spring elections for Caernarvorishire, Essex, Berkshire,

Norfolk, Cheshire, and Knaresborough and autumn elections for Oxfordshire, Great Marlow, Worcestershire, Bridgnorth, and Cambridgeshire, among others, could provide additional examples. Gruenfelder, "The Election for Knights of the Shire for Essex in the Spring, 1640," pp. 143–46; Ketton-Cremer, *Norfolk in the Civil War*, pp. 105–13, and sources cited therein; Davies to Owen Wynn, NLW, Wynn MSS (9062E), 1657; Sawyer to Read, 13 Dec. 1639, P.R.O., St. P. Dom. 16/435:72, in Hedges, *Hist. Wallingford*, 2:167–68; D. Parsons, ed., *The Diary of Sir Henry Slingsby of Scriven, Bart.*, pp. 50–51; Brerewood to [Sir Thos. Smith], 10 Mar. 1640, P.R.O., St. P. Dom. 16/442:46; "Whitelock's Annals," BM ADD MSS 37, 343, fols. 206–11; Russell to Pakington?, 26 Oct. 1640, Worcestershire RO, Berington Family Papers, 705: 24/623(30); Henry Oxenden to His Cousin Henry, n.d. fall 1640, BM ADD MSS 28,000, f. 41; Thynne to Totty at Bridgnorth, 30 Sept. 1640, Shropshire RO, Bridgnorth Borough MSS, 26/1; Peyton to Dering, 25 Oct. 1640, BM ADD MSS 44,846, f. 5; Raven, *Hist. Suffolk*, pp. 205–6; D'Ewes to Littleton, 10 Oct. 1640, Littleton to D'Ewes, 29 Oct. 1640, D'Ewes to His Wife, 14 Dec. 1640, in Halliwell, ed., *Autobiography of D'Ewes*, 2:246–49, 255; North to Crane, 29 Sept. 1640, Bodleian Library, Tanner MSS 65, f. 124; North to Jo. Hobart, 29 Sept. 1640, Bodleian Library, Tanner MSS 115, f. 131; D'Ewes to Littleton, 10, 29 Oct. 1640, BM Harleian MSS 374, f. 160; Barnardiston to D'Ewes, 30 Oct. 1640, BM Harleian MSS 384, f. 66; Keeler, *Long Parliament*, pp. 33, 35–36, 50, 52, 59–60, 64, 79; Bodleian Library, MS top. Kent e. 6, 81–87; Hirst, *Representative of the People?*, pp. 36, 99–100.

38. I am indebted to Mr. Kenneth Shipps for the information and reference for Thomas Ball's electioneering in the Northamptonshire spring election. Ball had been a weekly lecturer in Northampton for about ten years by the time of the election and was the joint editor of John Preston's works; Oxford University, Banks MSS 44/13; Gruenfelder, "The Election to the Short Parliament, 1640," in Reinmuth, ed., *Early Stuart Studies*, pp. 208–10, 212, 214, and sources cited therein; Everitt, *Kent and the Great Rebellion*, pp. 72, 73, 77–78, and sources cited therein; Bodleian Library, MS. Top. Kent e. 6, 85, 87; Gruenfelder, "The Election for Knights of the Shire for Essex in the Spring, 1640," pp. 143–46. Mr. Shipps has also been kind enough to bring to my attention the activities of one of the earl of Warwick's ministers, one "Pontie, a Scottish man," in that Essex election, PAO/PC/2, entry for 17 Apr. 1640; Pearl, *London and the Outbreak of the Puritan Revolution*, pp. 169, 175–93; *Commons Journal*, 2:10; petition of the freemen of Northampton, Oct. 1640, Northamptonshire RO, Finch Hatton MSS, FH 3501; Rushworth, *Collections*, 4:38; Dillingham to Sandecroft, 3 Nov. 1640, Bodleian Library, Tanner MSS 65, f. 175; "Whitelock's Annals," BM ADD MSS 37,343, fols. 211–12; Bodleian Library, Rawlinson MS D. 141, fols. 6–7; Barnardiston to D'Ewes, 30 Oct. 1640, BM Harleian MSS 384, f. 65.

39. Gruenfelder, "The Elections to the Short Parliament, 1640," in Reinmuth, ed., *Early Stuart Studies*, pp. 207–8, and sources cited therein; Martyn to Davies, 13 Jan. 1640, *HMC, 3rd Report*, 258–59; "Whitelock's Annals," BM ADD MSS 37, 343, fols. 207–8,211–12; Francis Read to Robt. Read, 4 Oct. 1640, P.R.O., St. P. Dom. 16/469:31; Colepeper to Dering, 14 Oct. 1640, BM Stowe MSS 743, f. 156; Smyth to Appleton, 20 Oct. 1640, Bodleian Library, Tanner MSS 65, f. 164; Maurice Wynn to Owen Wynn, n.d. 1641, NLW, Wynn MSS (9062E), 1680; Keeler, *Long Parliament*, p. 138; Stone, "The Electoral Influence of the Second Earl of Salisbury, 1614–68," pp. 393–94; *HMC Portland*, 3:66; *VCH Derbyshire*, 2:136; Bodleian Library, MS Top. Kent e. 6, 81; Hirst, *Representative of the People?*, p. 119; Fletcher, *County Community*, pp. 243, 248; for a more detailed account of Abingdon's spring 1640 election, see Gruenfelder, "The Spring, 1640, Parliamentary Election at Abingdon," pp. 41–47.

40. J. Thirsk, ed., *The Agrarian History of England and Wales, 1500–1640*, vol. 4. (Cambridge, 1967), pp. 291, 652; C. Russell, *The Crisis of Parliaments*, pp. 14–15; Hirst, *Representative of the People?*, pp. 118, 119. No earlier detailed bills, as for Hertford, Derbyshire, and Hertfordshire, have apparently survived. The Kent election, so it was claimed, cost Sir Albertus Morton between £200 and £300, and Sir John Wynn spent over £100 trying to win the Caernarvonshire election of 1621. Canterbury candidates, in

1625 and 1626, spent a total of £150, if Scott is correct. He claimed that his campaign in 1626 had cost him £100, but none of these bills (save for Kent, and that was based on rumor) touch what the earl of Salisbury spent or, for that matter, what Derbyshire cost Sir John Coke the younger.

41. Gruenfelder, "The Elections to the Short Parliament, 1640," in Reinmuth, ed., *Early Stuart Studies*, p. 206, and sources cited therein; Gruenfelder, "The Spring Parliamentary Election at Hastings, 1640, pp. 49–55; Rolle to Wise, n.d. Dec. 1640, in R. N. Worth, ed., *The Buller Papers*, p. 29; *Commons Journal*, 2:51; Rushworth, *Collections*, 4:111–12; Edw. Pitt to His Cousin, 2 Oct. 1640, BM ADD MSS 29,974, f. 319; Keeler, *Long Parliament*, pp. 42, 45, 67, 76, 329; Hirst, *Representative of the People?*, p. 119. Another bribery case arose in Arundel's election in November 1641 that was serious enough to provoke a House of Commons investigation and an apparent lawsuit against Arundel's mayor (G. W. Eustace, *Arundel, Borough and Castle*, pp. 149–50; Horsfield, *Hist. Sussex*, vol. 2, app. 3, p. 20).

# SIX

## Conclusion

Patronage and influence, the electoral power of the elite, the court, peerage, gentry, and borough oligarchies, all dominated parliamentary elections from 1604 through 1640. However, the rivalry for electoral influence among that elite was fierce. The number of places available at Westminster was limited and increased but slightly through 1640. But that, alone, hardly accounted for the growing competition. The gentry, leaders of their local communities, were confronted by other patrons, the peerage, and, in contrast to the Elizabethan past, the court itself, which became an aggressive patron in its own right. The success of such influence aroused fears, vociferously expressed in the Parliament of 1614, of parliament's survival as a "free" institution. And, given the influence of the peerage and court in early Stuart elections, the local community's fears were not exaggerated.[1]

Nicholas Fuller charged, in the Addled Parliament, that the "undertaking he feared was a report that some one great man had, by letters, procured sixty voices" in the House of Commons. Fuller had marvelously inflated his unnamed peer's influence, but another member, Francis Ashley, claimed, with greater accuracy, that "noble men engrossed the burgess-ships, some 8, some 10."[2] Their remarks were appropriate to any parliament through 1628 but applied with special force to the Parliaments of 1624–28, when the peerage was consistently involved in more than 45 percent of all elections for parliament.[3] It is probable that, in the Parliaments of 1625 and 1626, as many as 148 members owed their places, in part at least, to the backing of the peerage. From 1604 to 1628, the peerage was involved in from 38 to 48 percent of all elections; its nominees probably secured between 24 to 30 percent of the places available in those elections. In 1628, however, the story changed. Despite their customary high level of intervention, the number of places won or probably won by their candidates fell to only 123, a decline of about 20 percent from 1626. The downward trend continued in the elections of 1640, when their candidates or those that had their support accounted for 118 places in the spring and only 109 in the autumn. Indeed, if the "reform" peers had not enjoyed the success they did in 1640, the record would have been much worse.

Court electioneering, especially as practiced from 1614 through 1624 and again in 1640, was the notable innovation of early Stuart elections. Central planning was, like the electoral tactics of the elite, still in its infancy, but Bacon's suggestions had some effect. The court was concerned that the right men were chosen; the list of nominees sent to a surprised Zouch in 1620 and the lists of candidates backed by the Duchy of Cornwall and the Prince's Council suggested central direction. Such planning did not affect the outlying councils or, it seems, the Duchy of Lancaster, although it was certainly possible. It is clear, however, that court electioneering in the early seventeenth century sharply contrasted with the immediate Elizabethan past. The court's electoral influence was substantial. Its agencies and the lord wardens probably were involved in as many as 216 elections (12.7 percent of all elections) through 1628.[4] From 1614 through 1624, when the Duchy of Cornwall and Prince's Council were active, it was involved in 17 percent of all elections, a figure it slightly exceeded in 1640 when it intervened in 92 of 520 elections, or nearly 18 percent (17.7%). Comparisons of this electioneering in 1614–24 and 1640 are instructive. On average, it intervened in 43 elections for a harvest of 43 places from 1614 through 1624. In 1640, again on average, it intervened in 46 elections, but its nominees secured only 26 places. The electoral climate for the court had changed, and, though political questions undoubtedly played a major role in its 1640 defeat, other problems too plagued its electioneering and that of the peerage, as well.

In spite of differences from county to county, England was still a provincial country whose local elite, the gentry, were more loyal to their community and responsive to its wishes than they were to the more abstract conception of the state. Local families, connected by friendship, marriage, interests, and education, ruled every aspect of county life. It was no accident that the county is usually referred to as the "country" in their correspondence; for a Sir Thomas Barrington or a Sir Edward Dering, that was where their loyalties, connections, and interests truly rested.[5]

The county community's influence, however, came under a growing challenge from the central government in the reigns of Elizabeth, James, and Charles. In almost every sphere of county life, the encroachments of the central authority were increasingly felt. The grain trade was regulated, the administration of justice reviewed, and military matters reformed under a crown-appointed lord lieutenant. Even the customary pattern of county religious life was challenged, especially by Laud's innovations. Cheshire's gentry were upset by the actions of the Council of the Marches of Wales; Yorkshire's gentry, in Charles's reign, disputed the powers of the Council of the North. In Durham the crown's authority, expressed through the bishop, threatened the local community's cohesion; indeed, the divisions among Durham's gentry may have paralleled those noted in Elizabethan Norfolk.[6]

If one issue focused the minds of the local gentry "wonderfully" on parliament's usefulness, it was the crown's incessant and growing demands for financial support. Members found themselves weighing not only the king's requirements but those of their constituents, who would expect an answer for their actions in parliament. Defense burdens had already increased county costs; after 1604 loans, gifts, contributions, and benevolences were repeatedly extracted from the county community's pockets and, moreover, without its consent. Ship money, however, had the greatest impact and finally provoked the greatest resistance.[7]

Parliament, thanks to the impact of taxation and the intervention of the government in county affairs, became all the more important to the local community. Parliament was, in Elton's apt phrase, "a point of contact between rulers and ruled"; and if and when the community felt its wishes were being ignored at court, parliament became even more valuable as the community's forum wherein its political voice could be heard. A segment of Durham's gentry, frustrated by the bishop's power, campaigned for parliamentary representation; it was their only way of gaining political influence. As tension developed, however, parliament was in danger of becoming a "point of friction" between "rulers and ruled"; it was becoming, for the county community, a barrier against an innovative, centralizing government.[8] However, the barrier itself was threatened by influence in elections, influence that, if unchecked, could lead to servile, packed parliaments, as many an anxious member noted in the Parliaments of 1614 and 1621. The court's electioneering could be seen as another threat to the local community's autonomy, as another sign of the government's determination to extend its authority. The resistance aroused by other innovations of the central government also surfaced in the struggle against influence in elections.

The House of Commons responded to the threat of influence by attempting to reform the statutes governing elections and by widening borough franchises. Its retention of Gatton and Blechingley's narrow franchises was for the same reason, to end "aristocratic or other unwanted influence." Bills were repeatedly introduced to deny the choice of candidates nominated by the great; in 1606 a bill would have prevented the return of a peer's "servant or retainer" or of anyone employed by a member "of this house." If influence was not eliminated, another member observed in 1614, it would only "bring in servitude." Similar sentiments were expressed in 1621, probably in 1624, and in 1640. The House of Commons' recurring anxiety over influence in elections was a clear signal of the county community's concern for parliament's survival as a "free" institution.[9] Such concerns also appeared in elections. Thomas Scott, defeated in Canterbury's 1626 election by an outsider, James Palmer, the nominee of the earl of Montgomery, bitterly complained that the choice of such "usurpers and intruders" meant the "loss of our fundamental liberty, and of free parliaments."[10]

Opposition to the return of outsiders marked many an election; it was an expression of the county community's loyalty to its own and of its determination to have its views expressed in parliament. It may also have been a sign of its increasing fear of the centralizing tendencies of early Stuart governments. Such factors may explain the fate of the outsiders nominated in 1621 and 1624 by the Duchy of Cornwall and the Prince's Council. Of the nominees listed by the duchy in those elections, seven were local men and all were returned; however, of the twenty-one outsiders nominated, only nine were elected, four in 1621 and five in 1624. The Prince's Council fared even worse; it intervened in thirteen borough elections in 1624, nominating strangers to all save one (Bewdley). Only four of the boroughs, Bewdley included, accepted its candidates. Lord Conway, governor of the Isle of Wight, had his nominees, outsiders all, refused by the island's three boroughs in 1628; they preferred instead to fill five of their six burgess-ships with members of leading local families. Buckingham's nominees in the Cinque Ports ran into trouble for the same reason; they were usually outsiders.[11]

Other patrons suffered reverses for similar reasons. Somersetshire's gentry refused to return the earl of Hertford's nominee, his nephew Lord Beauchamp, in 1621 because "the place of knight for the shire, do properly belong unto the gent[lemen] inhabiting in the country"; indeed, if Beauchamp were chosen, "the liberty of our country" would be jeopardized. Like sentiments were expressed in Anglesey's 1624 election, and Dorsetshire's contested 1626 election revolved around the fact that Sir George Morton "lived in Oxfordshire wholly and was scarce known in this county." St. Albans took a similar stand with its patron, the second earl of Salisbury, in 1628.[12]

The success or failure of outsiders in elections is a good barometer of the county community's electoral record. Victory for an outsider was a triumph for influence in elections, the influence of the local elite's competitors, the peerage, and court. It could also signal another successful challenge to the concept of "free" parliaments. And from 1604 through 1628, such fears seemed justified. On average, 122 outsiders were chosen by all constituencies for each parliament. But the story dramatically changed in the elections of 1640. Taking the figure 122 as the base figure, the number of outsiders chosen in 1640 fell by about one-third (33.6 percent in the spring and 35.2 percent in the autumn).[13]

The decline in the number of outsiders returned, an indication of the decline in the influence of the peerage and the court, can also be traced in the returns for two member borough constituencies. Using average figures for the elections of 1604–28, 84 borough residents, 168 county residents, and 112 outsiders were usually chosen for each parliament. Taking the number of county residents customarily chosen (168) as the base figure, the number of county gentry elected in the spring 1640 election rose by 22 percent and by nearly 30 percent in the autumn election. In the same elections, the number of outsiders returned dropped by almost 35 percent. In actual figures, 158 county residents were elected in 1624, a number that gradually increased until, in the spring of 1640, it reached 205, a total exceeded in the autumn when 218 county residents were returned. In the same elections, the number of outsiders chosen dropped from 118 in 1624 to 103 in 1628 and then fell to its early seventeenth-century low of 72 in the autumn 1640 election.[14] The resident gentry, the elite of the county community, had won the battle for influence with the peerage and the court; indeed, they had captured the dominant electoral role in early Stuart England.

The elections of 1640, as Hirst remarked, "reveal a new world when compared with their immediate predecessors."[15] And, in terms of patronage and influence, they clearly did. The influence of a great peer, a Buckingham, Pembroke, or Arundel, was hardly what it was before. The court's agencies, too, were made aware of the change: in 1640, the Duchy of Cornwall was humiliated; the Duchy of Lancaster saw to the return of fewer candidates than in any other early seventeenth-century election; and the lord wardens suffered similar rebuffs. In 1640 the influence of a Fairfax or Belasyse in Yorkshire, a Barnardiston in Suffolk, or a Pelham in Sussex counted for more than the power and prestige of an earl of Northumberland or an earl of Huntingdon. The influence that counted in 1640 was the influence of the gentry, of the county residents who, because of their close ties to their communities, were regarded by an active and interested electorate as the men who could put things right in a troubled England.

The gentry's very closeness to their communities was an incomparable advantage in elections. They could appeal to an electorate that, as Hirst observed, "was gradually coming to think in terms of national issues." Indeed, his very qualification, that the electorate's "reaction was often localist resentment at the impact of national policies," served the local gentry well. Who could better serve the community and voice the local grievances that vexed an increasingly aware electorate? The "larger political nation was increasingly becoming involved," and its very involvement served the local gentry well.[16] An outsider, nominated by a court agency or by a patron linked to the court — a court that was readily (and rightly) blamed for wrongheaded religious policies, an unpopular war with the Scots, and ship money — had little chance of winning the support of an electorate already discontented, if not outraged, by those very policies.

The involvement of the electorate served, too, as a forecast of things to come. Indeed, it perhaps suggested the day when even the influence of the county elite would be at risk. In the spring elections, a group of "factious nonconformists," including a saddler, a turner, a hemp dresser, and a glover, had played a significant role in Sandwich's election, and in Essex, Lord Maynard was appalled at the electioneering of "fellows without shirts." Similar incidents occurred in the fall; "men of so mean condition" helped wreck Robert Read's candidacy at Hastings, and Bulstrode Whitelocke's campaign for a place at Great Marlow was orchestrated by one Toucher Carter, "a country fellow in a plain and mean habit" who organized "the ordinary sort of townsmen" in Whitelocke's behalf, including "the bargemen of the town [who] came in one and all for Mr. Hoby and me." Lord Paget's nominee (he was lord of the borough) was refused because, so Whitelocke was told, Paget's recommendation "will not do it in these times, blessed be God." Thus, the "country fellow" in humble garb, with the aid of the bargemen and ordinary folk, turned Great Marlow's election upside down. So much for the influence of a peer in 1640. As Christopher Hill had realized, to borrow his phrase, "the many-headed monster," the humble folk so feared by Tudor and Stuart society, was coming on stage.[17]

1. Between 1604 and 1628, the court, on average, intervened in 11.6% of all elections, and the peerage, again on average, was involved in 43% of the elections. Together, then, the peerage and court intervened in over half the elections held before the Parliaments of 1604–28. See Appendix Two.

2. *Commons Journal*, 1:470–71; Notestein et al., eds., *Common Debates, 1621*, 7:643.

3. The figures in this paragraph are taken from the tables evaluating the electioneering of the peerage in Appendix Two.

4. These figures and those that follow are based on the table assessing the court's electioneering in Appendix Two.

5. L. Stone, *The Causes of the English Revolution, 1529–1642*, pp. 106–8; James, *Family, Lineage, and Civil Society*, p. 190; Fletcher, *County Community*, pp. 151, 213, 224; Coate, *Cornwall*, p. 9; Morrill, *Cheshire*, pp. 2–4; Hassell Smith, *County and Court*, pp. 61, 108, 112, 181, 247–76; I. Roots, "The Central Government and the Local Community," in E. W. Ives, ed., *The English Revolution, 1600–1660*, pp. 37, 40, 41, 42; A. Everitt, "The County Community," in Ives, ed., *English Revolution*, pp. 51, 54; A. Everitt, "Social Mobility in Early Modern England." pp. 59, 60, 62.

6. Morrill, *Cheshire*, pp. 2–4, 26–27, 30; Fletcher, *County Community*, pp. 76–93, 148–49, 179, 185, 186–87, 188, 195, 200–201, 224–25; Hassell Smith, *County and Court*, pp. 16–19, 121–24, 126–33, 137–38, 147–48, 157–200, 242, 245–46, 247–76, 277, 285–86, 314–30, 336–37, 338–39; Cliffe, *Yorkshire Gentry*, pp. 296–300, 302; James, *Family, Lineage, and Civil Society*, pp. 156–57, 160–61, 164–68, 190; Ketton-Cremer, *Norfolk in the Civil War*, pp. 62–88; Roots, "The Central Government and the Local Community," in Ives, ed., *English Revolution*, p. 45; L. M. Hill, "County Government in Caroline England," in Russell, ed., *Origins*, pp. 78, 79; C. Russell, *The Crisis of Parliaments*, pp. 214–16; N. Tyacke, "Puritanism, Arminianism, and Counter-Revolution," in Russell, ed., *Origins*, pp. 119–43.

7. Hassell Smith, *County and Court*, pp. 245, 275–76, 334; Fletcher, *County Community*, pp. 205, 211, 212, 213; Cliffe, *Yorkshire Gentry*, pp. 285, 287–90, 291–93, 296–97, 305, 313, 316; Coate, *Cornwall*, p. 22; Hirst, *Representative of the People?*, pp. 166, 170, 171, 172–74; Russell, "Parliamentary History in Perspective, 1604–1629," pp. 13–14, 25–26; Morrill, *Cheshire*, pp. 28, 30; James, *Family, Lineage, and Civil Society*, pp. 172–73; L. M. Hill, "County Government in Caroline England," pp. 79, 85–86.

8. Stone, *Causes*, p. 108; Zagorin, *Court and Country*, pp. 85–86; Hassell Smith, *County and Court*, pp. 245, 275–76, 323, 330 31, 333–36; James, *Family, Lineage, and Civil Society*, pp. 164–67, 190; M. Hawkins, "The Government: Its Role and Its Aims," in Russell, ed., *Origins*, pp. 40, 42, 44; J. H. Elliott, "England and Europe: A Common Malady?," in ibid., pp. 253, 254; Elton, "Tudor Government: The Points of Contact: I. Parliament," p. 200; Russell, "Parliamentary History in Perspective, 1604–1629," pp. 26–27.

9. Hirst, *Representative of the People?*, pp. 66, 67, 73–75, 83, 88, app. 7, pp. 229–31; D. H. Willson, ed., *The Parliamentary Diary of Robert Bowyer, 1606–1607*, pp. 88, 100; *Commons Journal*, 1:463, 470, 471, 477, 478, 478–479, 513, 649–50; Notestein et al., eds., *Commons Debates, 1621*, 2:277–78, 431; 3:411–12; 4:421–22, 446–47; 6:193; Plumb, "The Growth of the Electorate in England from 1600 to 1715," pp. 98–99, 100.

10. Scott's election bid was supported by a number of Canterbury clergymen who, following Preston's admonitions on elections, preached against the election of a stranger since such choices might "quench . . . the light or lamp of England." Free parliaments, one clergyman claimed, were doomed "until free and legal elections be recovered." Scott MSS, 55v, 57, 58–59v, 89, 90, 91v, 113v, 120–21, 122, 125v. For Preston's admonitions on elections, see C. Hill, *Puritanism and Revolution*, pp. 262–63, and Walzer, *The Revolution of the Saints*, pp. 259–60.

11. Pontefract, after choosing the prince's candidate in 1624, refused his second nominee in a subsequent bye-election. Hertford could be added to Bewdley as a borough where the prince backed a local man since, when the prince's original

nominees (both outsiders) were withdrawn, the Prince's Council nominated Sir William Harrington. It made no difference; Harrington was still refused. Lord Conway to the Mayor and Burgesses of Newport, 1 Feb. 1628, the same to the Mayor and Burgesses of Yarmouth, 1 Feb. 1628, the same to Leigh, 2 Feb. 1628, the same to the Mayor and Burgesses of Newton, 2 Feb. 1628, the same to the Deputy Lieutenants of the Isle of Wight, 2 Feb. 1628, Oglander to Conway, 17 Feb. 1628, Conway to Oglander, 21 Feb. 1628, P.R.O., St. P. Dom. 16/92:4, 6, 15, 16, 17, 93:60, 94:9; "Sir John Oglander," *DNB*, 14:928; Black, *Parl. Hist. Isle of Wight*, pp. 5, 11–13, app. 2, pp. 32–33. Conway nominated Robert Read and his cousin Greville at Yarmouth, his son Sir Edward Conway, junior, at Newport, and Thomas Mallett at Newtown. Hirst, *Representative of the People?*, pp. 8, 140–41.

12. Horner and Others to the Earl of Hertford, 14 Dec. 1620, House of Commons Library Manuscript No. 19, in the custody of the House of Lords Record Office; Owen Wynn to Sir Jo. Wynn, 3 Dec. 1623, NLW, Wynn MSS (9059E), 1172; *Somerset and Dorset Notes and Queries* 4 (1894–95): 23–24; Stone, "The Electoral Influence of the Second Earl of Salisbury, 1614–68," pp. 389–90; Hirst, *Representative of the People?*, pp. 160, 164, 179–81.

13. The number of outsiders returned fell from 132 in 1624 to 113 in 1628 and to but 81 in the spring of 1640 and 79 in the autumn. These figures are taken from the table showing the number of outsiders elected for all constituencies, 1604–40, in Appendix Three.

14. These figures are taken from Appendix Four.

15. Hirst, *Representative of the People?*, p. 147.

16. Ibid., p. 153.

17. The Mayor and Jurats of Sandwich to Nicholas, 19 Mar. 1640, P.R.O., St. P. Dom. 16/448:33 and enclosure i; Philpot to Nicholas, 19 Mar. 1640, P.R.O., St. P. Dom. 16/448:34; Maynard to Barrington, 19 Mar. 1640, BM Egerton MSS 2646, f. 142; Robt. Read to the Mayor of Hastings, 11 Oct. 1640, P.R.O., St. P. Dom. 16/469:86 and enclosure i; M. R. Frear, "The Election at Great Marlow in 1640," pp. 433–48 and sources cited therein; C. Hill, "The Many-Headed Monster in Late Tudor and Early Stuart Political Thinking," in C. H. Carter, ed., *From the Renaissance to the Counter-Reformation: Essays in Honour of Garrett Mattingly*, pp. 296–317; C. Hill, *The World Turned Upside Down*, passim. For the continuing struggle against centralization and influence, among the "middle sort of people," see B. Manning, *The English People and the English Revolution, 1640–1649*, passim, especially pp. 234, 236, 268, 269, 276, 278, 302, 305, 306, 307–12.

# Appendix One

This appendix suggests the patronage, certain, probable, and possible, that accounted for elections to the Parliaments of 1604–40.[1] It includes those members returned for all constituencies. The letter N identifies those whose elections are credited to the influence of the peerage; a G indicates gentry influence; a T the intervention of a borough corporation; the U for those few members who owed their choice to the university electorates; an R for those chosen thanks to the intervention of a court agency or the lord warden; a C suggests that a clerical peer (bishop, archbishop) was probably responsible; and ? indicates that it is impossible to even suggest the influence behind the particular return.

| Election | N | G | T | U | R | C | ? | Parl. Places |
|---|---|---|---|---|---|---|---|---|
| 1604 | 112 | 215 | 107 | 4 | 28 | 5 | 2 | 473 |
| 1614 | 114 | 218 | 77 | 1 | 48 | 7 | 8 | 473 |
| 1621 | 107 | 236 | 81 | 2 | 40 | 9 | 6 | 481 |
| 1624 | 123 | 213 | 96 | 2 | 42 | 9 | 4 | 489 |
| 1625 | 139 | 228 | 85 | 1 | 22 | 9 | 5 | 489 |
| 1626 | 134 | 237 | 89 | 2 | 19 | 6 | 2 | 489 |
| 1628 | 121 | 264 | 84 | 2 | 17 | 2 | 3 | 493 |
| s1640 | 113 | 246 | 91 | 2 | 30 | 5 | 6 | 493 |
| a1640 | 107 | 267 | 92 | 2 | 23 | 2 | 0 | 493 |

1. Certain evidence of electioneering is based on direct evidence only. Probable electoral patronage is based on family connection, clientage, or service connections, and possible electoral patronage is determined by the choice of an outsider by a customary patronage borough controlled by a particular peer or manor lord.

# Appendix Two

The influence of the peerage, both clerical and lay, and the court in elections, 1604–40.

| Election | Elections | Elections involving peerage | Identified places | Places won, or possibly won, through peerage influence |
|---|---|---|---|---|
| 1604 | 250 | 102 (40.8%) | 471 | 117 (24.8%) |
| 1614 | 251 | 103 (41.0%) | 465 | 121 (26.0%) |
| 1621 | 254 | 99 (38.9%) | 475 | 116 (24.4%) |
| 1624 | 258 | 116 (44.9%) | 485 | 132 (27.2%) |
| 1625 | 258 | 124 (48.0%) | 484 | 148 (30.5%) |
| 1626 | 258 | 116 (44.9%) | 487 | 140 (28.7%) |
| 1628 | 260 | 112 (43.0%) | 490 | 123 (25.1%) |
| s1640 | 260 | 104 (40.0%) | 487 | 118 (24.2%) |
| a1640 | 260 | 94 (36.1%) | 493 | 109 (22.1%) |

The influence of the Lord Warden and the various court agencies.

| Election | Elections | Elections involving the court | Identified places | Places won, or possibly won, through court influence |
|---|---|---|---|---|
| 1604 | 250 | 26 (10.4%) | 471 | 28 (5.9%) |
| 1614 | 251 | 39 (15.5%) | 465 | 48 (10.3%) |
| 1621 | 254 | 41 (16.1%) | 475 | 40 (8.4%) |
| 1624 | 258 | 51 (19.7%) | 485 | 42 (8.6%) |
| 1625 | 258 | 21 (8.1%) | 484 | 22 (4.5%) |
| 1626 | 258 | 19 (7.3%) | 487 | 19 (3.9%) |
| 1628 | 260 | 19 (7.3%) | 490 | 17 (3.4%) |
| s1640 | 260 | 54 (20.7%) | 487 | 30 (6.2%) |
| a1640 | 260 | 38 (14.6%) | 493 | 23 (4.6%) |

The electoral patronage of the court, by agent or agency, 1604–1640.

| Patron | 1604 | 1614 | 1621 | 1624 | 1625 | 1626 | 1628 | s1640 | a1640 |
|---|---|---|---|---|---|---|---|---|---|
| D. Cornwall | | 10 | 15 | 15 | | | | 18 | 8 |
| D. Lancaster | 8 | 9 | 10 | 13 | 10 | 10 | 8 | 9 | 8 |
| Prince's C. | | | 2 | 13 | | | | 3 | 2 |
| C. North | 7 | 8 | 4 | 1 | 2 | | 1 | 9 | 8 |
| C. M. Wales | 1 | 1 | 1 | 1 | 1 | 1 | 1 | 3 | 2 |
| Privy C. | 3 | 4 | 2 | 1 | 1 | 1 | 2 | | |
| Ld. Wd. | 7 | 7 | 7 | 7 | 7 | 7 | 7 | 7 | 7 |
| Queen's C. | | | | | | | | 5 | 3 |
| Totals | 26 | 39 | 41 | 51 | 21 | 19 | 19 | 54 | 38 |

Places won, or probably or possibly won, through court intervention, 1604–1640.

| Patron | 1604 | 1614 | 1621 | 1624 | 1625 | 1626 | 1628 | s1640 | a1640 |
|---|---|---|---|---|---|---|---|---|---|
| D. Cornwall | | 12 | 14 | 10 | | | | 5 | |
| D. Lancaster | 9 | 10 | 11 | 16 | 12 | 12 | 9 | 8 | 6 |
| Prince's C. | | | 1 | 4 | | | | 1 | 1 |
| C. North | 9 | 10 | 2 | | | | 1 | 8 | 8 |
| C. M. Wales | 1 | 1 | 1 | 1 | 1 | 1 | 1 | 3 | 2 |
| Privy C. | 2 | 5 | 1 | 1 | 1 | 1 | | | |
| Ld. Wd. | 7 | 10 | 10 | 10 | 8 | 5 | 6 | 4 | 5 |
| Queen's C. | | | | | | | | 1 | 1 |
| Totals | 28 | 48 | 40 | 42 | 22 | 19 | 17 | 30 | 23 |

The electioneering of the peerage, both clerical and lay, divided into the certain, probable, and possible categories, 1604–1640.

| ELECTORAL INVOLVEMENT | | | | | PLACES SECURED | | | |
|---|---|---|---|---|---|---|---|---|
| Election | Certain | Probable | Possible | Total | Certain | Probable | Possible | Total |
| 1604 | 20 | 55 | 27 | 102 | 14 | 66 | 37 | 117 |
| 1614 | 27 | 59 | 17 | 103 | 23 | 73 | 25 | 121 |
| 1621 | 33 | 53 | 13 | 99 | 32 | 67 | 17 | 116 |
| 1624 | 32 | 63 | 21 | 116 | 24 | 80 | 28 | 132 |
| 1625 | 31 | 68 | 25 | 124 | 29 | 83 | 36 | 148 |
| 1626 | 31 | 69 | 16 | 116 | 29 | 78 | 33 | 140 |
| 1628 | 33 | 59 | 20 | 112 | 31 | 67 | 25 | 123 |
| s1640 | 32 | 58 | 14 | 104 | 22 | 76 | 20 | 118 |
| a1640 | 16 | 63 | 15 | 94 | 14 | 78 | 17 | 109 |

The court's electioneering, again divided into the certain, probable, and possible categories, 1604–1640.

| ELECTORAL INVOLVEMENT | | | | | PLACES SECURED | | | |
|---|---|---|---|---|---|---|---|---|
| Election | Certain | Probable | Possible | Total | Certain | Probable | Possible | Total |
| 1604 | 11 | 9 | 6 | 26 | 10 | 11 | 7 | 28 |
| 1614 | 10 | 18 | 11 | 39 | 12 | 26 | 10 | 48 |
| 1621 | 29 | 9 | 3 | 41 | 23 | 13 | 4 | 40 |
| 1624 | 37 | 8 | 5 | 50 | 25 | 12 | 5 | 42 |
| 1625 | 11 | 7 | 3 | 21 | 9 | 9 | 4 | 22 |
| 1626 | 9 | 8 | 2 | 19 | 7 | 9 | 3 | 19 |
| 1628 | 10 | 7 | 2 | 19 | 7 | 7 | 3 | 17 |
| s1640 | 33 | 17 | 4 | 54 | 8 | 17 | 5 | 30 |
| a1640 | 23 | 12 | 3 | 38 | 0 | 20 | 3 | 23 |

The N indicates the number of nominees; O indicates the number of outsiders among those nominees.

| | 1604 N–O | 1614 N–O | 1621 N–O | 1624 N–O | 1625 N–O | 1626 N–O | 1628 N–O | s1640 N–O | a1640 N–O |
|---|---|---|---|---|---|---|---|---|---|
| D. Cornwall | | 12–10 | 21–13 | 17–12 | | | | 20–18 | 8–8 |
| D. Lancaster | 10–9 | 12–9 | 13–10 | 19–14 | 14–12 | 13–10 | 10–7 | 9–7 | 8–7 |
| Prince's C. | | | 3–3 | 15–13 | | | | 2–2 | 2–2 |
| C. North | 9–1 | 11–5 | 4–0 | 1–0 | 1–0 | | 1–1 | 12–3 | 13–2 |
| C. M. Wales | 1–1 | | 1–1 | 1–0 | 1–0 | 1–0 | 1–0 | 5–2 | 2–0 |
| Privy C. | 2–0 | 5–1 | 3–0 | 1–0 | 1–0 | 1–0 | 1–0 | | |
| Ld. Wd. | 7–5 | 10–2 | 11–8 | 10–8 | 12–8 | 10–10 | 9–4 | 7–5 | 8–5 |
| Queen's C. | | | | | | | | 5–3 | 3–2 |
| Totals | 29–16 | 50–27 | 56–35 | 64–47 | 29–20 | 25–20 | 22–12 | 60–40 | 44–26 |

Total identified court nominees: 379

Total of outsiders nominated: 243 (64.1%)

# Appendix Three

The figures below represent the number of outsiders returned, all constituencies.

| 1604 | 1614 | 1621 | 1624 | 1625 | 1626 | 1628 | s1640 | a1640 |
|------|------|------|------|------|------|------|-------|-------|
| 102  | 131  | 122  | 132  | 129  | 124  | 113  | 81    | 79    |

# Appendix Four

These tables reflect the number of two-member boroughs that elected county residents (CR in the tables), borough residents (BR in the tables), and outsiders (O in the tables) and the number of county residents, borough residents, and outsiders, when identification was possible, that were returned. Following Neale, recorders were counted as borough residents. His tables, for the elections of 1584 and 1593, have been included for purposes of comparison.

| | Borough Returns | | | | | | | | | | |
| --- | 1584 | 1593 | 1604 | 1614 | 1621 | 1624 | 1625 | 1626 | 1628 | s1640 | a1640 |
| Two BR | 22 | 19 | 33 | 18 | 20 | 28 | 20 | 19 | 19 | 23 | 20 |
| BR & CR | 18 | 16 | 21 | 18 | 20 | 23 | 30 | 29 | 28 | 34 | 31 |
| BR & O | 21 | 20 | 18 | 17 | 16 | 15 | 12 | 17 | 15 | 12 | 13 |
| CR & O | 34 | 45 | 45 | 51 | 39 | 57 | 51 | 54 | 40 | 37 | 39 |
| Two O | 39 | 36 | 15 | 26 | 30 | 23 | 27 | 22 | 24 | 12 | 10 |

| | Places Won by County and Borough Residents and Ooutsiders | | | | | | | | | | |
| --- | 1584 | 1593 | 1604 | 1614 | 1621 | 1624 | 1625 | 1626 | 1628 | s1640 | a1640 |
| BR | 83 | 74 | 105 | 70 | 76 | 94 | 82 | 84 | 81 | 92 | 84 |
| CR | 116 | 105 | 156 | 158 | 167 | 158 | 169 | 175 | 192 | 205 | 218 |
| O | 133 | 137 | 93 | 120 | 115 | 118 | 117 | 115 | 103 | 73 | 72 |

# Appendix Five

The table below reflects the influence in county elections. G identifies those probably returned through resident gentry influence. An R marks those elected through the patronage of a court agency. An N suggests that the influence of the peerage, clerical and lay, was probably responsible for the choice. A U indicates that no patronage definition may be suggested. A number in parenthesis to the right of a given figure indicates the number of outsiders returned.

| | G | N | R | U | Total county members |
|---|---|---|---|---|---|
| 1604 | 59 | 27+(1) | 3 | 0 | 90 |
| 1614 | 63 | 22+(1) | 4 | 0 | 90 |
| 1621 | 64 | 26 | 0 | 0 | 90 |
| 1624 | 58+(3) | 27+(2) | 0 | 0 | 90 |
| 1625 | 54+(3) | 28+(2) | 0 | 0 | 90 |
| 1626 | 61+(2) | 27 | 0 | 0 | 90 |
| 1628 | 62+(3) | 25 | 0 | 0 | 90 |
| s1640 | 51+(1) | 34 | 3 | 1 | 90 |
| a1640 | 60 | 29 | 1 | 0 | 90 |
| Totals | 532+(12) | 249+(5) | 11 | 1 | 793+(17) |
| | 544 | 254 | 11 | 1 | 810 |

# Appendix Six

---

This appendix attempts to indicate both the patronage responsible, or probably responsible, for the candidate's election and his residency. The following letters suggest the patronage and residency of the members elected to the parliaments of 1603–40:

- N: This letter identifies the influence or probable influence of an aristocratic patron. When an N appears, it indicates that the member elected owed his return to aristocratic intervention and was, in addition, a kinsman of the peer involved and a resident within the county of the borough that returned him.
- T: A T suggests that the place was filled by a member of the town corporation or a resident of the town who was elected through his own or the borough corporation's influence.
- C: This letter signifies the successful patronage of a great cleric; if used alone, it also marks the election of a kinsman of a bishop or archbishop.
- G: The letter G indicates the influence of the neighbouring county squire. It also serves to identify the member chosen as a county resident who secured, or probably secured, his election through his own influence or that of the local gentry.
- R: An R reflects the intervention of a royal agency such as the Privy Council, the Duchy of Cornwall, or the Duchy of Lancaster. It is used solely as a patronage symbol and will appear, therefore, in combination with other letters signifying the member's residency.
- O: An O indicates the choice of an outsider, by definition a member of parliament who has no discernible connection with the borough or county that elected him. It is always used in combination with another letter indicating the patronage behind, or probably behind, the return of the outsider.
- U: This letter identifies those members elected by the universities who either were connected with the university or who were chosen, without evident outside interference, by the university electorate.

In order to suggest both patronage and residency, the letters are often employed in combinations of two letters. The first letter identifies the patronage thought responsible for a member's election, and the last letter marks him either as a resident (T for a borough resident, G for a county resident) or as an outsider (O). For example, if, after a member's name, the letters NO appear, it indicates that aristocratic influence was, or presumably was, responsible for that member's return and that the burgess or knight elected was an outsider. An RG signifies the election of a county resident (G) who was assisted, in his winning election bid, by a royal agency's patronage (R). A TO would reflect the election, thanks to the intervention of a borough's corporation, of an outsider. If local gentry were behind the return of an outsider, it would be shown by the letters GO. When no determination, of either patronage or residency, can be suggested, a question mark (?) is used; it is also employed when the identity of the burgess elected is unknown. For reasons of space, bye-elections are not included nor are the names of those elected. The letters used in the table follow the names as listed in the Official Return. Thus, for Bedfordshire in 1604, the two knights elected were Oliver St. John and Sir Edward Ratcliffe. Using the symbols, N is employed for St. John, G for Ratcliffe. The entry for the table (see page 230 ff.) for Bedfordshire under 1604 would be N.G.

| | 1604 | 1614 | 1621 | 1624 | 1625 | 1626 | 1628 | s1640 | a1640 |
|---|---|---|---|---|---|---|---|---|---|
| Bedfordsh. | N.G. | N.G.N.G. | N.NG. | N.NG. | N.NG. | N.NG. | N.NG. | N.NG. | N.NG. |
| Bedford | G.T. | N.G. | N.NT. | N.NT. | N.NT. | N.NT. | N.NT. | N.NG. | N.NG. |
| Berkshire | N.G. | G.G. | G.N. | G.G. | N.G. | G.G. | G.G. | G.G. | G.G. |
| Abingdon | G. | N. | G. | N.T. | N.T. | N.T. | N.T. | G. | G. |
| Reading | NG.G. | G.N. | NG.T. | N.G. | NO.G. | NO.G. | N.G. | CO.NO. | G.G. |
| Wallingfd. | G.T. | NO.G. | G.NG. | NO.T. | G.NG. | NO.T. | NO.?O. | G.G. | G.T. |
| Windsor | G.NT. | G.T. | NO.T. | G.G. | G.G. | G.G. | G.G. | NO.G. | NO.T. |
| Buckinghamsh. | G.G. | G.G. | G.G. | GO.G. | GO.GO. | G.G. | G.G. | G.G. | G.G. |
| Amersham | | | | G.GO. | GO.GO. | G.NO. | G.NO. | G.G. | G.G. |
| Aylesbury | G.G. | G.G. | G.G. | G.NO. | G.NO. | N.G. | G.G. | G.N. | G.G. |
| Buckingham | G.G. | G.G. | G.NO. | G.NO. | NO.G. | G.G. | G.T. | GO.G. | NO.G. |
| Gt. Marlowe | | | | G.G. | G.G. | G.T. | GO.T. | G.T. | G.G. |
| Wendover | | | | G.G. | G.T. | GO.GO. | NO.U. | NG.G. | G.T. |
| C. Wycombe | G.G. | GO.G. | GO.G. | G.G. | GO.T. | NO.U. | G.G. | GO.TO. | NG.G. |
| Cambridgesh. | G.G. | G.G. | G.G. | T.T. | CO.NO. | G.G. | T.T. | U.NO. | T.TO. |
| Cambridge | T.T. | NO.T. | T.NO. | NG.G. | G.G. | T.T. | G.NG. | G.G. | U.NO. |
| Cambridge U. | U.U. | NG.NO. | NO.U. | NCO.U. | T.T. | NG.G. | G.NO. | T.T. | G.G. |
| Cheshire | G.G. | G.G. | G.G. | G.G. | G.G. | GO.GO. | G.NO. | G.RO. | T.T. |
| Chester | T.T. | T.T. | T.T. | T.T. | NO.GO. | NO.G. | GO.G. | G.G. | G.G. |
| Cornwall | G.G. | G.G. | G.G. | NG.G. | NO.GO. | G.NO. | GO.GO. | GO.GO. | G.G. |
| Bodmin | G.T. | G.RO. | GO.GO. | NG.GO. | GO.NGO. | GO.GO. | NO.NO. | RO.G. | GO.GO. |
| Bossiney | NO.GO. | G.G. | G.G. | RO.RG. | G.G. | NO.G. | G.G. | RO.T. | NO.GO. |
| Callington | G.NO. | CO.RO. | G.NO. | GO.RO. | NO.GO. | G.G. | NO.T. | G.G. | GO.G. |
| Camelford | CO.G. | G.? | RO.GO. | RG.NO. | G.T. | G.T. | NO.G. | G.G. | G.G. |
| Fowey | G.G. | RO.G. | G.G. | G.G. | NG.G. | T.NO. | GO.NO. | ?.T. | G.G. |
| Grampound | G.NO. | G.GO. | GO.RO. | RO.GO. | NO.GO. | NO.GO. | G.NO. | G.T. | G.G. |
| Helston | NO.T. | RO.RO. | RG.NG. | RO.NO. | GO.NO. | NO.NO. | G.G. | G.G. | G.T. |
| Launceston | NO.G. | G.T. | G.RG. | T.G. | ?.? | NO.G. | G.GO. | ?.T. | T.T. |
| Liskeard | G.GO. | G.G. | RO.G. | RO.G. | GO.G. | GO.GO. | GO.GO. | G.T. | G.G. |
| E. Looe | GO.NO. | RO.G. | RO.RO. | NO.NO. | NG.G. | G.GO. | G.GO. | G.G. | G.G. |
| W. Looe | NO.NO. | NO.RO. | G.RO. | RO.GO. | GO.GO. | G.NGO. | | RO.? | G.G. |
| Lostwithiel | NO.G. | NO.GO. | G.RO. | G.G. | CO.GO. | GO.GO. | | G.T. | G.G. |
| Michael | G.GO. | RO.GO. | G.? | NG.T. | NO.G. | NG.GO. | | GO.GO. | G.GO. |
| Newport | NG.GO. | G.GO. | RO.G. | GO.G. | | GO.GO. | | G.CO. | GO.G. |
| Penryn | NO.? | NG.GO. | GO.GO. | NO.CO. | | CO.GO. | | RO.GO. | G.GO. |
| St. Germans | CO.G. | CG.CO. | CO.G. | G.? | | NG.GO. | | | GO.GO. |
| St. Ives | NO.T. | RO.G. | NO.GO. | | | G.NO. | | | G.GO. |

| | 1604 | 1614 | 1621 | 1624 | 1625 | 1626 | 1628 | s1640 | a1640 |
|---|---|---|---|---|---|---|---|---|---|
| St. Mawes | NO.G. | G.RO. | RO.RO. | G.RO. | NO.NO. | NO.NO. | G.NO. | CO.NO. | G.CO. |
| Saltash | G.NO. | RO.RO. | RO.GO. | RO.G. | T.G. | T.GO. | T.NO. | G.G. | G.GO. |
| Tregony | T.T. | GO.GO. | GO.GO. | G.G. | G.NO. | G.N. | G.G. | G.G. | G.G. |
| Truro | T.T. | ?.T. | CO.G. | T.T. | G.NG. | G.NG. | T.G. | NG.G. | NG.G. |
| Cumberland | G.G. | G.G. | G.G. | G.G. | G.G. | G.G. | G.G. | G.G. | G.G. |
| Carlisle | T.T. | NO.NO. | NO.NO. | NO.T. | NO.T. | NO.NG. | G.NG. | G.G. | G.G. |
| Derbysh. | G.G. | NO.N. | N.G. | N.N. | N.N. | N.NG. | NO.G. | ?.G. | T.T. |
| Derby | T.T. | G.T. | T.NO. | NO.T. | NO.T. | G.NO. | NO.T. | ?.G. | G.G. |
| Devonsh. | G.G. | G.G. | G.G. | G.G. | G.G. | G.G. | G.G. | T.T. | T.T. |
| Barnstaple | NO.T. | NO.T. | T.T. | T.T. | T.T. | NO.T. | G.G. | G.G. | GO.G. |
| Beeralston | NO.G. | GO.GO. | GO.G. | GO.G. | GO.G. | G.G. | NO.T. | G.G. | G.T. |
| Dartmouth | NO.T. | GO.GO. | T.T. | T.T. | G.T. | G.T. | G.G. | G.T. | T.T. |
| Exeter | T.T. | T.T. | T.T. | T.T. | T.T. | T.T. | G.T. | T.T. | T.T. |
| Plymouth | T.T. | T.T. | T.T. | T.T. | T.T. | T.T. | T.T. | T.T. | T.NO. |
| P.¹ Earl | G.GO. | G.G. | G.G. | G.NO. | G.G. | G.G. | T.T. | T.G. | N.NO. |
| Tavistock | NO.NO. | G.NO. | G.NO. | NO.G. | G.NO. | NO.NO. | G.NG. | G.NO. | T.G. |
| Tiverton | ..... | ..... | G.G. | G.T. | NO.G. | G.G. | G.NO. | NO.G. | NO.G. |
| Totness | T.T. | TO.T. | G.T. | G.G. | G.G. | G.T. | G.G. | G.N. | G.N. |
| Dorsetsh. | G.G. | N.G. | G.G. | G.G. | G.G. | GO.G. | G.T. | G.G. | T.G. |
| Bridport | T.T. | G.T. | G.G. | GO.GO. | T.NG. | NG.NG. | G.G. | GO.G. | GO.G. |
| Corfe C. | GO.T. | G.GO. | GO.G. | T.T. | GO.GO. | GO.T. | GO.G. | T.T. | T.T. |
| Dorchester | T.T. | T.G. | GO.T. | G.T. | T.T. | T.T. | G.GO. | G.G. | T.G. |
| Lyme Regis | T.T. | G.G. | GO.T. | NO.T. | G.GO. | G.GO. | T.T. | GO.T. | GO.T. |
| Poole | T.T. | G.GO. | G.G. | G.GO. | G.GO. | G.GO. | G.GO. | T.NO. | T.NO. |
| Shaftesb. | NO.T. | NO.NO. | T.NO. | T.T. | NO.T. | NO.T. | G.GO. | G.T. | G.G. |
| Wareham | G.NO. | G.G. | G.G. | G.T. | G.GO. | G.GO. | NO.NO. | NG.NG. | G.G. |
| Weymouth | T.T. | GO.GO. | T.T. | G.GO. | G.GO. | G.GO. | G.G. | NG.T. | T.G. |
| Melcombe R. | NO.NG. | T.G. | GO.GO. | T.T. | GO.T. | T.T. | T.NG. | NG.NO. | N.NG. |
| Essex | T.TO. | NO.NO. | NG.G. | NG.NG. | NG.NG. | NG.NG. | NG.NG. | G.T. | NG.T. |
| Colchester | NO.NO. | T.TO. | T.TO. | T.TO. | T.TO. | NG.T. | NG.TO. | NG.NG. | NG.NG. |
| Harwich | NO.G. | NG.NO. | NG.G. | N.G. | NO.G. | N.G. | N.G. | NG.T. | G.NO. |
| Maldon | NO.G. | G.G. | GO.G. | NG.NG. | NG.G. | NG.NG. | NG.NG. | NG.NG. | NO.NO. |
| Gloucestersh. | N.NG. | G.NG. | G.NG. | G.G. | NG.G. | G.G. | G.G. | G.T. | G.G. |
| Bristol | T.T. | T.T. | T.T. | T.T. | T.T. | T.T. | T.T. | T.T. | T.T. |
| Cirencester | NO.G. | NO.G. | GO.G. | G.T. | G.T. | G.T. | GO.T. | T.T. | T.T. |
| Gloucester | T.T. | T.T. | T.T. | T.T. | T.T. | T.T. | G.T. | NO.NO. | NO.NO. |
| Tewkesbury | NO.G. | GO.NO. | GO.NO. | GO.G. | GO.G. | GO.G. | G.GO. | NO.NO. | NO.NO. |

| | 1604 | 1614 | 1621 | 1624 | 1625 | 1626 | 1628 | s1640 | a1640 |
|---|---|---|---|---|---|---|---|---|---|
| Hampshire | G.G. | NG.NG. | G.G. | G.G. | G.G. | G.G. | G.G. | G.G. | G.G. |
| Andover | NO.G. | G.T. | T.G. | G.T. | G.T. | N.T. | G.NO. | NO.G. | G.G. |
| Christch. | NO.NG. | NG.NG. | NO.NO. | NO.GO. | NO.NO. | NO.G. | NO.NO. | NO.T. | GO.T. |
| Lymington | G.G. | G.GO. | G.G. | NO.G. | G.? | G.G. | G.G. | G.G. | G.G. |
| Newport IW | T.NT. | G.G. | G.G. | NO.G. | NO.G. | GO.G. | G.G. | NO.NG. | NO.G. |
| Newton IW | NO.G. | G.G. | NO.G. | G.G. | NO.G. | G.NO. | G.G. | NO.NO. | NO.NO. |
| Petersfld. | N.G. | G.G. | G.GO. | G.GO. | G.G. | G.G. | NT.NT. | NO.NO. | G.G. |
| Portsmouth | NO.T. | NO.T. | G.NO. | G.NO. | NO.G. | NO.T. | T.T. | NO.NO. | NO.NO. |
| Southampton | G.G. | G.NO. | G.T. | T.T. | T.T. | T.T. | G.G. | T.T. | T.T. |
| Stockbridge | RO.NO. | RG.RO. | RG.RO. | G.RO. | G.RO. | G.RO. | G.G. | G.G. | G.G. |
| Whitchurch | G.T. | GO.G. | G.RO. | G.G. | G.G. | G.G. | NG.T. | T.G. | G.G. |
| Winchester | T.T. | G.CG. | G.G. | N.T. | NO.NG. | NG.G. | NG.G. | NG.NG. | T.G. |
| Yarmouth IW | NO.NG. | NG.NO. | G.T. | NO.NO. | G.NO. | NG.NG. | NG.GO. | T.T. | G.NO. |
| Herefordsh. | G.G. | G.G. | NG.NO. | G.NG. | NG.GO. | T.T. | G.G. | G.G. | NG.NG. |
| Hereford | T.G. | G.T. | G.G. | T.T. | | G.GO. | GO.G. | NG.NG. | T.T. |
| Leominster | G.T. | G.G. | T.T. | NO.G. | G.T. | | GO.G. | N.G. | G.G. |
| Weobley | | | NO.G. | | G.GO. | NG.NG. | NG.NG. | NG.NG. | G.GO. |
| Hertfordsh. | NG.G. | NG.G. | NG.NG. | NG.NG. | NG.NG. | G.GO. | NO.G. | N.G. | NG.NG. |
| Hertford | | | | NO.G. | NO.G. | NG.NG. | NG.G. | G.G. | N.G. |
| St. Albans | NG.T. | G.NO. | NO.NO. | G.NG. | NG.NG. | N.NG. | NG.NG. | G.T. | G.G. |
| Huntingdonsh. | G.G. | G.G. | G.G. | N.G. | N.G. | RO.T. | N.G. | G.RO. | N.G. |
| Huntingdon | G.G. | GO.NO. | N.G. | N.RO. | N.NG. | G.G. | NG.G. | G.RO. | N.N. |
| Kent | G.T. | G.G. | N.NG. | G.NG. | N.NG. | RO.T. | G.T. | NG.G. | G.G. |
| Canterbury | RO.G. | CT.G. | T.CT. | T.T. | NO.G. | G.G. | RO.RO. | G.NO. | G.T. |
| Dover | G.RG. | RG.RG. | RO.RO. | RO.RO. | RO.RO. | G.G. | G.G. | G.T. | G.G. |
| Hythe | G.T. | G.RO. | RG.RO. | RG.RO. | G.RO. | T.G. | G.G. | RG.T. | G.RO. |
| Maidstone | RO.T. | G.G. | G.G. | G.G. | T.T. | NG.NO. | NG.G. | NG.NG. | N.G. |
| N. Romney | NO.G. | RO.T. | G.RO. | RO.T. | RO.T. | T.G. | G.G. | G.G. | RO.G. |
| Queenborough | G.G. | NG.G. | NO.NO. | NG.NO. | G.NG. | RO.T. | G.G. | G.RG. | G.NO. |
| Rochester | RG.T. | G.NG. | G.T. | G.G. | G.T. | T.G. | G.T. | RO.G. | G.G. |
| Sandwich | G.NG. | RG.G. | G.RG. | RG.?O. | RG.G. | RO.T. | G.G. | RO.RO. | G.T. |
| Lancashire | RO.G. | G.NG. | G.NG. | G.G. | G.G. | N.NG. | RO.G. | G.G. | G.G. |
| Clitheroe | RT.RO. | NG.GO. | G.RO. | RO.RO. | RO.G. | G.RO. | G.RO. | G.RG. | G.G. |
| Lancaster | T.T. | RO.RO. | RO.RO. | RO.G. | RO.RO. | RO.RO. | RO.GO. | RO.G. | RO.RG. |
| Liverpool | GO.G. | RO.RG. | GO.RG. | RO.RO. | N.T. | RCG.G. | RO.? | RO.RO. | T.RO. |
| Newton-Makers | RO.G. | G.G. | RO.RO. | G.RG. | GO.RO. | GO.RO. | RO.RO. | G.G. | G.RO. |
| Preston | | RO.G. | RO.RO. | RO.RO. | RO.G. | RO.RO. | | | G.G. |

| | 1604 | 1614 | 1621 | 1624 | 1625 | 1626 | 1628 | s1640 | a1640 |
|---|---|---|---|---|---|---|---|---|---|
| Wigan | RO.RO. | G.G. | G.RG. | G.RO. | RO.RCG. | G.RO. | G.RCG. | RCG.T. | RCG.T. |
| Leicestersh. | G.G. | N.G. | G.N. | G.N. | N.G. | N.G. | N.G. | G.N. | G.N. |
| Leicester | G.G. | NO.RO. | NG.G. | RO.T. | RO.N. | RO.N. | RO.N. | RO.NO. | N.NO. |
| Lincolnshire | N.N. | N.NG. | N.G. | NG.CO. | G.NG. | G.G. | RO.N. | G.G. | G.G. |
| Boston | T.G. | T.G. | NO.T. | N.G. | TO.CO. | TO.CO. | T.CO. | T.T. | T.T. |
| Grantham | N.NO. | NO.NO. | NG.G. | G.NG. | N.G. | NG.G. | G.T. | NO.NT. | G.NT. |
| G. Grimsby | G.G. | G.G. | T.NG. | NO.G. | G.NG. | G.?O. | G.NG. | T.G. | T.T. |
| Lincoln | G.NO. | G.NO. | NO.G. | NO.G. | G.G. | G.G. | G.G. | NT.G. | T.G. |
| Stamford | NG.G. | N.NO. | N.NG. | NO.G. | NG.NG. | NG.NO. | NO.NO. | NO.G. | NO.G. |
| Middlesex | G.RG. | RG.RG. | G.G. | NO.G. | NG.G. | G.G. | G.G. | G.G. | G.G. |
| London | T.RT. | T.RT. | T.RT. | T.RT. | T.RT. | T.RT. | T.T. | T.T. | T.T. |
| Westminster | T.T. | RO.T. | T.T. | N.T. | N.T. | NO.T. | T.T. | T.T. | T.T. |
| Norfolk | NO.NO. | G.G. | N.T. | NG.G. | G.NG. | G.G. | G.G. | NG.G. | G.G. |
| C. Rising | G.NG. | G.NO. | G.NG. | NO.NG. | G.NG. | NG.G. | NO.NG. | NG.NO. | NG.NO. |
| King's Lynn | NO.G. | T.T. | NO.NO. | T.T. | T.T. | T.T. | G.T. | NG.NO. | NG.G. |
| Norwich | T.G. | NO.G. | T.T. | T.T. | T.T. | T.TO. | T.T. | T.T. | T.T. |
| Thetford | G.NO. | NO.T. | T.T. | G.NG. | NO.G. | NG.G. | NO.G. | G.G. | G.G. |
| G. Yarmouth | T.T. | NG.G. | NG.G. | T.T. | G.T. | G.T. | G.T. | T.T. | T.T. |
| Northamptonsh. | NG.NG. | N.NO. | T.T. | N.NG. | N.NG. | N.NG. | G.G. | NG.NG. | NG.NG. |
| Brackley | N.G. | NG. | N.NG. | N.GO. | G.N. | N.G. | GO.GO. | GO.GO. | GO.G. |
| H. Ferrers | G. | T.TO. | N.GO. | N. | N. | GO. | N.NO. | G. | G. |
| Northampton | T.T. | ?O.?O. | G. | T.N. | N.T. | T.N. | T.N. | NG.NG. | NG.NG. |
| Peterborough | N.GO. | G.G. | N.G. | GO.?O. | ?O.G. | N.?O. | N.?O. | NG.G. | NO.G. |
| Northumberld. | G.G. | G.T. | GO.G. | G.G. | G.NG. | G.G. | G.GO. | NG.G. | N.G. |
| Berwick | G.T. | NO.NO. | G.T. | T.GO. | G.T. | T.G. | GO.GO. | RT.NO. | RT.RO. |
| Morpeth | GO.NO. | T.T. | G.T. | G.NO. | NO.NO. | NO.NO. | NO.NO. | RO.? | G.G. |
| Newcastle-T. | T.T. | G.G. | G.G. | T.T. | T.T. | T.T. | T.T. | T.T. | T.RO. |
| Nottinghams. | G.G. | N.NO. | GO.NO. | G.G. | G.N. | T.T. | G.G. | G.N. | N.G. |
| E. Retford | G.G. | T.T. | G.G. | N.GO. | N.NO. | N.NO. | N.NO. | N.T. | N.G. |
| Nottingham | T.T. | G.G. | G.G. | G.N. | T.T. | G.G. | N.G. | N.G. | N.G. |
| Oxfordshire | G.G. | N.NO. | G. | G.GO. | G.G. | N.G. | N. | N. | N. |
| Banbury | G. | NO.T. | NO.T. | GO. | T.T. | T. | T.T. | N.T. | T.N. |
| Oxford | NO.T. | NU.U. | U.NO. | NO.U. | CNO.U. | CNO.U. | NO.U. | CO.U. | CO.U. |
| Oxford U. | U.U. | GO.T. | T.GO. | GO.T. | GO.GO. | GO.NO. | GO.NO. | T.GO. | T.NO. |
| Woodstock | G.G. | NG.G. | NG.G. | NG.NG. | NG.NG. | NG.G. | NG.NG. | N.NG. | N.NG. |
| Rutlandsh. | G.G. | | | | | | | | |

| | 1604 | 1614 | 1621 | 1624 | 1625 | 1626 | 1628 | s1640 | a1640 |
|---|---|---|---|---|---|---|---|---|---|
| Shropshire | NG.G. | G.G. | G.G. | G.G. | G.G. | G.G. | G.G. | N.G. | G.G. |
| Bp's Castle | NO.G. | NO.G. | NO.G. | G.CG. | G.T. | G.T. | G.G. | G.T. | G.T. |
| Bridgnorth | GO.G. | T.T. | G.G. | G.GO. | G.?. | GO.G. | GO.GO. | G.G. | G.G. |
| Ludlow | T.T. | T.T. | RO.TO. | TO.RT. | TO.RT. | TO.RT. | TO.RT. | G.RT. | G.RT. |
| Shrewsbury | T.RO. | T.T. | G.T. | T.T. | T.T. | T.T. | T.T. | G.T. | G.TO. |
| G. Wenlock | G.G. | G.G. | G.G. | G.T. | G.G. | G.G. | G.T. | T.G. | T.N. |
| Somersetsh. | G.G. | G.G. | G.G. | G.G. | G.G. | G.G. | G.NG. | G.NG. | N.NG. |
| Bath | T.T. | GO.GO. | ?.?. | GO.G. | GO.GO. | T.T. | G.G. | G.G. | G.G. |
| Bridgwater | G.T. | T.G. | CO.CO. | G.T. | CO.CO. | CO.G. | T.NG. | G.G. | G.TO. |
| Ilchester | ...... | ...... | ...... | CO.CO. | G.CO. | G.GO. | G.G. | NO.G. | G.G. |
| Milborne Pt. | ...... | ...... | CO.CGO. | CO.CGO. | G.G. | ...... | N.G. | G.G. | NO.N. |
| Minehead | GO.G. | ?.?. | T.?. | G.T. | G.G. | G.G. | G.G. | NG.T. | NG.T. |
| Taunton | G.T. | G.G. | G.T. | T.G. | G.CO. | G.T. | G.T. | NG.T. | NG.NG. |
| Wells | GO.NG. | T.CO. | NG.G. | NG.NG. | NG.G. | G.CO. | G.T. | NG.NG. | G.NG. |
| Staffordsh. | NG.G. | G.NG. | G.NG. | NO.NG. | NT.NG. | NG.NG. | NG.G. | N.T. | N.T. |
| Lichfield | T.GO. | G.NG. | RO.NO. | RO.NG. | G.T. | NT.NG. | NO.NT. | NO.RO. | G.NO. |
| Newcastle-L. | G.RO. | RO.G. | T.NG. | T.NT. | T.NO. | G.T. | G.G. | G.G. | G.G. |
| Stafford | NO.G. | NG.NO. | G.G. | NO.G. | T.NO. | G.NO. | T.NG. | NG.NG. | NO.NO. |
| Tamworth | NO.G. | GO.NO. | NG.NG. | G.G. | G.G. | G.N. | G.N. | G.G. | NO.G. |
| Suffolk | G.NG. | G.G. | G.G. | T.T. | NG.NG. | G.G. | GO.G. | GO.T. | GO.T. |
| Aldeburgh | G.G. | G.NG. | GO.T. | G.G. | G.G. | NG.NO. | G.GO. | G.T. | G.G. |
| B. St. Edmunds | ...... | ...... | T.GO. | G.RO. | G.NGO. | G.NGO. | G.G. | G.G. | G.G. |
| Dunwich | GO.G. | G.NO. | T.T. | T.T. | G.NGO. | G.NGO. | G.NO. | RG.G. | RG.G. |
| Eye | GO.GO. | NO.G. | G.G. | T.G. | T.T. | G.T. | G.NGO. | T.G. | T.G. |
| Ipswich | NG.NG. | T.G. | T.G. | G.RG. | T.G. | T.G. | T.G. | G.G. | G.G. |
| Orford | G.G. | G.G. | G.NG. | G.G. | G.G. | T.G. | G.G. | G.G. | G.G. |
| Sudbury | G.G. | G.RO. | G.G. | NO.NT. | G.G. | G.T. | G.RG. | G.?. | G.G. |
| Surrey | G.G. | G.G. | G.GO. | G.G. | G.G. | G.NT. | G.G. | G.G. | G.G. |
| Blechingley | NO.NO. | NO.N. | G.G. | G.G. | NG.NO. | NG.G. | G.NO. | G.GO. | G.G. |
| Gatton | G.G. | G.NO. | NO.NO. | T.NO. | G.G. | GO.G. | G.G. | G.G. | G.G. |
| Guildford | G.G. | G.G. | T.T. | T.T. | G.NT. | G.N. | G.GO. | G.G. | G.G. |
| Haslemere | NG.G. | N.NO. | N.N. | N.G. | T.T. | T.T. | T.NO. | NO.T. | G.GO. |
| Reigate | N.G. | T.T. | NO.NO. | NO.G. | G.G. | G.G. | T.T. | G.G. | GO.GO. |
| Southwark | T.?. | G.NG. | G.G. | G.G. | NO.G. | G.G. | G.NG. | N.NG. | G.T. |
| Sussex | N.N. | NO.G. | N.N. | N.G. | G.G. | G.N. | N.G. | N.NG. | T.T. |
| Arundel | G.NO. | NO.G. | NO.NO. | NO.G. | NO.G. | G.G. | N.G. | G.NO. | G.G. |
| Bramber | G.G. | NG.G. | G.G. | G.G. | G.G. | G.G. | G.NO. | G.NO. | G.G. |

| | 1604 | 1614 | 1621 | 1624 | 1625 | 1626 | 1628 | s1640 | a1640 |
|---|---|---|---|---|---|---|---|---|---|
| Chichester | T.T. | G.T. | NO.T. | NO.T. | N.NO. | N.NO. | T.T. | T.NO. | T.G. |
| E. Grinstead | NG.NO. | NG.NG. | NG.G. | NO.G. | NG.NG. | NG.G. | NG.G. | NG.G. | N.G. |
| Hastings | RO.T. | RO.T. | RO.T. | G.RO. | G.RG. | RO.G. | RG.G. | RO.G. | RG.G. |
| Horsham | NO.NO. | NO.T. | NO.T. | NO.T. | NO.T. | NO.T. | NO.T. | T.T. | T.T. |
| Lewes | G.NG. | N.NT. | NG.NT. | N.NG. | NG.NG. | NG.NG. | NG.NG. | G.G. | G.G. |
| Midhurst | NO.NG. | G.NO. | G.NO. | NO.G. | NO.G. | NO.G. | G.NO. | G.NO. | G.NO. |
| Rye | T.RO. | RO.RO. | RO.RO. | RO.RO. | RO.NO. | RO.NO. | NO.RO. | NO.G. | NO.RO. |
| Shoreham | G.NO. | N.G. | G.NG. | G.T. | G.T. | G.T. | G.T. | G.T. | G.T. |
| Steyning | G.G. | G.NG. | G.NG. | NG.T. | NG.T. | NG.G. | T.G. | G.T. | G.N. |
| Winchelsea | T.RO. | RO.RO. | RG.RO. | G.RO. | RO.GO. | RO.GO. | RO.RO. | G.RO. | NG.RO. |
| Warwicksh. | G.G. | G.G. | G.G. | NG.G. | NG.G. | NG.G. | NG.G. | NG.NG. | N.NG. |
| Coventry | T.T. | TO.T. | T.T. | T.T. | T.T. | T.T. | G.N. | T.T. | T.T. |
| Warwick | T.T. | G.T. | G.GO. | NG.NG. | NG.NG. | NG.NG. | G.N. | NG.NG. | NG.NG. |
| Westmorland | G.NG. | N.N. | N.N. | G.G. | G.G. | G.G. | G.G. | NG.G. | NG.G. |
| Appleby | NO.NO. | NO.NO. | NO.NO. | NO.NO. | NO.NO. | NO.NO. | G.NO. | NO.G. | NO.NO. |
| Wiltshire | G.G. | N.G. | N.G. | G.NO. | N.NG. | G.G. | N.NG. | N.N. | G.G. |
| G. Bedwin | G.G. | NG.G. | G.NG. | G.NO. | NO.G. | NO.GO. | NO.G. | NG.N. | NG.G. |
| Calne | T.NO. | GO.T. | G.GO. | N.G. | N.T. | G.T. | GO.T. | G.T. | T.G. |
| Chippenham | G.T. | GO.GO. | G.G. | GO.G. | G.GO. | G.G. | G.G. | G.G. | G.G. |
| Cricklade | G.G. | NO.NO. | N.NO. | N.G. | N.NO. | N.NO. | G.G. | G.GO. | G.GO. |
| Devizes | G.T. | G.NG. | G.T. | G.T. | G.T. | G.T. | G.T. | G.G. | G.T. |
| Downton | NG.G. | NG.GO. | NG.G. | G.NO. | NO.NO. | NO.NO. | NO.NO. | NO.G. | NO.N. |
| Heytesbury | G.G. | G.G. | G.G. | G.G. | GO.G. | GO.G. | GO.G. | G.G. | G.G. |
| Hindon | G.G. | G.GO. | G.G. | G.G. | G.G. | G.G. | G.G. | NO.NO. | NO.NO. |
| Ludgershall | MO.G. | NG.NO. | G.NO. | NO.G. | NO.G. | NO.G. | NO.G. | NO.G. | NO.G. |
| Malmesbury | NO.NO. | G.NT. | N.NT. | N.NT. | NT.NO. | NT.NO. | N.NT. | G.G. | G.G. |
| Marlborough | G.NT. | G.NT. | N.NT. | N.NT. | N.T. | NT.NO. | N.NT. | N.NO. | N.T. |
| Old Sarum | NO.NO. | NO.NO. | NO.NO. | NO.NO. | NO.NO. | NO.NO. | NO.NO. | N.NO. | NO.NO. |
| Salisbury | T.T. | T.T. | T.T. | T.T. | T.T. | T.T. | T.T. | T.NO. | T.NO. |
| Westbury | G.G. | G.G. | G.GO. | G.GO. | G.GO. | NO.GO. | NO.G. | ?O.G. | GO.G. |
| Wilton | NO.NO. | NO.NO. | GO.NO. | NO.NO. | NO.NO. | NO.NG. | NO.NO. | NO.NO. | NO.NO. |
| W. Bassett | NO.G. | G.G. | NO.G. | NO.NO. | NO.NO. | NO.NO. | NO.NO. | NO.G. | NO.NO. |
| Worcestersh. | CG.CG. | G.G. | G.G. | NG.G. | G.G. | G.G. | G.G. | G.G. | G.G. |
| Bewdley | NO. | RO. | RO. | RG. | G. | G. | G. | RO. | RO. |
| Droitwich | G.G. | G.G. | G.G. | G.G. | T.G. | G.T. | T.G. | T.G. | NO.G. |
| Evesham | G.G. | G.G. | G.G. | GO.T. | T.G. | GO.G. | NO.T. | G.G. | T.G. |
| Worcester | T.T. | T.T. | T.T. | T.T. | NG.GO. | GO.T. | T.T. | T.T. | T.T. |

| | 1604 | 1614 | 1621 | 1624 | 1625 | 1626 | 1628 | s1640 | a1640 |
|---|---|---|---|---|---|---|---|---|---|
| Yorkshire | RG.RG. | RG.RG. | GO.G. | G.G. | G.G. | G.G. | G.G. | RG.G. | G.G. |
| Aldborough | RN.G. | G.RG. | G.T. | G.T. | G.T. | G.T. | G.G. | G.G. | G.RG. |
| Beverley | NG.RT. | ?.RO. | G.?. | RO.?. | G.G. | G.G. | G.G. | G.G. | G.G. |
| Boroughbg. | RG.G. | G.G. | G.RG. | G.RO. | RO.G. | G.RO. | G.G. | G.G. | G.G. |
| Hedon | G.G. | RO.RN. | G.G. | G.G. | G.G. | G.G. | G.G. | G.G. | G.G. |
| Hull | T.T. | G.T. | T.CO. | NO.CO. | T.CO. | T.CO. | T.T. | T.NO. | T.NO. |
| Knaresboro. | G.G. | G.RO. | G.G. | G.G. | G.G. | G.T. | G.T. | G.T. | G.T. |
| Pontefract | | | G.GO. | G.RO. | T.G. | T.G. | T.G. | G.RG. | RG.RG. |
| Richmond | T.RO. | RO.T. | T.TO. | T.G. | T.G. | G.T. | T.RO. | RG.RG. | RG.RG. |
| Ripon | RG.C. | CG.G. | CG.G. | CG.G. | CG.G. | CG.G. | CG.G. | G.C. | G.G. |
| Scarborough | RN.RG. | RG.T. | RG.T. | G.T. | G.NG. | G.G. | NG.NO. | G.G. | G.G. |
| Thirsk | G.G. | G.RO. | G.G. | N.G. | NO.G. | G.G. | G.G. | G.G. | G.G. |
| York | T.T. | T.T. | T.T. | T.T. | T.T. | T.T. | T.T. | RG.RT. | T.T. |
| Anglesey | G. | G. | G. | G. | G. | G. | G. | G. | G. |
| Beaumaris | G. | G. | GO. | T. | T. | T. | T. | T. | RG. |
| Breconshire | G. | G. | GO. | G. | G. | G. | G. | RG. | G. |
| Brecon | G. | GO. | G. | GO. | GO. | GO. | GO. | G. | G. |
| Cardigansh. | G. | G. | GO. | G. | G. | G. | G. | G. | G. |
| Cardigan | T. | ?. | G. | GO. | GO. | GO. | G. | G. | G. |
| Carmarthensh. | NO. | NO. | G. | G. | G. | G. | G. | G. | G. |
| Carmarthen | G. | G. | G. | G. | G. | G. | G. | G. | G. |
| Caernarvonsh. | G. | G. | T. | GO. | GO. | GO. | GO. | G. | G. |
| Caernarvon | G. | T. | T. | T. | T. | T. | G. | G. | G. |
| Denbighshire | T. | T. | G. | GO. | GO. | GO. | T. | GO. | GO. |
| Denbigh | T. | T. | NG. | NG. | NG. | NG. | GO. | G. | N. |
| Flintshire | G. | G. | NG. | NG. | NG. | NG. | NG. | NG. | NG. |
| Flint | GO. | G. | NG. | GO. | GO. | GO. | NG. | GO. | G. |
| Glamorgansh. | N. | NG. | G. | NO.G. | NO.G. | N.G. | NG. | RG.G. | NG. |
| Cardiff | NO. | NO. | NG.G. | RO. | RO. | RO. | G.G. | RO. | RO. |
| Merionethsh. | NG. | G. | ?. | N. | N. | N. | N. | N. | NG. |
| Monmouthsh. | N.NG. | G.G. | N. | NO. | NO. | NO. | G. | G. | N. |
| Monmouth | RO. | RO. | NG. | N. | N. | T. | G. | G. | G. |
| Montgomerysh. | N. | N. | G. | G. | G. | G. | G. | G. | G. |
| Montgomery | NO. | NO. | G. | G. | G. | G. | T. | G. | T. |
| Pembrokesh. | G. | G. | G. | NO. | G. | G. | G. | G. | NG. |
| Haverfordw. | G. | NO. | G. | G. | G. | G. | G. | NG. | NO. |
| Pembroke | G. | G. | G. | G. | G. | G. | T. | G. | T. |
| Radnorshire | G. | G. | G. | G. | G. | G. | G. | NG. | NG. |
| New Radnor | NO. | NO. | G. | G. | G. | G. | G. | G. | NO. |

# Appendix Seven

This appendix sets out the certain, probable, and possible electoral involvement of the lay and clerical peerage from 1604 through 1640. The influence of peers who served as lord wardens or who headed the Duchy of Lancaster or the Councils of the Marches of Wales or the North is not included; that is included with the influence of the court. Certain electoral involvement is marked by an asterisk, probable involvement by a °, and no mark at all indicates possible intervention. An (I) indicates electoral involvement only and does not suggest that a peer's influence was of primary importance in the election.

Arundell, Thos., Ld. Arundell of Wardour
    Christchurch, 1604*, 1614*, 1621*, 1624*, 1625°, 1626*, 1628*
    Somersetshire, 1614 (I)*

Arundell, Thos., 2d Ld. Arundell of Wardour
    Christchurch, s1640*, a1640*

Bacon, Francis, Ld. Verulam, Visct. St. Albans
    Cambridge, 1621*
    St. Albans, 1621*, 1624(I)*

Berkeley, Henry, Ld. de Berkeley
    Gloucestershire, 1604°

Berkeley, Geo., 8th (4th) Ld. de Berkeley
    Gloucestershire, 1614°, 1621°, 1625°, s1640*

Bertie, Robt., Ld. Willoughby de Eresby, earl of Lindsey
    Lincolnshire, 1614°, 1624°
    Stamford, 1625°, 1626°
    Berwick, s1640*
    Grantham, s1640, a1640

Bourchier, Wm., earl of Bath
    Barnstaple, 1604, 1614

Bourchier, Edward, 4th earl of Bath
    Barnstaple, 1626, 1628

Bridges, Grey, Ld. Chandos
    Tewkesbury, 1614, 1621*

Browne, Anthony, Visct. Montague
    Midhurst, 1604°, bye-elect. 1604°, 1614, 1621, 1624, 1625, 1626°, 1628

Browne, Francis, 3d Visct. Montague
  Midhurst, s1640, a1640

Carew, Geo., Ld. Carew, Earl of Totness
  Helston, 1621°
  Bodmin, 1624°

Carey, John, Ld. Hunsdon
  Hertfordshire, 1604°, 1614(I)°

Cavendish, Wm., Ld. Cavendish, earl of Devonshire
  Derbyshire, 1614°, 1621°, 1624°, 1625°, 1626°
  East Retford, 1614°
  Somersetshire, 1614(I)*
  Bishop's Castle, 1621°

Cavendish, Eliz., countess of Devonshire
  Leicester, 1621*, s1640*, a1640*
  East Retford, 1621*, 1624*, 1625, 1626, 1628°

Cavendish, Wm., Ld. Cavendish, Visct. Mansfield, earl of Newcastle-on-Tyne
  Nottingham, 1624*, 1625*, 1628*, s1640°
  East Retford, a1640°

Cecil, Thos., Baron Burghley, earl of Exeter
  Stamford, 1614°, 1621°
  Boston, 1621*

Cecil, Wm., 2d earl of Exeter
  Stamford, 1624°, 1625°, 1626°, 1628°, s1640
  Peterborough, s1640°

Cecil, David, 3d earl of Exeter
  Stamford, a1640

Cecil, Robt., Ld. Cecil, Visct. Cranborne, earl of Salisbury
  1604: Bossiney, Callington, Grampound, Helston, Launceston°, East Looe°,
    West Looe°, Lostwithiel°, Penryn°, St. Ives, St. Mawes°, Saltash,
    Beeralston°, Queenborough°, Stamford°, Westminster°, Peter-
    borough°, Stafford°, Bewdley°
  1605: Queenborough, Hereford*, Newcastle-under-Lyme*, St. Albans*,
    Beeralston*, West Looe*, Evesham*
  1606: Helston°
  1607: Hull*
  1609: Boroughbridge*, Bossiney*, Ludlow*, Penryn*
  1610: Hedon*, Eye*, Weymouth*, Evesham, Stafford°, Stamford°, Tewkes-
    bury°, St. Albans

Cecil, Wm., 2d earl of Salisbury
  Hertfordshire, 1614°, 1621*, 1624*, 1625*, 1626*, 1628°, s1640*, a1640°
  Old Sarum, 1614°, 1621*, 1624*, 1625*, 1626*, 1628*, s1640*, a1640°
  Chippenham, 1614(I)*
  Hertford, 1624*, 1625°, 1628°, s1640°, a1640*
  St. Albans, 1624*, 1625*, 1626°, 1628*, a1640*

Clifford, Geo., earl of Cumberland
  Appleby, 1604
  Yorkshire, 1604(I)*

Clifford, Francis, 4th earl of Cumberland
  Carlisle, 1614°, 1621°, 1624, 1625, 1626, s1640*
  Appleby, 1614°, 1621°, 1624°, 1625°, 1626°, 1628°, s1640°, a1640°
  Westmorland, 1614°, 1621°
  Yorkshire, 1614(I)*, 1621(I)*, 1625(I)*, 1628(I)°
  Richmond, 1621(I)*
  Pontefract, 1624(I)*

Clinton, Henry, earl of Lincoln
  Lincolnshire, 1604°
  Boston, 1614

Clinton, *alias* Fiennes, Theophilus, 4th earl of Lincoln
  Boston, 1621*

Compton, Wm., Ld. Compton, earl of Northampton
  Chester, 1621*
  Bewdley, 1624*
  Coventry, 1625*

Compton, Spencer, Ld. Compton, 2d earl of Northampton
  Warwickshire, s1640°, a1640*

Conway, Edward, Baron Conway of Ragley, Visct. Conway
  Newport, IW, 1625*, 1626*, 1628*
  Newton, IW, 1625*, 1626*, 1628*
  Yarmouth, IW, 1625*, 1626*, 1628*
  Southampton, 1628*
  Andover, 1628*
  Evesham, 1628*

Cottington, Francis, Ld. Cottington of Hamworth
  Berkshire, s1640*
  Hindon, s1640*, a1640°

Coventry, Thos., Ld. Coventry of Aylesborough
  Coventry, s1640*
  Tewkesbury, s1640

Coventry, Thos., 2d Ld. Coventry of Aylesborough
  Tewkesbury, a1640°

Cranfield, Lionel, Ld. Cranfield, earl of Middlesex
  Steyning, 1624*
  Hull, 1624*
  Tewkesbury, s1640*, a1640*
  Liverpool, s1640

Danvers, Henry, Ld. Danvers of Dantsey, earl of Danby
  Cirencester, 1604, bye-elections, 1604, 1610, 1614
  Ludgershall, 1614

Darcy, Thos., Ld. Darcy of Chiche, Visct. Colchester, earl Rivers
  Essex, 1604(I)*, bye-election 1605(I), 1625(I)*, 1628(I)*

Darcy, Jo., Ld. Darcy and Meinill
    Nottingham, 1624*
    East Retford, 1624

Devereux, Robt., earl of Essex
    Radnor, 1604, 1614°
    Staffordshire, bye-election 1610°, 1621°, 1624°, 1625°, 1626°, 1628°, s1640°, a1640°
    Stafford, 1614°, 1621°, 1624°, 1625, 1626, 1628
    Lichfield, 1614, 1621, 1624, 1625°, 1626°, 1628°, s1640°, a1640°
    Newcastle-under-Lyme, 1621°, 1624, s1640°, a1640°
    Tamworth, 1604°, 1614°, 1624, 1626°, 1628°, s1640°
    Pembroke, 1614°, 1624°
    Worcestershire, 1624°
    Worcester, 1625
    Herefordshire, a1640*

Digby, Jo., Ld. Digby of Sherbourne, earl of Bristol
    Bridport, 1625°, 1626°
    Weymouth, 1628°
    Milborne Port, 1628°, a1640°
    Dorsetshire, s1640°, a1640°

Egerton, Thos., Ld. Ellesmere, Visct. Brackley
    Oxford, 1604*
    St. Albans, 1604°, bye-election, 1610°, 1614°
    Cambridge, 1614*
    Oxford, U., 1614*

Egerton, Jo., Ld. Ellesmere, Visct. Brackley, earl of Bridgewater
    Flint, 1621*, 1624°, 1625°, 1626°, 1628°
    Brackley, 1624(I), 1625*, 1626

Fane, Francis, Ld. Burghersh, earl of Westmorland
    Kent*, 1625
    Northamptonshire, 1626*
    Peterborough, 1626°, 1628°, a1640
    Higham Ferrers, 1628
    Maidstone, s1640°

Feilding, Susan, countess of Denbigh
    Dunwich, 1628*

Fiennes, Wm., Visct. Saye and Sele
    Oxfordshire, 1626°, 1628°, s1640°, a1640*
    Banbury, 1628, s1640°, a1640°

Finch, Jo., Ld. Finch of Fordwich
    Cambridge, a1640*
    Winchelsea, a1640°

Goring, Geo., Ld. Goring of Hurstpierpoint
    Lewes, s1640*
    Portsmouth, a1640°

Greville, Fulke, Ld. Brooke of Beauchamps Court
  Warwickshire, 1624, 1625, 1626, 1628
  Warwick, 1624°, 1625°, 1626*, 1628*
  Coventry, 1628°

Greville, Robt., 2d Ld. Brooke of Beauchamps Court
  Warwickshire, s1640°, a1640*
  Warwick, s1640°, a1640°

Grey, Henry, Ld. Grey of Groby, earl of Stamford
  Leicester, a1640*

Grey, Wm., Ld. Grey of Werke
  Northumberland, 1625°

Hastings, Geo., earl of Huntingdon
  Leicester, 1604*

Hastings, Henry, 5th earl of Huntingdon
  Leicester, bye-election, 1610*, 1614*, 1621*, 1624*, 1625*, 1626*, 1628°,
  s1640*, a1640*
  Leicestershire, 1614*, 1621°, 1624°, 1625*, 1626°, 1628°, s1640*, a1640°
  Rutlandshire, 1614°, 1621°, 1624*, 1625°, 1626°, 1628°, s1640°, a1640°

Herbert, Edward, Ld. Herbert of Cherbury
  Montgomeryshire, s1640°, a1640°
  Montgomery, a1640°

Herbert, Wm., earl of Pembroke
  Glamorganshire, 1604°, bye-election 1605°, 1614°, 1621°, 1624°, 1625°, 1626°,
1628°
  Merionethshire, 1604
  Montgomeryshire, 1604°, 1614°, 1621°, 1624°, 1625°, 1626°, 1628°
  Cardiff, 1604, 1614, 1621*, 1624°, 1625°, 1626°, 1628°
  Wilton, 1604°, bye-election 1607°, 1614°, 1621°, 1624°, 1625°, 1626*, 1628°
  Old Sarum, 1604°, 1614°, 1621*, 1624*, 1625*, 1626*, 1628*
  Downton, 1604, 1614, 1621, 1614, 1625°, 1626°, 1628°
  Shaftesbury, 1604°, 1614°, 1621°, 1624°, 1625°, 1626*, 1628°
  Lostwithiel, 1614°, 1626*
  Devizes, 1614°
  Montgomery, 1604, 1614°, 1621°, 1624°, 1625°, 1626°
  Callington, 1621, 1626*
  Derby, 1621°, 1624°, 1625°, 1626°, 1628
  Portsmouth, 1621*, 1624°, 1625°, 1626*
  Oxford U., 1621, 1624, 1625°, 1626*, 1628*
  Monmouthshire, 1621°, 1624°, 1625°, 1626°
  Wiltshire, 1621(I)°, 1624, 1625*, 1628(I)°
  Cornwall, 1624, 1626, 1628
  West Looe, 1624°
  St. Germans, 1624°
  Liskeard, 1625, 1626*, 1628°
  St. Mawes, 1625°

Fowey, 1626*
Grampound, 1626*
Salisbury, 1626*
East Looe, 1628°
Derbyshire, 1628(I)°

Herbert, Phillip, earl of Montgomery, 4th earl of Pembroke
Queenborough, 1614*, 1621*, 1624*, 1625*, 1626*, 1628°, s1640, a1640
Woodstock, 1614*, 1626°, 1628°, a1640°
Kent, 1625(I)*, s1640*, a1640*
Canterbury, 1625*, 1626*, s1640*
Gloucestershire, s1640*, a1640(I)
Wiltshire, s1640°
Old Sarum, s1640°, a1640°
Shaftesbury, s1640, a1640°
Wilton, s1640°, a1640°
Salisbury, s1640*, a1640°
Downton, 1640°, a1640°
Glamorganshire, s1640°, a1640°
Radnorshire, s1640, a1640
Cardiff, s1640°, a1640°
St. Mawes, s1640
Callington, a1640
Plympton Earl, a1640°
Christchurch, a1640*
Monmouthshire, a1640°
Radnor, a1640

Hicks, Baptist, Ld. Hicks of Ilmington, Visct. Campden
Tewkesbury, bye-election 1628°

Holles, Jo., Ld. Haughton, Earl of Clare
East Retford, 1625°, 1626°

Howard, Charles, Ld. Howard of Effingham, earl of Nottingham
Scarborough, 1604*
Windsor, 1604, bye-election 1610°
Harwich, 1604°, bye-election 1605, 1614°
Portsmouth, 1604°, bye-election 1607°
Blechingley, 1604°, bye-election 1610°, 1614°, 1621°
Shropshire, 1604
Reigate, 1604°, 1614°, 1621
Sussex, 1604°
Shoreham, 1604°, 1614°
Carmarthenshire, 1604°, 1614°
Newport, 1614°
Gatton, 1614°

Howard, Margaret, countess of Nottingham
Blechingley, 1624*, 1626°
Reigate, 1624°, 1626°, 1628°

Howard, Chas., 2d earl of Nottingham
 Gatton, 1625°, 1626°, 1628°
 Reigate, 1625°
Howard, Henry, earl of Northampton
 Bishop's Castle, 1604°, bye-election 1610*, 1614*
 Dartmouth, 1604°, 1614*
 Norfolk, 1604°
 Castle Rising, 1604°, 1614°
 Thetford, 1604°, 1614*
 Suffolk, 1604
 Cambridge U., 1614*
 Totness, 1614*
 Portsmouth, 1614*
 Gt. Yarmouth, 1614*
 Stafford, 1614°
 Eye, 1614
Howard, Thos., Visct. Howard of Bindon
 Weymouth, 1604(I)*
 Wareham, 1604
Howard, Thos., earl of Arundel and Surrey
 Steyning, 1624*, 1625*
 Horsham, 1604, 1614, 1621°, 1624°, 1625*, 1626°, 1628
 Aldeburgh, 1614°, 1621*, 1624*, 1625°, 1626°, s1640°, a1640°
 Arundel, 1614°, 1621°, 1624°, 1625*, 1628°, s1640°
 Bramber, 1614°
 Norfolk, 1621, 1624*, 1625, s1640
 Castle Rising, 1621*, 1624*, 1625, 1626, 1628°, s1640, a1640*
 Thetford, 1621°, 1624°, 1625*, 1626°, 1628*
 Reigate, 1621*, 1624*
 Chichester, 1621°, 1624°, 1625*, 1626°
 Shoreham, 1621°
 Morpeth, 1624°, 1625°, 1626°, 1628°
 King's Lynn, s1640*, a1640*
Howard, Thos., Ld. Howard de Walden, earl of Suffolk
 Essex, 1604*
 Maldon, 1604*, bye-election 1605(I)*
 Ipswich, 1604°, 1614*
 Malmesbury, 1604°, 1614°, 1621°, 1624°, 1625°, 1626°
 Wootton Bassett, 1604, 1621, 1624, 1625, 1626°
 Calne, 1604, 1624°, 1625°
 Morpeth, 1604,°, 1614°, 1625°, 1626°
 Harwich, 1605
 Norfolk, 1614*
 Dunwich, 1614*
 Wiltshire, 1614°
 Cricklade, 1614°, 1621°, 1624°, 1625°, 1626°

Howard, Theophilus, 2d earl of Suffolk
Dorchester, 1628*

Howard, Thos., Ld. Howard of Charlton, Visct. Andover, earl of Berkshire
Malmesbury, 1628°
Wootton Bassett, 1628, s1640
Wiltshire, 1628
Morpeth, 1628°
Oxford, s1640*, a1640°

Kerr, Wm., Visct. Rochester, earl of Somerset
Rochester, 1614*

Knollys, Wm., Visct. Wallingford, earl of Banbury
Reading, 1604°, 1614°, 1621°, 1624*, 1625*, 1626*, 1628*
Berkshire, 1604°, 1621°, 1625°
Abingdon, 1614°, 1624°, 1625°, 1626°
Wallingford, 1614*, 1621*, 1624°, 1625°, 1626°, 1628°
Oxford, 1614°, 1621°
Windsor, 1621°

Ley, Jas., Ld. Ley, earl of Marlborough
Devizes, 1626°
Westbury, 1628°

Longueville, Chas., Ld. Grey of Ruthin
Leicestershire, s1640°, a1640°

Manners, Roger, earl of Rutland
Lincolnshire, 1604
Grantham, 1604°

Manners, Francis, 6th earl of Rutland
Lincolnshire, 1614°, 1621*, 1625
Grantham, 1614°, 1621*, 1624°, 1625°, 1626°
Lincoln, 1614, 1621°, 1624°
Somersetshire, 1614(I)*
Chippenham, 1614(I)*
Yorkshire, 1614(I)*
Gt. Grimsby, 1621°, 1624°, 1625°, 1626°, 1628°

Manners, Geo., 7th earl of Rutland
Grantham, s1640°, a1640°
Lincoln, s1640

Montagu, Henry, Ld. Montagu of Kimbolton, Visct. Mandeville, earl of Manchester
Huntingdonshire, 1624°, 1625°, 1626°
Huntindgon, 1628°, s1640°, a1640°
Dartmouth, 1628*

Montagu, Sir Edward, Ld. Montagu of Boughton
Northamptonshire, 1624*, 1625(I)°, 1626*, 1628°, s1640, a1640
Higham Ferrers, 1624°, 1625°

Huntingdonshire, 1626°, 1628, s1640, a1640°
Northampton, 1628°, s1640°, a1640°
Huntingdon, s1640°, a1640°

Mordaunt, Henry, Ld. Mordaunt
Northamptonshire, 1604*

Nevill, Edward, Ld. Abergavenny
Lewes, 1604°, 1614°, 1621°
Midhurst, 1604°
Sussex, 1614, 1621°

Nevill, Henry, 9th (2d) Ld. Abergavenny
Lewes, 1624°, 1625°, 1626°, 1628°
Sussex, 1628°

Noel, Edward, Visct. Campden
Rutlandshire, s1640°, a1640°

North, Dudley, Ld. North de Kirtling
Cambridgeshire, s1640°, a1640°

Paget, Wm., Ld. Paget de Beaudesert
Staffordshire, 1604*
Gt. Marlowe, 1624, 1625, 1626°

Paget, Wm., 6th Ld. Paget de Beaudesert
Gt. Marlowe, s1640°, a1640*

Paulet, Wm., marquis of Winchester
St. Ives, 1604, 1621°, 1626
Andover, 1604, 1626°
Winchester, 1625, 1626, 1628

Paulet, John, 5th marquis of Winchester
Andover, s1640

Percy, Henry, earl of Northumberland
Haslemere, 1604°
Beverley, 1604(I)
Steyning, 1614°, 1621°, 1624°, 1625°, 1626°
Sussex, 1624°
Chichester, 1625°, 1626°

Percy, Algernon, 4th earl of Northumberland
Christchurch, s1640*
Gt. Yarmouth, s1640*, a1640°
Dover, s1640*
Rye, s1640*
Sandwich, s1640*
Hull, s1640*, a1640°
Scarborough, s1640*
Berwick, s1640°
Northumberland, s1640°, a1640°
Portsmouth, s1640°, a1640°

Yarmouth, IW, s1640*, a1640°
Chichester, s1640°
Harwich, s1640°

Pierrepoint, Robt., Ld. Pierrepoint, Visct. Newark, earl of Kingston-upon-Hull
Nottingham, 1628°
East Retford, s1640°
Shropshire, s1640°
Gt. Wenlock, a1640°

Poulett, John, Ld. Poulett of Hinton St. George
Somersetshire, 1628, s1640°, a1640°
Bridgewater, 1628°
Taunton, s1640, a1640
Wells, s1640, a1640

Radcliffe, Robt., earl of Sussex
Essex, 1604(I)°
Colchester, 1625*

Ramsay, John, Ld. Ramsay of Kingston-upon-Thames, Visct. Holderness
Scarborough, 1625*

Rich, Robt., Ld. Rich, earl of Warwick
Essex, 1604*, bye-election 1605, 1614°
Maldon, 1610°
Harwich, 1614°

Rich, Robt., 2d earl of Warwick
Essex, 1621°, 1624°, 1625*, 1626°, 1628*, s1640*, a1640*
Harwich, 1621*, 1624°, 1626°, s1640°, a1640°
Maldon, 1624°, 1625°, 1626°, 1628°, a1640°
Colchester, 1626°, 1628*, s1640°, a1640*

Rich, Henry, Ld. Kensington, earl of Holland
Windsor, s1640*, a1640°
Reading, s1640*, a1640*
Colchester, s1640*, a1640*
Cambridge U., s1640°, a1640°

Robartes, Richard, Ld. Robartes of Truro
Truro, 1625, 1626, s1640, a1640
Bossiney, 1626°, 1628°

Russell, Edward, earl of Bedford
Tavistock, 1604°, 1614°, 1621, 1624°, 1625°, 1626°
Lyme Regis, 1610°
Tiverton, 1625

Russell, Francis, Ld. Russell of Thornhaugh, 4th earl of Bedford
Tavistock, 1628°, s1640°, a1640°
Totness, s1640°, a1640°

St. John, Oliver, Ld. St. John of Bletsoe
  Bedfordshire, 1604°, 1614°
  Bedford, 1614°
  Higham Ferrers, 1614°
  Huntingdon, 1614

St. John, Oliver, 4th Ld. St. John of Bletsoe, earl of Bolingbroke
  Bedfordshire, 1621°, 1624°, 1625°, 1626°, 1628°, s1640°, a1640°
  Bedford, 1621°, 1624°, 1625°, 1628*, s1640°, a1640°
  Huntingdon, 1621°, 1624°, 1625°

Sackville, Thos., Ld. Buckhurst, earl of Dorset
  Arundel, 1604*
  Sussex, 1604°
  E. Grinstead, 1604°
  Newcastle-under-Lyme, 1605*

Sackville, Robt., 2d earl of Dorset
  Sussex, 1608

Sackville, Richard, 3rd earl of Dorset
  Arundel, 1610
  E. Grinstead, 1614°, 1621°, 1624°
  Lewes, 1614°, 1621°
  Sussex, 1621°

Sackville, Edward, 4th earl of Dorset
  Kent, 1625(I)*, s1640*
  E. Grinstead, 1625°, 1626°, 1628°, s1640°, s1640°
  Rye, 1625*, 1626*, 1628*, s1640*, a1640°
  Lewes, 1625°, 1626°, s1640*
  Bramber, 1628, s1640*
  Arundel, a1640°
  Gt. Yarmouth, s1640*, a1640°
  Steyning, a1640°

Savage, John, Visct. Savage, earl Rivers
  Cheshire, s1640*

Savile, Thos., Ld. Pomfret, Visct. Savile
  Southwark, s1640*

Seymour, Edward, Ld. Beauchamp, earl of Hertford
  Wells, 1604°
  Marlborough, 1604°, 1614°, 1621°
  Ludgershall, 1604°, 1614°
  Gt. Bedwin, 1614°, 1621°
  Somersetshire, 1614(I)*, 1621*
  Wiltshire, 1621°

Seymour, Wm., 10th earl of Hertford, marquis of Hertford
  Gt. Bedwin, 1624, 1625, 1626°, 1628°, s1640°, a1640°
  Marlborough, 1624°, 1625°, 1626°, 1628°, s1640°, a1640°

Ludgershall, 1624°, 1625°, 1626°, 1628°
Wiltshire, 1625*, 1628°, s1640°
Milborne Port, s1640°, a1640°

Sheffield, Edmund, Ld. Sheffield of Butterwicke, earl of Mulgrave
Scarborough, 1624*, 1625*, 1628*
Thirsk, 1624°

Sidney, Robt., Ld. Sidney of Penshurst, Visct. L'Isle, earl of Leicester
Kent, 1621°

Somerset, Edward, earl of Worcester
Monmouthshire, 1604°

Spencer, Robt., Ld. Spencer of Wormleighton
Northamptonshire, 1604*, 1614°, 1621°, 1624*, 1625°, 1626*
Brackley, 1604*, 1614*, 1621°, 1624°, 1625°
Northampton, 1621*, 1624°, 1625°, 1626°

Spencer, Wm., 2d Lord Spencer of Wormleighton
Northamptonshire, 1628°
Northampton, 1628*

Stanhope, Philip, Ld. Stanhope of Shalford, earl of Chesterfield
Derbyshire, 1624°, 1625°
Nottinghamshire, 1625°, 1626°
East Retford, 1628°
Nottingham, a1640°
Tamworth, a1640°

Stanley, Wm., earl of Derby
Lancashire, 1604, 1614°, 1621, 1626°, s1640°, a1640°
Clitheroe, 1614
Liverpool, 1625°
Thirsk, 1625°

Stanley, Eliz., countess of Derby
Brackley, 1604*

Stuart, Ludovic, duke of Lennox
Canterbury, 1621*, 1624*
Queenborough, 1621*
Rye, 1621(I)*

Stuart, James, 4th duke of Lennox
Southampton, s1640*
Christchurch, a1640*

Talbot, Gilbert, earl of Shrewsbury
Yorkshire, 1604(I)*
Nottinghamshire, 1604(I)*
Worcestershire, 1604(I)*

Tufton, Nicholas, Ld. Tufton, earl of Thanet
Rye, 1628°

Kent, 1628(I)*
  Maidstone, a1640°
Tuchet, Geo., Lord Audley
  Dorsetshire, 1614°
Villiers, Geo., Ld. Whaddon of Whaddon, Visct. Villiers, earl and duke of Buckingham
  Buckingham, 1621°, 1624°, 1625°, 1626, 1628°
  Leominster, 1621°, 1624°
  Westminster, 1621*, 1624°, 1625°, 1626°, 1628*
  Cambridge U., 1621, 1624*, 1625°, 1626°, 1628*
  Windsor, 1624, 1625*, 1626°, 1628
  Scarborough, 1624, 1626*, 1628°
  Launceston, 1624
  Newport, 1624°, 1625°, 1626*, 1628
  West Looe, 1624°, 1625, 1626, 1628
  Plympton Earl, 1624, 1628*
  Herefordshire, 1624, 1625, 1626, 1628
  Kent, 1624, 1625*, 1626*, 1628*
  Winchelsea, 1624(I)*
  Boston, 1624
  Middlesex, 1624*, 1625°
  Hull, 1624*
  Bossiney, 1625
  Callington, 1625
  Camelford, 1625
  East Looe, 1625°, 1626°
  Lostwithiel, 1625, 1628
  St. Ives, 1625
  St. Mawes, 1625, 1626
  Harwich, 1625
  Eye, 1625, 1626, 1628
  Essex, 1625(I)*
  St. Germans, 1626
  Carlisle, 1626°, 1628°
  Bridport, 1626*
  Bury St. Edmunds, 1626
  Tiverton, 1626*
  Cornwall, 1628(I)
  Grampound, 1628*
  Saltash, 1628*
  Rochester, 1628*
  Portsmouth, 1628*
Wentworth, Thos., Ld. Wentworth, earl of Cleveland
  Bedford, 1628*
  Bedfordshire, s1640°, a1640°

Weston, Jerome, 2d earl of Portland
  Newport, IW, s1640, a1640
  Newton, IW, s1640\*, a1640°
  Yarmouth, IW, s1640°, a1640°

Wharton, Philip, Ld. Wharton
  Westmorland, 1604°, 1614°, 1621°

Wharton, Philip, 4th Ld. Wharton
  Westmorland, s1640°, a1640°

Windsor, Thos., Ld. Windsor
  Droitwich, a1640

Wriothesley, Henry, earl of Southampton
  Yarmouth, IW, 1604\*, 1614\*, 1621°, 1624°
  Newport, IW, 1604\*, 1624\*
  Newton, IW, 1604\*, bye election 1605°, 1614, 1621
  Stockbridge, 1604
  Southampton, 1614
  Hampshire, 1614\*
  Lymington, 1624°
  Winchester, 1624°

Wriothesley, Eliz., countess of Southampton
  Petersfield, 1604

Wriothesley, Thos., 4th earl of Southampton
  Winchester, 1625

Abbot, Geo., archbp. of Canterbury
  Canterbury, 1614°, 1621°, 1626\*
  Hull, 1621\*, 1624\*, 1625°, 1626\*
  Oxford U., 1625(I), 1626(I)

Babington, Gervase, bp. of Worcester
  Worcestershire, 1604\*

Baylay, Lewis, bp. of Bangor
  Caernarvonshire, 1621(I)\*, 1624(I)°, 1625(I)°, 1626(I)°, 1628(I)°

Bennett, Robt., bp. of Hereford
  Hereford, 1605(I)\*

Bilson, Thos., bp. of Winchester
  Winchester, 1614°

Bridgeman, John, bp. of Chester
  Wigan, 1625(I)°, 1628(I)°, s1640(I)°, a1640(I)°
  Liverpool, 1626(I)°

Carey, Valentine, bp. of Exeter
  St. Germans, 1624\*, 1625°, 1626\*

Cotton, Wm., bp. of Exeter
  St. Germans, 1604°, 1614°, 1621
  Camelford, 1604, 1614°
  Truro, 1621°

Dove, Thos., bp. of Peterborough
  Northamptonshire, 1604*

Goldsborough, Godfrey, bp. of Gloucester
  Gloucester, 1604*

Hall, Jos., bp. of Exeter
  St. Germans, 1628*
  Penryn, s1640°
  St. Mawes, s1640°, a1640°

Harsnett, Samuel, bp. of Norwich
  Gt. Yarmouth, 1621*, 1624*, 1625*

Hutton, Matthew, archbp. of York
  York, 1604*
  Ripon, 1604°

Lake, Arthur, bp. of Bath and Wells
  Minehead, 1621°, 1624°
  Somersetshire, 1624(I)*
  Wells, 1625*, 1626*
  Bridgewater, 1625°, 1626°

Laud, Wm. archbp. of Canterbury
  Reading, s1640*
  Canterbury, s1640*
  Oxford U., s1640*, a1640°

Matthew, Tobias, archbp. of York
  Ripon, 1614, 1621, 1624, 1625, 1626, 1628

Montagu, Jas., bp. of Bath and Wells
  Somersetshire, 1614*
  Wells, 1614°

Morton, Thos., bp. of Coventry and Lichfield
  Coventry, 1625*

Neile, Richard, bp. of Durham, Archbp. of York
  Yorkshire, 1621(I)*
  Ripon, s1640°

Piers, Wm., bp. of Bath and Wells
  Wells, s1640*

Williams, John, bp. of Lincoln
  Ilchester, 1621*, 1624°, 1625*
  Westminster, 1621(I)*, 1624(I)*, 1625(I)*, 1626(I)°, 1628(I)*
  Caernarvonshire, 1621(I)*, 1624(I)*, 1625(I)*, 1626(I)
  Cambridge U., 1624(I)*, 1625°
  Boston, 1624°, 1625°, 1626°, 1628°
  Hertford, 1624*
  Bishop's Castle, 1624°
  Caernarvon, 1624(I)*

# Appendix Eight

The following table, based on direct evidence for 440 elections from 1604 through 1628 and for 166 of the 1640 elections, sets out the tactics employed, along with similar figures for the seven preceding elections.

| Method | Employment in Number of Elections | | | |
|---|---|---|---|---|
| | 1604–28 | Spring 1640 | Autumn 1640 | Total |
| Aristocratic, court, clerical letters of recommendation ............ | 307 | 68 | 52 | 427 |
| Gentry letters of recommendation ............ | 106 | 39 | 21 | 166 |
| Canvassing and campaigning ............... | 150 | 35 | 31 | 216 |
| Intimidation and the creation of voices ........... | 82 | 11 | 8 | 101 |
| Interception of the writ ...................... | 14 | 6 | 0 | 20 |
| Violence ..................... | 12 | 2 | 5 | 19 |
| Use of blanks ................ | 10 | 0 | 2 | 12 |
| Employment of office: Sheriff ..................... | 40 | 6 | 7 | 53 |
| JP, deputy lt. .............. | 29 | 2 | 0 | 31 |
| Borough office or corporation decision ................... | 92 | 11 | 11 | 114 |
| Employment of ministers as campaign agents ......... | 10 | 4 | 1 | 15 |
| Financial intervention: Serve without pay .......... | 49 | 5 | 3 | 57 |
| Entertainment .............. | 25 | 11 | 9 | 45 |
| Bribery ................... | 2 | 2 | 2 | 6 |

# Bibliography

---

*Original Manuscript Materials*

Bodleian Library, Oxford
  Firth MSS
  Tanner MSS
  Rawlinson MSS
  MS Top. Kent e.6

British Museum
  Additional MSS
  Cottonian MSS
  Egerton MSS
  Harleian MSS
  Hatfield House (Salisbury) MSS (microfilm)
  Stowe MSS

Duchy of Cornwall Record Office
  Letters and Patents, 1620–1621
  Burgesses for Parliament, 1623–1624
  Letters and Warrants, 1639–1643

House of Lords Record Office

Lambeth Palace Library
  Shrewsbury and Talbot MSS

National Library of Wales
  Additional MSS
  Wynn of Gwydir MSS

Public Record Office
  State Papers Domestic, Reign of James I, SP 14
  State Papers Domestic, Reign of Charles I, SP 16
  Star Chamber cases, St. Chamber 8
  Venice Correspondence, St. P. Dom. 99
  Privy Council Registers, P. C. 2

Oxford University, Banks MSS
  Thomas Scott, "Canterbury Citizens for Parliament, 1626," MSS in the possession of Mr. William Urry of St. Edmunds Hall, Oxford

*County Record Office Materials*

Bedfordshire Record Office, various MSS
Berkshire Record Office
  Borough of Reading MSS
  Borough of Wallingford Minute Book
  Agnes Baker MSS
Cheshire Record Office
  Grosvenor MSS
Cornwall Record Office
  MSS of Sir John G. Carew Pole, Bart.
Devon Record Office
  Dartmouth Borough MSS
  Exeter City MSS
Essex Record Office
  Morant MSS
  Borough of Maldon MSS
Hampshire Record Office
  Whitehead's Letter Book
Hertfordshire Record Office
  Borough of Hertford MSS
Suffolk Record Office, Ipswich Branch
  Borough of Dunwich MSS
  Borough of Ipswich MSS
Isle of Wight Record Office
  Yarmouth Borough MSS
  Newtown Borough MSS
  Oglander MSS
Kent Record Office
  Sandwich Borough MSS
  New Romney Borough MSS
  Queenborough Borough MSS
  Dering MSS
  Darell of Colehill MSS
Lancashire Record Office
  Clitheroe Borough MSS
Northamptonshire Record Office·
  Ellesmere (Brackley) MSS
  Finch Hatton MSS
Shropshire Record Office
  Borough of Ludlow MSS
  Borough of Bridgnorth MSS
Somersetshire Record Office
  Phelips MSS
  Sanford MSS

Staffordshire Record Office
  D593S/4/60
East Sussex Record Office
  Winchelsea Borough MSS
  Corporation of Rye MSS
Warwickshire Record Office
  Warwick Borough MSS
Worcestershire Record Office
  Berington Family Papers
Yorkshire, East Riding Record Office
  Beverley Borough MSS

*Borough and City MSS*

Bedford Borough MSS
Bishop's Castle Corporation MSS
  First Minute Book of the Corporation
Boston Borough MSS
  Council Minute Books
Bradford City Museum, Cartwright Memorial Hall
  Spencer Stanhope MSS
Bristol Record Office
  Bristol Corporation MSS
Canterbury Cathedral Archives
  Canterbury City MSS, Burghmoot Book
Carlisle City MSS
Chippenham Borough MSS, Yelde Hall
Christchurch Borough MSS
Colchester Borough MSS
  Assembly Books of the Corporation
Coventry Libraries, Arts, and Museums Department
  Coventry Borough MSS
Evesham Public Library
  Barnard Collection
Gloucester Public Library
  Gloucester City MSS
  Gloucester City Minute Book of the Corporation
Grantham Borough MSS
  Court Minute Book I
Grimsby Borough MSS
Great Yarmouth Borough MSS
Guildford Museum and Muniment Room
  Loseley MSS
Harwich Borough MSS

Hastings Corporation MSS
  Common Books of Assembly
Hull Corporation MSS
  Corporation Letters
  Bench Book of the Corporation
Hythe Corporation MSS
  Borough Assembly Books
King's Lynn Borough MSS
  Hall Books of the Corporation
Leicestershire Museums, Art Galleries, and Records Service
  City of Leicester MSS
  Hall Papers Bound
  Hall Book of the Corporation
Norwich and Norfolk Record Office
  City of Norwich MSS
Salisbury Corporation MSS
Scarborough Borough MSS
  General Letters, B. 1
Sheffield City Library
  Wentworth-Woodhouse MSS
Shrewsbury County, Local Studies Library
  Shrewsbury Corporation MSS
St. Albans Public Library
  St. Albans Borough Records
Stamford Borough MSS
  Hall Books of the Corporation
Tewkesbury Corporation MSS
Worcester City MSS
  Worcester City Chamber Orders Books
York City Library
  City of York Housebooks

*Original Printed Materials*

*Acts of the Privy Council of England*
Bacon, Francis. *The Works of Sir Francis Bacon.* Ed. J. Spedding et al. 14 vols. London, 1849.
Batho, G. R., Ed. *The Household Papers of Henry Percy, Ninth Earl of Northumberland, 1564–1632.* Royal Historical Society, Camden Third Series, Vol. 43. London, 1962.
Birch, T. *The Court and Times of James I.* Ed. R. F. Williams. 2 vols. London, 1849.

_____. *The Court and Times of Charles I.* Ed. R. F. Williams, 2 vols. London, 1848.

Brown, R., G. C. Bentinck, H. F. Brown, and A. B. Hinds, eds. *Calendar of State Papers and Manuscripts relating to English Affairs, Existing in the Archives and Collections of Venice, and in Other Libraries of Northern Italy.* 38 vols. in 40. London, 1864 ff.

Bruce, J., ed. *Liber Familicus of Sir James Whitelocke.* Camden Society, Old Series, vol. 70. London, 1858.

_____, W. D. Hamilton, and S. C. Lomes, eds. *Calendar of State Papers, Domestic Series, of the Reign of Charles I, Preserved in the State Paper Department of Her Majesty's Public Record Office.* 12 vols. London, 1858–97.

*Cabala Sive Scrinia Sacra: Mysteries of State and Government in Letters of Illustrious Persons.* London, 1654.

*Calendar of Wynn of Gwydir Papers, 1515–1690.*

Clive, R. D., ed. *Documents Connected with the History of Ludlow.* London, 1841.

Collier, J. P., ed. *The Egerton Papers.* Camden Society, Old Series, vol. 12. London, 1840.

Collins, A., ed. *Letters and Memorials of State.* 2 vols. London, 1746.

Crossley, J., ed. *The Diary and Correspondence of Dr. John Worthington.* 2 vols. Chetham Society, Old Series. Manchester, 1847–55.

Dennett, J., ed. *Beverley Borough Records, 1575–1821.* Yorkshire Archaeological Society, Records Series, vol. 84. 1933.

East, R., ed. *Extracts from Records in the Possession of the Municipal Corporation of the Borough of Portsmouth.* Portsmouth, 1891.

Foster, E. R. *Proceedings in Parliament, 1610.* 2 vols. New Haven, Conn., 1966.

Foster, J., ed. *The Register of Admissions to Gray's Inn, 1521–1889.* London, 1889.

Gardiner, S. R., ed. *Debates in the House of Commons in 1625.* Camden Society, New Series, vol. 6. London, 1873.

Gibbs, A. E. *Corporation Records of St. Albans.* St. Albans, 1890.

Gilmore, G. D., ed. *The Papers of Richard Taylor of Clapham.* Bedfordshire Record Society, vol. 25. 1947.

Goldney, F. H., ed. *Records of Chippenham.* London, 1889.

Goodman, Godfrey. *The Court of King James the First.* Ed. J. S. Brewer. 2 vols. London, 1839.

Green, M. A. E., ed. *The Diary of John Rous.* Camden Society, Old Series, vol. 66. London, 1856.

Guilding, J. M., ed. *Reading Records: Diary of a Corporation.* 4 vols. 1892–96.

Halliwell, J. O., ed. *Autobiography and Correspondence of Sir Simonds D'Ewes.* 2 vols. London, 1845.

*Harleian Society*. Publications.

Heywood, J., and T. Wright, eds. *Cambridge University Transactions during the Puritan Controversies of the 16th and 17th Centuries*. 2 vols. London, 1854.

*Historical Manuscripts Commission*. Publications.

Hobbes, Thomas. *Behemoth*. Ed. W. Molesworth. B. Franklin rpt. New York, 1963.

————. *Leviathan*. Ed. A. R. Waller. Cambridge, 1904.

Howells, B. E., ed. *A Calendar of Letters Relating to North Wales*. University of Wales History and Law Series, vol. 23. Cardiff, 1967.

Hull, F., ed. *The White and Black Books of the Cinque Ports*. London, 1966.

Johnson, G. W., ed. *The Fairfax Correspondence*. 2 vols. London, 1848.

*Journals of the House of Commons, 1547–1714*. 17 vols. London, 1742 ff.

*Journals of the House of Lords, 1578–1714*. Vols. 2–19. London, 1767 ff.

Kemp, T., ed. *The Black Book of Warwick*. Warwick, 1898.

Knowler, W., ed. *The Earl of Strafford's Letters and Despatches with an Essay towards His Life by Sir George Radcliffe*. 2 vols. London, 1739.

Lemon, R., and M. A. E. Green, eds. *Calendar of State Papers, Domestic Series, of the Reigns of Edward VI, Mary, Elizabeth, and James I, Preserved in the State Paper Department of Her Majesty's Public Record Office*. 12 vols. London, 1856–72.

Lewis, T. T., ed. *Letters of the Lady Brilliana Harley*. Camden Society, Old Series, vol. 58. London, 1854.

Lodge, E., ed. *Illustrations of British History*. 2d ed. 3 vols. London, 1838.

Macray, W. D., ed. *Beaumont Papers*. Roxburgh Club. London, 1884.

Manship, Henry. *History of Great Yarmouth*. Ed. C. R. Palmer. 2 vols. Great Yarmouth, 1854–56.

Markham, C. A., and J. C. Cox, eds. *The Records of the Borough of Northampton*. 2 vols. Northampton, 1897.

Matthews, J. H., ed. *Records of the County Borough of Cardiff*. 6 vols. Cardiff and London, 1905.

McClure, N. E., ed. *The Letters of John Chamberlain*. 2 vols. Philadelphia, 1939.

Nalson, J., ed. *Affairs of State*. 2 vols. London, 1682.

Nichols, J., ed. *The Progresses, Processions, and Magnificent Festivities of King James the First, His Royal Consort, Family, and Court; Collected from Original Manuscripts, Scarce Pamphlets, Comprising Forty Masques and Entertainments; Ten Civic Pageants; Numerous Original Letters; and Annotated Lists of the Peers, Barons, and Knights Who Received Those Honours during the Reign of King James*. 4 vols. London, 1828.

Notestein, W., F. H. Relf, and H. Simpson, eds. *Commons Debates, 1621*. 7 vols. New Haven, Conn., 1935.

Ogle, O., W. H. Bliss, and C. H. Firth, eds. *Calendar of the Clarendon State Papers*. 4 vols. Oxford, 1872–1938.

Parsons, D., ed. *The Diary of Sir Henry Slingsby of Scriven, Bart.* London, 1836.

*Persecuto Undecima.* London, 1648.

Raine, J., ed. *The Correspondence of Dr. Matthew Hutton, Archbishop of York.* Surtees Society, vol. 17. London, 1843.

Roberts, G., ed. *The Diary of Walter Yonge.* Camden Society, Old Series, vol. 41. London, 1848.

Rushworth, J., *Historical Collections of Private Passages of State . . . .* 8 vols. London, 1659–1701.

Rymer, T., and R. Sanderson, eds. *Foedera, conventiones, literae, et sujuscunque generis acta publica, inter reges Anglise et alios quosvis imperatores, reges, pontifices, principes, vel communitates ab anno 1101, ud nostra usque tempora, habita aut tractata; ex autographis, fideliter exscripta.* 20 vols. London, 1704–32.

Salter, H. E., ed. *Oxford Council Acts, 1583–1626.* Oxford Historical Society, vol 87. 1928.

Saunders, H W., ed. *The Official Papers of Sir Nathaniel Bacon of Stiffkey, Norfolk, 1580–1620.* Camden Society, Third Series, vol. 26. London, 1915.

Scrope, R., and T. Monkhouse, eds. *State Papers Collected by Edward, Earl of Clarendon, Commencing 1621.* 3 vols. Oxford, 1767–86.

Somers, Lord. *A Collection of Scarce and Valuable Tracts.* Ed. W. Scott. 2d ed. 13 vols. London, 1810.

Spedding, J., et al. *See* Bacon, Francis.

Stanewell, L. M., *Calendar of the MSS of Kingston Upon Hull.* Hull, 1951.

Stevenson, W. H., et. al., eds. *Records of the Borough of Nottingham.* 9 vols. London and Nottingham, 1882–1956.

Stocker, J. J. "Pedigree of Smythe of Ostenhanger, Kent; of Smythe of Bidborough and Sutton-At-Hone, Kent; and of the Smythes, Viscounts Strangford, of Dormore, Ireland." *Archaeologia Cantiana,* vol. 20, 1893.

Sturgess, H. A. C., ed. *Register of Admissions to the Honourable Society of the Middle Temple, from the Fifteenth Century to 1944.* 3 vols. London, 1949.

Thomson, T. R., ed. *Materials for a History of Cricklade.* Oxford, 1958–61.

Tibbutt, H. G., ed. *The Life and Letters of Sir Lewis Dyve, 1599–1669.* Bedfordshire Historical Record Society, vol. 27. 1948.

Tyrwhitt, T., ed. *Proceedings and Debates.* 1621. 2 vols. 1766.

Whitelock, B. *Memorials of English Affairs.* 4 vols. Oxford, 1853.

Willson, D. H., ed. *The Parliamentary Diary of Robert Bowyer, 1606–1607.* Minneapolis, 1931.

Winthrop Papers, 5 vols. Massachusetts Historical Society, 1925–47.

Wood, Anthony, *Athenae Oxonienses,* ed. P. Bliss. 5 vols., London, 1813–20.

Worth, R. N., ed. *Calendar of the Plymouth Municipal Records.* Plymouth, 1893.

————, ed. *The Buller Papers.* Privately printed, 1895.

Yorke, P., earl of Hardwick, ed. *Miscellaneous State Papers.* 2 vols. London 1778.

*Secondary Authorities*

Albery, W. *A Parliamentary History of Horsham, 1295–1885.* London, 1927.

Alexander, J. J. "Dartmouth as a Parliamentary Borough." *Reports and Transactions of the Devonshire Association,* vol. 43, 1911.

———. "Members of Parliament for Exeter." *Reports and Transactions of the Devonshire Association,* vol. 61, 1929.

———. "Bere Alston as a Parliamentary Borough." *Reports and Transactions of the Devonshire Association,* vol. 41, 1909.

Allen, J. *History of the Borough of Liskeard.* London, 1856.

Aspinal, A., ed. *Parliament through Seven Centuries: Reading and Its MP's.* London, 1962.

Atkinson, W. A. "A Parliamentary Election in Knaresborough in 1628." *Yorkshire Archaeological Journal,* vol. 34, 1938–39.

Aubrey, E. R. *Speed's History of Southampton.* Southampton Record Society, vol. 8. Southampton, 1909.

Aylmer, G. E. *The King's Servants.* London, 1961.

Bacon, N. *Annals of Ipswich.* Ed. W. W. Richardson. Ipswich, 1884.

Bailey, T. *Annals of Nottinghamshire.* 4 vols. London and Nottingham, 1852–55.

Baines, E. *The History of the County Palatine and Duchy of Lancaster.* Ed. J. Croston. Rev. ed. 5 vols. London and Manchester, 1888–93.

Baines, T. *History of the Commerce and Town of Liverpool.* London and Liverpool, 1852.

Baker, A. C. *Historic Abingdon.* Abingdon, 1963.

Baker, G. *The History and Antiquities of the County of Northampton.* 2 vols., London, 1822–41.

Baker, J. B. *The History of Scarborough.* London, 1882.

Bankes, G. *The Story of Corfe Castle.* London, 1853.

Barnes, T. G. *Somerset, 1625–1640.* London, 1961.

Bates Harbin, S. W. "Knights of the Shire for Somerset." *Somersetshire Archaeological and Natural History Society,* 1939.

Bean, W. W. *The Parliamentary Representation of the Six Northern Counties of England and Their Cities and Boroughs (1603–1886). With Lists of Members and Biographical Notices.* Hull, 1890.

Beaven, A. *The Aldermen of the City of London.* 2 vols. London, 1908–13.

Beesley, A. *The History of Banbury.* London, 1841.

Bennett, J. *History of Tewkesbury.* Tewkesbury, 1830.

Black, Sir F. *The Parliamentary History of the Isle of Wight.* Newport, 1939.

Blackner, J. *The History of Nottingham.* Nottingham, 1815.

Blomefield, F. *An Essay Towards a Topographical History of the County of Norfolk.* 5 vols. London, 1739–75.

Bohannon, M. E. "The Essex Election of 1604." *English Historical Review,* vol. 48, 1933.

Boys, W. *Collections for an History of Sandwich in Kent. With Notices of the Other Cinque Ports and Members, and of Richborough.* Canterbury, 1792.

Bradfer Lawrence, H. L. *Castle Rising.* King's Lynn, 1932.

———. *The Merchants of Lynn.* Ed. C. Jussey. London, 1929.

Brand, J. *The History and Antiquities of Newcastle upon Tyne.* 2 vols. London, 1878–81.

Brayley, E. W. *A Topographical History of Surrey.* Rev. and ed. Edward Walford. 4 vols. London, 1878–81.

Brooke, F. W. *The Council of the North.* Historical Association Pamphlet. 1953.

Brown, A. *The Genesis of the United States.* 2 vols. Boston and New York, 1891.

Brunton, D., and D. H. Pennington. *Members of the Long Parliament.* Cambridge, 1954.

Burke, J., and J. B. Burke. *A Genealogical and Heraldic Dictionary of the Peerages . . . Extinct, Dormant, & in Abeyance.* 2d ed. London, 1840.

Burton, G. *Chronology of Stamford.* Stamford and London, 1846.

Carroll, R. "Parliamentary Elections for Yorkshire, 1625–1660." Ph.D. dissertation, Vanderbilt University, 1964.

Carroll, R. "Yorkshire Parliamentary Boroughs in the Seventeenth Century", *Northern History,* vol. 3, 1968.

Cartwright, J. J. *Chapters in the History of Yorkshire.* Wakefield, 1872.

Cave-Brown, J. "Knights of the Shire for Kent." *Archaeologia Cantiana,* vol. 21, 1895.

Chandler, G. *Liverpool under James I.* Liverpool, 1960.

———. *Liverpool under Charles I,* Liverpool, 1965.

Cholmley, Sir H. *The Memoirs of Sir Hugh Cholmley.* Privately printed, 1870.

Clarke, G. R. *The History of Ipswich.* Ipswich, 1830.

Cliffe, J. T. *The Yorkshire Gentry.* London, 1969.

Clodd, H. P. *Aldeburgh, The History of an Ancient Borough.* Ipswich, 1959.

Clutterbuck, R. *The History and Antiquities of the County of Hertford.* 3 vols. London, 1815–27.

Coate, M. *Cornwall in the Great Civil War, 1642–1660.* Oxford, 1933.

———. "The Vyvyan Family of Trelowarren." *Transactions of the Royal Historical Society,* 4th Series, vol. 32, 1950.

Cokayne, G. E. *The Complete Peerage of England, Scotland, Ireland, Great Britain, and the United Kingdom.* 8 vols. London, 1887–98.

Collinson, P. *The Elizabethan Puritan Movement.* London, 1967.

*Complete Parochial History of the County of Cornwall, A.* 4 vols. London and Truro, 1867–72.

Cooper, C. H. *Annals of Cambridge.* 5 vols. Cambridge, 1842–53.

Copinger, W. A. *Manors of Suffolk.* 7 vols. London and Manchester, 1905–12.

Courtney, W. P. *The Parliamentary Representation of Cornwall to 1832.* London, 1889.

Cross, C. *The Puritan Earl,* London, 1966.

Cussans, J. E. *History of Hertfordshire.* 3 vols. London and Hertford, 1870–81.

Dodd, A. H. *Studies in Stuart Wales.* Cardiff, 1952.

_____. "Wales's Parliamentary Apprenticeship." *Transactions of the Honorable Society of Cymmrodorion,* London, 1944.

_____. "Wales in the Parliaments of Charles I," pt. 1, *1625–1649. Transactions of the Honorable Society of Cymmrodorion,* London, 1946.

Drakard, J. *The History of Stamford.* Stamford, 1822.

Edwards, E. *Parliamentary Elections of the Borough of Shrewsbury,* Shrewsbury, 1859.

Elliott, J. H. "England and Europe: A Common Malady?" *In* C. Russell, ed. *The Origins of the English Civil War.* London, 1973.

Elton, G. R. "Tudor Government: Points of Contact: I. Parliament." *Transactions of the Royal Historical Society,* fifth series, vol. 24, 1970.

Eustace, G. W. *Arundel, Borough and Castle.* London, 1922.

Evans, J. *A Chronological Outline of the History of Bristol.* Bristol, 1824.

Everitt, A. *The Community of Kent and the Great Rebellion, 1640–1660.* Leicester, 1966.

_____. "Social Mobility in Early Modern England." *Past & Present,* vol. 33, 1966.

_____. "The County Community." *In* E. W. Ives, ed., *The English Revolution, 1600–1660.* New York, 1971.

Farnel, J. E. "The Aristocracy and Leadership of Parliament in the English Civil Wars." *Journal of Modern History,* vol. 44, 1972.

Farnham, E. "The Somersetshire Election of 1614." *English Historical Review,* vol. 46, 1931.

Ferguson, R. *A History of Cumberland.* London, 1898.

Finch, M. E. *The Wealth of Five Northamptonshire Families, 1540–1640.* Northamptonshire Record Society, vol. 19. Oxford, 1956.

Fitch, E. A. "The Lords Lieutenants of Essex." *Essex Review,* vol. 7, 1898.

Flemion, J. S. "The Struggle for the Petition of Right in the House of Lords: The Study of an Opposition Party Victory." *Journal of Modern History,* vol. 45, 1973.

Fletcher, A. *A County Community in Peace and War: Sussex 1600–1660.* London, 1975.

Fletcher, A. J. "Sir Thomas Wentworth and the Restoration of Pontefract as a Parliamentary Borough." *Northern History,* vol. 6, 1971.

Forster, J. *Sir John Eliot.* 2 vols. London, 1864.

Fosbrook, T. *History of the City of Gloucester.* London, 1819.

Fox, G. *History of Pontefract.* Pontefract, 1827.

Frear, M. R. "The Election at Great Marlow in 1640." *Journal of Modern History,* vol. 14, 1942.

Gardiner, S. R. *History of England from the Accession of James I to the Outbreak of the Civil War, 1603–1642.* 10 vols. London, 1883–84.

Gaskin, R. T. "The Cholmleys of Whitby." *Bradford Antiquary,* New Series, vol. 2, 1905.

Gleason, J. H. *The Justices of the Peace in England, 1558–1640.* Oxford, 1969.

Gooder, A., ed., *The Parliamentary Representation of the County of York, 1258–1832,* vol. 2. Yorkshire Archaeological Society, vol. 96, 1938.

Gribble, J. *Memorials of Barnstaple.* Barnstaple, 1830.

Grimwood, C. G., and S. A. Kay. *History of Sudbury.* Sudbury, 1952.

Groome, A. N. "Higham Ferrers Elections." *Northamptonshire Past and Present,* vol. 2, 1958.

Gruenfelder, J. K. "The Parliamentary Election at Chester, 1621." *Transactions of the Historical Society of Lancashire and Cheshire,* vol. 120, 1968.

_____. "Rye and the Parliament of 1621." *Sussex Archaeological Collections,* vol. 107, 1969.

_____. "The Parliamentary Election in Northamptonshire, 1626." *Northamptonshire Past and Present,* vol. 4, no. 3, 1968–69.

_____. "The Spring Parliamentary Election at Hastings, 1640." *Sussex Archaeological Collections,* vol. 105, 1967.

_____. "The Election for Knights of the Shire of Essex in the Spring, 1640." *Transactions of the Essex Archaeological Society,* vol. 2, third ser., part 2, 1967.

_____. "The Spring, 1640, Parliamentary Election at Abingdon." *Berkshire Archaeological Journal,* vol. 65, 1970.

_____. "The Election to the Short Parliament, 1640." *In* H. Reinmuth, Jr., ed. *Early Stuart Studies.* Minneapolis, 1970.

_____. "The Electoral Influence of the Earls of Huntingdon 1603–1640." *Transactions of the Leicestershire Archaeological Society,* vol. 50, 1974–75.

_____. "The Lord Wardens and Elections, 1604–1628." *Journal of British Studies,* vol. 16, 1976.

_____. "The Electoral Patronage of Sir Thomas Wentworth, Earl of Strafford, 1614–1640." *Journal of Modern History,* vol. 49, 1977.

_____. "Two Midland Parliamentary Elections of 1604, Northamptonshire and Worcestershire." *Midland History,* vol. 3, 1976.

_____. "Gloucester's Parliamentary Elections, 1604–1640." *Transactions of the Bristol & Gloucestershire Archaeological Society,* vol. 96, 1978.

_____. "The Parliamentary Election for Shrewsbury, 1604." *Transactions of the Shropshire Archaeological Society,* vol. 59, 1978.

## 264    Bibliography

_____. "Yorkshire Borough Elections, 1603–1640."*Yorkshire Archaeological Journal*, vol. 49, 1977.

_____. "Dorsetshire Elections, 1604–1640." *Albion*, vol. 10, 1978.

_____. "The Wynns of Gwydir and Parliamentary Elections in Wales, 1604–1640." *Welsh History Review: Cylchgrawn Hanes Cymru*, vol. 9, 1978.

_____. | "Boston's early Stuart Elections, 1604–1640." *Lincolnshire History and Archaeology*, vol. 13, 1978.

_____. "Radnorshire's Parliamentary Elections, 1604–1640." *Transactions of the Radnorshire Society*, vol. 47, 1977.

Hacket, J. *Scrinia reserata: A Memorial Offered to the Great Deservings of John Williams, D.D., Containing a Series of the Most Remarkable Occurences and Transactions of His Life.* 2 parts. London, 1693.

Harrison, W., ed. *Ripon Millenary Record*, 2 parts in one vol. Ripon, 1892.

Hassell Smith, A. *County and Court: Government and Politics in Norfolk, 1558–1603.* Oxford, 1974.

Hasted, E. *The History and Topographical Survey of the County of Kent.* 2d ed., 12 vols. Canterbury, 1797–1801.

Hawkins, M. "The Government: Its Role and Its Aims." *In* C. Russell, ed. *The Origins of the English Civil War.* London, 1973.

Hedges, J. K. *History of Wallingford.* 2 vols. London, 1881.

Hembry, P. M. *The Bishops of Bath and Wells.* Oxford, 1967.

Hexter, J. H. *The Reign of King Pym.* Cambridge, Mass., 1961.

Hill, C. *Puritanism and Revolution.* London, 1958.

_____. *The Economic Problems of the Church from Archbishop Whitgift to the Long Parliament.* Oxford, 1956.

_____. "The Many-Headed Monster in Late Tudor and Early Stuart Political Thinking." *In* C. H. Carter, ed. *From the Renaissance to the Counter-Reformation: Essays in Honour of Garrett Mattingly.* London, 1966.

_____. *Society and Puritanism in Pre-Revolutionary England.* London, 1964.

_____. *The World Turned Upside Down.* London, 1972.

Hill, J. W. F. *Tudor and Stuart Lincoln.* Cambridge, 1956.

Hill, L. M. "County Government in Caroline England." *In* C. Russell, ed. *The Origins of the English Civil War.* London, 1973.

Hills, W. H. *History of East Grinstead.* East Grinstead, 1906.

Hirst, D. "The Defection of Sir Edward Dering, 1640–41." *Historical Journal*, vol. 15, 1972.

_____. "Elections and the Privileges of the House of Commons in the Early Seventeenth Century: Confrontation or Compromise?" *Historical Journal*, vol. 18, 1975.

_____. *The Representative of the People?* Cambridge, 1975.

Hoare, R. C., et. al. *The Modern History of South Wiltshire.* 6 vols. London, 1822–43.

Hodgson, J. *A History of Northumberland.* 2 parts in 6 vols. Newcastle-on-Tyne and London, 1820–58.

Horsfield, T. W. *The History, Antiquities, and Topography of the County of Sussex.* 2 vols. Lewes and London, 1835.

Howell, R., Jr. *Newcastle-Upon-Tyne and the Puritan Revolution.* Oxford, 1967.

Hulme, H. *The Life of Sir John Eliot, 1592–1632.* New York, 1957.

Hunter Blair, C. H. "Knights of the Shire for Northumberland." *Archaeologia Aeliana,* 1945.

_____. "Members of Parliament for Morpeth." *Archaeologia Aeliana,* 1945–46.

Hutchins, J. *The History and Antiquities of the County of Dorset.* 3d ed., 4 vols. Westminster, 1861–70.

James, M. *Family, Lineage, and Civil Society.* Oxford, 1974.

Jefferson, S. *The History and Antiquities of Carlisle.* Carlisle and London, 1838.

Jones, E. G. "County Politics and Electioneering, 1558–1625." *Caernarvonshire Historical Society, Cymdeithas Hanes Sir Caernarfon Transactions,* 1939.

Jones, J. B. *Annals of Dover.* Dover, 1916.

Keeler, M. F. *The Long Parliament, 1640–1641.* Memoirs of the American Philosophical Society, vol. 36. Philadelphia, 1954.

Kenny, R. W. "Parliamentary Influence of Charles Howard, Earl of Nottingham, 1536–1624." *Journal of Modern History,* vol. 39, 1967.

Kershaw, R. N. "The Elections for the Long Parliament, 1640." *English Historical Review,* vol. 38, 1923.

Ketton-Cremer, R. W. *Norfolk in the Civil War.* Hamden, 1970.

Kingston, A. *Herefordshire during the Great Civil War.* London, 1894.

Lambert, U. *Blechingley: A Parish History.* 2 vols. London, 1921.

Latimer, J. *Annals of Bristol in the Seventeenth Century.* Bristol, 1900.

Lawrance, W. T. *Parliamentary History of Cornwall.* Truro, 1925.

Lawson-Tancred, Sir T. *Records of a Yorkshire Manor.* London, 1937.

_____. "Parliamentary History of Aldborough and Boroughbridge." *Yorkshire Archaeological Journal,* vol. 27, 1923.

Lehmberg, S. E. *The Reformation Parliament, 1529–1536.* Cambridge, 1970.

Lipscombe, G. *The History and Antiquities of the County of Buckingham.* 4 vols. London, 1847.

Lloyd, H. A. *The Gentry of south-west Wales.* Cardiff, 1968.

Lowndes, G. A., ed. "The History of the Barrington Family." *Transactions of the Essex Archaeological Society,* New Series, 2, 1884.

MacCaffrey, W. *Exeter, 1540–1640,* Cambridge, Mass., 1958.

Maclear, J. F. "Puritan Relations with Buckingham." *Huntingdon Library Quarterly,* vol. 21, 1958.

Manning, B. *The English People and the English Revolution, 1640–1649.* London, 1976.

## 266　Bibliography

Manning, Q., and W. Bray. *The History and Antiquities of the County of Surrey*. 3 vols. London, 1804–14.

Mason, R. H. *History of Norfolk*. London, 1884.

Mathew, D. "Wales and England in the early Seventeenth Century." *Transactions of the Honorable Society of Commrodiorion*. London, 1955.

May, G. *A Descriptive History of the Town of Evesham, from the Foundation of Its Saxon Monastery; with Notices of the Ancient Deanery of Vale*. Evesham, 1845.

Mayo, C. H. "Shaftesbury." *Proceedings of the Dorset Natural History and Antiquarian Field Club*, vol. 15, 1894

McKisack, M. *The Parliamentary Representation of the English Boroughs*. Oxford, 1932.

Merewether, H. A., and A. J. Stephens, *The History of the Boroughs and Municipal Corporations of the United Kingdom*. 3 vols. London, 1835.

Moir, T. *The Addled Parliament of 1614*. Oxford, 1958.

Morant, P. *The History and Antiquities of the County of Essex*. 2 vols. London, 1768.

Morrill, J. S. *Cheshire, 1630–1660*. Oxford, 1974.

Muir, R. *History of Liverpool*. 2d ed. London, 1907.

Mullinger, J. B. *The University of Cambridge*. 3 vols. Cambridge, 1873–1911.

Nash, T. R. *Collections for the History of Worcestershire*. 2 vols. London, 1781–82.

Neale, Sir John. *The Elizabethan House of Commons*. London, 1949.

———. *Elizabeth I and Her Parliaments*. 2 vols. London, 1953–57.

Nevinson, C. *History of Stamford*. Stamford and London, 1879.

Newton, A. P. *The Colonising Activities of the English Puritans*. New Haven, Conn., 1914.

Nichols, J. *The History and Antiquities of the County of Leicester*. 4 vols. London, 1795–1815.

Nicholson, J., and R. Burn, *The History and Antiquities of Westmorland and Cumberland*. 2 vols. London, 1777.

Notestein, W. *The House of Commons, 1604–1610*, New Haven, Conn., 1971.

Oliver, G. *The History and Antiquities of the Town and Minster of Beverley*. Beverley, 1829.

Oliver, G. *The History of the City of Exeter*. Exeter, 1861.

"Orders of the Corporation of Shrewsbury, 1511–1735, The." *Shropshire Archaeological and Natural History Society*, vol. 11, 1888.

Ormerod, G. *The History of the County Palatine and City of Chester*. 2d ed., rev. T. Helsby, 3 vols. London, 1875–82.

Page, W., et al., eds. *The Victoria History of the Counties of England*. Westminster, 1900–.

Palmer, C. J. *The History of Great Yarmouth*. Great Yarmouth and London, 1856.

Pape, T. *Newcastle-under-Lyme in Tudor and Early Stuart Times*. Manchester, 1938.

Pearl, V. *London and the Outbreak of the Puritan Revolution*. Oxford, 1961.

Pink, W. D., and A. B. Beavan, *The Parliamentary Representation of Lancashire, County and Borough, 1258–1885*. London, 1889.

Pink, W. D. *Notes and Queries for Somerset and Dorset*. Vol. 2, 1891.

Plumb, J. H. "The Growth of the Electorate in England from 1600 to 1715." *Past & Present*, vol. 45, 1968.

Porritt, E. and A. G. *The Unreformed House of Commons*. 2 vols. Cambridge, 1903–9.

Prestwich, M. *Cranfield: Politics and Profits under the Early Stuarts*. Oxford, 1966.

Pryce, G. *A Popular History of Bristol*. Bristol, 1861.

Raven, J. J. *History of Suffolk*. London, 1895.

Reid, R. R. *The King's Council of the North*. London and New York, 1921.

*Return of the Names of Every Member of the Lower House of Parliament of England, Scotland, and Ireland, with Name of Constituency Represented, and Date of Return from 1213–1874*. 2 vols. London, 1878.

Rex, M. B. *University Representation in England, 1604–1690*. New York, 1954.

Rickwood, G. "Members of Parliament for Colchester." *Essex Review*, vol. 5, 1896.

Richards, W. *The History of Lynn*. 2 vols. London, 1812.

Rogers, A., ed. *The Making of Stamford*. Leicester, 1965.

Roots, I. "The Central Government and the Local Community." *In* E. W. Ives, ed. *The English Revolution, 1600–1660*. New York, 1971.

Roskell, J. S. *The Commons in the Parliament of 1422*. Manchester, 1954.

Rowe, V. A. "The Influence of the Earls of Pembroke on Parliamentary Elections 1625–41." *English Historical Review*, vol. 50, 1935.

Rudge, T. *The History and Antiquities of Gloucester*. Gloucester, 1803.

Ruigh, R. *The Parliament of 1624*. Cambridge, Mass., 1971.

Russell, C. "Parliamentary History in Perspective, 1604–1629." *History*, vol. 61, 1976.

————. ed. *The Origins of the English Civil War*. London, 1973.

————. *The Crisis of Parliaments*. Oxford, 1971.

Sainty, J. C. *Lieutenants of Counties, 1585–1642*. Special Supplement no. 8, *Bulletin of the Institute of Historical Research*. London, 1970.

Schwarz, M. L. "Viscount Saye and Sele, Lord Brooke, and the Aristocratic Protest to the First Bishop's War." *Canadian Journal of History*, vol. 7, 1972.

Seddon, P. R. "A Parliamentary Election at East Retford 1624." *Transactions of the Thoroton Society of Nottinghamshire*, vol. 76, 1972.

Sharpe, R. R. *London and the Kingdom*. 3 vols. London, 1894.

Simpson, R. *A Collection of Fragments Illustrative of the History and Antiquities of Derby, Compiled from Authentic Sources*. 2 vols. in 1. Derby, 1826.

Slack, P. "Poverty and Politics in Salisbury, 1597–1666." *In* P. Clark and P. Slack, eds. *Crisis and Order in English Towns, 1500–1700*. London, 1972.

Slack, P. "An Election to the Short Parliament." *Bulletin of the Institute of Historical Research*, vol. 46, 1973.

Snow, V. F. *Essex the Rebel*. Lincoln, 1970.

Somerville, R. *Office-Holders in the Duchy and County Palatine of Lancaster*. London and Chichester, 1972.

Sperling, F. C. D. *Hodson's History of the Borough of Sudbury*. Sudbury, 1896.

Stephen, L., and S. Lee. *Dictionary of National Biography*. 22 vols. New York, 1908–9.

Stirling, A. M. W. *The Hothams*. 2 vols. London, 1918.

Stone, L. "The Electoral Influence of the Second Earl of Salisbury, 1614–68." *English Historical Review*, vol. 71, 1956.

————. *The Crisis of the Aristocracy, 1558–1641*. Oxford, 1964.

————. *An Elizabethan, Sir Horatio Palavicino*. Oxford, 1956.

————, *The Causes of the English Revolution, 1529–1642*. New York, 1972.

————. *Family and Fortune*. Oxford, 1973.

Styles, P. "The Corporation of Bewdley under the Later Stuarts." *University of Birmingham Historical Journal*, vol. 1, 1947.

Suckling, A. *The History and Antiquities of the County of Suffolk*, 2 vols. London, 1846–48.

Tighe, R. R., and J. E. Davis, eds. *Annals of Windsor*. 2 vols. London, 1858.

Thompson, C. "The Origins of the Politics of the Parliamentary Middle Group." *Transactions of the Royal Historical Society*, fifth ser., vol. 22, 1972.

Thompson, J. *The History of Leicester from the Time of the Romans to the End of the Seventeenth Century*. Leicester and London, 1849.

Townsend, G. F. *The Town and Borough of Leominster*, Leominster, n.d.

Trevor-Roper, H. R. *Archbishop Laud*. 2d ed. London, 1962.

Turnor, E. *Collections for the History of the Town and Soke of Grantham*. London, 1806.

Tyacke, N. "Puritanism, Arminianism, and Counter-Revolution." *In* C. Russell, ed. *The Origins of the English Civil War*. London, 1973.

Upton, A. F. *Sir Arthur Ingram*. Oxford, 1961.

De Villiers, Lady E. "Parliamentary Boroughs Restored by the House of Commons, 1621–41." *English Historical Review*, vol. 68, 1952.

Walzer, M. *The Revolution of the Saints*. Paperback ed. New York, 1968.

Waylen, J. *Launceston, Past and Present*. London, 1884.

Wedgwood, J. C. *The Parliamentary History of Staffordshire*. 2 vols. Birmingham, 1919–20.

Weeks, W. S. *Clitheroe in the Seventeenth Century*. Clitheroe, n.d.

Weyman, H. T. "Members of Parliament for Ludlow." *Transactions of the Shropshire Archaeological and Natural History Society*, 2d ser., vol. 7, 1895.

_____. "The Members of Parliament for Bishop's Castle." *Transactions of the Shropshire Archaeological and Natural History Society*, 2d ser., vol. 10, 1898.

Whitaker, T. D. *A History of Richmondshire in the North Riding of the County of York*. 2 vols. London, 1823.

Whitley, T. W. *Parliamentary Representation of the City of Coventry*. Coventry, 1894.

Wilks, G. *The Barons of the Cinque Ports and the Parliamentary Representation of Hythe, 1265–1892*. Folkestone, 1892.

Willcox, W. B. *Gloucestershire: A Study in Local Government, 1590–1640*, New Haven, Conn., 1940.

Williams, J. *History of Radnorshire*. 2d ed. Brecknock, 1905.

Williams, P. *The Council in the Marches of Wales under Elizabeth I*. Cardiff, 1958.

Williams, W. R. *The Parliamentary History of the County of Gloucester*. Hereford, 1898.

_____. *The Parliamentary History of the County of Hereford*. Brecknock, 1896.

_____. *The Parliamentary History of the County of Oxford*. Brecknock, 1899.

_____. *The Parliamentary History of the Principality of Wales, 1541–1895*. Brecknock, 1895.

_____. *The Parliamentary History of the County of Worcester*. Hereford, 1897.

Willson, D. H. *The Privy Councillors in the House of Commons, 1604–1629*. Minneapolis, 1940.

_____. *King James VI & I*. London, 1956.

Wood, A. *The History and Antiquities of the University of Oxford*. Ed. J. Gutch. 3 vols. Oxford, 1792–96.

Worth, R. N. *History of Plymouth*. Plymouth, 1890.

Wright, T. *The History and Topography of the County of Essex*. 2 vols. London, 1831–35.

Zagorin, P. *The Court and the Country*. London, 1969.

# Index

Abingdon, 152, 198, 199

Abbot, George, archbishop of Canterbury, 4, 10–11, 26 n. 29, 68; and elections of 1625 and 1626, 128

Aldborough, 45, 46, 84, 94, 97, 98, 99, 100

Aldeburgh, 135–36, 193

Alford, Edward, 11, 158, 180 n. 68

Alford, Sir William, 99, 100, 101, 119 n. 98

Anglesey, 14, 25 n. 19, 216

Andover, 20

Appleby, 166–67, 181 n. 79

Aristocratic electoral influence, 84, 85, 90, 95, 96, 109; and Charles I, 184, 189; in county elections, 8; in elections of 1604–10, 33, 35–41, 52, 53 n. 7, 54 n. 10, 55 nn. 14 and 17, 221, 222; in elections of 1604–28, 213, 219 n. 1; in elections of 1614–28, 123–69, 182 n. 84, 182 n. 86, 213; in elections of 1604–40, 223, 237–51; in elections of 1640, 189, 193–95, 203 n. 7, 204 n. 11, 205 n. 13, 207 n. 20, 207 nn. 23–24, 208 n. 25, 210 n. 34, 213, 218; in Elizabethan elections, 34–35, 123; and nomination of outsiders, 216, 217; of opposition peers (1640), 65, 189, 190, 191–93, 204 n. 10, 205 n. 14, 206 n. 17, 206 nn. 18–19, 213–14. See also under individual peers

Arundel, 15, 40, 132, 172 n. 19, 212 n. 41

Arundell, Thomas, Lord Arundell of Wardour, 5, 23 n. 7, 37, 38, 166, 207 n. 24

Ashton, William, 96, 161, 166

Askwith, Sir Robert, 7, 51, 57 n. 37

Bacon, Sir Francis: and Caernarvonshire, 105; and Cambridge, 5; and Cecil, earl of Salisbury, 34; and election planning, 34, 59, 60–61, 62, 63, 64, 65, 66, 86, 109, 214; as M.P. for Ipswich, 41; and parliament, 34, 60; and Prince's Council, 95; and St. Albans, 161; on Stockbridge election of 1614, 74

Badger, Sir Thomas, 82, 148, 177 n. 49

Bagg, Sir James, 129, 146, 147–48

Banbury, 152, 153, 206 n. 18

Barnardiston family, 84, 85, 197, 217

Barnstaple, 197, 210 n. 36

Barrett, Sir Edward, Lord Newburgh, 88, 185–86, 187–88

Barrington family, 49, 155

Barrington, Sir Francis, 155, 156–57, 158

Barrington, Sir Thomas, 191–92, 200, 206 n. 19, 214

Bash, Sir Edward, 164, 166, 203 n. 7

Bath, 51

Bayly, Lewis, bishop of Bangor, 17, 21, 105, 106

Bayntun, Sir Edward, 27 nn. 33–34, 95

Bedford, 5–6, 23 n. 9, 199, 206 n. 18, 210 n. 37

Bedfordshire, 23 n. 9, 25 n. 19, 206 n. 18

Beecher, Sir William, 75, 126, 145, 146, 202 n. 5

Beeralston, 36, 37, 179 n. 62, 202

Berkshire, 25 n. 19, 38, 139, 152, 154, 182 n. 82, 194, 210 n. 37

Berwick-upon-Tweed, 187, 198, 208 n. 25

Bewdley, 36, 90, 96, 121 n. 111, 184, 216, 219 n. 11

Bishop's Castle, 18, 40, 136–37, 173 n. 26, 209 n. 32

Blechingly, 17, 20, 39, 40, 139, 140

Bodmin, 87, 177 n. 47, 184

Borough elections, 4, 22 nn. 3–4, 50, 217, 226; contested elections in, 10–13, 30 n. 47, 44–45, 46–47, 50–51, 73–75, 80–81, 90–91, 94–96, 114 n. 56, 114 n. 59, 131, 134, 140, 145–46, 147, 148, 149, 153, 154, 158, 176 n. 45, 179 n. 59, 185, 186–88, 193, 195, 197–98, 204 n. 10, 210 n. 37, 216, 218, 219 n. 10 (expenses of, 19, 20); effect of wages and costs on, 7–8, 24 n.

Borough elections (*continued*)
16, 25 n. 17, 27 n. 33, 57 n. 40; election of legal officers and their connections in, 3, 5–7, 23 n. 10, 24 n. 11, 24 n. 13, 93–94, 94–95, 100, 148, 153, 154, 163, 165, 192, 197–99, 210 n. 35; election of outsiders in, 52, 58 n. 41, 82, 87–88, 89–90, 96–97, 126, 128, 141, 142, 148, 161, 162, 163, 165, 166, 194, 195, 196, 216, 217, 219 n. 11; electorate and electoral tactics in, 4–5, 7–8, 15, 16–17, 18, 19, 20, 29 nn. 41–42, 30 n. 47, 55 n. 16, 96–97, 125, 129, 133, 135, 137, 147, 178 n. 50, 198, 199, 200, 201, 202, 209 n. 32, 210 n. 37, 211 n. 40, 212 n. 41; influence of aristocracy on, 3, 5, 23 n. 9, 24 n. 16, 25 n. 17, 26 n. 32, 27 n. 33, 27 n. 35, 54 n. 10, 55 n. 14, 55 n. 17, 57 n. 40 (in 1604, 33, 35–41, 53 n. 7; in 1614–28, 80–82, 83–85, 101–2, 110 n. 16, 118 n. 89, 119 n. 100, 122 n. 113, 124–42, 145–50, 151, 152–54, 157–59, 161–63, 164–67, 169 n. 5, 170 n. 6, 172 n. 15, 172 n. 19, 174 n. 34, 175 n. 39, 176 n. 46, 177 n. 49, 180 n. 74, 180 n. 75, 181 n. 76, 181 n. 78, 181 n. 79, 216; in 1640, 191–92, 193–95, 203 n. 7, 204 n. 10, 205 n. 12, 206 nn. 18–19, 207 nn. 23–24, 208 n. 25, 210 n. 34, 218); influence of borough corporations on, 3, 6–7, 21, 23 n. 8, 26 n. 30, 27 n. 34, 51, 57 n. 37, 57 n. 40, 120 n. 103, 136, 145–46, 149, 154, 158, 165, 176 n. 45, 197–98, 221; influence of court on, 3 (in 1604, 43–47, 55 nn. 19–20; in 1614–28, 73–99, 103–4, 107, 114 n. 58, 114 n. 69, 116 n. 76, 117 n. 86, 121 n. 111, 122 n. 113, 129, 178 n. 52, 178 n. 58; in 1640, 184–88, 189, 196, 202 n. 5, 203 n. 9, 205 n. 12); influence of gentry on, 3, 8–9, 25 n. 20, 27 n. 34, 57 n. 40 (in 1604, 50, 51–52; in 1614–28, 79, 80, 82, 83, 84, 85, 89–90, 94, 95–96, 97, 99–102, 112 n. 38, 115 n. 61, 116 n. 72, 119 nn. 95–96, 119 n. 100, 120 n. 103, 121 n. 111, 122 n. 113, 129, 144, 166, 173 n. 26, 177 nn. 47–48, 178 nn. 52–53, 179 n. 62, 180 n. 68, 180 n. 75); reasons for contested elections in, 10–13, 24 n. 14, 26 n. 29, 57 n. 36, 117 n. 83, 121 n. 111, 193, 195, 198, 199, 203 n. 8, 207 n. 23, 219 n. 10; of 1604, 51, 57 n. 40; of 1640, 193, 195, 198, 199
Bossiney, 4–5, 36, 86, 88, 89, 115 n. 69, 147, 202 n. 5
Boston, 142, 165, 210 n. 36
Brackley, 22 n. 4, 39
Bramber, 132, 202

Breconshire, 25 n. 19, 203 n. 9
Bridgeman, Sir Orlando, 78, 187, 189, 196
Bridgnorth, 210 n. 37
Bridport, 20, 148–49
Bristol, 6, 7, 51, 57 n. 40
Brooke, Christopher, 7, 51, 57 n. 37
Brooke, Henry, Lord Cobham, 33, 41–42, 68
Brooke, Sir John, 139, 141, 153–54, 162
Brooke, William, Lord Cobham, 41–42
Buckingham, 146, 151
Buckinghamshire, 25 n. 19, 47, 48, 57 n. 31, 141, 142
Buller, Sir Richard, 6, 148
Bury St. Edmunds, 92, 149–50

Caernarvon, 106
Caernarvonshire, 9, 13, 14, 17, 18, 19, 20, 22 n. 1, 25 n. 19, 28 n. 39, 29 nn. 41–42, 105
Caesar, Sir Julius, 89, 107, 122 n. 13, 158
Callington, 36, 129, 147, 202 n. 5, 209 n. 32
Calne, 41, 138
Calvert, Sir George, 16, 18, 100, 101, 102
Cambridge, 5, 6, 23 n. 8, 57 n. 40
Cambridge University, 136, 140, 141, 142–43, 186, 206 n. 18
Cambridgeshire, 13, 15, 25 n. 19, 28 n. 39, 30 n. 47, 200, 210 n. 37
Camelford, 86, 88, 89, 92, 115 n. 69, 177 n. 48, 184
Canterbury, 4, 10–11, 17, 19, 20, 26 n. 29, 131, 193, 216, 211 n. 40, 219 n. 10
Cardiff, 39, 124, 126
Cardiganshire, 25 n. 19
Carey, Sir Henry, 88, 89, 90–91, 95, 117 n. 86, 160–61, 162
Carleton, Sir Dudley (father), 35, 71, 130
Carleton, Sir Dudley (son), 187, 196, 202 n. 5
Carlisle, 57 n. 40, 95, 185, 196
Carmarthenshire, 25 n. 19, 39, 139
Carvile, John, 94, 100, 119 n. 96
Castle Rising, 40, 132, 133, 134–35, 137, 201
Cave, Sir Alexander, 159–60
Cecil, Sir Edward, 69–70, 132
Cecil, Robert, Lord Cecil, Viscount Cran-

borne, earl of Salisbury, 33, 35, 45, 53 n. 1, 59, 64, 125, 146, 150, 151, 166; and bye elections of 1609, 4–5; and earl of Essex, 34, 59; electoral influence of (1604–10), 33–37, 40, 43, 53 n. 7, 54 n. 10, 121 n. 111

Cecil, William, Lord Burghley, 46, 122 n. 113, 164

Cecil, William, 2d earl of Salisbury, 123, 152, 170 n. 6; electoral influence of (1614–28), 12, 27 n. 33, 95, 96, 125–26, 160–62, 167, 170 n. 6, 180 n. 72, 216; and election costs of 1640, 200, 201, 211 n. 40

Chamberlain, John, 61, 63, 73, 92, 142

Charles, duke of Cornwall, Prince of Wales, king of England, 86, 87, 90, 92, 95, 183; alliance of, with "popular" or "reform" group, 63, 64, 169; attempts reconciliation between Buckingham and Pembroke, 124; and authority of central government, 214, 215; election intervention by, 59, 64, 184; electoral influence of, as prince, 90, 93, 94; foreign policy of, 99; interest of, in elections of 1640, 64, 183, 186, 203 nn. 8–9; opposes James I, 64; and parliament, 183, 184; and parliament of 1625, 64; and Sir Edwyn Sandys, 143; summons Council of Peers (1640), 183; and support of peerage in 1640, 189, 197

Cheeke, Sir Thomas, 38, 54 n. 10, 155, 157, 158, 165, 179 n. 62, 206 n. 19

Chelmsford, Essex, 156, 157

Cheshire, 10, 25 n. 19, 210 n. 37, 215

Chester, 6, 10, 20 n. 41, 57 n. 40, 90–91, 93, 96, 185, 197, 203 n. 6

Chichester, 57 n. 40, 132, 208 n. 25, 210 n. 36

Chippenham, 11–12, 27 n. 33, 57 n. 36, 162, 181 n. 78, 182 n. 81

Chipping Wycombe, 210 n. 36

Christchurch, 5, 23 n. 7, 37, 194, 195, 207 n. 24, 208 n. 25, 209 n. 32

Cinque Ports, the, 22 n. 7, 35, 41–42, 52, 60, 63, 65, 66, 67, 70, 71, 72, 144, 146, 184; electoral influence of lord warden of, 22 n. 4, 33, 41–42, 47–48, 52, 55 nn. 17–19, 59, 65, 66–67, 70–73, 108, 140, 160, 183–84, 188, 189, 195, 204 n. 11, 205 n. 13, 216, 217

Clarke, Edward, 20, 148–49

Clifford, Francis, Lord Clifford, 4th earl of Cumberland, 45–46, 166–67

Clifford, Henry, Lord Clifford, 5th earl of Cumberland, 166–67, 181 n. 79, 182 n. 81

Clitheroe, 43, 45, 75, 77–78, 79–80, 85, 187, 189

Cockermouth, 208 n. 25

Coke, Sir Edward, 50, 57 n. 34, 61–62, 63–64, 87, 88, 93, 119 n. 100

Coke, Sir John the younger, 200–201, 211 n. 40

Colchester, 11, 98, 155, 156, 157, 158, 180 n. 68, 190–91, 206 nn. 18–19, 210 n. 36

Colepeper, Sir John, 188, 200, 204 n. 11

Combes, William, 192–93

Commons, House of, 38, 60, 76, 93, 144, 168; and Arundel's election (1624), 15, 172 n. 19; and Blechingley's election (1624), 17, 20, 140, 215–16; and bribery case at Arundel (1641), 212 n. 41; and Bridport's election (1626), 20, 149; and Chippenham's elections (1625–28), 12; and Colchester's election (1628), 11, 158; and the county community, 216; and Dover's election (1624), 69, 70; and election practices, 13, 17–18, 57 n. 31, 197; and electoral reform, 169, 215, 216; and free elections, 169; and Gatton's election (1628), 122 n. 113, 215–16; and Gloucester's election (f1640), 210 n. 35; and Leicestershire's elections, (1621) 159, (1626) 180 n. 70; and Ludgershall's election (1626), 163; and Ludlow's election (1614), 103; and narrow franchises, 70, 215; and Newport elections, (1626) 147, (1628) 148; and Norfolk's election (1626), 147; opposition of, to influence of the "great," 216; opposition of, to "undertaking," 61, 63, 213; and Oxford's elections, (1621) 154, (1626) 128–29; and Pembroke's election (1621), 15; and Pontefract's election (1624), 15, 95; and restoration of Hertford as parliamentary borough, 95; and Sandwich's election (1621), 69, 70; and Shrewsbury's election (1604), 47; and Stockbridge's election (1614), 74; and Warwick's elections (1625–28), 12, 19; and Warwickshire's election (f1640), 193; and Westminster's election (1621), 176 n. 45; and Winchelsea's election (1624), 15

Community, the (county or local), 97, 196, 213, 214–15, 218; and aristocratic influence, 169; crown's financial demands on, 215; opposition of, to election of out-

Community (*continued*)
siders, 194–95, 196, 216, 217; opposition of, to Stuart policy, 169; parliament's importance to, 169, 215, 216; threatened by court's electioneering, 215

Compton, William, Lord Compton, earl of Northampton, 90, 92, 103, 104, 105, 106

Contested elections, 3, 9–20, 52, 68–69, 69–70, 70–71, 74, 90–91, 93, 94, 105, 107–8, 133–34, 140, 143, 145–46, 147–48, 153–54, 156–57, 158, 159, 163, 172 n. 19, 186–87, 187–88, 192–93, 195, 197–98, 199–200, 201

Conway, Sir Edward, Lord Conway, 6, 20, 37, 89, 93, 149, 216, 219 n. 11

Conyers, William, 20, 98, 119 n. 100

Cope, Sir Walter, 36, 74, 107

Cornwall, 13, 17, 29 n. 41, 30 n. 47, 130, 146, 184; gentry influence in, 25 n. 19, 108–9, 129

Cornwall (duchy), 48, 52, 60, 64, 86, 91–92, 96, 108, 129, 146, 147, 149, 150, 167, 202 n. 4; electoral influence of, 59, 63, 64, 86–90, 108, 109, 117 n. 90, 184–85, 202 n. 5, 217; nomination of outsiders by, 87, 90, 196, 216; nominees of, 65, 87–88, 89–90, 170 n. 6, 202 n. 5, 214

Coryton, William, 14, 129, 130, 184–85

Cottington, Sir Francis, Lord Cottington of Hamworth, 6, 26 n. 32, 89, 92, 147–48, 194

Cotton, Sir Robert, 134, 135, 136, 145, 170 n. 6

County elections, 3–4, 9, 48–50, 57 n. 31, 197, 226, 227; aristocratic influence in, (1604) 38, 39, 40, 54 n. 12, (1614–28) 124, 126–27, 128, 131, 133–34, 137–38, 143–45, 149, 152, 154–57, 159–61, 163–64, 165, 166, 167–68, 169, 178 n. 56, 180 n. 70, 181 n. 78, 182 nn. 81–82, 216, (1640) 191, 194, 198, 206 nn. 18–19, 207 n. 20, 208 n. 25, 209 n. 32; contested elections in, 9–10, 22 n. 1, 25 nn. 24–25, 26 n. 26, 105, 106, 133–34, 137–38, 143, 156–57, 159, 192–93, 198–201, 216; court influence in, (1604) 45–46, 47, (1614–28) 97, 98, 102, 107–8, (1640) 186; electorate and electoral tactics in, 13–15, 15–20, 28 nn. 38–39, 28 n. 42, 30 n. 47, 197–201, 210 n. 37, 211 n. 38, 211 n. 40; gentry influence in, 8, 25 n. 19, 170 n. 9

Court, the: attempts by, to prevent some members' attendance in parliament, 60, 63–64, 93; electoral influence of, (1604–
10) 41–48, 52, 55 n. 17, 57 n. 30, 59, (1604–28) 108, (1614–40) 59, 60, 61, 63, 64, (1640) 183–89, 196, 202 nn. 4–5, 203 n. 6, 203 n. 8, 204 n. 11, 205 n. 12, 217, 218; electoral influence of, through Council of the Marches of Wales, 103–7; electoral influence of, through Council of the North, 97–102, 114 n. 58, 118 n. 93, 119 n. 96, 119 n. 98, 120 n. 103; electoral influence of, through Duchy of Cornwall and Prince's Council, 85–97, 115 n. 69, 116 n. 72, 116 n. 75, 117 n. 86, 118 nn. 89–90, 121 n. 111, 122 n. 113; electoral influence of, through Duchy of Lancaster, 73–85, 112 nn. 39–40, 113 n. 51, 114 n. 54, 114 n. 56, 114 n. 59, 115 n. 63; electoral influence of, through lord wardens, 65–73, 110 n. 20, 111 n. 36; electoral influence of, through Privy Council, 107–8, 116 n. 76, 121 n. 111, 157; as electoral patron, 59, 64, 65, 96, 108–9, 109 n. 1, 122 n. 114, 150, 168, 214, 215, 219 n. 1, 221; electoral planning by, 60–61, 62–63; nominates outsiders, 65, 87–88, 89–90, 92, 94, 96–97, 109, 110 n. 18, 122 n. 115, 196, 216; reactions to electioneering of, 61–62, 64–65, 70, 90, 109; reviews nominees of Lord Zouch (1621), 63, 65, 67, 111 n. 22, 214. *See also* Appendix Two

Coventry, 57 n. 36, 57 n. 40, 93–94, 117 n. 83, 185

Coventry, Sir Thomas, Lord Coventry of Aylesborough, 5, 23 n. 8, 24 n. 16

Crane, Sir Francis, 86, 89, 116 n. 72

Cranfield, Sir Lionel, Lord Cranfield, earl of Middlesex, 66, 76, 87, 88, 132, 139, 143, 146, 195

Crew, Sir Thomas, 23 n. 10, 89, 122 n. 113, 140

Cricklade, 138

Crofts, William, 86, 89, 174 n. 34

Cumberland, 25 n. 19, 166


Dallison, Sir Roger, 41, 138, 174 n. 34

Darcy, Thomas, Lord Darcy of Chiche, Viscount Colchester, earl Rivers, 149, 155, 156

Darley, Henry, 100, 119 n. 96, 119 n. 100, 120 n. 101

Dartmouth, 13, 27 n. 35, 40, 136

Denbighshire, 25 n. 19, 29 n. 41

Derby, 124, 127–28, 210 n. 36

Derbyshire, 25 n. 19, 201, 211 n. 40

Dering, Sir Edward, 144, 145, 194–95, 197, 200, 214

Devereux, Robert, earl of Essex, 34–35, 41, 59, 64, 123

Devereux, Robert, 2d earl of Essex, 24 n. 16, 83–84, 114 n. 59, 152, 162, 163, 180 n. 74, 189, 201, 206 n. 17

Devizes, 124

Devonshire, 4, 25 n. 19

Digby, Sir John, Lord Digby of Sherbourne, earl of Bristol, 37, 149, 178 n. 50, 206 n. 17

Dorchester, 17, 57 n. 40

Dorsetshire, 8, 9, 17, 18, 25 n. 19, 29 n. 41, 168, 206 n. 18, 216

Dover, 42, 66, 67, 68, 69–70, 111 n. 28, 121 n. 111, 188, 204 n. 11, 208 n. 25

Downton, 39, 124, 125, 169 n. 5, 193

Dunwich, 33, 50, 57 n. 34, 137, 138

Durham, 215

Dyve, Sir Lewis, 20, 149, 178 n. 50

East Grinstead, 38, 43, 200

East Looe, 36, 88, 89, 115 n. 69, 130, 147, 202, 202 n. 5, 209 n. 32

East Retford, 20, 29 n. 42

Edmondes, Sir Thomas, 10, 53 n. 7, 90–91, 93, 95, 108, 122 n. 113, 128, 132, 170 n. 5

Edward IV, king of England, 59

Egerton, John, Lord Ellesmere, Viscount Brackley, earl of Bridgewater, 5, 22 n. 1, 203 n. 9

Egerton, Thomas, Lord Ellesmere, Viscount Brackley, 5, 23 n. 8, 35, 38, 62

Electoral tactics: "blanks" as, 4–5, 14, 21, 35, 40, 63, 97–98, 125, 147, 197, 252; canvassing and campaigning as, 3, 10, 14, 15–16, 17, 18, 21, 29 nn. 41–42, 48, 50, 156, 196, 198, 199–200, 202, 210 n. 37, 252; clerical and ministerial influence as, 11, 14, 17, 18, 21, 29 n. 43, 68, 69, 105, 140, 191, 196, 200, 211 n. 38, 252; creation of freeholders as, 17, 19, 21, 29 n. 42, 94, 143, 156, 199; financial intervention and bribery as, 20, 21, 140, 196, 201–2, 212 n. 41, 252; food, drink, entertainment at elections as, 3, 14, 19–20, 50, 196, 200–201, 202, 211 n. 40, 252; influence of high steward as, 5, 38, 41, 127–28, 132, 137, 138, 145, 152–53, 153–54, 157–58, 167, 193, 195; influence of jus-

tices of peace and deputy lieutenants as, 14, 21, 28 n. 38, 156–57, 197, 252; influence of lord lieutenants as, 38, 131, 133, 143, 160, 162–63, 167, 182 n. 32; influence of manor lords as, 3, 5, 37, 38, 40, 124, 125–26, 133, 136–37, 139, 140, 146, 163, 185; influence of mayors as, 14, 15, 69, 111 n. 26, 147–48; influence of recorders as, 3, 5–6, 23 n. 10, 24 n. 11, 197–99, 210 n. 36; influence of sheriffs as, 14–15, 18, 21, 28 n. 39, 46, 47, 48, 137–38, 143, 156, 159–60, 180 n. 70, 186, 192–93, 197, 200, 252; interception of writ as, 14, 19, 21, 47, 192, 252; intimidation as, 3, 17–18, 47, 50, 74, 140, 200, 252; offer of service without pay as, 5, 7–8, 38, 101, 103, 104, 133, 135, 137, 197, 209 n. 32, 252; patron support of candidate as, 46, 68, 71, 81, 105, 113 n. 51, 130, 134, 137, 141, 142, 145, 160–61, 164–65, 171 n. 10, 185, 197, 209 n. 32; violence as, 20, 30 n. 47, 47, 50, 74, 200, 252

Eliot, Sir John, 146, 147, 148, 176 n. 46

Elizabeth I, queen of England, 41, 48, 59, 214

Essex, 13, 14, 17, 25 n. 19, 28 n. 39, 29 n. 21, 33, 40, 48, 49, 137, 142, 149, 191, 200, 205 n. 16, 206 nn. 18–19, 210 n. 37, 218; aristocratic electoral influence in, 25 n. 19, 154–57; creation of freeholders in, 19 n. 42, 156

Eure, Ralph, Lord Eure, 37, 46, 57 n. 30

Eversfield, Nicholas, 72, 73, 195

Evesham, 6, 149

Exeter, 11, 26 n. 30, 57 n. 36, 57 n. 40, 198

Eye, 37, 92, 96, 137, 149–50, 186

Fane, Sir Francis, Lord Burghersh, earl of Westmorland, 12, 143–44

Fairfax, Sir Ferdinando, 83, 94, 100, 186

Fairfax, Sir Thomas, 98, 102, 217

Fanshawe, Thomas, 96, 156–57

Fanshawe, Sir Thomas, 45, 75, 77, 187

Fanshawe, William, 75, 77, 78

Fiennes, William, Viscount Saye and Sele, 153, 189, 190, 206 n. 17

Finch, Francis, 92, 149–50

Finch, Sir Heneage, 26, 88, 107

Finch, John, Lord Finch of Fordwich, 26 n. 29, 193, 195, 197

Finch, Sir Thomas, 68, 144–45

Fleetwood, Sir Miles, 140, 146, 17–4 n. 35, 194

Flint, 5

Flintshire, 14, 25 n. 19, 28 n. 39

Forced loan, the, 107, 146, 147, 148, 169, 190

Fortescue, Sir John, 44, 47, 48, 80

Fowey, 88, 89, 115 n. 69, 129, 130, 184

Franklin, Sir John, 143, 174 n. 34, 176 n. 46

Gatton, 122 n. 13, 139, 140

Gawdy family, the, 84–85, 134

Gentry, the: ambitions of, for place in parliament, 72, 73, 135; attitude of, to central government influence, 214–15; and borough elections, 8, 12–13, 51–52, 57 n. 40, 99–102, 120 n. 103, 122 n. 113, 184, 209 n. 32, 226; and county elections, 3–4, 8, 9–10, 13, 16, 25 n. 19, 133, 159–60, 167, 227; electoral influence of, 8–9, 79, 80, 83, 84, 85, 89, 90, 94, 97, 109, 133, 166, 213, 217–18, 221, 228–36; and letters of recommendation in elections, 21, 252; and local community, 106, 109, 214, 218

Gifford, Emanuel, 111 n. 28, 141, 149–50

Gifford, Sir Richard, 74, 82, 112 n. 38, 114 n. 56

Glamorganshire, 25 n. 19, 124, 126–27

Glemham, Sir Henry, 41, 135–36

Gloucester, 6, 7, 10, 16, 19, 30 n. 47, 50–51, 57 n. 40, 198, 199, 210 n. 35

Gloucestershire, 13, 25 n. 19, 25 n. 38, 197, 199–200, 205 n. 16

Goring, George, Lord Goring of Hurstpierpoint, 164, 194, 197

Government, central, 214–15, 216

Grampound, 36, 86, 89, 115 n. 69, 129, 130, 147, 148, 177 n. 49, 184, 196, 202 n. 5

Grantham, 142, 165, 185, 198, 203 n. 7, 210 n. 36

Great Bedwin, 162–63

Great Contract, the, 34

Great Grimsby, 165, 209 n. 32

Great Marlow, 200, 206 n. 18, 210 n. 37

Great Wenlock, 198, 210 n. 36

Great Yarmouth, 25 n. 19, 57 n. 40, 137, 194, 208 n. 25, 210 n. 36

Greville, Sir Fulke, Lord Brooke, 11–12, 26 n. 32, 87, 88, 93

Greville, Robert, 2d Lord Brooke, 189, 190, 192–93

Grey, Henry, Lord Grey of Groby, earl of Stamford, 192, 204 n. 10, 206 n. 17

Grimston, Sir Harbottle, 156–57, 158, 159, 180 n. 68, 191, 206 n. 19

Hampshire, 9–10, 13, 18, 25 n. 19, 29 nn. 41–42

Harley, Sir Robert, 3–4, 6, 149, 199, 201

Harrington, Sir William, 80, 96, 97, 128, 219 n. 11

Harris, Sir Arthur, 155, 158, 179 n. 62

Harrison, John, 102, 141–42, 187

Harwich, 39, 40, 55 n. 14, 139, 142, 157, 159, 168, 206 nn. 18–19, 208 n. 25

Hastings, 33, 42–43, 55 n. 19, 66–67, 71, 72, 188, 195, 197, 202, 204 n. 11, 218

Hastings, George, 4th earl of Huntingdon, 44, 45, 74, 123

Hastings, Sir George, brother to 5th earl of Huntingdon, 23 n. 7, 75, 81–82, 159–60

Hastings, Henry, 5th earl of Huntingdon, 44–45, 75, 80–82, 159–60, 187–88, 189, 192, 207 n. 20, 217

Hastings, Sir Henry, nominee of 5th earl of Huntingdon, 159, 160, 180 n. 70

Hatton, Sir Christopher, 78, 185–86, 196, 201, 203 n. 8

Haverfordwest, 19

Heath, Sir Robert, 6, 107, 195

Hedon, 4, 37, 97, 98

Helston, 5, 36, 88, 89, 115 n. 69, 196, 202 n. 5

Henry IV, king of England, 43

Henry VIII, king of England, 59

Herbert, Sir Arnold, 138, 139, 207 n. 24

Herbert, Sir Edward, 124, 127, 169 n. 5, 170 n. 9, 189, 195, 205 n. 12

Herbert, Phillip, earl of Montgomery, 4th earl of Pembroke, 4, 6, 10–11, 123, 130–32, 143, 144, 170 n. 5, 172 n. 15, 184, 189, 193, 199, 205 n. 12, 207 nn. 23–24, 208 n. 25, 210 n. 34

Herbert, William, 3d earl of Pembroke, 3, 5, 16, 33, 34, 39, 53 n. 7, 91, 103, 104, 106, 108–9, 118 n. 90, 123, 124–30, 132, 141, 147, 148, 150–52, 162, 164, 168, 169, 169 n. 5, 170 n. 6, 170 n. 9, 171 n. 10, 171 n. 12, 172 n. 18, 175 n. 39, 178 n. 56

Herbert, Sir William, 39, 125, 126, 127, 170 n. 5

Hereford, 37

Herefordshire, 4, 25 n. 19, 149, 199, 201

Hertford, 95–96, 161–62, 180 n. 72, 201, 219 n. 11, 211 n. 40

Hertfordshire, 25 n. 19, 160–61, 167, 190, 201, 211 n. 40, 206 n. 18, 209 n. 32

Hesilrige, Arthur, 81, 168, 192

Heyman, Sir Peter, 72–73, 204 n. 11

Heyrick, Sir William, 75, 80–81, 113 n. 51

Higham Ferrers, 43, 84, 85, 185–86, 196, 201, 203 n. 8

Hindon, 194, 197

Hippisley, Sir John, 70, 130, 143, 144, 208 n. 25

Hirst, Derek, 6, 8, 10, 13, 16, 22 n. 1, 55 n. 16, 118 n. 89, 121 n. 111, 133, 198, 217, 218

Hobart, Sir Henry, 84, 89, 158

Hobart, Sir John, 23 n. 8, 89, 95–96, 134

Hoby, Sir Thomas Posthumous, 40, 46, 99–100, 119 n. 95

Holcroft, Sir Henry, 79, 82, 94, 95, 114 n. 56

Holland, Sir Thomas, 40, 133–34

Horsham, 53 n. 7, 98, 132, 133

Howard family, the, 39–40, 41, 132, 135, 136, 140, 174 n. 36

Howard, Charles, Lord Howard of Effingham, earl of Nottingham, 33, 39–40, 45, 46, 55 n. 14, 86, 122 n. 113, 123, 133, 139, 140

Howard, Charles, 2d earl of Nottingham, 122 n. 113, 135, 139, 140

Howard, Sir Edward, 138, 139, 152, 180 n. 72

Howard, Henry, earl of Northampton, 27 n. 35, 33, 39, 40, 42–43, 45, 55 n. 20, 66–67, 68, 70, 71, 110 n. 20, 111 n. 22, 111 n. 36, 123, 134, 136–37, 138, 140, 174 n. 30

Howard, Lady Margaret, countess of Nottingham, 20, 135, 139, 140

Howard, Theophilus, 41, 188, 195, 204 n. 11

Howard, Thomas, Lord Howard of Charlton, Viscount Andover, earl of Berkshire, 45, 123, 137, 138, 139, 152–53, 174 n. 34

Howard, Thomas, earl of Arundel and Surrey, 39, 41, 123, 128, 132–36, 140–41, 150–52, 172 n. 19, 172 n. 22, 173 n. 27, 178 n. 56, 189, 193, 217

Howard, Thomas, Lord Howard de Walden, earl of Suffolk, 39–41, 49, 50, 122 n. 13, 123, 137–39, 140, 174 n. 34

Howard, Lord William, 41, 136, 137, 138

Hull (Kingston Upon), 45, 57 n. 40, 97, 141, 208 n. 25

Huntingdon, 43, 80, 84, 85

Huntingdonshire, 18, 25 n. 19, 29 n. 41, 200

Hythe, 22 n. 1, 42, 66, 67, 68, 71, 72–73, 111 n. 31, 142, 148, 188, 204 n. 11

Ilchester, 180 n. 75

Influence. *See* Electoral tactics: "influence" items

Ingram, Sir Arthur, 7, 66, 166, 170 n. 6, 191

Ipswich, 41, 137, 138

Jacob or Jacobs, Sir John, 177 n. 49, 204 n. 11, 208 n. 25

James I, king of England, 4, 33, 34, 37, 40, 49, 52, 59–60, 61, 62, 63–64, 65, 67, 74, 76, 105, 107, 109 n. 5, 165, 214

Jermyn, Sir Thomas, 77, 82, 92, 114 n. 54

Kent, 25 n. 19, 66, 67, 72, 141, 143–44, 197, 199, 200, 201, 211 n. 40

Killigrew family, the, 85–86, 89

Killigrew, Sir Robert, 86, 116 n. 72, 144, 177 n. 47

King's Lynn, 193

Kirton, Edward, 83–84, 162, 163, 180 n. 75

Knaresborough, 43, 75, 84, 85, 94, 120 n. 103, 200, 203 n. 8, 210 n. 37

Knollys, Sir Francis, 38, 154, 195

Knollys, William, Lord Knollys, Viscount Wallingford, earl of Banbury, 38, 139, 152–54, 167, 182 n. 82

Lake, Sir Thomas, 35, 61, 107, 122 n. 13, 130, 139

Lambe, Sir John, 185, 186, 196

Lancashire, 25 n. 19, 43, 76, 79, 80, 168

Lancaster (duchy), 43, 60, 95, 102, 150; electoral influence of, 43–45, 59, 64, 65, 73, 76, 79–80, 85, 100, 167, 178 n. 52, 214 (in elections of 1604, 33, 52, 53 n. 7; in

Lancaster (duchy) (continued)
elections of 1621, 1624, 63; in elections of 1614–28, 73–85, 94; in elections of 1640, 185–86, 187–88, 189, 205 n. 12, 217; in elections outside Lancashire, 85; in elections within Lancashire, 85; at Stockbridge, 18, 73, 74)

Lancaster, 43, 45, 75, 76–77, 79, 187

Laud, William, archbishop of Canterbury, 183, 184, 189, 190, 193, 195, 215

Launceston, 35, 86, 88, 89, 90, 115 n. 69, 146, 196, 202 n. 5, 210 n. 36

Leech, Sir Edward, 128, 129, 170 n. 6

Leicester, 43, 44–45, 74–75, 80–82, 85, 187–88, 204 n. 10

Leicestershire, 25 n. 19, 159–60, 180 n. 70, 192, 200, 206 n. 18, 207 n. 20

Leigh, Sir Francis, 75, 82, 112 n. 39

Lenthall, William, 198, 199, 210 n. 35

Leominster, 146, 151, 176 n. 46, 205 n. 12

Lewes, 18, 30 n. 47, 194, 197

Lichfield, 163, 206 n. 18

Lincoln, 165, 166

Lincolnshire, 8, 25 n. 19, 39, 166

Liskeard, 87, 88–89, 128–29, 130, 196, 202 n. 5

Liverpool, 43, 57 n. 40, 75, 78–79, 187

London, 43, 47, 107, 121 n. 11, 157, 198, 200

Lostwithiel, 35, 86, 88, 89, 115 n. 69, 129, 147, 148, 177 n. 47, 196, 202 n. 5

Lovell, Henry, 20, 139, 140

Ludgershall, 162, 163

Ludlow, 37, 46, 51, 57 n. 4, 103–4, 200, 203 n. 9

Lyme Regis, 25 n. 19, 57 n. 40

Lymington, 70 n. 5


Maidstone, 200

Mainwaring, Sir Arthur, 84, 94, 115 n. 60

Mainwaring, Sir Henry, 68, 69–70, 111 n. 28, 115 n. 60

Mainwaring, Sir Philip, 83, 94, 100, 114 n. 58, 128, 133

Maldon, 29 n. 42, 40–41, 47, 55 n. 16, 122 n. 113, 154, 157–58, 206 nn. 18–19

Malmesbury, 41, 138, 139, 174 n. 34

Manners, Francis, 6th earl of Rutland, 123, 164–66, 181 n. 78, 182 n. 81

Manners, George, 7th earl of Rutland, 165–66, 185, 203 n. 7

Mansell, Sir Robert, 126–27, 129, 139

Marlborough, 162, 163, 180 n. 74, 206 n. 18

Masham, Sir William, 11, 158, 159, 191, 206 n. 19

Maynard, Sir William, Lord Maynard, 27 n. 33, 37, 218

May, Sir Humphrey, 37, 65, 73, 76, 96, 107; in Lancashire's boroughs, 76–80; outside Lancashire, 80–85

Melcombe Regis, 25 n. 19, 57 n. 40, 210 n. 36

Merionethshire, 15, 19, 22 n. 1, 25 n. 19, 29 n. 41

Michael, 86, 176 n. 46, 202 n. 5

Midhurst, 46, 122 n. 113

Middlesex, 25 n. 19, 47, 107–8, 141, 143

Milborne Port, 206 n. 18

Mildmay, Sir Henry, 122 n. 113, 157–58

Monmouth, 43, 45, 75, 80, 83, 85, 188

Monmouthshire, 25 n. 19, 126, 203 n. 9

Montagu family, the, 3, 48, 84

Montagu, Henry, Lord Montagu of Kimbolton, Viscount Mandeville, earl of Manchester, 13, 27 n. 35, 47, 107, 121 n. 111

Montgomery, 124, 127

Montgomeryshire, 25 n. 19, 39, 126, 127

Morpeth, 41, 53 n. 7, 135, 136, 138, 139, 173 n. 26, 187

Morton, Sir Albertus, 19, 131, 143–44, 211 n. 40

Naunton, Sir Robert, 4, 86, 87, 88, 116 n. 71

Neale, Sir John, 14, 15, 34, 50, 51, 59, 64

Newcastle-under-Lyme, 43, 45, 53 n. 7, 75, 80, 83, 84, 85, 114 n. 59, 162, 188, 206 n. 18

Newcastle-upon-Tyne, 6, 7, 24 n. 14, 51, 57 n. 40, 187

Newport, 54 n. 10, 86, 88, 90, 115 n. 69, 139, 147, 148, 202 n. 5

Newport, Isle of Wight, 38

Newton-in-Makersfield, 43, 79, 80, 85, 187

Newtown, 38, 54 n. 10

New Romney, 42–43, 55 n. 19, 66–67, 70, 71, 188, 204 n. 11

Nicholas, Edward, 68, 83, 142, 146, 195, 202 n. 5, 204 n. 11, 208 n. 25

Norfolk, 13, 14, 15, 25 n. 19, 28 n. 39, 29 n. 41, 33, 40, 132, 133, 137–38, 210 n. 37, 215

North, Council of the: electoral influence of, (1604) 45–46, 57 n. 30, 97, (1614–28) 97–102, (1640) 64, 186–87, 189, 203 n. 8 (1604–28) 108; electoral influence of its lord presidents, 5, 41, 45–46, 55 n. 17, 57 n. 30, 97–99, 102, 187

Northampton, 6, 23 n. 10, 30 n. 47, 197, 200

Northamptonshire, 3, 9, 14, 16, 18, 19, 38 n. 49, 39 nn. 42–43, 33, 48–49, 200, 211 n. 38

Northumberland, 25 n. 19, 28 n. 39, 132, 208 n. 25

Norwich, 57 n. 40, 71, 138

Nottingham, 7–8, 25 n. 17, 25 n. 19, 57 n. 40

Nottinghamshire, 25 n. 19, 39, 199


Old Sarum, 35, 39, 124, 125–26, 170 n. 6, 193, 205 n. 12

Oldsworth, Michael, 124, 125–26, 129, 170 n. 6, 207 n. 23, 208 n. 35

Opposition group. *See* Reform group

Outsiders (foreigners, strangers): elected to parliaments of 1604–28, 8, 25 n. 25, 70, 217, 220 n. 13, 220 n. 14; elected to Parliament of 1640, 52, 58 n. 41, 217, 219, 220 n. 13, 220 n. 14; as nominees of the court, 65, 109, 110 n. 18, 122 n. 115, 194, 195, 196, 224; as nominees of 4th earl of Northumberland, 208 n. 25; opposition to election of, 72, 73, 89–90, 96–97, 147–48, 162–63, 216, 219 n. 10; returned, 225, 226, 227

Oxford, 38, 57 n. 36, 152, 153–54, 179 n. 59, 198

Oxford, University of, 124, 128–29, 170 n. 5, 193

Oxfordshire, 25 n. 19, 26 n. 25, 152, 182 n. 82, 200, 206 n. 18, 210 n. 37


Palmer, Sir Roger, 130, 131, 172 n. 15, 187, 193

Parliament: fear of influence in elections of, 215–16, 217; and financial demands of crown, 215; as free institution, 213, 216, 217, 219 n. 10; importance of, to local community, 215, 216; importance of, to reform group, 190; increase of representation in, 213; and recusancy, 49; summons of, urged, 34, 190–91; of 1478,

59; of 1584, 59; of 1614 (Addled Parliament), 61, 65, 67, 73, 98, 137, 168, 213, 215, 216; of 1621, 215, 216; of 1624, 165, 216; of 1625, 213; of 1626, 64, 213; Short Parliament, 183, 184, 190; Long Parliament, 189, 197, 200

Parry, Sir Thomas, 73–77, 80, 112 n. 39

Patronage. *See* Electoral tactics: patron support of candidate as

Peers, Council of, 183

Pelham, Henry, 165, 185, 203 n. 7

Pembroke, 15, 30 n. 47

Pembrokeshire, 18, 25 n. 19, 29 n. 41

Penryn, 5, 35, 36–37, 86, 116 n. 72, 144, 202 n. 5

Percy, Algernon, 4th earl of Northumberland, 189, 193–94, 204 n. 11, 207 n. 24, 208 n. 25, 217

Peterborough, 36

Phelips, Sir Robert, 9, 14, 28 n. 38, 86–87, 163, 178 n. 53, 180 n. 75, 181 n. 78

Plymouth, 6, 24 n. 13, 26 n. 30, 57 n. 40, 88, 89, 90, 115 n. 69, 202 n. 5

Plympton Earl, 147, 177 n. 49, 236 n. 10

Poley, Sir William, 77, 78, 84

Pontefract, 15, 22 n. 4, 82, 94–95, 96, 97, 120 n. 103, 203 n. 8, 219 n. 11

Poole, 29 n. 41, 25 n. 19, 57 n. 40, 122 n. 113, 210 n. 36

Portsmouth, 39, 124, 128, 137, 175 n. 39, 208 n. 25

Poulett, Sir John, Lord Poulett of Hinton St. George, 9, 27 n. 38, 163–64

Prestigne, 17, 18

Preston, 43, 45, 53 n. 7, 75, 76–77, 78, 79, 148, 187, 189

Preston, John, 169, 173, 211 n. 38, 219 n. 10

Price, James, 15, 16–17, 18

Prince's Council, 48, 52, 64, 65, 108, 146, 147, 149, 150, 202 n. 4, 214; electoral influence of, (1604–28) 108, (1621–24) 10, 26 n. 32, 63, 82, 90–97, 100, 118 n. 90, 122 n. 111, 122 n. 113, 219 nn. 111–12, (1640) 64, 109, 184, 185, 203 n. 6; and Hertford, 95, 161; nomination of outsiders by, 97, 216

Privy Council, 15, 42, 65, 183; and Caernarvonshire election of 1621, 105; debate of 1615 over electoral management, 61–62; electoral influence of, (1604–10) 47, (1604–28) 108, (1614–28) 107–8, 116 n. 76; intervenes in elections, (Canter-

Privy Council (*continued*)
bury) 26 n. 29, (Chester) 10, (Essex) 47, 48, 49, 50, 107, 154, 157, (Gatton) 122 n. 113, (Gloucester) 50, (Hastings) 204 n. 11, (Maldon) 40–41, 47, (Middlesex) 107; James I urges electoral intervention by, 51; members of, as nominees, 62, 87, 89; Sir Thomas Parry suspended from 74

Proclamation summoning parliament, (1603) 35, 110 n. 8, (1621) 62–63

Provis, Thomas, 35, 36–37

Pye, Sir Robert, 145–46, 147, 148, 163, 177 n. 49, 178 n. 53

Pye, Sir Walter, 147, 149, 199

Queenborough, 35, 130–31, 170 n. 5, 209 n. 32

Queen's Council, 48, 64, 184, 185–86, 196

Radnorshire, 15, 17, 18, 19, 22 n. 1, 25 n. 19

Read, Robert, 186, 197, 202, 204 n. 11, 218, 219 n. 11

Reading, 28, 38, 152, 153, 178 n. 58, 193, 194, 195, 206 n. 18

Reform group, 190–91, 205 n. 16

Reigate, 39, 135, 139, 140

Religion: as election issue, 49–50, 52, 104, 111 n. 26, 193, 195, 196, 197, 199

Rich family, the (earls of Warwick): electoral influence of, at Essex, 48, 49, 154, 159, 182 n. 81; electoral influence of, at Harwich (1604–28), 55 n. 14, 154

Rich, Henry, Lord Kensington, earl of Holland, 44–45, 137–38, 158, 191–92, 193, 195, 206 n. 17

Rich, Robert, Lord Rich, earl of Warwick, 155, 157, 159

Rich, Robert, 2d earl of Warwick, 11, 17, 29 n. 43, 142, 155–59, 182 n. 82, 189, 190, 191–92, 206 n. 19, 211 n. 38

Richmond, 46, 53 n. 7, 97, 98, 99, 100, 101, 102

Ripon, 45, 46, 97, 98, 99–100

Rochester, 131, 142, 143

Rudyerd, Sir Benjamin, 124, 126, 128, 129, 130, 169 n. 5, 170 n. 6, 171 n. 10

Rutlandshire, 25 n. 19, 160

Rye, 22 n. 1, 33, 42, 55 n. 19, 66, 67, 68, 70, 71, 143, 188, 204 n. 11, 208 n. 25

Sackville, Edward, 4th earl of Dorset, 29 n.

43, 70, 143–44, 177 n. 48, 188, 193–94, 197, 204 n. 11

Sackville, Thomas, Lord Bickhurst, earl of Dorset, 38, 51, 57 n. 38, 83

Salisbury, 3, 6–7, 24 n. 13, 26 n. 30, 57 n. 40, 124, 193, 197–98, 199, 207 n. 23, 210 n. 34

Saltash, 6, 36, 86–87, 88–89, 115 n. 69, 147–48, 202 n. 5

Sandwich, 12, 16, 17, 42, 43, 55 nn. 19–20, 66, 67, 68–69, 70, 71, 72, 144, 175 n. 42, 195, 197, 204 n. 11, 208 n. 25, 218

Sandys, Sir Edwyn, 63–64, 68, 69–70, 71, 73, 143, 144, 145, 175 n. 42

Savile, Sir Henry, 100, 101, 115 n. 61

Savile, Sir John, 16, 17, 25 n. 24, 45–46, 97

Scarborough, 5, 20, 33, 40, 46, 97–98, 99, 100, 101, 119 n. 100, 141–42, 186, 208 n. 25

Scotland, revolution in, 183, 190, 218

Scott, Thomas, 11, 19, 211 n. 40, 216, 219 n. 10

Scrope, Emanuel, 97–102, 118 n. 93, 187

Selden, John, 77, 162, 163, 180 n. 75

Seymour family, the (earls of Hertford), 162–64, 167, 180 n. 74, 182 n. 81

Seymour, Edward, Lord Beauchamp, earl of Hertford, 124, 162–64, 180 n. 74, 216

Seymour, Sir Francis, 124, 163, 164

Seymour, William, 10th earl of Hertford, marquis of Hertford, 16, 84, 123, 124, 162–64, 180 nn. 74–75, 182 n. 82, 206 n. 17, 216

Selwyn or Selwin, Sir Nicholas, 202 n. 5, 204 n. 11, 208 n. 25

Shaftesbury, 39, 124, 126, 193, 210 n. 36

Sheffield, Edmund, Lord Sheffield of Butterwicke, earl of Mulgrave, 5, 39, 45, 46, 55 n. 17, 57 n. 30, 97–99, 102

Ship money, 190, 215, 218

Shoreham, 36, 40, 132–33, 139

Shrewsbury, 12, 16, 30 n. 47, 46–47, 103

Shropshire, 4, 25 n. 19, 27 n. 33, 29 n. 41, 39

Slingsby family, the, 85, 102, 120 n. 103

Slingsby, Sir Henry, 75, 94, 119 n. 100, 203 n. 8

Smyth or Smith, Sir Richard, 66, 67, 89, 176 n. 46

Smyth, Sir Thomas, 66, 88–89, 116 n. 72

Somersetshire, 9, 13, 14, 25 n. 19, 28 n. 38, 29 nn. 41–42, 163–64, 181 n. 78, 216

Southwark, 206 n. 18

Spain: invades the Palatinate, 62; opposition to, 63, 111 n. 22, 189, 190

Spencer, Robert, Lord Spencer of Wormleighton, 3, 23 n. 10, 47–48

Spiller, Sir Henry, 132, 134, 138

St. Albans, 38, 95, 161, 216

Stamford, 36, 164

St. Germans, 124, 129, 147, 202 n. 5

St. Ives, 36, 86, 89–90, 115 n. 69, 147, 184

St. John, Oliver, Lord St. John of Bletsho, earl of Bolingbroke, 5–6, 23 n. 9, 206 n. 17

St. Mawes, 35, 86, 87, 88, 89, 147, 202 n. 5

Stanley, William, earl of Derby, 43, 79, 100

Stewell, Sir John, 14, 28 n. 38, 163–64

Steyning, 40, 128, 133, 180 n. 68

Stockbridge, 18, 43, 45, 73, 74, 80, 82, 85, 97, 107, 114 n. 56

Stone, Professor Lawrence, 123, 167, 170 n. 6

Stradling, Sir John, 124, 125–26, 127, 129, 170 n. 6

Strangways, Sir John, 8, 9, 25 n. 25

Stafford, 36, 137

Staffordshire, 4, 25 n. 19, 39, 84, 162, 206 n. 18, 209 n. 32

Strafford, Sir Thomas, 185–86, 196

Strode, Sir Richard, 20, 148–49, 178 n. 50

Stuart, Sir Francis, 128–29, 130

Stuart, James, 4th duke of Lennox, 188, 204 n. 11, 207 n. 24

Suckling, Sir John, 71, 89, 98, 139, 141, 143, 202

Sudbury, 43, 75, 77, 80, 84, 85, 197

Suffolk, 4, 25 n. 19, 29 n. 41, 40, 132, 197, 199, 200

Surrey, 8, 25 n. 19, 132

Sussex, 4, 25 n. 19, 38, 39, 66, 72, 132, 201

Swaffham, Norfolk, 138

Talbot, Gilbert, earl of Shrewsbury, 33, 39, 45–46

Tamworth, 26 n. 32, 197, 206 n. 18

Taunton, Somersetshire, 14

Tavistock, 206 n. 18

Tewkesbury, 20, 195

Thetford, 40, 43, 84–85, 132, 133, 134, 136, 137, 209 n. 32

Thirsk, 97, 98, 100

Thoroughgood, John, 124, 126, 128, 129

Tiverton, 146, 203 n. 8

Tomkins, Nathaniel, 23 n. 7, 147, 166, 180 n. 75

Totness, 25 n. 19, 57 n. 40, 136, 206 n. 18

Tregony, 25 n. 19, 57 n. 40

Trevor, John, 139, 163, 177 n. 48

Trevor, Sir Thomas, 40, 77, 86, 87, 88, 89, 139

Truro, 25 n. 19, 57 n. 40

Tufton, Cicely, countess of Rutland, 12, 27 n. 33, 181 n. 78, 182 n. 81

Vane, Sir Henry, 86, 87, 88, 94, 95, 134, 147, 166, 177 n. 47, 208 n. 25

Vavasour, Sir Thomas, 98, 114 n. 58, 133

Venetian ambassador, 63, 157, 190

Villiers, George, Lord Whaddon of Whaddon, Viscount Villiers, and earl and duke of Buckingham, 141, 146, 149, 154, 159, 177 n. 47; alliance of, with "popular" group, 63, 64, 65, 67, 142, 157, 169; electoral influence of, 20, 34, 64, 90, 102, 108–9, 110 n. 100, 119 n. 16, 119 n. 100, 129, 131, 141–52, 175 nn. 38–39, 176 n. 46, 178 nn. 54–56, 217; electoral influence of, as lord warden, 55 n. 20, 65, 66, 70–73, 78, 11 n. 36, 141, 150, 175 n. 38, 175 n. 42, 188; nominates outsiders, 72, 73, 216; opposes plan of James I, 64, 143; and Parliament of 1621, 62, 63; pro-Spanish views of, 111 n. 22; relationship of, to earl of Pembroke, 124, 129, 130, 147, 148, 169, 171 n. 12, 175 n. 39; suggests nominees to Lord Zouch, 59, 63, 65, 67

Wales, Council of the Marches of, 18, 45, 65, 103, 104–6; electoral influence of, (1604) 46–47, 52, 57 n. 30, 103, (1604–28) 108, (1614–28), 103–4, 106–7, (1640) 64, 189, 203 n. 9; Elizabethan electoral influence of, 46, 56 n. 26, 103; king urges electoral activity by, 184, 186

Wallingford, 152–53

Wallop, Sir Henry, 19, 26 n. 26, 74

Walrond, William, 28 n. 38, 163–64

Walter, Sir John, 87, 88, 89

Wandesford, Christopher, 94, 100, 119 n. 96

Wareham, 39, 202

Warwick, 11–12, 19, 25 n. 19, 26 n. 32, 57 n. 36, 58 n. 40, 92, 206 n. 18

Warwickshire, 25 n. 19, 168, 192–93, 197, 206 n. 18

Wells, 193, 194

Wentworth, Thomas, Lord Wentworth, earl of Cleveland, 5–6, 23 nn. 8–9

Wentworth, Sir Thomas, earl of Strafford, 13, 14, 15, 16, 17, 18, 19–20, 22 n. 4, 25 n. 24, 83, 97, 98, 100, 101, 102, 120 n. 3, 166, 186–87, 198, 199, 203 n. 8

West Looe, 5, 36, 37, 87, 88, 90, 115 n. 69, 129, 139, 146, 147, 148, 155, 170 n. 6, 184

Weston, Sir Richard, earl of Portland, 89, 147, 155, 156, 172 n. 19, 177 n. 47

Westminster, 36, 50, 107, 141, 145–46, 176 n. 45

Westmorland, 4, 25 n. 19, 166–67

Wethered, George, 98, 100, 114 n. 58, 118 n. 93

Weymouth, 25 n. 19, 39, 57 n. 40, 210 n. 36

Wharton, Sir Thomas, 101, 102, 119 n. 99

Whitby, Edward, 10, 90–91, 93

Whitchurch, 209 n. 32

Whitelock, Bulstrode, 183, 190, 198, 200, 218

Widdrington, Sir Thomas, 186–87, 198, 199

Wigan, 43, 45, 53 n. 7, 78, 79, 80, 108, 187, 189, 196, 204 n. 10

Williams, John, bishop of Lincoln and lord keeper, 64, 96, 106, 145–46, 171 n. 12, 176 n. 45, 180 n. 75

Wilsford, Sir Thomas, 23 n. 7, 69–70

Wilton, 5, 39, 53 n. 7, 125, 170 n. 5, 193

Wiltshire, 16, 25 n. 19, 124, 138, 164, 206 n. 18

Winchelsea, 15, 42, 55 n. 19, 66, 68, 70, 188, 204 n. 11

Winchester, 57 n. 40, 210 n. 36

Windebank, Sir Francis, 183, 184, 193, 194, 204 n. 11

Windsor, 40, 145, 146, 193, 206 n. 18, 209 n. 32

Wingfield, John, 164–65, 166

Woodstock, 6, 131–32, 198

Wootton Bassett, 41, 139, 174 n. 34

Worcester, 7, 24 n. 16, 50, 51, 57 n. 40

Worcestershire, 13, 14, 16, 18, 19, 25 n. 19, 29 n. 42, 30 n. 47, 48, 49, 50, 52, 210 n. 37

Wriothesley, Henry, earl of Southampton, 26 n. 26, 37–38, 54 n. 10

Wynn family, the, 15, 17, 19, 20, 25 n. 24, 105

Wynn, Henry, 15, 19, 170 n. 9, 196, 202 n. 5

Wynn, Sir John, 19, 20, 106, 211 n. 40

Wynn, Sir Richard, 180 n. 75, 184, 187, 202 n. 5

Yarmouth, Isle of Wight, 38, 54 n. 10, 208 n. 25

York, 6, 7, 16, 46, 51, 57 n. 37, 57 n. 40, 97, 186–87, 198, 199

Yorkshire, 9, 13, 14, 15, 16, 17, 20, 25 n. 24, 29 n. 41, 97, 99, 102, 182 n. 81, 186, 197; electoral influence of Council of the North in, 45–46, 97, 102, 186, 215; gentry electoral influence in, 25 n. 19, 94, 99–102, 115 n. 61, 119 nn. 95–96, 119 n. 100, 120 n. 101, 120 n. 103

Young, Sir Richard, 68, 69–70, 121 n. 111

Zouch, Edward, Lord Zouch, 61–62, 67, 70, 72, 96, 111 n. 22; electoral influence as lord president of Council of the Marches of Wales, 33, 46–47, 55 n. 17, 57 n. 30, 67, 103; electoral influence of, as lord warden, 55 n. 20, 65, 66, 67–70, 71, 73, 111 n. 28, 111 n. 36, 121 n. 111; nominees suggested to, by the king and the duke of Buckingham, 59, 63, 65, 67, 111 n. 22, 214